Advance praise for

"Some years age ... ... ecuted for
their religio: ... ere a Christian I would be a ... enough to alle-
viate the sorrow ... stian or of almost
any other religion, I think ou will finish ... ... to do more to ease
the suffering and murder of persecuted Christians."

—A.M. Rosenthal, formal executive editor of the *New York Times*

"Religion cannot flourish without democracy—thus there is an organic basis for
the unlikely alliance Allen Hertzke so powerfully depicts in this groundbreaking
book."

**—Ambassador Mark Palmer, author of *Breaking the Real Axis
of Evil: How to Oust the World's Last Dictators by 2025***

"How did American evangelicals and Jews join together to become one of the most
powerful human rights lobbies? Hertzke combines solid research, perceptive analysis, and eloquent prose to provide a difinitive answer. For anyone wishing to understand how religion is reshaping the US foreign policy agenda—often in suprising
ways—this book is a must read."

—Luis Lugo, director of The Pew Forum on Religion & Public Life*

"In the past decade, evangelical and other religious groups have played an increasingly central role in debates over global human rights. In this eloquent and thought-
ful book, Allen Hertzke offers an enlightening survey of the new politics of human
rights, and shows how religious activism has been translated into practical politics.
Freeing God's Children makes excellent reading for anyone interested in the inter-
face of religion and politics, and indeed for anyone who seeks to understand how
pressure groups of any shade make their voices felt in the American political system. This is a noteworthy study of how social movements work."

**—Philip Jenkins, Distinguished Professor of History and
Religious Studies, Pennsylvania State University**

"In lively prose, Freeing God's Children details the growth of one of the most significant, and ignored, developments in recent U.S. foreign policy, the growth of a
large, religion based human rights movement. The story it tells shows how religion
shapes American politics in ways not envisaged by either its admirers or detractors,
and how foreign policy cannot be interpreted apart from religion. Its lessons need

urgently to be digested in order to accelerate the too slowly growing realization that, without understanding religion, we cannot understand international politics."

—Paul Marshall, Center for Religious Freedom at Freedom House

"Allen Hertzke has once again struck paydirt with a riveting book that tells an engaging story about religious activists in the public arena. Journalists who thought all they needed to know about religion was its connection to a conservative domestic platform will be suprised by this book—and so will many social scientists. This is more than a story about singular or short-lived development. It suggests that America's "new world order"—like that of world powers in the past—is more influenced by religion than realpolitick and trade statistics would suggest. The story is well told; the implications are profound."

—Robert Wuthnow, Princeton University

"I have enjoyed reading Allen Hertzke's book on the faith-based movement for international human rights. *Freeing God's Children* is a first-rate work of investigative scholarship, combining impeccable research, skilled reporting, a compelling narrative, and eloquent advocacy for religious freedom. It is one of those rare books likely to make a real difference in the formation of public policy."

—A. James Reichley, Georgetown University

FREEING GOD'S CHILDREN

FREEING GOD'S CHILDREN

The Unlikely Alliance for Global Human Rights

ALLEN D. HERTZKE

ROWMAN & LITTLEFIELD PUBLISHERS, INC.
Lanham • Boulder • New York • Toronto • Oxford

ROWMAN & LITTLEFIELD PUBLISHERS, INC.

Published in the United States of America
by Rowman & Littlefield Publishers, Inc.
A Member of the Rowman & Littlefield Publishing Group
4501 Forbes Boulevard, Suite 200, Lanham, Maryland 20706
www.rowmanlittlefield.com

PO Box 317
Oxford
OX2 9RU, UK

Distributed by National Book Network

British Library Cataloging in Publication Information Available

Library of Congress Cataloging-in-Publication Data

Hertzke, Allen D., 1950–
  Freeing God's children : the unlikely alliance for global human rights / Allen D.
Hertzke.
    p. cm.
Includes bibliographical references and index.
  1. Human rights—Religious aspects—Christianity. 2. Evangelicalism—Political
aspects. 3. Human rights—Religious aspects. 4. Christianity and other religions.
I. Title.
BT738.15.H47 2004
261.7—dc22   2004003814

ISBN-13: 978-0-7425-0804-0 (cloth : alk. paper)
ISBN-10: 0-7425-0804-8 (cloth : alk. paper)
ISBN-13: 978-0-7425-4732-2 (pbk. : alk. paper)
ISBN-10: 0-7425-4732-9 (pbk. : alk. paper)

Printed in the United States of America

♾™ The paper used in this publication meets the minimum requirements of
American National Standard for Information Sciences—Permanence of Paper for
Printed Library Materials, ANSI/NISO Z39.48–1992.

To Barbara, Always . . .

CONTENTS

ACKNOWLEDGMENTS

It is humbling to note how many people and organizations it took to make this book possible. But in a way that befits research embedded in thick networks of advocates and scholars. This has been a communal enterprise.

During the past six years a number of students from the University of Oklahoma have aided my work. Two graduate students, Melissa Doll and Chris Grossman, conducted substantive research that was incorporated into chapters 2 and 7. No less than a dozen undergraduates served as research assistants at various times. Brevity requires that I only list them here, but they know how pivotal their work was for me. They include Northon Arbelaize, Marshall Camp, Michael English, Lindsay LaFevers, Jeff Mankoff, Kellie Moss, Amy Pharr, Anthony Schmidt, Hans Seidenstucher, Erin Spear, Karissa Story, and Kevin Watson. Special thanks goes to Lindsay LaFevers, who anchored the final manuscript preparation, rounded up photographs, and kept me organized in the final push to completion.

I could not have researched and written this book without considerable financial and institutional help from a variety of sources. Absolutely indispensable to this project was a generous grant by Fieldstead & Company, which funded much of my field research and supported unencumbered writing time. I am especially grateful to the foundation's program officer, Steve Ferguson, who has promoted a number of major initiatives advancing religious freedom and human rights.

At the University of Oklahoma my research was financially supported by the College of Arts and Sciences, the Graduate College Research Administration, and the Political Science Department.

In addition to direct grants, I received institutional support as well. Especially pivotal was the Ethics and Public Policy Center in Washington, D.C. Through the foresight of then President Elliott Abrams, the center sponsored scholarly conversations on religion and American foreign policy. Invited to present a paper at one such event, in January 1998, I found myself in the midst of the most prominent leaders of the nascent movement. That event literally plunged me into a six-year journey of discovery into the nexus of global religion, human rights, and American politics. That journey forever changed my life and scholarship.

Also crucial was a consultancy for the Pew Charitable Trusts Religion Program, directed by Luis Lugo, which widened my contacts in the religious advocacy community and helped shape my early thinking. A subsequent visiting fellowship at the Ethics and Public Policy Center provided a wonderful base of operation for interviews and meetings. Mike Cromartie, vice-president of the center, both shared his wealth of knowledge about the evangelical world and served as a sounding board for my ideas. I always value his sage advice.

I am also grateful for support closer to home. At the beginning of my research the Carl Albert Congressional Research Center at the University of Oklahoma provided an institutional home, while the newly created Religious Studies Program did so at the end. Special thanks go to Lee Green, administrative director for Religious Studies, who ran interference for me in the last stages of getting this manuscript out.

This book is immeasurably better because of the scholars who read and commented on various drafts. James Reichley and Steve Monsma read an early version of the manuscript for Rowman & Littlefield and provided invaluable feedback. Other reviewers included my colleague Ann Marie Szymanski, whose knowledge of social movements was most helpful; Dan Philpott, with whom I coauthored a piece defending the new thrust in American foreign policy; and Paul Sigmund, who commented on an early synopsis of the book. Robert Booth Fowler, my mentor and confidante, read the entire manuscript with a fine-tooth comb, offering a multitude of cogent, insightful, and gently critical suggestions.

I also shared my writing, both in published and draft form, with a number of activist leaders themselves. This somewhat unconventional strategy proved tremendously fruitful in correcting factual errors, triangulating on events, and furnishing sensitive insights that could only be gleaned from those living the story. Of course, by focusing on the big picture I had to exercise judgment over whether or how to incorporate such feedback. Limitations of space and thematic emphasis kept me from including more of their narrative material.

Though many persons improved this book, the deficiencies are mine alone. In particular, I am painfully aware of how much is left out, of other people I could have interviewed, of stories that needed chronicling, of activists who deserved fuller coverage. But at some point one must put a book to bed, trusting that it will be a point of departure, not the end, of inquiry.

Portions of this book have appeared earlier in other outlets. These included the *Weekly Standard*, the *National Interest*, *Wall Street Journal*, *Journal of Human Rights*, and *Extensions* (a publication of the Carl Albert Center). Writing for these more popular outlets helped me think through theoretical issues and sharpen the book's themes.

Several organizations and individuals provided the vivid photographs that grace this book. These organizations include Freedom House, the American Anti-Slavery Group, the United States Commission on International Religious Freedom, International Justice Mission, Voice of the Martyrs, the Union of American Hebrew Congregations, Prison Fellowship, the Hudson Institute, Equality Now, and the Salvation Army. Individuals who shared personal photos included Faith McDonnell of the Institute on Religion and Democracy, William Saunders of the Family Research Council, Sonam Zoksang (for the Tibetan photographs), and Eric Reeves.

I am deeply grateful to my publisher, Rowman & Littlefield, a class operation all the way around, and to my editors, Jonathan Sisk and Laura Roberts Gottlieb. Laura was a staunch advocate who took some risk in promoting this book for a general audience. Her good judgment and encouragement enabled me to get through the arduous final stages of adapting the manuscript.

Above all, I must express both gratitude and admiration for the many human rights heroes—both in the United States and around the globe—whom I have been graced to meet. Passionately devoted to the cause of human dignity, these people shared their time and insights with me. I felt humbled and honored to be in the presence of such courageous figures as Wei Jingsheng of China, Bishop Macram Gassis of Sudan, and Soon Ok Lee of North Korea. I also enjoyed the gracious hospitality of the many activists who let me into their lives—to learn from them, to observe their operations, and to eavesdrop on their ardent struggles. I feel deeply blessed to have been given this opportunity.

I owe a special debt to the irrepressible Michael Horowitz, who, upon my first meeting in 1998, urged me to be the chronicler of the movement and shared generously of his time and voluminous files, and also to the pioneering Nina Shea, who provided insights and access to pivotal documents at Freedom House. Another human rights stalwart, Rabbi David Saperstein, wisely pressed me to articulate a cogent argument worthy of the struggle.

Getting to know such smart committed people has been a richly rewarding experience. Among the others in the unlikely alliance who shared their insights with me are David Aikman, Bill Armstrong, Mariam Bell, Dennis Bennett, Francis Bok, Senator Sam Brownback, Stacie Burdette, John Busby, John Carr, Rich Cizik, Chuck Colson, Baroness Caroline Cox, Dave Dettoni, John Eibner, Sam Ericsson, Tom Farr, Deborah Fikes, Jerry Fowler, Getaneh Metafriah Getaneh, John Hanford, Laura Bryant Hanford, Tom Hart, Gary Haugen, Charles Jacobs, Richard Land, Laura Lederer, Joe Madison, Paul Marshall, Faith McDonnell, Steve McFarland, John Miller, Steve Moffitt, Andrew Natsios, Jessica Neuwirth, Senator Don Nickles, Congressman Donald Payne, Sharon Payt, Congresswoman Nancy Pelosi, Joseph Rees, Eric Reeves, Abe Rosenthal, Bill Saunders, Bob Seiple, Congressman Chris Smith, the late Steve Snyder, Norbert Vollertsen, Tom White, Roger Winter, and Congressman Frank Wolf. I am in awe of these, and the multitude of others not mentioned, who labor in the vineyards of humanitarian work.

My family, of course, made this journey with me. My sons, Patrick and Simon, endured my time away from home, as well as my frustrations when the writing slowed and deadlines were slipped. They cheered me up and cheered me on. But there is one person who literally made this book possible and without whom it would never have been written: my married partner of the past quarter century. It is something of a cliche for a writer to acknowledge his spouse. In my case the debt goes back a long way. Without Barbara's urging and sacrifice, I never would have embarked on my scholarly career in the first place, nor gained an entrée into the new human rights movement, nor written this book. Barbara lovingly handled family affairs, her studies, and her own work through my many trips away from home, the weekends and nights of writing, my writer's angst. She not only provided editorial advice and encouragement, but also surprised me with cunning gifts from time to time. Once when I was agonizingly slogging through a multitude of editorial changes—while trying to manage my university teaching and administrative duties—Barbara sent me on a week-long retreat to an Abbey. That block of uncluttered time got me through the thicket.

Since there is no way to adequately credit Barbara's influence, I am left simply to express my undying love—and dedicate this book.

May 2004, Norman, Oklahoma

1

HEROD'S CHALLENGE

Getaneh Metafriah Getaneh is a gentle man whose radiant face belies the horrors he experienced during the red terror of the Mengistu regime in Ethiopia. Arrested by the Communist authorities for preaching, he was repeatedly denied food, water, and sleep for days, tortured with boiling oil poured on the soles of his feet, and whipped with a metal cable during his many years in prison. He eventually escaped prison and fled to neighboring Djibouti. When the Communist government fell in 1994, he returned to Ethiopia, only to be arrested at the airport because an autonomous Islamist court in his home region had charged him with converting Muslims to Christianity.[1] He escaped again, and this time his exile led him to the United States, where he faced the threat of deportation. Through it all his commitment to "The Lord Jesus Christ" endured.[2]

Getaneh's story of faith amidst persecution has made him a familiar witness in Christian circles in the United States, one of the rising voices of a Christian solidarity movement highlighting the persecution of believers around the globe. He has spoken at numerous conferences, testified at congressional hearings, and been featured in religious publications that dramatize the plight of the "suffering church" abroad.

Getaneh's life is especially compelling because it seems to capture, in microcosm, so many of the forces at play in the faith-based human rights movement. He represents the new face of Christianity that has shifted demographically to the "global south" of Africa, Asia, and Latin America, where nearly two-thirds of all the world's

Getaneh Metafriah Getaneh of Ethiopia. Courtesy of Voice of the Martyrs.

Christians now live. He has suffered at the hands of Communists, dictators, and a militant Islam, but in the freer environment of the United States he joined with other refugees to create a new congregation that adds to the pluralist tapestry of American religion. The vitality of American church networks, moreover, ensured that his fledgling congregation was linked with more established churches that could provide assistance and exposure. In turn, the growing sophistication of international Christian advocacy groups, combined with global communications and travel, has meant that accounts like Getaneh's receive wide distribution in the United States, Britain, and elsewhere in the West. This publicity has dramatically heightened concern in the pews of American churches and sparked efforts to champion believers abroad who suffer for their faith.

But Getaneh is special for another reason. His desperate quest for asylum brought him, literally, into the suburban home of one Michael Horowitz, a seasoned Washington, D.C., insider with a potent combination of chutzpah and moral outrage (see chapter 5). It was this providential meeting that helped spark a new human rights movement that burst unexpectedly onto the international stage with the dawning of the twenty-first century.

Initially motivated by concern for persecuted Christians around the world, this movement now encompasses a broader faith-based quest for human rights, infusing new energy into a cause often trumped by economic and strategic calculations. Acting as a magnet for groups with diverse grievances and hopes, the movement sprouts congressional legislation, presidential initiatives, diplomatic moves, petition drives, international protests, stock divestment campaigns, and acts of civil disobedience. In the classic motifs of social movement, once obscure activists gain prominence, new constituencies are mobilized, alliances of "strange bedfellows" emerge, and confidence among advocates grows.[3] One cannot understand international relations today without comprehending the new faith-based movement—a bold assertion but one that will be borne out in the coming years.

PURPOSES OF THE BOOK

This book has several purposes. First, it provides a detailed account of the nature and impact of this movement, which arises out of the nexus of global religious developments, American church involvement, and national politics. From the mid-1990s onward successive campaigns by religious leaders addressed—and continue to press—human rights concerns through the machinery of American foreign policy. Central to the movement are American evangelicals, heretofore associated mostly with domestic skirmishes in the culture wars, but now increasingly engaged in international humanitarian and human rights causes.[4] In partnership with a broad array of other religionists, evangelical leaders mobilized grassroots pressure behind the successful enactment of legislation to stem the pandemic of global religious persecution. This success galvanized an increasingly diverse alliance to champion other human rights causes, from Sudanese atrocities to sex trafficking to massive abuses in North Korea. Given the depth and range of this activity, the movement seems poised to endure as a key presence in American foreign policy.

Second, this book offers an explanation for why this movement emerged when it did. What we will see is that a number of developments were flowing in parallel fashion, like tributaries of a river, until they finally converged. For example, over the past quarter century American evangelicals have built a thriving network of domestic organizations, both for ministry and social action. Parallel to this development, global Christianity has shifted "south" into the developing world,[5] where many indigenous believers face poverty, violence, exploitation, and persecution. As these two developments connect, the social networks of the evangelical world, born initially of conservative impulses, are increasingly put in service of human rights and justice concerns normally associated with the progressive spirit—a striking development indeed.

Third, the book demonstrates how committed individuals can make a difference. This seems like a truism, but it runs counter to much social science inquiry, which highlights impersonal "forces" at play in the world. As we will see, even though conditions were ripe for movement mobilization, it took leadership initiative to harness and channel those nascent forces. Individual agency thus is a central truth about the faith-based movement and undermines pessimists who believe it is irrelevant to public policy. That agency includes efforts of Jews, Catholics, and others who buoy—and sometimes even prod—evangelical leaders in their new international role. The motivation for much of this ecumenical activism, as I discovered in my interviews, appears to flow from authentic religious conviction and conscience, suggesting how American religious culture can nurture social movement leaders.

Fourth, *Freeing God's Children* provides a window into the changing religious landscape, at home and abroad. For the past three decades, much American religious commentary has focused on the clash between conservative and liberal religionists over the nation's meaning and direction.[6] In this book we will encounter alliances that belie that simplistic dichotomy. Liberal Jewish groups team up with conservative Pentecostals, the Catholic Church with Tibetan Buddhists, Episcopalians with the Salvation Army, black churches with secular activists, feminists with evangelicals. Especially robust is Jewish activism for persecuted Christians, which flows in part from Judaism's historical commitment to human rights, but also from a growing sense of kinship with those whose persecution is written off as inconvenient. These diverse alliances of "strange bedfellows" illuminate how religious currents around the globe are impinging on American society and politics.

Finally, this exploration has something to teach us about the role of transcendent faith in the new millennium. For much of the twentieth century, the dominant view among intellectuals was that modernization brings an inevitable secularization of society, a waning of religious salience. Thus one reason top journalists, scholars, and policymakers have been slow to grasp the import of this new religious engagement is that they have long operated with secular "pictures in their heads" that dismiss the force of religious commitments in people's lives.[7] Developments charted in this book not only challeng. this "secularization thesis" but also suggest the need to inco porate the role of faith, particularly global Christianity, into the calculus of human rights around the world.[8]

The job of a scholar is to make sense of complex things, to provide insight. One way to do that is to articulate a clear argument (buttressed with compelling evidence) that explains why something is occurring and what it means for the world. *My argument is that the new faith-based movement is filling a void in human rights advocacy, raising issues previously slighted—or insufficiently pressed—by secular groups, the prestige press, and the foreign-policy establishment.*

Sparked by identification with "suffering churches" abroad, diverse religious groups launched an ongoing campaign to promote religious freedom in American foreign policy. The energies unleashed by this campaign have injected a shot of adrenalin into the broader human rights quest. The movement plucked the tragedy in Sudan from the backwaters of international concern and into a high level of focus for American government. It is doing the same for the humanitarian tragedy in North Korea. The faith-based constituency also joins with feminist groups to fight international sex traffic, which swallows up millions of vulnerable women and children in grotesque forms of modern servitude. From India to Thailand to Eastern Europe, local Christian groups link up with American advocates to attack this and other forms of slave labor practices and exploitation.[9]

Moreover, alliances forged in those disparate campaigns facilitate co-operation on such international humanitarian efforts as debt relief and AIDS funding for Africa.[10] Thus the supposedly "parochial" concern for fellow believers abroad produces an ecumenical quest to have "the globe's indispensable nation" act more vigorously on behalf of human dignity.

The significance of this phenomenon should be obvious. Unparalleled in its global influence, the United States is also an exceptionally religious society with deepening links to religious communities abroad. To comprehend the new politics of human rights we must thus appreciate how American churches operate within a global context. To grasp something of the global future, we must understand American religion.

HOW I DID THE RESEARCH

Before I develop these themes it is necessary to say a few words about how I conducted research for this book. For the past six years I have followed the new faith-based movement from its early stirring through its halting steps to its notable policy triumphs. This book has thus evolved with the movement it chronicles, and the narrative takes the reader on a journey quite similar to the one I experienced.

I began my journey by investigating the legislative campaign to advance religious freedom through American foreign policy, and much of my narrative develops that story and its significance. As events unfolded, however, I realized that this campaign had galvanized the religious community into successive waves of human rights initiatives—initiatives that were achieving some dramatic results, such as potentially ending a civil war in Sudan and shutting down child prostitution rings in Asia. I had stumbled onto the most significant human rights movement of our time.

To capture this evolving movement, I took numerous trips to interview activists in Washington, D.C., and elsewhere. I blended these with forays to grassroots events in places ranging from Tulsa, Oklahoma, to Midland, Texas, where I observed the interaction of local activists, national movement leaders, and representatives of religious communities from around the world. Ultimately I interviewed scores of leaders and activists, both from the United States and abroad, some multiple times. These included Christian evangelicals, Jews, Catholics, mainline Protestants, Mormons, Muslims, Buddhists, and Baha'is, as well as journalists, human rights activists, feminists, academics, executive branch officials, presidential aides, and members of Congress and their staffs. I have been humbled to meet many courageous leaders—Chinese dissidents, Sudanese exiles, North Korean refugees—who have championed the cause of human dignity despite enormous personal suffering.

I also attended a host of functions to record observations and chat with participants. Thus in addition to formal interviews, I had many conversations with activists on the fly, before or after meetings, in taxi cabs, and so on, and I observed the same people in a variety of contexts. When it is feasibly possible, I provide endnote citations of these sources.[11] This "soaking and poking"[12] provided rich detail, which I weave together with material from internal documents, a mushrooming public record, and voluminous e-mail traffic among the activists.

Because I attended so many functions, I got to know well a number of the religious activists and their allies, not only as an "objective scholar" but as a sympathetic witness in the process, hanging around meetings, sharing work I had written, passing along information that might be of value. I became, in the language of ethnographic research, a "participant observer," a small part of the movement I was studying. Indeed, I published articles in outlets read by policymakers that made the case for U.S. promotion of religious freedom, leadership against Sudanese genocide, and the like.[13]

Although "participant observation" research can compromise scholarly objectivity, it also provides the enormous benefit of special access. On a number of occasions I attended strategy sessions where no other scholar or journalist was present, providing me with a unique vantage point on the movement's evolution. Because I was in the information loop, I was able to schedule research trips to numerous public events: congressional floor debates, hearings, National Press Club speeches, rallies, demonstrations, executive briefings, religious conferences, prayer services for the persecuted, advocacy group meetings, and the like. Moreover, by sharing writings with the activists themselves, I received helpful corrections and clarifications and fresh insights.

While acknowledging the potential pitfalls of this kind of research, I do not apologize for it. Past scholars have capitalized on their personal involvement in labor organizations, social movements, civil rights, or party politics to develop insights that enlighten us about crucial trends in politics. It is in this tradition that I am situated. Keenly aware of legitimate concerns about bias coloring my analysis, I have consciously sought out diverse persons and perspectives, including those highly critical of the movement and its leaders. I also made sure to confirm key events through several sources.

In my writing I often present the story from the vantage points of the actors themselves, as faithfully as possible.[14] If I have done my work well, activists will see themselves here. But I also hope they will see their work situated in a broader framework. Of course, no research project is wholly objective, and even the decision to study a particular phenomenon is laden with the values and biases of the researcher. The reader can judge whether, or where, I have succeeded in providing insight and explanation.

Every research project must define and limit the phenomena it considers. Since this book addresses the new faith-based human rights movement in foreign policy, it does not cover the entire landscape of religious forces in global politics, nor is this an account of the entire international agenda of religious organizations, though it has profound implications for that agenda.[15]

CAPTURING THE MOVEMENT

To get a flavor of how successive faith-based initiatives are transforming the politics of human rights, consider the stories of four individuals:

- Baroness Caroline Cox is a nurse, social scientist, grandmother, and member of the British House of Lords. As head of Christian Solidarity Worldwide, she personally ferries relief supplies to forbidden places where war, famine, and ethnic violence make relief efforts dangerous. Christian audiences, from Washington, D.C., to Los Angeles to Midland, Texas, are riveted by her accounts of the courage of believers amidst horrible suffering. Her documentation of religious persecution, especially of Christians in forgotten places, helped move Congress to pass the International Religious Freedom Act (1998).

- Gary Haugen is a human rights lawyer who served as UN genocide investigator for the Rwanda war crimes tribunal. This experience moved him, as an evangelical Christian, to create the International Justice Mission, an organization that intervenes on behalf of exploited people. On his desk is a busted padlock, a vivid symbol of the need for action against the global sex trafficking industry. During an investigation of a notorious Asian brothel, Haugen personally wielded bolt cutters to bust the lock that imprisoned young girls inside, who were in wretched shape after weeks of repeated rapes. It was this kind of documentation that led Congress to pass the Trafficking Victims Protection Act (2000).

- Charles Jacobs created the American Anti-Slavery Group when he discovered that secular human rights groups were largely ignoring widespread slavery in Sudan and Mauritania. As a Jew he feels profound kinship with people whose stories of captivity and deliverance echo Hebrew scripture. He has traveled to the Sudanese bush to redeem slaves, sponsored Sudanese exiles to tell their stories across the country, pressed major investment managers to divest stock in Sudanese oil, and enlisted the participation of African American preachers in the coalition that lobbied for the Sudan Peace Act (2002).

- Norbert Vollertsen is a German doctor who spent eighteen months working in North Korea for a medical aid group. In hospitals he saw children who looked like Nazi concentration camp victims, operations with no anesthesia, horrific conditions. But he was also shocked by the shameless lives of the party elite, who enjoyed sumptuous banquets, posh hotels, casinos, and luxury cars in a nation of famine and torture. Vollertsen's exposé of this outrage was met with indifference in Europe but was quickly embraced by the American faith-based community. He was featured in Christian publications, cited in congressional hearings, consulted for commission recommendations, and invited to speak at religious conferences. As a result of this exposure, congressional legislation was introduced in 2003 to promote human rights in North Korea and facilitate asylum for refugees.

These profiles capture something of the spirit and range of the faith-based quest for human rights. A sense of *religious calling* has drawn these people to places where they become witnesses to injustice—injustice often overlooked by others. Religious networks, in turn, enable them to fill those voids by mobilizing for initiatives in American foreign policy. Taken together, these vignettes illustrate how struggles that seem disparate can be part of a wider movement. To understand the origins of this movement, I now turn to the conditions that shaped its emergence.

RESPONDING TO HEROD'S CHALLENGE

My first inquiry into the movement occurred when I was asked to present a paper on the Christian response to global persecution, at a 1998 conference on religious groups and American foreign policy.[16] That conference was held on January 6, the date that traditionally marks the feast of Epiphany in the Christian calendar. To Christian believers this coincidence might seem providential. For as recounted by Matthew, the manifestation of Christ's divinity by the Magi becomes inextricably linked to political oppression. Indeed, divine promise and earthly persecution arise simultaneously, as King Herod, deeply troubled by the news of the royal birth, orders the slaughter of all male infants in Bethlehem and its environs. For the next three centuries various Caesars would compete with Herod to inflict brutality on Christ's followers, who dangerously believed in the equality of all souls before God and proclaimed allegiance to a power higher than the state. From the start, one might say, the Christian message has threatened tyrants.

While comfortable Christians in the West may read accounts of early martyrs as part of some bygone age of heroic faith, for many believers around the world today persecution is a concrete reality. Autocratic regimes cannot tolerate citizens who embody free civil society—and a number of those people happen to be indigenous Christians. Ironically, these regimes sometimes have a keener, if perverse, appreciation for the character of their Christian citizens than many who live comfortably in free democracies. Chinese authorities, for example, watched in horror as Christian churches in Eastern Europe helped topple those Communist regimes. "If China does not want such a scene to be repeated in its land," the state-run press admonished in 1992, "it must strangle the baby while it is still in the manger."[17] Clearly the authorities knew which figure in the nativity story they would emulate.

Many of today's foreign-policy challenges were anticipated in the waning days of the Cold War.[18] The emergence of a religious movement to confront global religious persecution, however, took the foreign affairs community by surprise. No less surprising is how the energy unleashed in that faith-based campaign has propelled the religious alliance into the vanguard of human rights advocacy in American foreign policy.

In the annals of the bloody twentieth century, of course, there is nothing novel about religious persecution, whether against Jews, Christians, Buddhists, Hindus, or Muslims. Religious persecution has been a leitmotiv of the century past. What cries out for an answer is why a religious movement to challenge this persecution emerged when it did and with the expressions it took.

To answer these questions requires that we understand the nature of social movements. There is "power in movement,"[19] which takes people out of their routines. Movements excite, buoy confidence, forge new relationships, strengthen organizations, and force the system to respond.[20]

What distinguishes a social movement from other forms of political advocacy? Social movements seek broader goals than interest groups; they strive for fundamental change. And movements depend on grassroots mobilization to exploit political opportunities. But mobilization requires resources—energetic leaders, ardent followers, informational networks, credibility. Where in the American social landscape do we find institutions that share these attributes? *In American churches.* Entrepreneurial church leaders strive for broad normative change, seek sweeping goals (like salvation), and organize multitudes of citizens. Though most of these efforts are nonpolitical, they represent a unique potential resource for movement mobilization when favorable opportunities present themselves.

Successful social movements are rare because they require the convergence of underlying conditions, resources, political opportunities, and choices by leaders. The new faith-based movement has had all of these, but with an international twist. The movement focuses on the plight of people far beyond the shores of the United States through the linkages of global church networks that have blossomed in the post–Cold War era. Understanding this movement, consequently, will not only explain a surprising thrust of American foreign policy, but will tell us something about broader forces afoot in the world today.

The underlying conditions for the movement include a revival of religion around the world, the globalization of Christianity, an enduring human rights crisis, and a shift toward a more faith-friendly intellectual climate in the United States. The fall of the Iron Curtain and the revolution in global communications in turn converged to open far corners of the world to scrutiny by a growing array of religious groups with access to American religious networks and political leaders. The emergence of the United States as the globe's preeminent power provided a pivotal opportunity to leaders to focus nascent movement energies on tangible foreign-policy goals.

The Resurgence of Global Religion

For much of the twentieth century, intellectuals and policymakers were guided by a powerful if mistaken vision that with modernization would come an inexorable decline in religious faith and adherence.[21] Indeed, it was an article of faith among some of the West's great thinkers that as societies embraced modern technology and rational forms of social organization, religious "superstition" would increasingly recede into the narrow recesses of the private sphere, losing its power over how people organized their collective lives. Communist ideology, of course, sought to accelerate the secularization process by force. But elsewhere, technological, rational, and bureaucratic organizations pushed religious culture to the margins of society as "the link between religion and civic order seemed to grow increasingly tenuous."[22] Deemed of decreasing power in people's lives, religion was ignored or trivialized by the most well-educated of the globe's scholars, policymakers, diplomats, and journalists.

This secular worldview is so powerful that it blinds otherwise intelligent policymakers. Thus American officials were caught flat-footed by the Iranian Revolution of 1979 because they dismissed the power of Shiite religious forces building against the Shah. Indeed, an attempt within the CIA to assess the activities of religious leaders in Iran was even vetoed as a waste of time. Why study religious factors that "we know" are politically irrelevant to a modernizing society?[23]

The shock of the Iranian revolution was but one of many events that undermined the secularization assumption. The resurgence of Islam, the dramatic growth of Christianity in the developing world, the role of churches in undermining Communist and authoritarian regimes, and the rise of various fundamentalist expressions all testify to the salience and power of religious devotion.[24] But fundamentalist movements, while visible and dramatic, represent only "the surface waves of the much broader and more fundamental religious tide," in which people are "reinvigorating" or "giving new meaning to the traditional religions of their communities."[25]

As we move into the third millennium it is clear that religion endures as a pervasive dimension in the lives of "the overwhelming majority of the human race." Indeed, secularizing trends in Western Europe and among a thin, if influential, community of global intellectual elites now stand out as exceptions to more general patterns. Paul Johnson concluded that "the outstanding event of modern times was the failure of religious belief to disappear." Today what looks "antiquated" is "not religious belief but the confident prediction of its demise once provided" by a host of Western intellectuals.[26]

Faith has not only endured; in many places it is powerfully resurgent. Now scholars speak of the "unsecularization of the world" or even "the Revenge of God."[27] The vacuum created by the collapse of the Soviet system, for example, is being filled by resurgent faith. In the new republics of Central Asia, there were only 160 functioning Islamic mosques in 1989; four years later there were an estimated

10,000.[28] In Africa and Asia, meanwhile, Christian churches are sprouting apace in societies plunged into the chaos of globalization. A single Christian evangelist draws over a million Nigerians to revivals in Lagos; the Pope has entertained the largest crowds in history, from Africa to Latin America to Asia.[29]

Not only is religion resurgent in people's daily lives, in many cases it is increasingly assertive, political, and the focus of government initiatives. French scholar Gilles Kepel suggests that beginning in the 1970s religious leaders around the world took on a new, more assertive posture toward secular society. Rather than accommodating religion to secularization, they moved in the reverse and sought to reevangelize the world, to Christianize or "Islamize modernity."[30] This more confident and assertive posture emerged from a disillusionment with secular society itself—with the shallowness of its materialism, its lack of communal solidarity, its moral relativism, and the perceived spiritual cul-de-sac of its radical skepticism. Moreover, we see around the globe the same phenomenon noticed by scholars of American religion: religious bodies that offer a vivid alternative to the secular realm grow, while churches that accommodate themselves to modernity decline. Writes Paul Johnson: "What the world witnessed, during the late 1970s, throughout the 1980s and into the 1990s, was a widespread retreat from the churches and established religious bodies which had sought to rationalize their beliefs" and the simultaneous growth of bodies that "bypassed rationalism [and] stressed the overwhelming importance of faith and miraculous revelation."[31]

The price of the growing salience and public assertiveness of religion, however, is increased scrutiny by fearful government authorities. When religion matters to people, authoritarian governments "will insist on controlling it, suppressing it, regulating it, prohibiting it, and manipulating it to their own advantage."[32] Thus, we should not be surprised that governments engage in egregious religious persecution, lesser forms of discrimination, and the manipulation of religious rivalries in many places around the globe.[33] A Freedom House survey in 2000 found that 36 percent of the world's population live in places where religious freedom is fundamentally violated, and another 39 percent reside under conditions that are only partly free.[34]

The revival of religion has also fed into, and intensified, the cultural cleavages that characterize the post–Cold War world. Rather than eliminating ethnic, national, or religious identities, the disruptions of modernization have intensified the yearning for a sense of belonging and identity, often provoking clashes on the fault lines of culture and civilizations.[35] This reality has shaped the perception of American constituencies as they respond to accounts of the suffering of fellow believers abroad. Christian minorities have come under increasing pressure in Islamic lands as political movements there assert the primacy of Islamic civilization over the West. Chinese authorities, in turn, clamp down on independent Christian churches, both because they represent independent civil society and because they are perceived as outposts of Western influence.

This pattern has led some to see the religious freedom movement in the United States as an overt attempt to protect the frontiers and outposts of Western Christian civilization in a world where civilizational conflict may take on the dynamic of "the West versus the rest."[36] In the literature of Christian advocacy groups, in fact, we see the twin specters of militant Islam and the Communist remnant as the key threats to the faithful abroad. The September 11 attack by Islamic radicals only crystallized an emerging ecumenical consciousness among disparate Christian groups. Thus highly sectarian evangelicals who would have castigated Catholics as "papists" in the past now count them among the "faithful" and routinely highlight the depredations suffered by these "brothers and sisters in Christ." Similarly, Pope John Paul II, in spotlighting the "ecumenism of Christian martyrdom," has lauded the witness of Christians of all stripes.[37]

But even if we grant that the movement is colored by a Christian solidarity defense of the faith's outposts, its efforts advance a more general vision of human rights. This is due in part to the fact that Christian churches in the developing world increasingly are not appendages of the West but, rather, local institutions blossoming with indigenous cultural expressions.[38] To defend those communities, advocates embrace the vision of free civil society contained in UN declarations and international covenants.[39] Moreover, despite crude depictions of Islam in some born-again circles, the global threat of radical fundamentalist movements is drawing some evangelicals into dialogue with moderate Muslims who are often common targets of militant intimidation and violence.[40]

The unexpected attention on Sudan in the new century illustrates these themes. American religious leaders with links to Sudanese Christian communities are, in one sense, "defending Christianity" against the tide of militant Islam. But they also are championing the broader cause of human rights. In 2002 the fundamentalist regime in Sudan was named the "world's most violent abuser of the right to religious freedom and belief" because of its brutal attempt to subjugate its southern African population—whether animist, Christian, or Muslim.[41] While harrowing tales of Christians subject to ethnic cleansing, slaughter, starvation, slavery, and forced conversion touch a deep chord in the American religious community, that chord generates pressure on American officials to act on behalf of all African Sudanese, not just Christians.

The case of Sudan also points to a second development of enormous import for American foreign policy: the globalization of the Christian churches. The growth of Christianity outside the West, coupled with the immediacy of global communication, ensures that American church networks will publicize persecution of vulnerable believers and convey that message to policymakers. A new constituency for international human rights has thus arisen in American religious circles that once were preoccupied with domestic concerns.

A Christian Demographic Revolution

Christianity is so closely associated with Western civilization that it is easy to forget that indigenous Christian communities existed for centuries in North Africa, the Middle East, and Asia, in many cases predating the introduction of the faith in Northern Europe. In fact, in the first centuries after Christ, the faith spread from Mesopotamia (modern Iraq) into the Persian Empire, where it suffered harsh persecutions, on to India, then into China by the seventh century. It spread from North Africa to the Nuba regions of what is now Sudan, where it antedated Islam by 500 years, and then into Ethiopia.[42] Christianity was thus "in Africa before Europe, India before England, China before America."[43] Over time, of course, the evangelization of

Christian worship service in China. These are among the growing millions of Chinese Christians who assemble in unregistered congregations. Courtesy of Voice of the Martyrs, www.persecution.com.

Europe and the Americas, coupled with depredations elsewhere, concentrated the faith in the traditionally Christian countries of the "global north."

That is no longer the case. An unheralded demographic revolution, which accelerated in the last half of the twentieth century, has produced a tectonic shift of the Christian population toward the "global south." A function both of lapsing faith in the West and dramatic indigenous growth elsewhere, this shift has momentous implications for both U.S. domestic politics and international relations. Consider the trends. In 1900, 80 percent of the world's Christian population resided in Europe and North America. By 2000, that figure was down to a rapidly declining 40 percent, leaving a rising 60 percent of the world's Christians living in Latin America, Africa, and Asia.[44] The most dramatic demographic transformation is occurring in Africa. While Christianity comprised less than 10 percent of the continent's population in 1900, it is now nearly half, with over a majority in sub-Saharan Africa professing Christianity.[45] Because Christianity is the largest world religion, with about two billion adherents, its concentration in the global south makes it one of the major faiths in the developing world today; it certainly is more broadly dispersed than Islam, Hinduism, or Buddhism (see appendix tables).

In the sweep of two millennia of Christian history, this demographic transformation is striking for its "suddenness and rapidity." And it may be comparable in significance to other epochal events in the shaping of Christendom because the growth of Christianity in the developing world has occurred simultaneously with its dramatic decline in Western Europe. If demographic trends continue, there will be more practicing Muslims than Christians in France and other European countries. As a leading scholar of missions observed, "one has to go back centuries" to find such a "radical shift in the cultural and demographic composition of the Christian church since 1900."[46] Just as Christianity was shaped by its successive implantation into Greek and Roman cultures, the British Isles, or North America, its indigenous growth beyond the West will usher in a new chapter for the faith. That is the message of Phillip Jenkins, who argues that the movement of the faith to the global south will constitute nothing less than a "New Christendom," a "Second Reformation" as potentially world-shaping as the first.[47]

The character of this New Christendom is strikingly akin to that of the early Church. Living amidst poverty, oppression, and violence, believers in the developing world experience the faith in literalist "New Testament" terms. Their world is one of divine power and evil; of miracles, prophecy, faith-healing, and the expulsion of demons; of persecution and martyrdom. Because of this, Jenkins predicts that a gulf will emerge between the Christianity of the global south and modernist churches of the West.

The crucial exception to this looming divide are those churches in the United States that have resisted, to a degree, modernist religious impulses. Thus in Pentecostalism, evangelicalism, and traditional Catholicism and Anglicanism, we find parishioners who especially identify with believers in the global south. It is this identification that helps animate the Christian solidarity impulse in the faith-based movement.

Some scholars believe that current figures even underestimate the extent to which the bulk of Christian adherents now live outside the West. Because demographers rely on self-identification, their figures include many nominal Christians in the West who scarcely practice their faith. On the other hand, the "cost of discipleship" can be high for Christians elsewhere, so those figures reflect people who *actively* practice their faith, often under conditions of discrimination and persecution.

Paul Marshall thus argues that the concentration of global Christianity is closer to 75 percent in the developing world. He suggests that "more people take part in Christian Sunday worship in China than do people in the entirety of Western Europe."[48] The same may be true for Nigeria, India, and Indonesia. We see the same stark contrasts within denominations. For example, on a given Sunday, "more Anglicans attended church *in each* of Kenya, South Africa, Tanzania, and Uganda than did Anglicans in Britain and Episcopalians in the United States combined."[49] Nigeria's Anglican population dwarfs that in the West. Thus the "typical Anglican is not drinking tea in an English vicarage. She is a twenty-six-year-old African mother of four."[50] More Presbyterians attend church in Ghana than in Scotland; more Assemblies of God members worship in Brazil than in the United States (the Pentecostal denomination's birthplace); more Lutherans now worship in Africa than in America.[51]

Given that about a third of the globe's population is Christian, changes in the composition of the faith also bear watching. Over 80 percent of the world's Christians are either Roman Catholics or evangelicals. Half, or about a billion, are Catholics while another 650 million are evangelicals and Pentecostals. The remaining believers are scattered among Orthodoxy and various Protestant denominations. In terms of growth, the most dramatic trend is among the evangelical and Pentecostal population. Since 1970 the evangelical population has grown 207 percent in Africa, 233 percent in Latin America, and 326 percent in Asia, so that perhaps 70 percent of Protestant evangelicals now live in Asia, Africa, and Latin America.[52]

In part this growth reflects the fact that theologically conservative evangelicals take seriously the great commission to "make disciples of all nations." When leaders of the so-called mainline denominations— Episcopalians, Presbyterians, Lutherans, United Methodists, Congregationalists—embraced more liberal theology and engaged in "worldly" ecumenical enterprises, they left the missionary field to theologically traditional Protestants, who quietly went about the business of spreading the "Good News" in Asia, Africa, and Latin America. This has produced a dramatic transformation of missionary activity. At the end of World War I, eight out of ten of the Protestant missionaries sent from the United States were sponsored by the historically mainline churches. By 1996, those same mainline churches mustered less than 3,000 missionaries out of more than 40,000 sent abroad (not counting Mormons[53]), indicating that theologically conservative evangelicals virtually dominate the Protestant mission field today. Notably, the Southern Baptist Convention alone, by fielding some 3,500 missionaries annually, dwarfs the *combined* missionary effort of the mainline denominations. The U.S. Catholic Church also operates a sizable missionary enterprise, but it has declined after a peak in the late 1960s, now numbering just over 4,000 sent abroad annually.[54]

The crucial story is not about western missionary activity, however, but about indigenous Christian evangelization. This was epitomized by the gathering, sponsored by the Billy Graham Evangelistic Association, of some 10,000 church leaders who traveled from 190 countries to Amsterdam in the summer of 2000. Capturing the flavor of the gathering was the story of a single pastor from Papua New Guinea, who had personally founded over 300 churches in the past two decades.[55] This indigenization has profound implications for the politics of developing nations. Whereas scholars of African politics in the 1950s referred to Christianity as a missionary phenomenon, by the 1990s Christianity had become an intimate "part of the fabric of sub-Saharan African life," often one of the most visible forms of "civil society when other forms had collapsed." Though churches do become enmeshed in violent ethnic strife,[56] they also serve as "umpires," "vehicles of change," and "catalysts in times of transition."[57]

One of the most rapidly growing expressions of Christianity in the developing world is Pentecostalism, which is particularly appealing because it provides a vivid emotional experience, makes the church the center of community life, and provides a strict code of personal morality. Once introduced by missionaries, it quickly becomes an indigenous movement, owing to heavy emphasis on lay involvement and few formal requirements for ministers.[58] In fact, the growth of Pentecostalism in Latin America may represent a net increase in faith practice, as "nominal and passive Catholics become active and devout Evangelicals."[59]

Because Christianity often elevates the status of women in traditional societies, believers in non-Western societies are disproportionately female. Thus "there is absolutely no excuse for thinking of Christianity as either Western, white, or male."[60] The majority of the world's Christians, indeed, are females of color.

Demographic shifts have profoundly affected denominations. As late as the 1960s roughly half of the world's Catholic population resided in the European heartland and North America. Today the vast majority live elsewhere, as the Roman Catholic Church has become a truly global religious community. Catholic leadership reflects this trend, with an increasing proportion of bishops and cardinals from Latin America, Africa, and Asia. Protestant church bodies are experiencing similar globalization, with American churches increasingly discovering that they are in fact national branches of larger global ministries.

One exception to these demographic trends is Eastern Orthodoxy, which has declined significantly as a proportion of world Christianity.[61] This decline flowed in part from the devastating effects of Soviet repression and persecution in the Middle East, but there are other reasons. Orthodoxy developed a different trajectory from Western Christianity, one more dependent on a melding of church and nation.[62] Thus is it less able to operate in the more entrepreneurial environment of global Christianity. Threatened by the new environment, Orthodox societies have attempted to prevent inroads by other Christian groups. Some Western Christian solidarity organizations, in response, depict Orthodox discrimination against Catholics and evangelicals (in such places as Russia) as part of the story of the "suffering church" abroad, barely acknowledging Orthodoxy as part of the Christian family. More astute Western advocates, on the other hand, champion the cause of minority Orthodox communities under increasing pressure in Islamic lands even as they criticize Orthodox governments that harass non-Orthodox believers.

This extended discussion of Christian demographics points to a stunning reality: The Christian churches most intimately associated with Western civilization are now most populous and most vibrant *outside* the

West. Christianity is now predominately a *non-Western* faith, but one with linkages to established bodies in the West, especially in America where religious practice remains far more vibrant than in Western Europe. We cannot understand the new interfaith engagement in international human rights without appreciating this reality.

Explanations for the indigenous growth of Christianity vary. Some see the Christian message of love and transcendent reward as especially appealing to the vulnerable. Perhaps this is why, as a scholar of missions noted, Christianity tends to "wither at center," where it becomes established and comfortable, and grow "at or beyond the circumference."[63] Others look to more proximate causes of the demographic growth of Christianity. Forces of mass communication, technology, and capitalism uproot people and weaken ancestral faiths tied to village or place. This produces a spiritual vacuum that the great proselytizing and cosmopolitan faiths, such as Christianity and Islam, rush in to fill.[64]

Because of this demographic revolution, American church leaders are coming to approach Christian communities abroad less as "leaders" sending missionaries and more as "servants" providing support to heroic indigenous believers. Vivid models of courage and fidelity among modern martyrs and "Christians in catacombs," it turns out, serve evangelical aims. As one parishioner observed, "It's done me a world of good in my commitment to see the examples of these people who have joy and strength in their faith while they daily face the threat of personal disaster."[65] Indeed, at some evangelical events in the United States, the featured speakers are likely to be foreign Christians, often treated like celebrities and role models, who share poignant testimony of how God sustained them in prison, of how the spirit worked to gain souls despite persecution. With Protestant evangelicalism at the cutting edge of church growth in the United States, it is not surprising that grassroots concern for the "suffering church" has increasingly percolated up through the political system.

The metaphor of the "suffering church" captures a genuine consequence of the demographic revolution. In the midst of globalizing markets, ideas, and migrations, autocrats often repress the independence of Christian churches or incite mob violence as a way to maintain their hold on power. The result is that today as many as 250 million Christians live at the mercy of hostile regimes in the Middle East, Africa, and Asia, while an additional 400 million face nontrivial restrictions on their religious freedom. Christians are among the most numerous victims of religious persecution in the world today.[66] In another sense the "suffering church" metaphor captures the extent to which the growth of global Christianity nests the faith among the world's poor and vulnerable. Because these believers are linked with counterparts in the West, they help expose other forms of exploitation, such as sex trafficking, previously hidden in dark corners of the global marketplace.

Intellectual Mood

Though hard to measure, changes in the intellectual climate also facilitated the new interfaith human rights movement. Since at least the 1970s an avalanche of commentary and scholarship has fostered a new intellectual mood—one less hostile to religion and more open to serious discussion of its impact in public life.

One aspect of this mood is simply an appreciation of the political relevance of religion. On the negative side, we see how religiously infused ethnic conflict has provoked horrendous atrocities, from the Balkans to Central Africa. Also obvious is the power of militant fundamentalist movements to create disorder and violence.[67] On the positive side, we see how churches nurtured dissent and contributed to peaceful democratic transitions—from the velvet revolution in Eastern Europe to the Philippines to South Africa. Clearly religion cannot be ignored by foreign-policymakers.

On the diplomatic front, there has been a new awareness of the unheralded role of churches as mediators of conflicts and agents of social and economic development. Religious groups have been instrumental in a wide array of successful mediation efforts.[68] The pivotal role of churches in relief and development work is also receiving positive attention. The faith-based "nongovernmental organizations" (NGOs) operate a formidable array of humanitarian programs in some of the most remote corners of the globe. Such groups as Catholic Relief Services and World Vision have some of the best networks on the ground in hot spots and areas hit by natural disasters, and governments rely upon them to deliver foreign aid and relief services. These faith-based partnerships with government have been going on for years, with millions of U.S. aid dollars funneled annually through religious institutions. Without religious NGOs, numerous efforts—from refugee services to agricultural development to health care—would be less effective at reaching those in need.[69]

Another shift in intellectual mood has come from the critique of the perceived failures and blinders of the secular project. To be sure, this critique is not universally shared, but a vast scholarship, along with a proliferating array of opinion journals and think tank symposia, catalog the fallout from the abandonment of transcendent societal anchors. Epitomizing this thought is Paul Johnson's magisterial book *Modern Times*, which attacks the common Enlightenment assumption that *less* religious faith necessarily equals *more* human freedom or democracy. The collapse of the religious impulse among the educated classes in Europe at the beginning of the twentieth century, he argues, left a vacuum that was filled by politicians wielding power under the banner of totalitarian ideologies—whether "blood and soil" fascism or atheistic Communism. Thus the attempt to live without God made idols of politics and produced the century's "gangster statesmen"—Stalin, Hitler, Mao, Pol Pot—whose "unappeasable appetite for controlling mankind" unleashed unimaginable horrors.[70] Or as T. S. Eliot put it, "If you will not have God (and he is a jealous God) you should pay your respects to Hitler or Stalin."[71]

The new intellectual mood is reinforced by a growing receptivity of government officials to work through faith-based organizations. It is striking that during the 2000 U.S. presidential election both Al Gore and George W. Bush campaigned on developing partnerships with religious charities. These programs, they argued, can better attend to the whole person, body and soul. As president, Bush made the faith-based initiative the centerpiece of his noneconomic domestic agenda, defending his approach on the basis of Catholic social teaching that the state should support, but not supplant, the healing work of families, communities, and religious voluntary associations. This dovetails with how America's sprawling global commitments require work through religious relief and development organizations, which in turn provide valuable information for foreign-policy deliberations.

Growing concern about citizen disengagement and cynicism has also sparked a fresh exploration of the religious contribution to a healthy civil society.[72] This exploration often takes as its point of departure the thought of Alexis de Tocqueville, who stressed the role of churches as the crucial mediating institutions of civil society. More recently, Robert Putnam popularized the idea that trusting relationships among citizens are essential to healthy democracies, and he found that religious institutions produce roughly half of such "social capital" in America.[73] Other political scientists have found that civic engagement is facilitated by participation in religious activities that teach civic skills and connect people to public affairs. That hardheaded empirical political scientists document this contribution to American democracy represents a departure from the previous generation that largely ignored the religious dimension.[74]

Intellectual trends within the religious community have also been important to the altered climate. Pope John Paul II has repeatedly argued that the primacy of religious freedom is "a point of reference of the other fundamental rights" and in some way "a measure of them."[75] A cadre of influential evangelical thinkers have joined Pope John Paul II in promoting a more theologically grounded civic consciousness among the faithful. Central here has been Charles Colson, who seeks to recover for Bible-believing Christians the heritage of social engagement from the eighteenth and nineteenth centuries when evangelicals fought against the evils of slavery and exploitation of children.[76] Others are working to help the pietistic community develop a vocabulary that will anchor political activism against injustice and the denial of human dignity.[77] Though certainly not a dominant force in a constituency known as the bulwark of "Christian Right" moral causes, this impulse nonetheless facilitates evangelical participation in ecumenical initiatives on international human rights.

Further spurring ecumenical cooperation is a deeper appreciation that all faiths have a stake in the protection of religious liberty. Ironically, it was a U.S. Supreme Court decision that crystallized this understanding on the domestic front. In 1990 the Court shocked the religious community by narrowing the grounds of its religious freedom guarantees, which sparked a decade-long struggle to reestablish more generous contours of religious protection.[78] Not only did this struggle forge relationships among diverse faith representatives, it helped sharpen the sense of religious liberty as the "first freedom" in the American experience.[79]

Another shift in intellectual mood has come from a fresh understanding of the centrality of religious freedom to the broader cause of human rights, producing a more congenial attitude toward the religious sector, notably by the human rights establishment.[80] While this centrality was boldly asserted by the United Nations in the Universal Declaration of Human Rights in 1948,[81] some secular human rights activists have been ambivalent. This ambivalence stems from a view that religion is a "problem"—a contributor to intolerance, ethnic strife, and war. Moreover, because expanding religious freedom also facilitates proselytization, some seem reticent to promote it.[82] But religious freedom, many now appreciate, is less about missionary activity than the rights of local peoples. As the revolutions in Eastern Europe showed and as Chinese dissident Wei Jingsheng has argued, allowing freedom for religious communities simultaneously opens space for political dissidents, labor organizers, and other human rights advocates.[83]

This brings us to one of the most consequential intellectual developments buoying the movement: a vibrant scholarly inquiry into the contribution of Christianity to global democracy and freedom.[84] The Christian emphasis on the dignity of the human person, the equality of all souls before God, and the autonomy of churches from state control (now embraced by both Protestant and Catholic traditions) fosters civic culture and institutional pluralism. As Samuel Huntington has shown, Western Christianity is strongly associated with democracy around the world. This relationship strengthened dramatically when the Catholic Church joined Protestantism as a major cultivator of democratic culture. After the Second Vatican Council endorsed human rights and democratic governance, the Catholic Church became a forceful advocate of change in Latin America, Eastern Europe, and the Philippines.[85] As a consequence, well over 80 percent of the countries that Freedom House categorizes as "free" are majority Christian.[86] Other democracies have substantial Christian minorities that played a role in democratic transition. The almost simultaneous growth of Christianity and democracy in South Korea and Taiwan, for example, culminated in the election

of Christian politicians (who championed the democracy movements) to head both governments in the 1990s.[87]

One implication of this pattern is that support for besieged religious minorities, many of them Christian, might serve the broader
aim of "democratic enlargement" in American foreign policy by
helping to nurture incipient civil societies in authoritarian lands. This
prospect at least provides ammunition both to those who dispute the
pessimistic "realism" in foreign-policy circles that dismisses promotion of democracy as utopian and counterproductive.[88]

Curtains Opened

The changes noted above—the revival of religion around the
globe, the Christian demographic transformation, the reality of widespread persecution, and the shift toward a more faith-friendly intellectual climate—prepared the ground for the new religious human
rights movement. Epochal changes in a new global environment, in
turn, opened up new opportunities for human rights advocacy.

No event is as central to this new environment as the end of the
Cold War. The Iron Curtain, representing a world of barriers, was an
apt metaphor for closed systems and hidden realities. The new global
environment is best captured by metaphors of openness: We hear of
walls falling, curtains torn open, and veils lifted. The fall of the Iron
Curtain exposed the appalling human rights record of collectivist
systems and highlighted continuing abuses in the Communist remnant. The end of the Cold War also meant that the quest for human
rights would no longer be submerged within superpower rivalry.
The endless and often debilitating debate between liberals and conservatives about the relative evil of superpower clients—of right
wing versus left wing dictatorships—was rendered moot. As these
ideological veils were lifted, new alliances for the cause became possible.

But the end of the bipolar world also tore open curtains that separated cultures and civilizations, heightening ethnic and religious
identities. As despots exploited ethnic animosities, religious minorities
became vulnerable targets. The opening of the globe also accelerated
the disruptions of modernization, sparking fundamentalist religious

movements that seek, in a sense, to erect new curtains against disruptive change. When armed with political power this impulse threatens the rights of those deemed as alien or impure, as we see from the "ethnic cleansing" of Muslims in the Balkans, Hindu militant attacks on Muslims in India, and Shiite persecution of Baha'is in Iran.

The most powerful expression of this impulse is militant Islam, which employs Muslim symbols and networks to advance its radical political ideology. The rich heritage of Islam has many sides, but various fundamentalist Muslim movements deeply threaten human rights because they are unabashed about using violent intimidation and coercive state power against those deemed infidels, including other Muslims. It is not surprising that as Islamic societies come under pressure from these disruptive movements, all religious minorities become victims.

For the global Christian community the lifting of veils has produced an awareness of a shared crucible. From Indonesia to Nigeria, China to Cuba, local church leaders now see their struggles in a wider and more ecumenical context. Expanded travel, communication, and advocacy networks connect these vulnerable Christian communities to more powerful bodies in the West. From remote Sudanese villages to Uzbekistan prisons, reports circle the globe at the speed of light as on-the-ground groups link up with international church ministries. These international Christian networks, moreover, move beyond succoring fellow believers to revealing human rights tragedies in some of the dark corners of the world. Such information becomes a source for policy consideration through the efforts of movement advocates.

CHURCH RESOURCES

Grievance alone does not guarantee the political system will respond. But business as usual can be shattered by the kind of mobilization and drama that social movements ignite. Successful movements need resources—leaders, energized followers, money, and networks of communication—to employ when political opportunities arise. Those resources often come from religious communities. Understanding the distinct resources of American churches is crucial to our story.

People

Unlike special interests with their Washington lobbies, social movements rely on mobilizing people, lots of them, to gain political clout. Movements need foot soldiers armed with information and a willingness to contact their elected representatives, give money, and enlist others in the cause. Letters, phone calls, e-mail, petitions, guest editorials, publicity, and demonstrations—these can grab the attention of election-minded politicians. But it is hard to mobilize people for a cause if they live in channel-surfing isolation, disengaged from society and cynical about politics.

That is why religious mobilization is potentially so momentous; it produces a new human rights constituency acknowledged and even celebrated by secular activists.[89] Churches are where many Americans congregate. The United States is unique in the Western world in the vitality of its religious life and the robustness of its church institutions. Over half of all Americans are church members, far surpassing participation in any other type of association, union, or group. It is in worship and religious fellowship that many citizens bond with one another and connect with their communities. Church attendees, for example, are far more likely than nonparticipants to socialize, volunteer, join other social groups, and give to charity.[90]

Church membership is a crucial pathway to broader civic engagement. There is something about the religiously observant that makes them more likely to go to meetings and to be community leaders than demographically matched people who do not attend religious services. Church attendees are a disproportionate share of those who serve on juries, vote, and engage in other political activities.[91] Thus, issues of concern to the religious community become magnified in a society where barely half of the adult population votes.

Churches are also incubators of civic skills. Local congregations provide opportunities for lay members to organize events, chair meetings, raise money, speak in public, and the like. Not only do these activities teach skills necessary for political participation, but they build confidence and a sense of efficacy, essential ingredients in politics.[92]

To be sure, people do not join churches to engage in politics, and ministers often shy away from overt political organizing in congregations. But praying for the "suffering church" abroad, listening to a guest speaker, or organizing letters of concern against persecution— these activities do not bear the stigma of partisan politics, even though they can foster civic involvement.

A dramatic illustration of this fact is the rapid growth of an annual event, the International Day of Prayer for the Persecuted Church, which raises awareness about the plight of believers abroad. Conceived as a worship activity, it is planned by a permanent organization that enlists congregations to participate and provides them with kits containing information about religious persecution and suggested activities of solidarity. Begun in 1996 with approximately 5,000 participating churches, organizers claimed that by 2002 it enlisted an estimated 100,000 participating congregations in the United States. Even accounting for exaggeration, perhaps a fourth to a fifth of U.S. houses of worship probably participate in this event, an enormous grassroots reach.[93] Leading the effort has been the Southern Baptist Convention, which sent packets to all of its 40,000 member congregations.

Organizers of the National Day of Prayer have also grown more politically sophisticated over time, as indicated by the selection of Midland, Texas, the hometown of President and Laura Bush, to pilot a community-wide weekend observance for the persecuted church during both 2001 and 2002.[94] With some forty churches participating, national and international speakers exhorted the local faithful to prayer and action. And a clear message was sent by friends of the new president: Do not abandon the cause of religious freedom in the war on terrorism.

Though mass mobilization is powerful, intense commitment by a smaller cadre is also a formidable resource for social movements. Intensity is a force magnifier, and the moral zeal of religious people has been a crucial ingredient in many of the great movements in American history. As we will see in this book, a fervent cohort of American believers is willing to organize events, donate to advocacy groups, organize petition drives, and even participate in demonstrations and arrests. These pockets of intense commitment provide energy and resources to the movement and enhance the publicity about human rights issues in foreign policy.

Leaders

Without leaders, sympathetic constituents remain disorganized and unfocused. Fostering a network of national leaders and local lieutenants is thus crucial to movement impact. The difficulty of creating such a network is one reason social movements are rare in American history. And it is precisely this kind of network that a church-based human rights movement offers. Pastors, ministers, bishops, rabbis, religious writers, denominational officers, and organizational heads represent a huge reservoir of leaders with considerable credibility. And they are often linked in dense organizational networks that facilitate coordination and grassroots reach.

Religious leadership thrives in the United States because unique historical circumstances fostered a robust entrepreneurial climate in church life. The American innovation in church-state practice, as embodied in the First Amendment, turned churches into volunteer societies, free from state interference or favoritism. In this dynamic environment the vitality of churches depends on the entrepreneurial efforts of ministers. Because of the wide-open religious marketplace in the United States, the axiom of church life is this: Grow, or lose market share and influence in the culture. Successful church leaders, therefore, must be entrepreneurs, and the most successful churches thrive in part because of the exceptional energy and skill of their pastors and evangelists.[95]

Because of this cultural context, American religious leaders represent a formidable resource for social movements. They are numerous and widely dispersed throughout the land. To sustain their churches they must hone skills in organization, fund-raising, and motivation, precisely the same leadership traits necessary for movement mobilization.

Ministers and religious leaders also enjoy a certain moral stature in American culture, despite the occasional scandal. Surveys show that ministers are among the more respected people in the country, and national church representatives have access to policy elites.[96] Church leaders are especially credible when their political witness flows from respected international humanitarian work and access to information through their missionary outreach to corners of the globe.

The moral authority of religious leaders plays a central role in the movement. When Charles Colson exhorts, his followers respond; when foreign bishops testify, policymakers listen; when rabbis speak out, elites notice; when black preachers join white evangelicals, journalistic interest is piqued. Because of its ecumenical appeal, the interfaith movement draws upon the pluralist strengths of the various religious communities. Catholics operate as leaders of vast institutions; evangelicals as entrepreneurs with grassroots reach; Episcopalians as heirs to the establishment; Jews as tough advocates and consciences; Buddhists and Baha'is as sympathetic minority voices. The unusual alliance of actors, some on opposite sides of the cultural wars, suggests how profoundly the movement transcends traditional ideological lines.

A less tangible but nonetheless notable resource for this faith-based movement has been a religious sense of calling among key leaders. In my research I continually discovered leaders who attributed their activism to the commitments and sensitivities they gleaned from their religious formation. Take three principal figures, Nina Shea, a Catholic, Charles Colson, an evangelical, and Michael Horowitz, a Jew. In her early work as a human rights lawyer, Shea felt a natural sensitivity to religious issues that her secular colleagues seemed to lack. As we will see in chapter 4, this sensitivity propelled her into a leading role in the religious rights campaign and made her program at Freedom House a center of organization and information. For Charles Colson a profound born-again experience in prison called him to champion the cause of those abandoned in jails around the world. Inspired by evangelicals who fought to free slaves and reform societies of the past, he feels a Christian duty to fight to "free God's children" from persecution, suffering, and contemporary forms of chattel slavery. Horowitz, as chapter 5 shows, sees his activism flowing deeply from his Jewish heritage, from its sense of justice and accountability. He also brings the memory of the Holocaust to bear when he depicts Christians as "the Jews of the twenty-first century" and the "new victims of choice for thug regimes."[97]

Horowitz's case epitomizes the crucial and fascinating role of the Jewish experience in the movement. Time and again I heard from numerous Jewish leaders that they felt compelled by their faith to take up the cause of persecuted Christians, especially when other liberal groups were ignoring it.

The vital role of leaders illustrates a key theme of this book, that movements are not just about impersonal forces, resources, or fortuitous opportunities, but that *human agency matters*. Throughout this book we will see how the passion, commitment, and strategic choices of leaders helped shape the trajectory of the movement, a phenomenon I only fully appreciated after more than five years of periodic interviewing, observing, soaking, poking, and participating.[98]

To provide but one illustration, from the late 1980s onward Christian presses, broadcast networks, and parachurch organizations highlighted the plight of believers abroad. These efforts remained somewhat fragmented, unfocused, and even competitive. Michael Horowitz seized on the idea of congressional legislation as a way to focus these disparate groups and energize the broader religious constituency. To Horowitz, the legislative campaign would serve as a *tool* both to energize the Christian community and transform the way "bigoted" secular elites view devout faith in the twenty-first century. This strategic analysis mirrored that of scholars who argue that social movement success depends on fostering "cognitive liberation"—a freeing of people from the fatalistic view that they cannot move the political system.[99] As we will see, successive legislative efforts did catalyze the movement, absorbing nascent energies and sending them out in magnified form.

This finding points to a further consequence of the movement. To a degree, the efforts of diverse activists helped awaken the sleeping giant of evangelicalism and connect it to a broader human rights alliance. This was fateful because of the resources that evangelical networks provide.

Evangelical Networks

Of all the religious communities in America, evangelicalism banks the resources most conducive to movement mobilization. It is the classic entrepreneurial faith, thriving in the American open marketplace because it is constantly renewed by revivals and religious visionaries. In

contrast to declining "mainline" denominations, its churches are growing, increasing their "market share" of the faithful.[100] The evangelical
emphasis on aggressive proselytizing also cultivates a large cadre of successful entrepreneurs. These energetic pastors and evangelists are skilled
in fund-raising, organization, and motivational techniques necessary to
maintain huge voluntary enterprises. Uninfected by the postmodern
malaise, evangelical leaders tend to be confident in their religious convictions, convinced there are fixed standards of right and wrong. Animated by passionate concerns about the drift of the culture, they have
created a booming network of schools, colleges, associations, publishing houses, direct-mail groups, parachurch organizations, and broadcast
ministries. Grassroots evangelicals are thus "readily available" for mobilization because they are "enmeshed in webs of local churches, channels of religious information, and networks of religious association."[101]

This evangelical network is a formidable political resource because of a dramatic reversal in patterns of civic engagement. While
evangelicals were *less* likely than others to vote and engage in political activities in the past, the reverse is now true. They are especially more likely to be recruited directly into political activity
through their congregations.[102] In cataloging the general decline in
social connectedness and civic engagement in the United States,
Robert Putnam summarized the significance of this pattern: "Religious conservatives have created the largest, best-organized grassroots social movement of the last quarter century." It is they, "rather
than the ideological heirs of the sixties," who represent an "up-
welling of civic engagement against the ebb tide" of broader disengagement.[103]

The evangelical world offers an additional resource for the religious freedom campaign: a sense of identification with the persecuted.
Odd as it may seem to those outside the camp, many American evangelicals feel themselves besieged by hostile forces. They are both "embattled and thriving."[104] Large majorities of evangelical ministers contend that religious freedom *in the United States* is threatened by
antireligious groups and that religious people need protection.[105]
Evangelicals are thus predisposed to believing, and heeding, reports of
persecution abroad. After all, if Christians are ridiculed or stigmatized
in a democratic United States, how much worse must Christians in

despotic lands be suffering? Evangelicals can also be shamed to action when forced to compare their own comfortable situations with those abroad who experience a severe cost for discipleship.

A final evangelical contribution to the movement is zeal. Throughout American history the pietist tendency to see worldly struggles in cosmic moral terms has infused social movements with energetic fervor.[106] From the Revolutionary War to the abolitionist movement we see how a searing moral clarity fostered political mobilization. In the antipersecution struggle this sense of moral clarity sometimes leads evangelicals to filter out ambiguity, to ignore fugitive instances when their Christian counterparts abroad participate in abuses or engage in unsavory practices.[107] But the aroused conscience of evangelical activists and their allies also drives a broader quest for human rights and humanitarian intervention, providing a storehouse of conviction in an often cynical political world.

To summarize: The community *most* likely to identify with the New Christendom of the global south, with the suffering church, is the *very one* with the social networks and motivation capable of mobilizing pressure on the political system.

Not surprisingly, a major survey of evangelical elites—prominent pastors, denominational heads, educators, broadcasters, and organizational leaders—found over 70 percent affirming the view that "stopping religious persecution should be given top priority in American foreign policy."[108] Though the issue does not reach as deeply into the pews, surveys show greater concern about religious freedom and human rights among born-again citizens than the general public.[109] Given the influence of evangelicals in Republican Party circles, these findings are of enormous import. In poking around Washington, I was struck by how frequently GOP members of Congress or their staffs would point to Charles Colson as an inspiration for their political careers, or cite the work of Franklin Graham. This access and credibility within the GOP, as we will see, sometimes serve as a counterweight to business and strategic impulses that resist an aggressive human rights posture. Most notably, the special access of evangelicals to the administration of George W. Bush produced major policy initiatives on Sudan and sex trafficking that surprised elite journalists and pleased human rights advocates.[110]

EXPLAINING THE ARGUMENT

How does the unlikely alliance fill voids in human rights advocacy? It does so by raising issues—religious persecution, Sudanese atrocities, North Korean gulags, and sex trafficking—that languished on the periphery of diplomacy. It does so by challenging the foreign-policy establishment, which often fails to press human rights out of geopolitical calculations. It does so by checking corporate business disdain for human rights intervention. Finally, it does so by providing a real grassroots constituency for American leadership on human rights.

The emergence of such an eventful movement cries out for systematic (even scientific[111]) explanation. In this chapter, I have outlined strands of that explanation: the resurgence of global religion, the nesting of Christian communities amidst the vulnerable and persecuted, the growth of evangelical social networks, and the rise of the United States as the global leader. Clearly conditions were ripening for a movement to emerge. But conditions, in and of themselves, do not create a movement. It takes the initiative of leaders to harness and sustain movement mobilization. With this new movement it is activists primarily inspired by faith convictions—driven, energetic, and passionate activists—who are connecting exploited people abroad with church networks and policy councils in the United States.

Evangelicals spearhead the grassroots vanguard of this movement, but as will be explained later, their engagement is prodded, buoyed, and channeled by leaders outside the evangelical world, helping transform what began as "parochial" concern for fellow religionists into the broader human rights campaign. This surprising development has sparked unusual alliances between evangelicals, Jews, Catholics, Anglicans, religious minorities, and even some secular activists against big business lobbies and devotees of realpolitik.

Because the United States stands at the apex of global influence—with a blend of military, economic, and cultural influence unsurpassed in world history—these developments have profound implications for the cause of human rights. Religious liberty, previously "the neglected stepchild of the human rights movement,"[112] now receives attention worthy of its place in the pantheon of free-

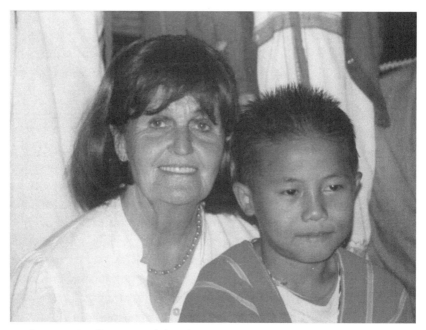

Baroness Caroline Cox with boy from Burma. Courtesy of Christian Solidarity International.

dom. Promotion of religious freedom is now statutorily a "basic aim" of American foreign policy. The debate now is not *whether* but *how best* to ameliorate the pandemic of global persecution. The fight for religious freedom, in turn, has galvanized faith-based activists into wider international engagement.

Significantly, because the movement mobilizes the most ardently religious Americans, it reaches into the very regions of the country thought to hold the most isolationist and nativist sentiment. Thus the religious heartland of America has become an unexpected breeding ground of internationalists and human rights advocates. Kansas senator Sam Brownback, himself a key leader of the movement, is not alone in being struck at how often people in town hall meetings in his state raise concerns about human rights in China and Sudan.[113]

This points to another item of significance: the development of a formidable new constituency for human rights. The human rights cause is always fragile, a potential victim of strategic calculations, business interests, and human selfishness. The secular human rights constituency, unfortunately, remains relatively small. A movement that mobilizes even a small portion of religious America will therefore dramatically expand backing for the international human rights cause.

The movement has also exposed ideological blinders in elite circles that filter out attention to some of the world's worst humanitarian abuses.[114] In particular, it has highlighted the vital use of American power in addressing such cases. In contrast, we see a preoccupation in certain human rights circles with mere statutory language in international covenants that suggests a naïveté about how despotic regimes will ignore such niceties.[115] Liberal secular groups, because of their skepticism about the U.S. role on the world stage, often resist its supposedly "unilateral" action. Many religious advocates, on the other hand, are less skittish about employing American leadership, providing real leverage for enforcement of international norms.

The benefit of political mobilization goes beyond specific policy changes. As Robert Putnam observes, social movements both *draw upon* the social capital of communities and *replenish* it.[116] As people are drawn into collective action they develop new relationships, trust, skills, and confidence—in a word, they build capital upon which they can draw for future initiatives. We see this exhibited in how the energies unleashed in the religious freedom campaign helped launch other human rights initiatives. As the movement took hold, the advocacy infrastructure swelled. From the mid-1990s onward group memberships boomed, funding flowed, leaders emerged, ecumenical alliances sprouted, publications proliferated, and élan among the activists blossomed. From local parishes to national organizations, the capacity for future collective action has grown, altering the politics of human rights and humanitarian intervention for the foreseeable future.

The most dramatic illustration of this capacity is the growing fight against human trafficking, which advocates characterize as nothing less than a modern version of the abolitionist movement that ended the African slave trade of generations past. This current effort, led by the United States and backed by a host of faith-based NGOs, is achieving unheralded but sweeping changes in national laws and practices, literally freeing vulnerable women and children held in horrible bondage around the world. Readers familiar with how the British navy enforced the ban on slave trafficking in the nineteenth century will recognize the significance of this effort. As of 2003 it is the stated policy of the American government to use all of its diplomatic and economic tools to "abolish modern-day slavery."[117] Such leadership, as we will see in chapter 8, is inconceivable without the efflorescence of the new interfaith movement.

Students of religion and politics no doubt will be struck by how the same evangelical constituency so identified with "Christian Right" domestic causes now joins, even leads, such progressive initiatives on international human rights. This fascinating, if ironic, prospect may seem inconceivable in the newsrooms and faculty clubs of the literati, where evangelical Christianity is widely caricatured.[118] To capture what is happening, therefore, we can imagine the following news headlines:

- Evangelicals, Jews, and Catholics press landmark religious freedom legislation
- Conservative churches, Congressional Black Caucus campaign against Sudanese atrocities
- Born-again leaders join feminists to curb global sex trafficking
- Missionaries expose North Korean abuses, champion refugees

In a sense, evangelical engagement is not only improving the prospects for human rights and dignity, but international engagement is improving evangelicalism by broadening its horizons and drawing upon its best instincts. The growing Christian consciousness of vulnerability to persecution seems to have cultivated a nascent kinship with other religious and ethnic minorities, from Tibetan Buddhists to Iranian Baha'is, from Chinese Falun Gong to Muslim Sufis. And it has connected believers to broader human rights challenges. Perhaps this sympathy is what naturally comes of responding to Herod's challenge.

2

THEIR BLOOD CRIES OUT[1]

Lee Soon Ok grew up in North Korea "without knowing God." A Communist until a minor infraction sent her into the gulags of the totalitarian regime, she witnessed brutal treatment meted out to those who professed a belief in Christ. "Many of the prisoners were beaten by the authorities to confess they would not believe in God but Kim Il Sung." Sometimes even the families of believers were exterminated. Lee's observation reflected the pervasive enforcement of Juche ideology, a kind of North Korean state religion in which Kim Il Sung and Kim Jong Il are considered gods and in which those who do not pay homage are treated as heretics.[2] Where a sizable Christian community once thrived, North Korea is now a place where mere profession of faith is a death warrant.[3]

What impressed Lee was the comportment of believers who refused to yield to demands that they deny Christ.[4] "I have observed that the Christians who were beaten to death would not denounce believing in God until they died." At the time she "did not know who their God was or whom these people risked their lives to believe in." Now a fervent Christian herself, she has emerged as one of the many voices calling upon American believers to pray for and champion their suffering brothers and sisters in North Korea. With a trembling voice she offered a moving benediction, through a translator, opening the Second Summit of Christian Leaders on Religious Persecution on May 1, 2002, in Washington, D.C. "Oh, God," she prayed, "those who are burned to death cry unto you." Those whose "faces were kicked and broken" sing "hymns to you." We pray the day will come when all will "be free" to "raise voices to you, to sing your praise."[5]

Variations on Lee's story, repeated in disparate places around the world, inspire American believers to press their government to respond. One cannot understand the new movement for global human rights without glimpsing this story of persecution because it was the common quest for greater religious freedom that first sparked the unlikely alliances we see throughout this book.

It is, of course, impossible to survey in a single chapter the complex picture of religious persecution and discrimination around the world. There are other, more comprehensive sources of such information that I cite throughout this chapter. Instead, I offer an account that limns the general contours of the global religious condition and illustrates how abuses motivated national religious leaders and local laity to press the cause of human rights in American foreign policy. This account catalogs abuses against a wide array of religionists. It also spotlights the persecution of Christian minorities since that problem especially animated American religionists to greater international attentiveness.

One result of the faith-based movement is that we now have a burgeoning documentary record on the status of religious freedom around the world, with the United States as the major repository of such country-by-country information.[6] This record is cataloged in both government and nongovernment sources, all headquartered in Washington, D.C. These sources include the State Department, the U.S. Commission on International Religious Freedom, Freedom House's Center for Religious Freedom, and published congressional hearings. Because these sources differ in tone, scope, and thematic emphasis, the most complete picture of the religious situation around the world draws from all of them, as I do below.

THE GLOBAL RELIGIOUS PICTURE

While the global record on religious freedom is complex, nonetheless we can distill the distinct sources and types of religious violations.[7] One group of countries, representing the Communist remnant, restrict all religion. Another group exhibits "state hostility" to unapproved or minority faiths. Many of these are in Islamic lands governed by authoritarian regimes or beset by militant movements. Other nations infringe religious liberty because they are conventional despotisms fearful of losing power (such as Burma and Turkmenistan), have state-affiliated churches resisting competition (such as Orthodox Russia), or promote policies that incite communal violence against minorities (India and elsewhere). A number of violent ethnic conflicts have religious dimensions, such as the brutal Russian effort to crush Islamic separatists in Chechnya and the ethnic cleansing by Serbian forces of Muslims in Bosnia and Kosovo. Some ethnically driven abuses are not included in the catalog of religious persecution because they lack clear religious lines. International norms sought by the faith-based movement, however, strive to keep such atrocities from happening again.[8]

The Communist Remnant

While Communism as an ideology is largely defunct, its remnant resists abandoning power. However much they liberalize their economies, therefore, the Communist governments of China, North Korea, Vietnam, Laos, and Cuba continue to repress religious civil society. In addition to various forms of harassment and overt persecution, these countries attempt to domesticate religion, often by creating state-sanctioned and regulated churches that must register prior to legal operation. This is an attempt to make religious communities an arm, in a sense, of the state apparatus.

Communist Cuba continues to view religion as a source of opposition and consequently suppresses any religious group that it perceives as a potential threat. Castro's regime, originally somewhat tolerant of the Catholic Church, shut down all private religious schools and arrested many members after the Bay of Pigs invasion. Cuba is the only country in the Americas that has attempted to impose state atheism, and since the 1960s onward its jails have been filled with pastors and other believers. Since the fall of the Soviet Union, the clause declaring Cuba an atheist state has been amended to declare it a "secular" state. On the books Cuba appears to protect religious freedoms, but in practice it continues its harsh repression of believers. It is noteworthy that, while Latin American countries virtually all have relatively high levels of religious freedom, Cuba is the conspicuous exception (with the Pope's visit only relaxing restrictions somewhat).[9]

We lack precise information about conditions inside North Korea, given how closed the country is, but the general picture is clear. The regime exercises total control over society, in Orwellian fashion. Its brutality extends beyond wide-scale arrests, torture, and killings; mass starvation has also resulted from policies engineered by the government, which has decided literally who eats and who doesn't. As German physician Norbert Vollertsen discovered in his tour of North Korea in 2001–2002, thousands of children starve while lavish facilities serve party elites and the military.[10]

There is a profound religious dimension to this abuse. The North Korea government not only imposed state-sanctioned atheism, it also mandated a totalitarian personality worship of Kim Il Sung and Kim Jong Il. This meant that the regime combined traditional Communist persecution of religion with a state-mandated faith we associate with Iranian mullahs or the Taliban. Thus "enemies of the state" are also treated as heretics.

When Mao established the People's Republic of China in 1949, the Communist government proceeded ruthlessly against religious institutions. Temples and churches were destroyed, with monks and clergy imprisoned or killed on a massive scale. This repression was especially devastating to the global fortunes of Buddhism, given China's giant population. As a share of the world's population, Buddhism declined significantly from 1900 to 2000, in large measure because of the rise of Communism in Asia.

Nowhere has the attack on religion been as systematic, or as enduring, as in Tibet, in which Chinese occupiers have sought to eradicate independent Buddhist culture by killing or arresting priests and nuns, confiscating property, and importing Chinese settlers. This effort to destroy the Tibetans as a religious group and end the influence of the Dalai Lama is ultimately an attempt to destroy them as a force of political opposition. Human rights advocates now fear that the Chinese may do the same with Muslim Uyghurs in the country's far western province. Authorities repress all activities suspected of supporting separatist Muslims, including peaceful religious gatherings.

With Mao's death and China's effort to enter the global economy, hopes were stirred about a flourishing of religious freedom in China. And things are certainly better than in the Maoist era. But the

Tibetan Buddhists lighting butter lamps. Groups representing persecuted Tibetan Buddhists joined with Christian organizations in support of international religious freedom initiatives. Courtesy of Sonam Zoksang.

regime continues to treat independent religious groups as a threat. Indeed, it was in the midst of China's rapid economic transformation that, in 1994, authorities promulgated tight restrictions against free religious practice. A subsequent State Department report in 1997 described the condition of religious freedom as "the most repressive period for them at any time since . . . the late 1970s."[11] This has led to skepticism that increased economic relations between the West and the Communist remnant will automatically enhance human rights. Indeed, while trade and free markets burgeoned in China and Vietnam in the 1990s, religious freedom in some cases deteriorated.[12]

Religious laws in China require all religious believers to belong to state-approved churches, which are heavily regulated, even to the point of the state running seminaries. The regime treats all other groups as banned cults. These anticult laws are used to discriminate against nonstate-run religion, resulting in confiscatory fines, arrests, severe economic discrimination, torture, imprisonment, and even execution. Roman Catholic priests are incarcerated for performing religious rites without authorization from the state. Bishops who refuse to renounce the authority of the Vatican have been sentenced to "reeducation through labor."[13] Protestant evangelical preachers are arrested for unauthorized preaching.

Those subject to this treatment include members of a wide array of religious groups—not only Catholics and Protestants associated with the West, but Muslim Uyghurs and the Falun Gong and Zhong meditation movements. Authorities have endeavored to convince the West that there is no longer state-imposed atheism or religious persecution, although party officials and all government workers are required by law to be atheist. Chinese officials point out that there are five authorized religions in China (Protestantism, Catholicism, Buddhism, Islam, and Taoism). Freedom House, however, notes that these groups are under tight control of the government. The government appoints mullahs for the Muslim population. Protestants in the official Three-Self Patriotic Movement are forbidden to speak of the Second Coming of Christ, the Biblical Creation story, and other elements inherent in that belief system. Members of the Catholic Patriotic Association must not pledge loyalty to the Pope.

China's treatment of unauthorized religion is not restricted to the underground Christian Church. In the wake of the country's disruptive modernization program, many Chinese turned to traditional meditation practices. One of the most fascinating episodes is the emergence of Falun Gong, which combines traditional Chinese breathing and movement exercises with claims of mystical healing and supernatural powers. Its millions of adherents follow the inspiration of a single charismatic leader, who lives in exile in the United States. When some 10,000 members appeared without notice on Tiananmen Square in a show of solidarity, authorities became upset that such an event could occur under its extensive radar. So the government declared the group illegal in 1999 and began a massive crackdown. Tens of thousands were arrested, many sent to reeducation camps, books were burned, and the airwaves filled with venom for the group (including footage of the Waco incident in the United States to show the global danger of cults). As of this writing more than a hundred "have died in police custody since 1999,"[14] and there are numerous reports of beatings, torture, and forced confessions. Concern about this treatment created unusual allies. While some Christians view Falun Gong as a false and even dangerous cult, the religious freedom movement has championed the cause of the group, with Freedom House even presenting a religious award to the Falun Dafa organization and its leaders.[15]

Like China, Vietnam and Laos have attempted to create the illusion of religious freedom as part of a strategy to attract foreign investment and trade, all the while routinely closing temples and churches and arresting clergy. Though Vietnam has released some long-term prisoners, it continues to victimize Christians and Buddhists of the Cao, Dai, and Hoa Hao branches. Leaders of these communities have suffered arrest, life sentences in labor camps, and death sentences. Vietnam both imprisons priests and monks and employs less overt tactics, such as barring bishop appointments or obstructing seminary entrants. For common villagers a tactic is to level outrageous ransoms, camouflaged as fines, resulting in indefinite imprisonments until sums equal to months, even years of their average income, are paid.[16]

The Islamic Arc

This section may offend some Muslims because it paints a rather bleak portrait of religious freedom in the Islamic world. Since I am keenly aware that this material can conjure up and exacerbate anti-Muslim and anti-Arab prejudice, I provide the following background. Islamic civilizations of the past practiced considerable religious tolerance at a time when Christendom did not.[17] Moreover, the Islamic world today is characterized by tremendous diversity, with a number of Muslims participating in pluralist democratic societies. Thus the problem is not the inherent tendency of Islam. Rather, the problem resides with the situation in a number of Islamic countries, which are led by despotic governments, under pressure from militant fundamentalists, or beset by factional strife.

Explanations for this sad situation are varied, including the colonial legacy, the distorting influence of oil, and lagging technological advancements.[18] Whatever the causes, the Islamic arc—from west central

Africa up through the Middle East, into Central Asia and down into Indonesia—has become an inhospitable place for many religious minorities, including Muslims who do not prescribe to the locally dominant interpretation of Islam. This latter point bears elaboration. Paul Marshall notes that "most of the Islamic regimes and groups" he cites as abusers of Christians *also* persecute moderate Muslims and Muslim minorities.[19] Samuel Huntington argues that more Muslims than Christians may be persecuted for their faith today, but primarily for being the wrong kind of Muslims in different parts of the Islamic world.[20] The beneficiaries of more tolerant Muslim practices, therefore, would include moderate Muslims, Shi'ite Muslims in Sunni lands, Sunnis in Shi'ite lands, Sufis, and Ahmadiya.

Considerable persecution stems from various Islamic militant movements that seek, through violence and intimidation, to restore what they see as the rightful place and glory of the Islamic world. Although Islamic militants share attributes characteristic of other religious fundamentalists, they represent the most destabilizing force on the globe today, according to Muslim scholar Bassam Tibi.[21] Frustrated in their attempt to unify the Islamic community, or Umma, they descend into ever harsher measures aimed at religious minorities and those they see as lax or unorthodox in their own faith. Beginning with the Shi'ite Revolution in Iran in 1979, which resulted in brutal treatment of Baha'is, Jews, and Christians, waves of repressive Islamist movements have washed over different parts of the Muslim world. Islamic militants provoked civil war in Sudan, imposed Taliban rule in Afghanistan, and slaughtered thousands in Algeria. Even where they have not taken power, these militants put pressure on governments to affirm Islamic fundamentals, which make religious minorities vulnerable. We see this from Nigeria to Egypt to Indonesia.

One of the most important developments arising out of the pressure by these movements is a move to declare Shari'a, or Islamic law, the official code of the state.[22] There is enormous debate among Islamic scholars regarding the proper interpretation and implementation of Shari'a and the way militants actually apply it.[23] Many Muslim scholars note that the harsh criminal penalties were rarely used at the height of Islamic civilization and were subject to contextual interpretation.[24] But driven by their fierce reaction against what they see as western decadence and liberality, fundamentalists administer Shari'a according to a literal reading of sacred texts, leading to amputations for theft and the stoning of women for adultery. Implementation of extreme Shari'a falls heavily on women, religious minorities, and moderate Muslims and dissenters.

Strife almost inevitably follows in the wake of extreme Shari'a. In the northern states of Nigeria, where Shari'a has been declared, Christian churches have been burned and people killed as vigilantes took ruthless measure to impose Shari'a on their own. The resulting strife between Muslims and Christians in Nigeria has ignited some of the worst communal violence in the world. One 2002 report cited 5,000 people killed, most of them Christians, and nearly half a million displaced.[25]

Religious freedom advocates note that the imposition of literalist Shari'a automatically bestows *dhimmi,* or a second-class citizenship, upon all non-Muslims, which provides them with inequitable protections and subjects them to harassment and abuse. While in some countries compliance with Shari'a is requisite only for Muslims, in other cases it is imposed upon non-Muslims, too, such as mandating Islamic dress for all women regardless of their religious affiliation. Such measures often serve as a pretext to punish dissenters and minorities, even to justify the torture of alleged transgressors on fabricated charges.[26]

Among the most persecuted religions within the Islamic world is Baha'i, a faith that emphasizes the unity of all religions, along with universal truth, peace, and brotherhood. Because it sprouted as an offshoot from Islam in the nineteenth century, it is treated as heretical by fundamentalist militants. Thus, Baha'is in revolutionary Iran are among the worst persecuted religious community in the world.[27] In Iran, officials claim that their treatment of Baha'is does not constitute religious persecution because they regard the religious minority as an illegal political group associated with the former Shah.[28] Moroccan Baha'is are forbidden to meet or participate in communal activities, contrary to the state's moderate legal code, and Indonesia, prior to 2001, had banned the Baha'i faith entirely.[29]

Dhimmi designates "people of the book" (primarily Jews and Christians) who, in the great Islamic civilizations of the past, were treated as a protected, but nonetheless second–class, group without full privileges of members of the Umma. While Islamic interpretation of *dhimmi* was notably tolerant in the past, today the remnants of that system provide avenues for harassment and severe discrimination. In a number of places *dhimmi* must carry identification cards denoting that standing. Many Islamic nations utilize requirements for such identification cards to discriminate against religious minorities. This makes Jews in Iran vulnerable, as economic hardship led the regime to intensify anti–Semitic propaganda. Indonesia requires disclosure of one's religious belief in order to obtain a national identification card, and employment is contingent upon possession of one. Some Islamic terrorist groups engage in mafialike extortion, demanding that these "subordinates" pay for "protection."[30]

An unfortunate legacy of so many authoritarian regimes in the Islamic world is that government officials exploit differences among the faithful or persecute those viewed as unorthodox or threatening. Thus many Muslims suffer abuse in Islamic lands. One way is to be declared non–Muslim or "Kafir" and thus stripped of many privileges and political rights. In Saudi Arabia, "members of the Shia minority are the subjects of officially sanctioned and political and economic discrimination."[31] Ahmadis are unorthodox Muslims who do not accept Mohammed as the last prophet of Islam. Pakistan authorities have at various times enforced blasphemy laws to threaten, punish, and intimidate them.[32] Before the 2003 war, Iraq's Sunni minority dominated economic and political life in that divided nation. Saddam Hussein was a nominal Sunni, and his government administered a harsh and repressive campaign against the subordinate Shi'a majority as well as many other religious groups. In fact, the State Department asserted that since the 1980s, the government attempted to eliminate the senior Shi'a religious leadership through killings, disappearances, and summary execution. In one instance the regime is alleged to have assassinated Grand Ayatollah Mohammad al-Sadr and later executed four innocent Shi'a men following a closed trial.[33] The regime in Sudan also engages in various repressive tactics against those who do not subscribe to its extremist version of Islam, often targeting Muslim moderates like Mahmoud Mohammed Taha, a scholar accused of apostasy and executed in 1985.[34]

Employing a selective interpretation of the Shari'a prohibition against defamation of Islam, some countries, such as Iran, Pakistan, Mauritania, Saudi Arabia, and Sudan, along with local governments elsewhere, have promulgated laws against blasphemy, proselytizing, conversion, or apostasy. Anyone expressing views which could be construed as antithetical to prevailing interpretations of Islam can be charged with blasphemy, which allows persecutions of religious minorities under ambiguous and often undefined charges. Charges of blasphemy have also resulted in assaults with impunity, leaving those accused with a "sense of helplessness, insecurity and anguish."[35] Under the sway of militant Shari'a, non–Muslims have been victims of forced conversion to Islam.

More covert methods are sometimes utilized by those in power to discourage dissent from their endorsed doctrine. In matters of family law, for instance, Shari'a requires that a Muslim male's betrothed be a Muslim or convert to Islam prior to the marriage. This stipulation was used against Dr. Nasr Hamed Abu Zeid, a relatively liberal Muslim and a professor of Islamic studies at Cairo University. He was declared an apostate for his views, and a convoluted interpretation was subsequently employed to justify ordering him to divorce his wife.[36]

It is important to note that moderate Muslim leaders have condemned the fundamentalist interpretation of Shari'a. To make their case, however, they must overcome a prominent source of militant Islamic thinking, the supposedly "conservative" kingdom of Saudi Arabia. As the State Department acknowledges, there is no religious freedom in Saudi Arabia.[37] Like other Arab nations, Saudi Arabia pronounces Islam its official religion. Its establishment, however, is guided by the austere and puritanical Wahhabi brand of Islam, which subjects all religious minorities, including Shia, to arrest and potential torture. Born on the Saudi peninsula in the eighteenth century, Wahhabism applies a literalist and harsh understanding of the faith. Under its influence the government denies religious freedom of Shi'ite and Sufi Muslims. Those found guilty of apostasy or proselytizing are subject to penalty of decapitation. Since Christian worship is also illegal, guest workers, such as Filipinos, are placed in an untenable position. In one case a Filipino pastor was spared execution only because of international opprobrium.[38] Human rights groups have documented over a thousand cases of Christian expatriates living and working there who have been incarcerated for refusing to comply with government edicts.[39] Non-Muslim foreigners on extended visas are pressured to convert to Islam. U.S. military and diplomatic personnel stationed in Saudi Arabia can only hold Jewish or Christian worship services in heavily cloistered circumstances. In one case Saudi authorities ordered that Christian worship services at the American Consulate desist; remarkably U.S. officials complied.[40]

Because Saudi Arabia is strategically important, its dismal record on religious freedom has largely been ignored by American policymakers. In the wake of September 11, however, there has been increasing scrutiny to the way in which Saudi oil wealth funds fundamentalist madrassas (religious schools) around the world and builds mosques that promote its brand of Islam, including in the United States. Influential sectors of Saudi society also are responsible in recent years for promoting virulent expressions of anti-Semitism not seen since the Nazi era, which do not bode well for the cause of human rights.[41]

While the State Department has resisted designating Saudi Arabia as a "country of concern," it has so designated Sudan because of its abhorrent record as a gross violator of religious liberty.[42] The fundamentalist Khartoum regime, anchored in the north, has been waging a war primarily against non-Muslims for two decades. This has resulted in an estimated two million deaths from fighting and famine. The conflict is decidedly religious in nature, as non-Muslims are often specific targets of government bombings and raids. Khartoum forces have resorted to massacres, enslavement of conquered peoples, forced religious conversion, and trafficking of women and children. The profligacy of these malefactions led the faith-based coalition to press successfully for congressional legislation in an attempt to induce Khartoum to relent (see chapter 7).

In recent years some of the worst religious violence has occurred in the sprawling archipelago of Indonesia, where militant fundamentalist movements have sprouted. Authorities themselves exploited religious strife in mostly Catholic East Timor prior to its independence in 1999. Strife then served as a pretext for repression and a formidable military presence. When the Timorese voted for independence, militias and renegade military units engaged in a horrible slaughter.

Since the settlement of the Timorese crisis, terrible violence has occurred in the Moluccas, spurred by jihad movements that have exacerbated Muslim-Christian tensions. Both Christians and Muslims have committed abuses—attacking churches and mosques, killing or maiming unarmed people—but the majority of victims have been Christians. Members of the Indonesian security forces have been implicated in attacks, along with militant Islamic groups. The appalling human rights picture is captured by statistics cited in the 2001 State Department Report: "From July to November 2000, the Government largely was ineffective in deterring interreligious violence that led to over 1,000 deaths, thousands of injuries, and tens of thousands of displaced persons in the Moluccas." In addition, forced conversions are common. The 2001 State Report notes "credible" reports that several hundred Muslims were forcibly converted to Christianity while thousands of Christians were forced to convert to Islam.[43]

Leading the militant fundamentalists in Indonesia has been Laskar Jihad, a violent group with ties to Osama bin Laden. It launched a series of bloody attacks in 2001–2002 on Christian villages in the Moluccas, indiscriminately killing with automatic weapons and machetes, destroying property, and spreading terror and displacement in its wake. At the time, few Laskar Jihad members were detained by authorities for these crimes. The group's actions intensified the conflict between Muslims and Christians and thwarted attempts by the government at a peaceful solution. Appalling carnage and massive destruction of property occurred before the government of Indonesia was finally able to stop it.[44] Religious freedom advocates repeatedly tried to gain greater exposure for these atrocities, and for the wider threat they represented.[45]

Other Contexts

Religious repression has many genitors, from secular dictatorships to interreligious violence to government efforts to halt competition to the dominant faith. In this section, I briefly catalog other threats to religious freedom.

One of the most dramatic instances of religious-imbued repression is when an entire people is targeted for ethnic cleansing by armies of another group, as we saw in the former Yugoslavia. In the case of Bosnia and Kosovo the victims, thousands of them, were Muslims, a fact widely seared into the consciousness of Muslims around the world. To Muslims and human rights observers, another tragedy is occurring in the breakaway Russian province of Chechnya. Widespread reports indicate indiscriminate killing of Muslims by the Russian army fighting rebels there, producing a massive humanitarian tragedy.

Another source of persecution flows from garden-variety despotisms, which may exploit interreligious rivalries or repress independent religious life. Burma is a classic example. Freedom House asserts that Burma's authorities have intentionally exacerbated friction between Buddhists and the Christian Karens for purely political purposes.[46] Authorities have also enforced legislation that discriminates against immigrants and in favor of ethnic Burmese. These enactments are tied to promotion of Buddhism—and religious animosity. Critics also charge that Burmese authorities have instigated anti-Muslim riots resulting in the destruction of several mosques.[47]

In Central Asia several of the former Soviet Republics employ remnants of Communist-era restrictions on religious freedom but with new twists. Turkmenistan, ruled by a former Communist boss under a cult of personality, channels religious practice into state-regulated Sunni Muslim and Orthodox groups, and harshly restricts all others. Intimidation, arrest, and physical abuse commonly afflict the Baha'is, Baptists, Hare Krishnas, Jehovah's Witnesses, Pentecostals, Seventh Day Adventists, and Muslims who operate independently of the state-sanctioned Sunni branch.[48] As in Turkmenistan, the government of Uzbekistan tightly controls religious activity. But there Muslims are the prime victims of a government crackdown on religionist communities viewed as a threat to the regime. Under the pretext of stemming fundamentalist radicals, detention and arrest of Muslim clerics, and even their family members, is widespread.

In Bhutan, where Buddhism is the state religion, the regime views the foreign Hindu population as a potential source of peril to Buddhist and ethnic hegemony. As a result, those in power have passed and enforced legislation to strip the Hindu population of its citizenship. Christian groups have also been plagued by harassment from the Bhutan government. When officials became concerned that

Christian learning centers were being used to organize campaigning activities, they shut them down.

Scholars of religious freedom have become concerned about the rise of a new form of discrimination—laws that distinguish between traditional or acceptable churches and new "cults," proscribing the latter or erecting barriers to their operation. In Russia and other Orthodox republics of the former Soviet Union, this kind of legislation gives officials carte blanche to act as they wish.[49] Only sanctioned churches benefit from tax breaks and exemption from military service for their clergy, are allowed to construct schools or receive government assistance for restoration of their religious structures. The 1997 "Law on Religion" in Russia, which replaced a more tolerant 1990 statute, reinstated Breshnev-era restrictions on religious minorities, which must demonstrate legal registration over the previous fifteen-year period to gain approval. The significance is that fifteen years prior marked a period of severe religious repression during which many of these groups (e.g., Jehovah's Witnesses) were completely illegal, and consequently, not registered. If religionists worship in unsanctioned churches, they are subject to harassment, arrest, and sometimes even torture, and their church property is destroyed.[50]

When a dominant faith allies itself with state power, repression of minority faiths can result. Because of its distinct historical roots, the Orthodox Church is deeply wedded to nations. Thus the administrative center of the Russian Orthodox Church had an active role in drafting the restrictive 1997 law, as well as in lobbying to see it passed over the objections of then-President Clinton and the Pope. One trend is to tag all other belief systems as "cults" or "sectarian," both of which are classed as illegitimate forms of faith. Discrimination is frequently shrouded by claims that religious groups are duping and victimizing people by employing malevolent means of manipulation. Such discrimination can take the form of either public statutes or such covert measures as inconsistent registration practices. The denial or delay of registration can result in deprivation of certain privileges inherent in basic theological practices, such as rights to property, access to media, rights to assembly, and rights to publish materials.[51]

As we see above, religious repression can result from the perceived threat unorthodox beliefs pose to the authority of the state.

The Jehovah's Witnesses, for example, are often the target of abuse due to their refusal of military service, which is frequently considered blatant repudiation of the legitimacy of the state. They have been proscribed and treated harshly, even by Western governments with democratic histories and fair levels of religious freedom.[52]

This treatment points to a new trend of democratically enacted intolerance, in which several states of the European Union have adopted "anticult" statutes. The State Department notes that in each of these states, existing criminal law is sufficient to address criminal behavior by groups or individuals, and that many unorthodox groups persecuted under these laws are actually "peaceful and straightforward."[53] Not only are these various statutes a threat to religious freedom in their own right, they offer a model, and perhaps a cover, for nondemocratic regimes elsewhere. How can champions of religious freedom chastise China for its anticult law if democratic France has one?

India presents an example of the consequences of politically backed religious extremism in an otherwise free society. India has a thriving democratic system, and its Hindu majority has long been viewed as tolerant of other religious faiths. The rise of Hindu nationalism, however, which equates Indian nationality with Hindu religion, has sparked attacks on Muslims and Christians, reprisals, and heartrending communal violence. This case also shows how political developments can undermine the enjoyment of religious freedom. Hindu nationalists, led by the BJP party, have maintained control of coalition governments in India from 1998–2004. The State Department reports that the BJP has "links to Hindu extremist groups that have been implicated in violent attacks against Christians and Muslims." The BJP also leads state governments where authorities have "not responded adequately to acts of violence against religious minorities by Hindu extremist groups," in part because of links between those groups and the BJP. In the state of Gujarat both Hindus and Muslims have died in these clashes, some burned alive. But Muslims have taken the brunt of the violence. In the spring of 2002, over a thousand Muslims were killed by Hindu mobs in the state.[54]

Religious nationalism has manifested itself elsewhere in Asia. In Nepal, Christians were arrested and forced to witness the severe beating of their pastor. They were threatened with the same manner of treatment if they refused to bow to a Hindu god.[55] Buddhism, also with a history of tolerance, claims its share of extremists. Sri Lankan monks mete out open hostility and harassment to Buddhists wishing to convert to another religion. While they do not force conversions of Christians, they have pressured the government to introduce a legal ban on converts away from Buddhism.[56]

Anti-Semitism has also reared its ugly head in the twenty-first century, thus undermining the security of Jewish life. The old blood libel against Jews has migrated from Europe to the Middle East, where the fraudulent Protocols of the Elders of Zion is sold extensively and mainstream media outlets propagate the most outlandish myths. In Saudi Arabia, for example, one commentator reported how Jews use the blood of Christian infants to prepare for the Passover meal. In Europe, meanwhile, a combustible mixture of anti-Zionist leftism, right-wing anti-Semitism, and hooliganism by alienated Muslim youth has resulted in numerous attacks against Jews and desecration of synagogues and graves. In Russia, Orthodox efforts to maintain religious dominance, along with the aggressive nationalist rhetoric of some politicians, has reignited anti-Semitism there. This recrudescence, when placed in the context of Jewish vulnerability in many parts of the Middle East, helps to explain the deep alliance between Jews and Christians in the antipersecution battle.

Of course, many Muslims point to widespread violations of Palestinian rights, including religious freedom. The State Department, in fact, reports that Muslims, Druze, and Arab Christians suffer from various forms of discrimination in Israel, and that the government's clampdown in the occupied territories inhibits Palestinians' ability to practice their faith. Palestinians and their sympathizers argue that Israeli policies constitute the oppression of an entire non-Jewish people.

FOCUS ON CHRISTIANS

In this section, I move from the general situation to the specific abuse of Christian minorities around the world. This focus makes sense on two levels. First, there are distinct contours of this problem, given the global dispersion of the faith and its association with independent civil society and the West. Second, the problem draws many American religionists into greater international engagement. As American believers become aware of persecuted coreligionists, they learn about the general plight of vulnerable people because the "persecuted church" also suffers amidst poverty, exploitation, and AIDS.

For faith-based activists, the need to highlight the persecution of Christians was crystallized in 1997 when the power of Hollywood was mobilized on behalf of another aggrieved religious minority. As Nina Shea observed: "Dustin Hoffman, Goldie Hawn, Oliver Stone, Larry King, and thirty other celebrities sponsored newspaper ads throughout Europe vehemently denouncing Germany's exclusion of Scientologists from government jobs, comparing the discrimination with the practices of the Nazis. Within hours, the U.S. State Department issued a public statement rebuking Germany." Shea complained that nothing comparable was being done on behalf of Christians "facing not simply discrimination but real terror in Sudan, China, Vietnam, Saudi Arabia, Pakistan, Egypt, and numerous other places."[57]

This terror was vividly displayed on September 25, 2002, when Pakistani gunmen entered the offices of the Organization for Peace and Justice in Karachi, a Catholic- and Protestant-supported group that provides free legal advice to poor workers and women. The gunmen methodically separated the seven Christian workers from the Muslims in the office, then bound and executed each of them. Pakistani intelligence officials suspected Islamic militants "who thrived under the Taliban regime who preached hate against non-Muslims."[58] This incident was but one of a number of murderous attacks on Christian groups in Pakistan that came in the wake of the international war on terrorism. What so shocked Pakistani officials and others was the calculated nature of the attack in which the gunmen took their time to segregate Christian from non-Christian workers at the charity. Also revealing, however, was the way in which the Western media often downplayed the religious nature of the attack. In a critique of media coverage of the event, Paul Marshall documented how often reports referred to murders of Christians in Pakistan as attacks on "Western interests."[59] All of those killed on September 25 and in prior assaults on Christian churches, however, were Pakistanis.

Since Christianity is the largest and most widely dispersed religious faith on the globe, with the cutting edge of its growth occurring outside of the West, numerous indigenous Christians live in hostile places without the protection of democratic rights. It has been estimated that some 200 million Christians live in countries where they face serious persecution, while another 400 million face nontrivial restrictions on their religious freedom. Probably thousands are killed annually, victims of despotic regimes or communal violence, an astonishing figure vastly underplayed by the Western press.[60] No wonder it has been asserted that the twentieth century produced more Christian martyrs than all the previous centuries combined, and that more are dying for their faith now than at any other time in history.[61] To be sure, one must place the situation in context. While more Christians in sheer number suffer persecution today, it is also true that most do not.[62] Still, the vulnerable percentage is striking. Taking the total of two billion Christians in the world, we see that the suffering church constitutes nearly a third of the total Christian population.[63]

One indicator of that suffering are the numbers seeking asylum. Richard Cizik of the National Association of Evangelicals claimed that evangelicals in the 1990s were the single largest group seeking asylum in the United States, yet their requests were routinely denied by a bureaucracy that he felt was "oblivious to religion around the world."[64] Before changes instituted by the International Religious Freedom Act, Christians fleeing repressive regimes were often deported back by the Immigration and Naturalization Service (INS), delivering "persecuted believers up like lambs to the slaughter."[65] Asylum seeking illustrates the vital link between the *suffering church* abroad and the *free church* in the West, which fuels the faith-based movement to harness the tools of American foreign policy in defense of global religious freedom.

Vivid stories play a crucial role in motivating American believers to action (see box 2.1). One report documented the confiscation and destruction of Bibles in China and arrest warrants naming 3,000 evangelical preachers. In Vietnam, Pastor Kon-Sa-Ha-Hak was photographed in a Vietnam prison camp with his hands bound behind his

---

Box 2.1.   Dateline: The World

Azerbaijan:	"Sixty Christians arrested at worship service."	1999
China:	"Largest mass arrest of Christians in recent years."	2000
China:	"Police destroy 15,000 religious sites in Zhejiang Province."	1998
Columbia:	"Christian leaders marked for assassination."	2000
Indonesia:	"Thousands of Christians attacked by Laskar Jihad."	2000
Laos:	"Christians forced to recant their faith."	2000
Nigeria:	"500,000 people uprooted, thousands dead in violence."	2002
Nigeria:	"Seventy churches destroyed."	1998
Saudi Arabia:	"Riyadh police break up Christian worship service."	2000
Sudan:	"4,119 more slaves liberated by Christian Solidarity International."	2001
Sudan:	"Over one hundred thousand killed, enslaved, displaced."	2002

These headlines, taken from newsletters of international Christian advocacy groups, news stories, and official reports, dramatize the plight of the "suffering church" abroad and create pressure for an American foreign-policy response.

---

back and lit cigarettes in his nose, being taunted by guards, while Dai Guillang was given a three-year prison term for propagating the book of Genesis.[66] In 1994 three Iranian evangelical pastors, Bishop Haik, Mehdi Dibaj, and Tateos Michaellian, all disappeared suddenly, only to be found dead a few days later.[67] The killing of such prominent leaders was viewed as a harbinger of threats to come by those in the nascent Christian solidarity movement.[68] And the words of Dibaj, who was imprisoned for ten years before his disappearance, inspired them. To his son he wrote: "I have always envied those Christians who all through the church history were martyred for Christ Jesus our Lord. What a privilege to live for our Lord and to die for Him as well."[69] In China, Bishop Fan Xueyan died in prison the day before his ten-year sentence was concluded. Photos indicative of torture evidenced that, among other things, both of his legs were dislocated below the knees.[70] Iranian Bishop Hovsepian-Mehr disappeared from Tehran in 1994, and his body was later found buried in a Muslim cemetery.[71] Indian Hindu fanatics have struck out at Catholic workers who pose a challenge to the caste system by providing relief to untouchables and women, and a number of nuns have been attacked by mobs.[72]

Where government brutality is not always present, sometimes cultural hegemony dramatically restricts religious freedom. In Egypt, for example, the Coptic community is beset by a combination of restrictive laws and local practices, as well as periodic communal violence that authorities do not always investigate. In Pakistan periodic raids on Christian villages by communally incited throngs produce terror, as homes are destroyed, females raped, and in some cases young girls kidnapped and forced to convert to Islam. The situation in Pakistan was dramatized when Catholic Bishop John Joseph committed suicide in protest of a conviction of one of his flock for blasphemy, which resulted in a death sentence for the parishioner.[73] While various laws on apostasy and blasphemy may not always be enforced by Islamic governments, they have made religious minorities more vulnerable to accusations and mob violence. The societal location of Christian minorities in such places as India and Pakistan results in discrimination and continued poverty. In Pakistan, for instance, 90 percent of Christians are either unemployed or have the basest positions, such as removing human excrement from the streets.[74] In India, the conversion to Christianity of Dalits, or those in the untouchable caste, produces deep resentment among Hindu traditionalists and sparks reprisals.

Christian solidarity activists often use these vivid accounts to rebuke comfortable believers. We see provocative references to the sleeping *free* Church "oblivious of their struggle and agony, just as Peter, James, and John slept in the moment of their Savior's agony. . . . Will you also sleep while the Underground Church, your brethren in Christ, suffer and fight alone for the Gospel?"[75] Others offer a more secular argument about why the faith community must awaken: otherwise the tyrants win. As Nina Shea observed, Hitler reassured his skittish generals that the world would be indifferent to the killing of civilians by retorting, "Who speaks today about the Armenians?"[76] In other words, in the economy of human rights, silence during the Armenian genocide emboldened Hitler; silence today in the face of contemporary abuses will do the same.

Attacks on Christian minorities do provide an early warning of wider threats. A vivid example concerns the rise of militant fundamentalist movements. In southeast Asia, as noted, militants spawned a variety of violent groups bent on enforcing their interpretation of Shari'a. To intimidate or subjugate Christian populations, these groups inaugurated a terror campaign of church bombings and indiscriminate killings, sometimes on a massive scale. Religious freedom advocates issued emergency alerts on these attacks and were aghast that the government of Indonesia refused to arrest Abu Bakar Bashir, the militant cleric who headed Jemaah Islamiyah, a group implicated in terrorist acts in Malaysia and Singapore. One reason was that Bashir, who often praised Osama bin Laden and castigated Americans and Jews as terrorists, was backed by the vice president of Indonesia, Hamzah Haz.[77] These warnings went unheeded until a terrorist bomb killed nearly 200 people on the Indonesian island of Bali in October of 2002. In the wake of the blast, the Indonesian government finally began to crack down on Jemaah Islamiyah. A collapsing Indonesian stock market, along with pressure from nations around the world whose citizens were killed, tilted the politics away from the relaxed response toward Islamic militancy.

The imposition of extreme Shari'a, sometimes on a local village level, not only falls harshly on women but can be manipulated in perverse ways to intimidate vulnerable Christian minorities. In one widely reported instance, a thirteen-year-old Christian girl in Bangladesh was raped and impregnated by a Muslim man. Unable to secure Muslim male witnesses to the rape, the girl was instead charged with adultery.[78] Harsh enforcement of family law can also disrupt marriages among Christians or result in forced marriages and conversions. In other cases blasphemy laws are selectively levied against Christians by unscrupulous neighbors as a means to ruin the reputation of rivals or in retaliation for personal grievances. Before its crackdown on Islamic militants, Pakistan's law led to arrests of numerous Christians for violations, including an illiterate eleven-year-old accused of blasphemous writings.[79] Even when the accused have been acquitted, some have been killed by vigilantes.

Such mob violence is another aspect of militant Shari'a. In Egypt mob attacks on Coptic people have killed scores, but have not been prosecuted aggressively by the authorities. Officials sometimes stand by, unable or unwilling to effectively intervene. Another form of intimidation is the murders of Muslims who convert to Christianity. In 1997, for example, a Pakistani man murdered his sister for her conversion to Christianity, but was never charged with a crime.[80]

Sometimes Christians are singled out because they represent independent civil society. A significant religious minority in North Korea before the Communist dictatorship took power, Christians have faced a regime that sought to wipe out all but a few Potemkin representations of the faith. Perhaps only 1 percent of North Korea's population are now Christians, yet Freedom House reports that "Christianity is perceived by authorities to be a dangerous threat, with the potential of undermining the Kim dynasty." The regime acts accordingly. To profess Christianity indicates insanity or status as an enemy of the state. Sent to labor camps, "Christians are given the heaviest work, the least amount of food, and the worst conditions in prison." Witnesses report Christians being executed with hot irons; children and grandchildren of Christians face life imprisonment for the beliefs and practices of their progenitors. A death sentence awaits those refugees forcibly returned by China who are suspected of being Christians.[81]

North Korean officials, however, strive to create a mirage of religious tolerance to impress the West, but have built only three Christian church structures since 1988 that are used solely as a facade for Western observers.[82] The government opened a seminary "only to train personnel to facilitate reception of assistance funds from foreign faith-based NGO's."[83]

In China restrictions have spawned a paradox in which the official churches register only a fraction of China's estimated 50–70 million Christians. Because of the size of the underground Christian church, the Chinese authorities keep busy arresting believers and destroying church sites. According to Freedom House, China owns the dubious distinction of having more Christian prisoners than any other country in the world.[84] To be sure, there is wide variability from region to region. A few prominent "underground" pastors operate above ground, while others must serve their flocks from secret forest sanctuaries or cramped rooms. And many of the devout do find spiritual succor in state-approved churches.[85]

Harsh treatment of Christians provides models of courage and faithfulness that inspire American believers. Reverend Tran Mai, sentenced to three years in Vietnam, testified that he had been beaten by security police, bound, left in the sun, and denied water for extended periods of time.[86] Commenting on this kind of thing, Pastor Dinh Thien Tu remarked in matter-of-fact fashion that persecution "is not a major issue for most Vietnamese pastors. It comes with the territory. It's part of our normal church life."[87]

Though American evangelicals see persecution and martyrdom as the "seeds" of church growth, sometimes the reverse is the case. This has been the story behind the decline of the Christian minority population in the Middle East. At the beginning of this century there were sizable Christian minorities from Turkey down to Egypt and across to Iraq. The environment turned far more hostile for such minorities with the collapse of the Ottoman Empire, the creation of autocratic new states, and the rise of Islamic militancy. The decline began dramatically in 1915 with the century's first genocide against Turkey's Armenian Christian population, which was largely eradicated or expelled. Since then, the Christian population elsewhere has declined precipitously as believers fled harassment by dictatorships, discriminatory treatment, or communal violence. In Syria, for example, more than 100,000 Christians have fled since 1975, leaving only 10,000 remaining.[88]

BRINGING THE SUFFERING CHURCH TO AMERICA

Stories of persecution are brought vividly to America through personal visits by those who themselves have suffered for the faith. Increasingly, pastors, bishops, and lay activists from abroad frequent the religious circuit in the United States to share poignant testimony of how God sustained them in suffering and how the Spirit works to gain souls despite persecution.

Voice of the Martyrs, one of the largest of the advocacy groups, vividly illustrates this phenomenon.[89] At one annual conference I noticed huge maps of the world, displays of Christian communities in Africa, the Middle East, and Asia in the lobby, and rooms brimming with books, tapes, and videos featuring Christian heroes abroad. The atmosphere in the conference was thoroughly evangelical, with lots of "amen"s and "praise the Lord," but it also exuded an international flavor, featuring a Hmong choir from Laos and a group of Persian musicians from Iran. The attendees (mostly from North America) were, in their own way, globalists who had come to hear and meet leaders of the persecuted church abroad.

There was a beaming Pastor Wally who suffered imprisonment, beatings, and near execution at the hands of authorities in Saudi Arabia for leading Christian worship services for Filipinos. There was Thuong Tram, a sophisticated young woman from Vietnam, who could pass for a political science graduate student or a representative at a feminist conference. A born-again Christian, she fled from a regime that sees religion as a threat to its hold on power. There was Noble Alexander, who spent over two decades in Cuban jails, testifying with amazing humor about the "power and love of the Holy Spirit" that sustained his missionary work despite excruciating torture. In one of his vignettes, he described being placed waist deep in a pool of raw sewage, but then recounted how God provided a sign, a fragrant blossom that bloomed during the night to overcome the stench.

There was Bob Fu, a born-again Christian from China who described how he led two lives—an English instructor for top party officials during weekdays, an illegal evangelist in off-hours. There was Brother Robak, who ministered at great peril to Persian Christians on the front lines of the Iran-Iraq war; Brother Kim and Sister Lee, who work to penetrate North Korea with Christian ministry; and Dr. Vang, a refugee from Communist Laos who led a team to produce the first Hmong Bible translation in the world.

It would take the most hardened skeptic to resist being touched and inspired by these believers, who seem to radiate good humor and conviction. And it is not hard to conceive the potential political clout of channeling concern for such people into a coordinated campaign to influence American foreign policy. Without realizing it, therefore, a number of American Christians are becoming internationalists, translating their relationships abroad into resources for foreign-policy influence.

THE CASE FOR AMERICAN LEADERSHIP ON INTERNATIONAL RELIGIOUS FREEDOM

Because a certain ambivalence toward religion exists in policy circles, it is helpful to outline the case for American leadership on behalf of religious freedom. One part of that case is suggested by the vulnerability of religious freedom. While Freedom House documents general advances in freedom and democracy over the past decades, its Center for Religious Freedom notes a lagging condition for religious freedom (see table 2.1).[90]

The case also rests on the international declaratory tradition of human rights. Virtually all of the globe's nations are signatories to documents that affirm religious freedom as a fundamental right. Thus by promoting Religious Freedom the United States can be viewed as nudging nations to live up to international covenants they agreed to. These covenants include the UN charter, the Universal Declaration of Human Rights of 1948, the International Covenant on Civil and Political Rights of 1966, the Helsinki Accords of 1975, and the UN Declaration on the Elimination of All Forms of Intolerance and Discrimination Based on Religion or Belief of 1981.[91]

The United States has been a central player in all of these initiatives. Eleanor Roosevelt, for example, helped guide the United Nations in drafting the universal declaration, whose Article 18 states: "Everyone has the right to freedom of thought, conscience and religion; this includes the freedom to change his religion or belief, and freedom whether alone on in community with others and in public

Table 2.1.   Comparison of Freedom House Indexes (Percent of World Population)

Index	Broad Freedom Index	Religious Freedom
Free	41%	25%
Partially Free	24%	39%

or private, to manifest his religion or belief in teaching, practices, worship, and observance."[92]

This ringing declaration provides a clear standard: religious believers should enjoy the right to worship freely; express their beliefs publicly; educate their children according to these beliefs; build and run houses of worship, schools, universities, and seminaries; enjoy freedom from discrimination in employment and political access; and retain the liberty to take up, abandon, proclaim, or dissent from their religion. By promoting this vision, the United States serves both its own interest and the good of humankind. A good case can be made that countries that generally respect these rights are less likely to pose a threat to neighbors or regional peace. Internal persecution often results in external instability. Or as elaborated by John Hanford, U.S. ambassador-at-large for International Religious Freedom, to the extent that American policy succeeds, it will provide one of the most "sustainable antidotes" to "religion-based violence and a potential clash of civilizations."[93]

Promoting religious freedom seems warranted by the corresponding priority the world's dictators place on denying it. Many of the victims of the twentieth-century's spectacular carnage were indeed "perversely singled out because of their faith."[94] This bloody legacy should spur us to fashion international norms to "make sure that the twenty-first century is not a repeat of the twentieth century."[95] In striving to achieve this aim, we should not gainsay the role of exposure, or what Robert Drinan calls the "mobilization of shame."[96]

Common European criticism of American initiatives is that they reflect unilateralism, self-righteousness, and inconsistency.[97] But this thrust in American foreign policy uniquely reflects the nation's distinct historical legacy, which treats free religious societies as a crucial foundation for pluralist democracy.[98] Deeply ingrained in the American experience, the constitutional guarantee of religious freedom is trumpeted by religious freedom advocates. Senator Joseph Lieberman asserted that the Bill of Rights "enshrines religious freedom as the First Freedom," a depiction more than mere rhetoric.[99] Some fear that this self-consciousness will lead America to impose its tradition on different cultures or to arrogate the role of "moral watchdog" for the world.[100] Viewed another way, however, the American model actually represents the cumulative and often painful struggle by religious minorities to achieve equal status in society. Thus there is nothing inherently wrong with American leaders drawing upon the nation's pluralist tradition in promoting the universal norm of religious freedom.

A key reason for American leadership on the issue is its preeminence in the post–Cold War world. When other nations complain about the American "hegemon" or "hyperpower," they concede the unique position of the United States as the globe's preeminent economic, military, and diplomatic power. If the United States uses that power to promote values held as "universal" in international covenants, its power will be more respected. Given the distinct constitutional tradition of the United States, it can offer a unique counterweight to the kind of soft hostility toward religious exercise that has begun to infect the increasingly secular nations of Western Europe.

The case for religious freedom extends beyond its intrinsic justice. Freedom of religion is a rich and potent human right, for its very practice entails other human rights as well: the right to assemble, to express oneself freely, to print literature, to own property.[101] Churches and religious organizations are vital to a healthy civil society, to the layer of mediating institutions whose importance to democracy Alexis de Tocqueville famously stressed.

Concern about persecution of Christians, to be sure, has been one of the driving forces for the movement to promote religious freedom in American foreign policy. This has led to the charge that the campaign involves "special pleading." But as one liberal writer noted, this "seems a remarkable attitude for a human rights activist, since, by definition, all arguments on behalf of all persecuted groups—racial minorities, political minorities, ethnic minorities, etc.—are 'special pleadings' intended to help 'certain classes' of victims."[102] Human rights campaigns on behalf of particular parties—South African blacks, Soviet Jews, East European dissidents, the Argentine disappeared, and victims of female circumcision—provide the primary energy for advances.

Behind the charge of special pleading is a view that the religious freedom movement is merely a Trojan horse to promote Christianity, especially missionary activity. As we will see, this is not an accurate depiction of the interfaith movement. But even if it is true that some advocates are motivated by the desire to protect Christianity abroad, their efforts promote free spaces for other religious minorities in civil society. An evenhanded policy promoting religious freedom should signal not only to Christian minorities, but Muslims, Buddhists, Jews, and others that the United States stands with their struggle for free expression.

While some charge that American initiatives create a "hierarchy of human rights," advocates respond that "religious freedom has been the orphan of human rights for so many years" that the United States is merely addressing a gap in its foreign policy. As Congressman Chris Smith observed, "When I joined with my colleagues in trying to stop apartheid back in the early 1980s, against the objections of the Reagan Administration, we weren't saying when you emphasize racism, somehow there's a diminution of concern about other human rights. Human rights all hang together. When we advance the ball in one area, we advance the ball in all other areas."[103] Advancing human rights, in other words, is not a zero-sum game in which the promotion of some rights involves the diminution of others. Rather than competing, different rights are mutually reinforcing.

A number of detractors emphasize the negative role of religion—its historic record as a major source of persecution. From the Spanish Inquisition to the Taliban of Afghanistan, religious institutions, when enmeshed with coercive state power, have harshly oppressed dissenters. This record leads some to believe that religion should not be treated as other human rights.[104] But acknowledging the sins of religion does not mean that religious freedom should be less vigorously promoted than other human rights. Rather, promoting it will further protect minority faiths from the abuses of state power.

Much criticism of the cause seems to reflect mistrust of its conservative religious supporters.[105] As we will see in subsequent chapters, evangelical motivation was not driven by eschatological or right-wing motives, and legislative initiatives were backed by a wide array of religious constituencies, including Jews, Catholics, Anglicans, Tibetan Buddhists, and Baha'is.

Good Friday services in the Nuba Mountains, Sudan. Courtesy of the Center for Religious Freedom at Freedom House.

The new human rights alliance spawned by the mobilization for religious freedom also serves as a valuable counterweight to corporate influence in foreign policy. While a case can be made that economic engagement, under the right circumstances, can promote liberalization in authoritarian regimes, businesses will make their peace with despots unless there are countervailing pressures. Today, mobilization through churches constitutes the only serious challenge to the periodic hijacking of foreign policy by global business interests perfectly content to ignore the sometimes abysmal human rights record of their trading partners. Ironically, by providing this counterweight, the faith-based movement may protect businesses from their own shortsighted practices. In celebrating the passage of the International Religious Freedom Act, Congressman Frank Wolf stressed that "when you're trading with a country that's respecting human rights, when you're trading with a country that's allowing people to worship . . . your business deals are better there than they are with a country that's throwing priests and bishops and evangelical pastors and Buddhist monks in jail."[106]

The faith-based coalition also offers a kind of sustained rebuke of those foreign-policy "realists" who would abandon the hope of ameliorating human rights abuses around the globe. Seared by the specter of bloody ethnic clashes and mob anarchy, some thinkers have come to the conclusion that Western efforts to promote democracy and human rights are doomed to failure or worse, likely to destabilize fragile regimes.[107] Churches, with their links to struggling communities abroad, are not willing to embrace this pessimistic resignation. They provide the leaven of hope without which progress is impossible.

Of course, the way the United States promotes religious freedom is crucial. Charges of hypocrisy will stick if U.S. policy lacks consistency. The U.S. Commission on International Religious Freedom, for example, has recommended that Saudi Arabia be included in the State Department's list of "Countries of Concern"—those nations that egregiously violate religious freedom. By refusing to do so, the State Department has invited criticism that it is not willing to offend a strategic ally. The consequences of such inconsistency go beyond public relations. As noted, the Saudi regime has been using petrodollars to promote its brand of Islam throughout the region and into the United States. By slighting harsh treatment of religious minorities in Saudi Arabia, the United States unintentionally acquiesced to this severe version of Islamic teaching.

It must be noted that Muslim groups often expressed suspicion for the legislative thrusts of this new movement. This is not surprising because Muslim countries are often charged with violations of religious freedom and listed as among the worst persecutors. Moreover, Christian advocates sometimes cast the entire Islamic world in a harsh light. As the movement takes hold in the administrative apparatus of U.S. government, however, Muslim concerns are being addressed and, indeed, atrocities against various Muslim groups abroad spotlighted. Equally important, the model of free religious societies promoted by the movement does not represent a vital challenge so much to Islam as to the authoritarian regimes that many Muslims live under. Movement activists note how they get back-channel communications from moderate Muslim leaders abroad, who say that they would have to denounce religious freedom legislation in public but supported it in private. In many parts of the Islamic world, indeed, governments under sway of fundamentalist radicals represent as much a threat to other Muslims as to non-Muslim minorities. A good case can also be made that Islamic terrorism thrives precisely where people are not free, so that to the extent American leadership can crack open spaces for broader human rights, it should do so.

A final argument in favor of this faith-based movement is that it has mobilized new grassroots support for the cause of human rights. Through the crucible of engagement, "parochial" concern for fellow believers has given way to broader human rights advocacy. We see this in broad alliances on human rights in China, Sudan, and North Korea. We see it in the "new abolitionist" movement against human trafficking that is literally freeing adults and children from brutal forms of modern slavery.[108] As secular human rights activists look beyond their suspicions, they will find in churches the potential for allies in a coalition far larger than their cause has hitherto enjoyed.

3

THE BARRIERS OF BABEL

When he first got to know Sudanese people, Charles Jacobs felt a deep emotional bond. He thought of them like fellow Jews, victims of a hidden holocaust ignored by the world, decent people lost in the bigger chessboard of international politics. This sense of kinship deepened when Jacobs, president of the Boston-based American Anti-Slavery Group, traveled to Sudan with a Christian group to redeem African slaves captured by militia of the fundamentalist regime. The trip coincided with Passover, so Jacobs conducted a service in the Sudanese bush, where he "drank the holy wine and broke the matzo" before purchasing the slaves freedom. Stunned by the symbolism, Jacobs thought to himself that this was occurring in a country adjacent to Egypt, "not so many hundreds of miles from where my people were freed."[1]

Jacobs did not foresee this life-altering activism when he wrote a 1994 op-ed piece in the *New York Times* on slavery and atrocities in Sudan.[2] He "naively" assumed that when the monstrous injustice perpetrated by this "fascist regime" was exposed, the cause would be seized by the major human rights groups, the United Nations, civil rights organizations, and the mass media. He had done his job. What he discovered, instead, were biases and blinders that kept these organizations from tackling one of the world's worst human rights situations. So Jacobs, girding for a long-term battle, formed a new organization devoted to fighting global slavery. Like his fellow activists, Jacobs learned that filling this void in human rights advocacy meant overcoming barriers unimaginable during the antiapartheid campaign.

All human rights activists must contend with potent resistance, but religious advocates face additional obstacles. There are sectarian divisions, disagreement about remedies, left-wing suspicion, and a secular bias among many journalists, intellectuals, and foreign-policymakers, who see religion as backward or problematic. To understand the striking achievements of the faith-based movement, one must appreciate the discordant babel of voices that threatened to stymie its promotion of religious freedom, and thus its subsequent initiatives.[3]

THE JEWISH EXAMPLE

Many advocates for persecuted Christians saw their initial endeavor modeled on the vigorous campaign for Soviet Jewry, when American Jews and their allies fought on behalf of those seeking to emigrate. Apparent similarities between the two issues are striking. Just as the

Abe Rosenthal, former New York Times *editor and columnist. He wrote numerous articles raising concern about persecution of Christians abroad.*

focus on persecuted Jews exposed cracks in the Soviet empire, today's advocates argue that pressing for greater freedom for Christians and other minorities abroad would foster new spaces for wider freedoms and general societal openness.[4] As with the campaign for Soviet Jewry, opposition to the movement for the persecuted arises from foreign-policy "realists" who see such "soft" initiatives as naive, or from corporate lobbies loath to offend foreign trading partners.

The focus on congressional legislation is another similarity. Advocates for Soviet Jewry gained passage of the Jackson-Vanik provision, which promised normalized trade relations and credit if the Soviet Union met open emigration guidelines.[5] Faith-based activists made the case that religious freedom legislation would provide the same kind of leverage for the persecuted that the Jackson-Vanik provided for Soviet Jewry.

Finally, campaign tactics on behalf of persecuted religious minorities mirror those employed by Jews nearly three decades previous— fostering public awareness through dramatic media exposure, personalizing the persecution, mobilizing congregations, and mounting constituency pressure—thus making the issue one that members of Congress and executive branch officials could not ignore.

Beyond these similarities, as I will show, there are a number of differences that must be understood. To highlight those differences it is helpful to chart what brought legislative success in the campaign for Soviet Jewry.

To begin with, Jews are a people whose shared crucible of persecution and Holocaust forged a profound solidarity on fundamental questions. Though diverse theologically and ideologically, on issues that touch on the survival of Israel and the Jewish people, Jews demonstrate unity and vigor. Indeed, among the ethnic lobbies that hope to shape U.S. foreign policy, the lament often heard is "why can't we be like the Jews."[6]

During the campaign for Soviet Jewry, active congregants heard poignant stories of oppressed brothers and sisters. Temples and synagogues sported banners demanding freedom for Jewish refuseniks, and Russian dissident Natan Sharansky became a living symbol of their plight. The message was proclaimed in books, internal news organs, congregational flyers, and in extensive popular press coverage. In addition, Jewish lobbyists in Washington brought to bear legendary skills and found ready allies among labor unions and anti-Communists.[7] These Washington insiders also capitalized on a vigorous grassroots response to keep the issue before Congress. A final feature of the campaign was its simplicity. Advocates focused on a single goal—the freedom to emigrate—and a single system—the Soviet Union and allied nonmarket regimes.

Jackson-Vanik was hailed both as a triumph for Jewish lobbies and a foreign-policy success, which kept economic and political pressure on the Soviet Union and its client states.[8] By shining light on how Communist systems prevented emigration, the law helped undermine the legitimacy of these regimes. When dissidents and others saw that the regime could not "pick on a few Jews" with impunity, cracks began to form in totalitarian systems that no longer looked ten feet tall.

Advocates for persecuted Christians echo these arguments, taking heart in the collapse of Communist regimes in the "velvet revolution" of 1989. In contrast to Jackson-Vanik, however, the current campaign for the persecuted is global in reach, multifaceted in its aims, and more complex in implementation. As a focus of American foreign policy, promoting religious freedom involves many nations with extraordinarily diverse strategic and commercial ties to the United States. This complexity enables skeptics to challenge the potential efficacy of the ongoing crusade. Moreover, Washington journalists and opinion leaders until recently have shown little interest in the issue, which receives less of the sustained publicity that the campaign for Soviet Jews did.

One might have anticipated, at least, Christian churches in the West mobilizing with unified vigor to champion persecuted brothers and sisters abroad, just as Jews did a generation earlier. While a formidable segment of American Christians did spring into action, the broader community remains divided or diverted.

Ironically, while the American Christian leadership evinced this mixed response, Jews have been among the most aggressive and effective advocates of persecuted Christians abroad. This high profile support challenged a standard journalistic story line—"Jews oppose evangelicals"—and overcame liberal suspicions that the movement was a Trojan horse for the Christian Right. Preeminent, of course, was Michael Horowitz, who made the problem his personal crusade. But Horowitz was joined by a broad cross section of Jewish leader-

Rabbi David Saperstein, director of the Religious Action Center of the Union of American Hebrew Congregations. As a key player in the initiatives of the faith-based movement, Saperstein enhanced its ecumenism.
Courtesy of the Religious Action Center.

ship. There was Charles Jacobs of the American Anti-Slavery Group, another figure hailed as a "Jew saving Christians." There was *New York Times* columnist Abe Rosenthal, who penned numerous *New York Times* columns on the issue.[9] There was Rabbi David Saperstein, the liberal mainstay for Reform Judaism who served as the first chair of the U.S. Commission on International Religious Freedom. He argued that support from Christians during the campaign for Soviet Jews commanded a response from Jews on behalf of persecuted Christians, and that "when God's children are imprisoned for praying, then Americans must speak out."[10] There was Elliott Abrams, who succeeded Saperstein as Chair of the Commission for International Religious Freedom. There was Stacie Burdette of the Anti-Defamation League, who listed implementation of the International Religious Freedom Act (IRFA) as a key organizational goal. Finally, there was Senator Joseph Lieberman, who cited sponsorship of the IRFA as one of his major legislative achievements.

Skeptics have ascribed self-interested political motives to this Jewish support, such as a payback for Christian conservative support of Israel or, less cynically, as a weapon to contain militant Islam. I have encountered little evidence of this first claim, while the latter dovetails nicely with traditional Jewish devotion to human rights and natural sympathy for the persecuted. Perhaps just as African Americans have second sight into America's soul, Jews have acute eyes for persecution. How else could we explain the fact that, at times, Jewish leaders have demonstrated more unity in the campaign against persecution of Christians than have American Christian leaders?

This brings into sharp relief the challenges faced by those seeking to mobilize American Christians on behalf of fellow believers abroad. Though notable mobilization is occurring, especially in the evangelical world, Christian solidarity activists have not approximated the level of Jewish unity and vigor in the campaign for Soviet Jewry. Christianity is simply too multifarious to engender the sense of peoplehood characteristic of Jews. And nowhere is the pluralism of Christian expression more evident than in the United States. To understand impediments to more unified and vigorous action by followers of Christ requires a venture into the sociological dynamics of American Christianity.

THE SOCIOLOGICAL CHALLENGE OF
AMERICAN CHRISTIANITY

A crucial feature of American religious life is its volunteer character, which arose in the eighteenth century when state governments ended "religious establishments" and ceased to provide financial support to churches. This created the first open religious marketplace in the world, where churches had to depend on member contributions to sustain them. Churches that lose their evangelical zeal, which cease to meet the spiritual hungers of people, thus lose "market share" to upstart entrepreneurs.[11] The experiment in religious freedom produced a bewildering pluralism of Christian expressions, with literally hundreds of different denominations and sects competing for the faithful. While this entrepreneurial environment ensures religious vitality, it also can undermine a unified and vigorous attention to international concerns.

Diffuse Focus

Successful political mobilization requires sustained focus and lay interest. American churches already invest impressive efforts in sustaining an array of congregations, religious schools, colleges, hospitals, charities, and world relief agencies. In addition, the growth of the administrative state in the United States has produced an unusually large and complex agenda for religious advocates as they respond to government impacts on their institutions, hospitals, schools, and the like. International engagement can be perceived as siphoning energies away from such institutional maintenance.

A review of church publications and news organs demonstrates the effort required to sustain large, complex church organizations. Consider the case of one denomination. As the persecution issue heated up, the Presbyterian General Assembly had before it some 130 resolutions for consideration, 95 of which concerned church governance, ministry issues, or internal policies.[12] We see this same pattern for the Methodists, Episcopalians, Lutherans, and Congregationalists.

Scholars also note how our "denominational" society represents a kind of détente between religious groups, as well as an unconventional pact with the broader polity.[13] In return for the nation's grant of broad religious freedom, groups tacitly agreed to be domesticated, to not challenge the fundamental premises of the regime, and generally to tolerate one another.[14] This can lead church leaders to mute vigorous and sustained political effort. Thus the great examples of successful religious mobilization—the abolitionist, temperance, and civil rights movements—are more the exception than the routine, with most of the visible political effort restricted most of the time to marginal adjustments in policy.

Even when churches are not fighting these institutional maintenance battles, the breadth of their political concerns can crowd out new issues. Among the so-called mainline churches,[15] for example, we see denominational resolutions dealing with an astonishing range of domestic and foreign-policy issues. In one year, for example, the Presbyterian church passed thirty-five resolutions encompassing domestic violence, movie ratings, poverty, homelessness, disarmament, sexual exploitation of women and children, Middle East relationships, and international family planning. Notably, three resolutions did deal with religious persecution—one concerned persecution of Christians generally, another advocating prayer for the persecuted church, and another focused on Sudan.[16]

The 1996 United Methodist General Conference, on the other hand, took positions on abortion, AIDS awareness, homosexuality, health care, substance abuse, immigration, and racism, but nothing on religious persecution.[17] Even as the issue of religious persecution percolated up in Congress, the response of some religious groups was silent. A month before a crucial House committee vote, the "Legislative Update" of the Lutheran Office for Governmental Affairs contained nothing about the issue, though it did feature articles on campaign finance reform, food stamps, child care, health care, Haitian refugees, the land mine ban, Cuban trade, and the earned income tax credit. From the "ecumenical" branch of Protestantism, initially at least, just about every liberal social concern was represented, with persecution of brethren largely pushed onto the margins.

Evangelicals and Catholics, similarly, operate with a huge agenda, encompassing broad issues of religious conscience and commitment. The Catholic Church, as the operator of the nation's largest nonprofit hospital system, the premier parochial school network, and a far-reaching charitable world relief enterprise, has huge stakes in health care, education policy, and international relations. It is also heavily invested in the abortion controversy. Evangelicals, meanwhile, see themselves defending the faith on numerous fronts against materialist trends and secular attacks.

For all religious groups, consequently, maintaining organizational focus on a single foreign policy is a daunting task. Equally challenging is generating lay interest in an issue so far from home. Not only are parishioners stretched thin by family and work obligations, but in some cases they may be too comfortable to relate to the persecution of brothers and sisters around the world.

The international nature of churches today can militate against taking on controversial issues that might threaten delicate relationships with particular state authorities. Some church relief organizations and foreign mission groups fear that making persecution a high profile focus of American foreign policy would undermine access, which in some cases is already tenuous, to the nations identified as persecutors. This honest, if excruciating trade-off can place religious leaders at odds with each other, even within denominations. Of course, this babel of contending views may also provide cover for politicians loath to act against economic interests or strategic nations.

The Scandal of Division

Another challenge for movement advocates remains the lack of unity among Christian groups. Unlike Judaism, which inheres in a distinct people, Christianity proclaims universal application. This represents both its strength and its potential weakness. Christianity may produce a broad civilization,[18] but because it spreads itself over such diverse cultures and nations, it does not produce a distinct people with natural solidarity—no "Next year in Jerusalem!"

Sociologists of religion, for example, have observed how the Christian faith has been molded to fit ethnic, class, sectional, or national identities. Christian sociologist H. Richard Niebuhr bemoaned the scandal of disunity, which he saw flowing from worldly compromises of the demanding ethical standards of Christ. But he also offered an astute empirical analysis of how differently the message was preached and practiced. Niebuhr noted how this pluralism produced profoundly different views of the Christian message itself. Thus solidarity is undermined as the faith is filtered through different ideological or cultural prisms.[19] The "social sources" of division would produce churches of the dispossessed, churches of the middle classes, nationalist churches, immigrant and ethnic churches, sectional churches, and so forth. While this was a worldwide phenomenon, nowhere has Christian pluralism flourished as it does in the United States.

To be sure, when just a fraction of the Christian population agitated for legislation on religious freedom, sex trafficking, and the Sudan cause, Congress acted. But disunity and waning interest in the pews may undermine robust follow-through, which flows from sustained pressure.

The Culture Wars

Religious divisions are exacerbated by competing visions of what America should become. Scholars note how domestic alliances have increasingly congealed into two divergent, mutually hostile camps of theological liberals and conservatives that cut across denominational lines. This great cultural divide is in part a legacy of the clash between modernists and fundamentalists earlier in this century, but has been sharpened and heightened by "the larger social unrest that emerged in the 1960s."[20]

This theological divide is evinced by the mutual stereotyping we see in church groups today. Sociologist Robert Wuthnow summarizes survey evidence to illustrate this phenomenon:

> People who identified themselves as religious liberals were prone to stereotype their conservative brethren as intolerant, morally rigid, fanatical, unsophisticated, closed-minded, and simplistic. The animosity recorded from the other side was equally blatant. Self-identified religious conservatives thought religious liberals were morally loose, were too hung up on social concerns rather than truly knowing what Christianity was all about, had only a shallow knowledge of the Bible, and were deeply compromised by secular humanism.[21]

This pattern produces deep suspicion, making coalitional efforts especially arduous.

This cultural clash gives religious divisions a harsh political edge. As James Davison Hunter has noted, skirmishes over abortion, homosexuality, pornography, public education, law, public expressions of faith, family structure, and welfare constitute a larger war over the culture. Thus partisans on opposite sides of the culture wars see each other as mortal adversaries in a struggle for the soul of the nation. The progressive coalition sees the Christian Right as a threat to gains in civil rights and liberties, women's liberation, gay rights, and tolerance for religious minorities. The orthodox coalition sees secularizing culture in a moral free fall, believers ridiculed and marginalized, and liberal religious opponents in league with forces that would plunge the nation into a decadent dark ages.[22]

Though the reality of a culture war among most lay people has probably been exaggerated, we have plenty of evidence that among clergy and church leaders the cultural divide is real and intense.[23] This is why in Washington, D.C., one finds liberal Protestant lobbyists at odds with evangelicals and fundamentalists on almost every contentious public question, with Catholics aligning with one or the other on the basis of issues.[24] The suspicions created by this divide can inhibit partnerships even when common ground exists.

Competing Impulses in the Evangelical World

With rich social networks and broadcast ministries, the evangelical world has no match in the capacity to mobilize grassroots pressure. From the mid-1990s onward born-again Protestants have provided the groundswell for initiatives against religious persecution, trafficking, and other abuses. This achievement is a testament to the growing reach and sophistication of evangelical leaders, but it did not come easy and is not necessarily sustainable. Despite the popular media image of a disciplined "Christian Right" drawing millions of evangelicals into its fold, Bible-believers have competing impulses toward politics in general and international engagement in particular. These tendencies had to be overcome during the antipersecution campaign and remain obstacles to sustained pressure for continued action.

One impulse in the evangelical community is to withdraw into personal piety or communal devotions detached from the wider world. Many evangelicals remain focused on the individual dimension of the faith, and their churches respond with spiritual succor, therapeutic ministries, family support, and in some cases even the promise of personal prosperity. Harvard political scientist Robert Putnam contends that evangelical congregations produce strong bonds among members but do less "bridging" outward.[25]

Contrary to their "fundamentalist" image, most evangelicals are neither militant nor overly focused on politics.[26] Indeed, overt political action often carries the taint of worldly preoccupation, which can distract the faithful from spreading the good news of salvation.[27] Evangelicals can also be hesitant to appear too self-interested in their political efforts. Michael Horowitz found evangelicals apologetic about the past sins of Christendom and sheepish about advocating for their fellow believers abroad.[28]

A second impulse for evangelicals, when they do engage in politics, is to focus on domestic issues. Thus the issue of persecution abroad does not always hit people where they live. Intensely concerned about their children, civic evangelicals invest heavily in battles over education, trash television, or religious rights at home. With popular culture seemingly inhospitable to "people of faith," enormous energies are spent either fighting rearguard actions against degradation of the moral ecology or carving out space for religiously grounded education. At the same time that evangelical leaders were mobilizing for international religious freedom legislation, for example, others were mounting campaigns for a "school prayer" amendment to the Constitution and legislation to broaden the judicial protection of the "free exercise" of faith.

Awareness of persecution against Christians abroad does not necessarily result in political action because a third impulse sees persecution and martyrdom as biblically foretold and even necessary for the faith. Tertullian's famous dictum—"The blood of the martyrs is the seed of the Church"—is often quoted by evangelicals and can be used to justify political quiescence. One can pray for the persecuted, feel inspired by their stories, even prepare for a similar fate. But to expect politics to ameliorate this situation may be fruitless or even counterproductive to God's plan of using martyrdom to build the global Church. This theological justification to eschew political action, in fact, was expressed by some evangelical leaders at the first strategy meetings convened by Freedom House in 1996.[29]

One practical problem with this theological view is that it is naive to think that persecution always results in the growth of the Church. Sometimes the opposite is the case. Thus, the pressure on Christians in the Middle East has resulted in a dramatic decline in their population. Since the early part of the twentieth century the Christian population declined from 35 percent to 5 percent in Iraq, 15 percent to 2 percent in Iran, 40 percent to 10 percent in Syria, and 32 percent to less than 1 percent in Turkey.[30]

Christian activist Gary Bauer takes issue with the "bizarre theological concept that we are promised persecution and thus should not resist it." To him this is a "strange" notion because "you can believe that we are going to be persecuted and still believe that good and decent people should still stand in defense of those being persecuted."[31] Charles Colson also disputes the theological justification for acquiescence. Believers are called to protect fellow members of the "body of Christ," and justice demands that the vulnerable be defended, whatever their faith. The fact that Colson had to assert this theological insight frequently in his lectures and writings testifies to the salience of the other impulse.[32]

A related obstacle to political activation is, in spite of formidable efforts by "Christian Right" leaders, a general reticence in the evangelical camp about engaging in "grubby" political controversy, out of fear that it is too worldly. Prominent evangelical figures, such as Cal Thomas, express the nagging suspicion that the blandishments of power will corrupt the faithful and detract them from the central task of saving souls.[33]

One intimation of this tendency came out in deep disputes over the timing of an event called the International Day of Prayer for the Persecuted Church. The most visible effort by the evangelical community to raise awareness in the pews about persecution abroad, the Day of Prayer seemed ideally suited to providing grassroots support for the policy initiatives of movement activists. But leaders of the Day of Prayer resisted any discussion of political aims in the packets sent to participating churches. Not only that, they decided to schedule the event in mid-November of each year, ensuring that biennial elections would not contaminate worship activities. For strategists this was a huge squandered opportunity because an event before elections would capture huge publicity as presidential and congressional candidates competed to demonstrate commitment to the cause. But to those who believe deeply in the power of prayer, such strategic calculations threaten to sully worshipful endeavors around the nation. Whatever one's view about this controversy, it illustrates a resistance to maximizing strategic clout among pietists whose kingdom is not of this world.

Spirited disagreements also exist among evangelicals about how best to approach international engagement. One view, reminiscent of "Fortress America," would eschew international entanglements entirely in the interest of maintaining national sovereignty. Driven by fear of the "new world order," this more "paranoid" branch often suspects that international engagement will end up ceding American sovereignty to the United Nations and, ultimately, to a world government inevitably hostile to Christianity. Several notable Christian Right leaders, such as Phyllis Schafly, withheld support for the IRFA precisely because it invoked United Nations covenants.[34]

If the above view tends toward paranoia, another civic impulse errs on the side of hope. It engages in quieter negotiation with foreign governments abroad, to create space for Christian witness, to free particular prisoners, and ultimately to change the hearts of leaders. Those who counsel quieter approaches fear unintended consequences, such as reprisals against vulnerable believers, which might flow from confrontation or sanctions. But part of the rationale involves a pragmatic calculus: the need for workable relations with nondemocratic governments to keep avenues of ministry open. Though acknowledging China's record of persecution, for example, evangelist Billy Graham wrote to members of Congress in the summer of 1997 urging support for granting Most Favorable Nation (MFN) status with China, arguing that open trade would tend to keep missionary lines open. Other advocates go farther to suggest that liberalized trade relations will help ameliorate persecution itself.[35]

But there is also an Augustinian theological perspective that justifies nonconfrontational engagement. Governments, in this view, are instituted by God. Who are we to claim that God is not working, say, through Chinese leaders as they struggle to maintain stability amidst forces that could plunge their nation into chaos? The Bible is also replete with stories of the faithful working through kings and princes blissfully unaware of their providential role. Thus some evangelicals counsel humility, oppose "demonizing" countries, and work to develop relationships that may bear fruit decades hence in God's enfolding plan.

This approach is exemplified by Advocates International, founded and headed by Sam Ericsson, former director of the Christian Legal Society. Contrary to some groups, Advocates International does not expose or criticize but rather seeks to nurture relationships with foreign leaders to help build infrastructures in various countries that will protect religious freedom. It also tries to foster trust with leaders abroad by appeals to common moral principles, especially the Golden Rule. The organization achieves noteworthy results in foreign countries by training local lawyers and judges and pressing for changes in laws or practices that harass religious minorities.

The philosophy undergirding this approach is remarkably optimistic.[36] However, Ericsson draws authority from the Bible, especially from Old Testament figures—such as Esther, Daniel, Joseph, Nehemiah, and Obadiah—whose faithful service to worldly leaders built a relationship that enabled them at critical junctures to advance justice for God's people.[37]

Here we can echo Lincoln: Evangelicals read the same Bible and pray to the same God, but come to different conclusions about what this means in concrete political terms. The debate over China provides a vivid illustration. Ericsson touted his cordial personal relationship with Ye Xiaowen, head of China's Religious Affairs Bureau, for why China made a key policy clarification in 1997 regarding the legality of Bible studies in homes. In stunning contrast, Voice of the Martyrs Director Tom White castigated Ye Xiaowen as "China's Caiaphas," a reference to the high priest who brought charges against Jesus.[38]

This narrative alludes to an enduring divide in the evangelical camp between those who endorse "quiet diplomacy" to ameliorate persecution versus those who favor tougher public initiatives. Not only was this a crucial difference among partisans in the congressional battle to enact religious freedom legislation, it remains a bone of contention over implementation. In the evangelical flagship publication, *Christianity Today*, Robert Seiple, former ambassador for International Religious Freedom, contrasted an approach "based on quiet diplomacy" (which he favored) with "public finger pointing." In stark terms he said that one approach "works with governments" while "the other castigates governments from afar." One "lights candles," while the other "feels obligated to curse the darkness" with condemnations or sanctions.[39] So many readers objected to Seiple's characterization of those who favor tough approaches as "cursing the darkness," that the magazine ran a succession of responses.[40] The debate within the evangelical world continues.

The entrepreneurial character of American evangelism presents another "source of babel" that challenges unified or credible engagement. Having founded ministries on their own vision and charisma, some religious entrepreneurs feel free to say and do things that undermine the collective efforts of others. There was nothing to prevent religious broadcaster Pat Robertson, for example, from capturing media attention as an "evangelical spokesman" with his outrageous claim in 2003 that Liberian dictator Charles Taylor "is a Christian statesman" being attacked by Muslims. Southern Baptist Convention leader Richard Land depicted Robertson as "way out on his own, in a leaking life raft" on the issue.[41] But the incident still played into negative stereotypes of evangelicals as simplistic, naive, and only concerned for their coreligionists.

In a similar vein, the relentless need for money to sustain their organizations tempts some leaders to exploit the plight of persecuted believers in blatant fund-raising appeals. James Kennedy used the Sudan tragedy in a rather unseemly effort to support his Coral Ridge Ministries. "Stop the brutal persecution of Christians," its banner headline said. In bold red letters, the letter began: "Kill the Christians. Enslave their children. How can we tolerate such an appalling agenda?" The answer was to contribute to Coral Ridge so that the ministry could "continue exposing this nightmare of Christian persecution on nationwide television, radio, and the printed page."[42] Because evangelical leaders must fight hard to maintain their credibility in elite circles, such seemingly self-serving appeals can hurt.

As we will see in later chapters, the babel of competing evangelical impulses has been overcome to a degree through the leadership of such widely respected figures as Charles Colson. But there is a revealing irony here, as a number of evangelical leaders will acknowledge. It took the prodding of Jews, the buoying alliances with Catholics, and the support of other religious minorities, such as Tibetan Buddhists, to help some evangelicals overcome their ambivalent or splintered responses toward the nascent political movement. The story is different for liberal Protestants.

Liberal Protestant Skepticism

Liberal leaders of the mainline Protestant denominations were among those most skeptical about the new faith-based thrust in foreign policy. For much of the twentieth century the well-established Protestant denominations—Methodists, Presbyterians, Congregationalists, Episcopalians, Lutherans, and Northern Baptists—constituted the vital heart of America religious life, earning them the appellation "mainline." These "theologically modernist" churches, however, have experienced such dwindling memberships that the term mainline no longer describes their position in the U.S. religious landscape. Still, they retain an important presence in American life. They enjoy an inherited capital of historic credibility, large financial endowments, and established institutions that provide their often highly educated and sophisticated leadership with access to Washington, D.C., policymakers and the elite press. Their world relief programs have for decades maintained ties to the American international aid apparatus.

A central feature of these established Protestant denominations is the well-documented gap between a moderate laity and their liberal representatives in Washington.[43] As with secular liberals, the legacy of the 1960s exercises a powerful hold on many of these church leaders. Civil rights, antiwar, feminist, and environmental causes animate many of these religious figures, and these denominations' national representatives advance a very liberal political agenda.

These church representatives see themselves as advocates of peace and justice for the oppressed, and they reacted vehemently against the emergence of the Christian Right and the conservative Reagan era. Equally troubling to them is the growth of thriving evangelical churches and denominations pursuing a religion they see as narrow and fundamentalist.

Given the visible involvement of evangelicals, it is not surprising that many mainline leaders initially reacted coolly to the new antipersecution movement. Indeed, liberal Protestants seemed caught off guard by a swift emergence of a human rights issue that they themselves did not identify or trumpet. Their voices were mixed or muted. Some raised legitimate concerns about unintended consequences and offered helpful ideas about how to refine the initiative.[44] But most expressed skepticism, trivialized the problem, or even opposed the entire thrust.

Animating some liberal leaders was a concern that movement activists exaggerated religious persecution or oversimplified a complex situation. In congressional testimony Albert Pennybacker of the National Council of Churches said that the "relationships between religious faith . . . and the cultural heritage of religions and nations are deep-seated, complex and defy easy assessment from afar."[45] Pennybacker was echoed by the Reverend Canon Patrick Mauney, Director of Anglican Global Affairs for the Episcopal Church. The troubles experienced by Christians around the world, he claimed, are not usually persecution. "In very few cases do you have systematic persecution of Christians as Christians. Most of the instances in which churches are burned or Christians put under arrest has to do with local conditions that are very complex."[46]

A different source of liberal skepticism lay in priorities of attention. Women, minorities, indigenous peoples, and peasants receive solicitude, but persecution of Christians does not usually rise to such prominence. Women and indigenous peoples, of course, can be persecuted *because of* their Christian faith, but this prospect has not been explicitly entertained that much in mainline literature. Indeed, during the antipersecution campaign in the late 1990s I noticed that the word "Christian" was often avoided in statements by mainline leaders. In commenting on legislation, one Lutheran advocate noted the special need to "defend the human rights of groups most susceptible to violations, especially all minorities, women and children." A United Methodist leader never mentioned Christians in a long letter on China policy, but did single out "ethnic and indigenous groups, especially Tibetans and others in border regions." Expressing skepticism of some aspects of the campaign on behalf of Christians, one liberal Protestant lobbyist observed that "some groups might be critical of persecution at the hands of Iraqis but not so critical at the hands of Israelis."[47]

One source of difference between liberal church groups and those evangelicals, Catholics, and Jews who took a more aggressive posture relates to how "constructive engagement" with totalitarian systems in the past affected relationships in Communist countries. In China, as we learned in chapter 2, evangelicals and Catholics who attempt to operate independently of government dictates face harsh penalties and destruction of their church property. Liberal church leaders, however, developed early relationships with the Three-Self Protestant churches (those sponsored and approved by Communist authorities). Indeed, one Chinese scholar found that liberal American denominations actually contributed to the formation of the Three-Self movement during the Maoist revolution.[48]

This involvement leads mainline visitors to China to attend state-sanctioned parishes, where there may be genuine spiritual succor but little talk of persecution. Moreover, close ties with the state churches can lead these denominations to eschew criticism of the regime. The Lutheran World Federation Assembly, for example, rejected a resolution of mild criticism of China when Chinese delegates argued that it would endanger relations between churches in Hong Kong and those in China.[49] A Methodist statement issued in Hong Kong observed that the body would continue to work through the officially sanctioned Council of Churches and Three-Self Patriotic movement.[50] In assuming this posture of constructive engagement, mainline Protestants have become allies of big business—an ironic outcome in light of their frequent criticism of corporate greed.

In some cases mainline Protestant leaders have acted like apologists for dictatorship. In 1997 Patrick Mauney denied that persecution is a problem in China because Christians "willing to register" with the government are free to worship. What looks like persecution is merely "the particular ways the Chinese state looks at its security interests."

This security concern is especially understandable with respect to Roman Catholics, the Episcopal leader observed, because they "are beholden to an outside power, even a foreign state in a way, because the Vatican is a nation." Thus "Catholics who insist on maintaining a tie with the Vatican are going to be persecuted" because they represent "outside interests," not "because they are Christians."[51] By definition, of course, faithful Catholics must "insist" on maintaining their ties with the universal church.

To activists against persecution, the above patterns illustrate how much some liberal mainline churches have been compromised by ties to persecuting countries. The National Council of Churches (NCC), for example, allowed itself to be used by the North Korean regime to fend off mounting international criticism of its human rights record. In 2003 the NCC received a letter from the government-created church in North Korea condemning America's "high-handed and imprudent acts" and thanking the Council for its "international solidarity movement for peace."[52] Thus policymakers and journalists hear different opinions from the religious community.

Animus toward proselytizing can also lead to the view that persecuted Christians "bring it on themselves," that they contribute to interreligious tensions. Albert Pennybacker expressed this sentiment in testimony before Congress: "The evangelistic zeal of outsiders, openly voiced or even subtly imposed, may encounter an authentic resistance as it moves on unfamiliar ground. What may appear as 'persecution' and indeed is resistance may in fact be the wish to preserve religious and cultural traditions."[53] Underlying this assessment, of course, is the image of Christianity as an import from the outside, from the West, rather than an increasingly indigenous phenomenon.

Though these skeptical denominational leaders mobilize few grassroots followers, they enjoy access to like-minded journalists who use them to produce a standard story line—"Mainline religious groups oppose the Christian Right." Babel still reigns.

The Catholic Voice

The international Catholic Church offers unique and formidable resources that can be put into service of international human rights. Since Vatican II it has helped to ignite and sustain a wave of democratization in a number of predominately Catholic countries around the world.[54] As a genuine global institution with a clear hierarchy, the Church speaks with considerable authority and enviable media coverage. Pope John Paul II has used his prominent pontificate to champion human rights, and he has specifically spoken against persecution of the faithful in Communist and certain Islamic societies. With its historic involvement with statecraft, the Church also has a range of diplomatic means to advance its concerns. Because of this institutional strength, the Church enjoys elite access to U.S. policymakers, who at least lend attentive ears to its pleas. Moreover, the National Conference of Catholic Bishops can speak with a clear voice on issues deemed important to the faith.

But even before the priest sex scandal rocked the American Church, divisions muted this Catholic witness. There are profound differences between liberal and conservative bishops. There are religious orders and lay groups that understand the social imperatives of Christ's teaching in radically different ways from Church officials. A case in point is the remarkable disparity in responses to China. The National Conference of Catholic Bishops officially opposed granting the United States normal trade relations with China, citing the regime's decrees that criminalize Catholics who swear allegiance to the Church of Rome. On the other hand, the Catholic Foreign Mission Society of America, Maryknoll, often a champion of human rights, nonetheless took a more accommodating posture toward the regime. In 1989 it depicted the underground Catholic Church, which is officially recognized by the Vatican, as merely a body that "refuses to go along with government regulations."[55]

The scholastic tradition of the Church is normally a strength, as it provides an infrastructure of theological grounding for foreign policy. But theological reflection takes time to form a consensus among leaders and even then sometimes produces a nuanced analysis not conducive to vigorous grassroots mobilization.[56] The Church's deliberative approach can make it a cautious coalition partner, which frustrates advocates who wish to strike when policy windows open up.[57]

Even when the Church takes a clear stand, its hierarchical ethos can lead to insufficient focus on lay mobilization, one of the greatest impediments to a strong voice. When the bishops "speak to the church," the laity does not always listen or respond, a reality that especially frustrates the Pope. Though the laity may sympathize with the bishops, as they probably do on promoting international religious freedom, they demonstrate little of the intensity and reach one finds in the evangelical world of entrepreneurial energy. And even if the bishops regain their now damaged credibility, they have shown little sign of promoting serious mobilization through parishes on any issue beyond abortion. To be sure, some individual priests may raise the issue of religious persecution in their parishes, but there is nothing comparable to what the Southern Baptist Convention did, when it distributed to all of its 40,000 congregations packets to raise awareness of suffering believers abroad.

Given its global stature and its domestic presence, the Roman Catholic Church's support for U.S. leadership against persecution in the late 1990s was pivotal. Since that time, however, Catholic activism has receded, especially in the wake of scandals that absorbed the energy and attention of leaders and will likely divert the Church for some time to come. The Catholic voice in the future may be muted.

Mixed Voices: The Black Church

Black community churches (and increasingly mosques) are renowned for robust political witness. But that witness, though growing, has been mixed. Black church advocates for African Christians, for example, were deeply disappointed by the silence of such figures as Jesse Jackson on slavery in Sudan or attacks on believers in Nigeria (see chapter 7).

In the broader black community, moreover, we have seen little of the kind of aggressive mobilization that occurred against apartheid in South Africa. Part of the reason stems from a pressing domestic agenda. Black religious leaders remain focused on economics, civil rights, and the daunting task of rebuilding the fabric of family and community life in America's troubled inner cities.

Another factor in muting black voices stems from budding alliances with Muslims, who fear that the movement to address persecution unfairly targets Islam. In many inner cities immigrant Muslims blend with African American converts and black Christians alike in common endeavors. Because of this affinity, some African American Christian leaders are loath to criticize Islamic governments. There are other, more peculiar international connections. The Nation of Islam, while scarcely a true expression of Islam, has nonetheless developed ties to militant regimes abroad. Louis Farrakhan has received money from the Middle East and been feted in Libya and Sudan, where he has publicly castigated "American attacks" on Islamic countries.

In certain circles, therefore, we see suspicion that the campaign for the persecuted is a white evangelical cause that singles out Muslim societies but ignores abuses against Palestinians. The growing profile of the Sudan cause, however, is helping link white and black Christian leaders, and black pastors increasingly are part of the advocacy infrastructure of the movement.

Secular Blinders

As if divisions in the Christian community are not enough, the secularization of major institutions, and those who lead them, presents another barrier to religious advocates.

While religious devotion persists at the mass level, an unmistakable *secularization at the elite level* has occurred, especially from the 1960s onward. From public schools to government bureaucracies, mass media to journalism, the academy to business, large institutions increasingly operate with purposes and logic largely detached from transcendent faith.[58] This can lead elite policymakers and opinion leaders to dismiss religious devotion.[59]

To be sure, in the United States faith is generally tolerated and religious practice protected by First Amendment guarantees. But believers, especially the most orthodox, must cross formidable cognitive barriers to get a hearing among policy elites or secular journalists. In his 1997 book Paul Marshall documented how the secular prism of elites had hidden or trivialized the problem of religious persecution abroad. From the press to the diplomatic corps to secular human rights organizations to the academy, Marshall heard a virtual "deafening silence" about this massive human rights tragedy.[60] Though a bit exaggerated,[61] Marshall's account captured the essence of a powerful barrier that groups are only now beginning to overcome.

The problem of secular blinders is especially real among those who fashion the news. Elite journalists largely inhabit a secular cosmos, and they often ignore what they cannot comprehend, or filter it through stereotyped frames of reference.[62] Consider the extensive media attention to atrocities against Bosnians, for example, with scant treatment at the time of similar treatment against Christians in Sudan. Especially surprising is the slighting of modern slavery, which one would expect to produce huge media exposure. Indeed, at the end of the twentieth century people were more likely to know that whales were endangered than that "you can buy a black woman as a slave for as little as fifteen dollars in Khartoum."[63] Nina Shea's 1990s survey of foreign coverage by the elite press confirms the scant attention to persecution, especially from the foreign desks where one would expect the greatest sensitivity.[64] A. M. Rosenthal took his fellow journalists to task for slighting both the story of persecution and mobilization against it. He contended that news media virtually ignored the International Day of Prayer for the Persecuted Church when it first surfaced, though organizers claimed the event had 50,000 participating churches in 1997 and 100,000 a year later.[65]

Even when the elite press finally paid attention to the movement's inescapable presence, coverage was often dismissive or patronizing in ways unimaginable during the earlier campaigns for Soviet Jewry or South African blacks. Persecution against Christians was "claimed" and "alleged"—or neatly dismissed in quotation marks as "persecution"—while evangelical backers were often depicted as earnest but ignorant of the complexities of the world. In one instance Laurie Goodstein of the *New York Times* wrote that American believers were mobilizing on behalf of "Christians *they are told* are suffering in countries like China, Saudi Arabia, and Sudan."[66] In another *New York Times* story the Sudan cause was described as a "pet cause of American religious conservatives."[67] It is hard to imagine the *Times* describing the plight of Soviet Jewry as a "pet cause" of American Jews or apartheid a "pet cause" of African Americans.[68] Criticism of such coverage, along with striking humanitarian breakthroughs on Sudan and human trafficking, however, finally seem to be resulting in more appropriate coverage.[69]

Secular blinders in the diplomatic corps represent another challenge. In 1995 President Clinton appointed former Senator James Sasser (D-TN) to be ambassador to China. After weeks of intensive briefings by specialists in the State Department, the designee demonstrated impressive knowledge of the human rights situation in China, until he was asked about the plight of the "house churches." His astonishing reply was, "What's a house church?"[70] Such striking ignorance in the mid-1990s, however, serves to underscore how much things have changed because of movement initiatives. New laws, exposure, and better training of diplomatic personnel ensure that the above vignette is now inconceivable, even if secular biases remain.

Secular blinders also operate, perhaps increasingly, in the world of business. Executives of multinational corporations operate in a powerful secular environment of global competition for capital, labor, and investment opportunities. It is easy for them to be ignorant of, or dismiss, human rights abuses in countries, such as China, Saudi Arabia, or Burma, where they do business. And this phenomenon is probably more than just self-interest. The high-tech vanguard of the new economy, as epitomized by the culture of Silicon Valley, apparently operates with secular visions and assumptions as powerful as those in elite academic circles.

Left-Wing Hostility

If secularism blinds elites to abuses of religious rights, left-wing hostility has presented another challenge. Opposition of some on the Left toward this new human rights effort might seem puzzling. After all, for years many liberals and those on the Left decried the abuses of dictatorships and demanded that human rights play a larger role in U.S. foreign policy. How can they explain their too frequent resistance toward protecting religious rights?

Part of the explanation lies in a long-standing animus among some on the Left toward religion in general and Christianity in particular. Many on the Left view religion as the enemy of abortion rights, gender equality, and gay rights. For them churches "oppress" their own members and relegate women to "second-class status." This new campaign for religious rights, they fear, might mask benighted attempts to turn back the clock on advances in cultural freedom.

This hostility seems especially evident when the persecuted are unfashionable evangelicals and traditional Catholics. A number of observers have noted that reports of persecution are often filtered through the Left's multicultural lens. In the increasingly dominant "politically correct" view, Christian missionaries were either accomplices of conquistadors in their genocide against indigenous peoples or cultural imperialists on the model of the minister in James Michener's *Hawaii*. Richard Land of the Southern Baptist Convention has argued that these images contribute to the anemic Western response to persecution: "[T]oo often people in the West, peering through the selective prism of Christian history in the West, reflexively think of Christians as persecutors rather than the persecuted."[71] The image of Christians qua Christians being persecuted does not easily pass through this ideological prism. Nina Shea found a similar mental barrier among journalists who view "Christianity as a white man's religion and a tool of Western imperialism." She noted that a top magazine's Middle East bureau chief, though aware of such beleaguered indigenous groups as Egypt's six million Copts, saw the campaign for persecuted Christians "as mainly a strategy for repressing the culture of the Third World—an attempt to force Muslim countries to allow proselytizing by American Christian missionaries."[72]

A huge, foundation-sponsored report on freedom of religion and belief, produced by the University of Essex Human Rights Centre in England, is a case in point of left-wing bias. The report begins by cataloging the daily occurrences of religious persecution: "forcible conversion, desecration of religious sites, the proscribing of beliefs and pervasive discrimination, killings and torture." But instead of identifying nondemocratic regimes as a prime source of this tragedy, the authors instead refer to "religious extremism," "intolerance," and "assertions of superiority of belief." The problem is that "crimes" are committed "under the mantle of religious freedom" by "groups bedecked with religiosity," which "inevitably provoke extreme reactions." In a bizarre twist, the authors devote almost as much space and concern for how the Catholic Church in Ireland exercises influence

over abortion and divorce policy as it does to some of the most egregious and violent abuses by governments around the world.[73]

We see similar bias in otherwise vigilant human rights groups.
Human Rights Watch, the premier secular organization, has a staff of
hundreds and a budget in the millions. It enjoys credibility in the elite
press and garners publicity in its annual reports on the status of human rights around the world. For years the organization's high priority items, to which special reports were devoted, included an array of
traditionally liberal concerns: women's rights, children's rights, abortion rights, rights of victims of multinational corporations, prisoners'
rights, gay and lesbian rights, AIDS sufferers, journalists' rights, artists'
rights, and so on. Religious abuses had not received the same systematic focus. Faith-based agitation and the 1998 religious freedom
law, however, seem to have increased the organization's systematic attention to religious freedom issues, if a bit haltingly.[74]

In attempting to understand "selective outrage" on the left,
Charles Jacobs of the American Anti-Slavery Group points to a syndrome he terms "the human rights complex." Why is it, asked Jacobs,
that "victims of slavery and slaughter" in Sudan are "virtually ignored, no, turned away, by American progressives?" How can it be
that "there is no storm of indignation at Amnesty International or
Human Rights Watch?" "How can it be that they have not raised the
roof about Khartoum's black slaves?" Why has the socialist Left not
championed "liberating the slaves or protecting black villages from
pogroms, even though Wall Street helps bankroll Khartoum's oil
business, which finances the slavery and slaughter? What is this literally murderous silence about?"[75]

While human rights leaders take issue with this characterization
of "silence,"[76] Jacobs argues that the severity of human rights abuses
has little to do with the degree of actual response by the liberal human rights groups. Rather, "to predict what the human rights community (and the media) focus on, look not at the oppressed; look
instead at the party seen as the oppressor." To illustrate this hypoth-
esis Jacobs suggests a scenario: "Imagine the media coverage and the
rights groups' reaction if it were 'whites' enslaving blacks in Sudan.
Having the 'right' oppressor would change everything." The human
rights community is "composed mostly of compassionate white

people" who seek "expiation" for the sins of the West, and thus feel "a special duty to protest evil done by those who are like 'us.'" Vigorous condemnation is meted out to "those like us"—whites in South Africa or Israelis—while Arabs, Muslims, or Asians are held to a different standard. Thus "slaves of Sudan are ignored because their masters' behavior has nothing to do with us." The slaves are simply unlucky to have the wrong oppressor.[77]

A related ambivalence on the Left is the sense that religion is somehow different from freedom of the press, assembly, or protest. At a conference devoted to a discussion of American government attempts to promote religious freedom abroad, one participant said this: "Religion is a deeply ambiguous, complicated aspect of human culture. I think we make a mistake if we try to wish that away, trying to look only at the good side of the story. You never get rid of the bad side. Religion is different. . . ."[78] She then went on to astonish other participants by asserting that religion *should not* be "on the list" of human rights because that denigrates nonreligious people.

When many liberal Protestant leaders took a left turn on foreign policy from the 1960s anti-Vietnam effort onward, they mirrored views of the secular Left. The National Council of Churches, for example, moved from a position of publicly criticizing the purges and religious persecution in the Soviet Union and its satellites in Eastern Europe in the 1950s to a posture of rather benevolent "silent diplomacy" toward totalitarian regimes. It also intensified its public denunciations of authoritarian regimes of the Right, a double standard that Amnesty International cautioned against. The World Council of Churches took an even more decisive turn, which critics charge was the result of an active and successful attempt by the Soviets to co-opt the body.[79]

Those who moved the farthest left softened criticism of the Soviet Union, chastised the capitalist United States, and embraced Marxist "liberation" struggles in the Third World. During the destructive cultural revolution in China, for example, a National Council of Churches booklet lauded "the Communist victory," which was producing a "government that was working for the interests of the ordinary people."[80]

When the Iron Curtain fell, this posture was discredited when the liberal churches came under criticism from former dissidents in

Eastern Europe. As one journalist noted: "Almost every Protestant leader that I met in Prague was bitter about the 'naive' and 'dangerous' role that liberal American Protestant leaders, especially the National Council of Churches (NCC), played during the Communist regime." One Czech Bible scholar, who had been imprisoned, told the reporter that "NCC people consistently refused to face the inconvenient fact that Christians were being persecuted in this country. . . . My colleagues and I will never forget the NCC's failure to recognize the antireligious actions of the Communists."[81]

Perhaps chastened by this record, some mainline leaders have moved away from the Left's ideological view from the Cold War. Old perspectives die hard, however, and a diluted version of this left-wing lens remains, explaining why some religious liberals have reacted so harshly to the new movement for the persecuted. Joan Brown Campbell, general secretary of the NCC, saw in the movement for persecuted Christians a dangerous "muscular Christianity," an attitude of Christian superiority that not only led to the Inquisition but eventually to the Nazi Holocaust.[82] The Reverend Jay Lintner, Washington representative for the United Church of Christ, opposed an early version of religious freedom legislation because, he said, it singled out persecution of Christians in China, North Korea, Vietnam, Laos, and Cuba, which he argued would "continue a hard-line Cold War sanctions strategy." And because it cites Muslim countries, he argued, the bill would "extend the Cold War to many Islamic countries."[83]

Business Opposition

If the Left resists the faith-based movement out of hostility toward traditionalist faith, the Right opposes it as interfering with business and the pursuit of "national interests." Thus bitter adversaries sometimes become unintentional allies—strange bedfellows in opposition to the new religious movement for human rights.

There are two variants of conservative opposition to the thrust of this movement—one self-interested, the other philosophical. Each is distinct, but they dovetail together in opposition to the thrust and tenor of religious human rights advocacy.

The most powerful self-interest in foreign policy is obvious:

money. Business has always enjoyed a "privileged position" in American politics.[84] It is not just another lobby; it is the lifeblood of a free economy. With globalism a dominant force in the twenty-first century, economic interests now exert enormous influence in international relations. With power to move capital and investment at the speed of light, multinational corporations are powerful players at home and abroad.

To update the adage of the 1920s, "the business of America is *international* business." The economic interest in American foreign policy cuts a wide swath: It encompasses the giants of American industry, finance, and high technology, but it also includes farmers seeking foreign markets for their produce, export-oriented small businesses, and consumers who enjoy inexpensive goods made by low-paid workers in China, Indonesia, or Vietnam.

When opportunities or threats arise, the business community can mobilize a vast lobby operation that spares no expense. A case in point was the successful effort to grant permanent normal trade relations (PNTR) to China in the summer of 2000. While there were compelling arguments on both sides of the issue, it was never a fair fight. Virtually the entire lobby infrastructure of business weighed in. Hundreds of millions of dollars were spent, and trade associations and agriculture groups sent delegations to the capital from every congressional district. Opposition from religious groups, labor unions, and Chinese dissidents was not able to resist such a force.

While such high profile cases do not arise every year, business lobbies constantly work in the quiet interstices of policy, securing a sanction exemption here, a favorable measure there. For example, in spite of the American government's designation of Sudan as a sponsor of terrorism, certain business lobbies won exemption from economic sanctions to allow the import of Sudan's gum arabic, an essential ingredient in soft drinks.

This analysis does not gainsay the enormous benefits of global trade and wealth creation, or even the potential that opening international trade may ultimately undermine the power of despotisms. The point, however, is that business interests will resist any measures that might undermine relationships with foreign trading partners, even with unsavory ones. Maintaining a strong focus on human rights concerns, therefore, requires constant pressure.

Conservative "Realist" Opposition

Dovetailing nicely with the economic critique of U.S. "meddling" in the affairs of other nations is a conservative "realist" understanding of the national interest. Both sides would have the American government refrain from attempting to impose human rights standards on other nations.

In certain respects one of the sharpest philosophical divides to emerge on foreign policy since the end of the Cold War is not between liberals and conservatives, but *among* conservatives. Oversimplifying a bit, a chasm separates certain "moralists" who champion American leadership on behalf of democratization and human rights versus those "realists" who see the world as "unamenable" to our liberal creed. This latter group begins with a pessimistic understanding of international statecraft, where niceties must give way to hardheaded calculations. Thus American attempts to impose human rights standards are often viewed as counterproductive. The best we can hope for is a modicum of stability, a balance of power, and a defense of the national interest understood narrowly in economic and military terms.

One variant on this theme sees the emerging world divided among competing civilizations—Western Christian, Islamic, Chinese—which must come to some "rapprochement" to avoid chaos and war.[85] One implication some draw from this analysis is that Western initiatives against nations that deny certain rights to their citizens would only further destabilize an already precarious situation, which is in no one's interest.

An even bleaker assessment questions the wisdom of even trying to promote democracy and human rights because we live "in a world moving toward authoritarian government." Animating this stark view is the specter of ethnic strife, war, crumbling infrastructures, environmental disaster, and a descent into anarchy in nations outside the affluent orbit. Central Africa provides a paradigm of this trend. Democracy is a luxury in such places, and Western attempts to impose it may only further undermine whatever order exists. Though U.S. diplomacy might conceivably ameliorate a few abuses in some stable authoritarian countries, such efforts are trivial compared to the broader catastrophes that threaten the world.[86]

Defenders of American leadership on human rights take issue with this tragic resignation. They note that time and again supposedly stable authoritarian regimes turned out to be anything but.[87] Thus, "nothing could be less realistic than the versions of the 'realist' view of foreign policy that dismisses human rights as a tool of American foreign policy."[88]

Institutional Resistance

Large institutions operate with their own internal logic and bureaucratic inertia that militate against changes imposed from the outside. The foreign-policy apparatus—encompassing the diplomatic corps, the National Security Council, military leaders, and presidential advisors—is a case in point. This hydra-headed system presents a major challenge to those wishing to advance human rights in American foreign policy. The system teems with established routines, norms of operation, and strategic imperatives. And some diplomats fear that "excessive" emphasis on human rights would compromise other aims and upset delicate foreign relationships. From the mid–1990s onward, State Department officials sought flexibility to "soften the blow" of antipersecution initiatives. They did the same with the human trafficking statute. Flexibility can be a virtue, but without constant outside pressure, policy will be diluted.

The new faith-based thrust can also be crowded out by national security concerns and military imperatives. Presidents and other policymakers seek maximum flexibility to chart their own course and response to developments around the world. Time and again administrations complain that congressional legislation on foreign policy will "tie the hands" of the president. Especially repugnant to presidential advisors and diplomats are automatic sanctions; sometimes even the hint of sanctions provokes opposition. Although promoting religious freedom and other human rights need not employ blunt and automatic sanctions, the foreign-policy system will resist even subtle forms of pressure. It is nettlesome for a president or ambassador to complain to heads of state that the United States objects to their internal human rights record, especially when other American objectives seem more central to the national interest.

The demand for maximum flexibility tends to delink human rights from policies deemed mutually beneficial to the United States and a foreign government. This can turn human rights policy into an "island" detached from high level negotiations.[89] This concern was expressed during the Clinton administration, but is a bipartisan affair. Prior to September 11, religious advocates expressed concern that some advisors to President George W. Bush embraced a narrow view of the national interest. After the terrorist attacks, they saw instances in which national security calculations threatened to undermine human rights considerations. Vigilance is required irrespective of which party occupies the White House.

SUMMARY

Barely a blip on the policy horizon in the early 1990s, the cause of international religious freedom now enjoys increasing notoriety and diplomatic attention. In light of the challenges cataloged in this chapter, this change is impressive. And because similar barriers present themselves on other human rights initiatives, subsequent achievements deserve note. From 1998 to 2002 the faith-based movement not only gained passage of religious freedom legislation, but successfully pressed congressional laws on human trafficking and peace in Sudan, and elevated diplomatic attention to human rights in China, North Korea, and elsewhere.

These achievements flow from the "power of movement" to take people out of their routines, to excite and energize, to reduce fatalism and buoy confidence, to empower leaders.[90] Most of the leaders I interviewed for this book, especially evangelicals, said they were more invested in international engagement as a result of their involvement in the movement's legislative campaigns. The faith-based effort also changed the policy context, altering perceptions and prejudices. While we once heard State Department officials criticizing the focus on re-ligious freedom as creating a "hierarchy of human rights," now some of them argue that religion is the "first freedom" and foundational to other rights.[91] Secular human rights groups, in turn, increasingly pay attention to issues advanced by the faith-based alliance.

This change is a testament to the impressive energy, passion, and strategic skills of movement leaders. But we must sound a cautionary note. Deep grassroots engagement will be required to overcome the continued barriers to sustained impact. It is here that the faith-based movement can do more. So far we see extensive leadership involve-ment, decent pockets of grassroots activism, and latent lay sympathy, but nothing comparable, say, to the mobilization for Soviet Jewry a generation ago. In a pattern that probably repeats itself on other issues, a 2002 survey revealed that some 70 percent of evangelical elites—prominent pastors, denominational heads, organizational leaders—had "heard a lot" about the Sudan crisis, while only 22 percent of the evangelical public had.[92] Given the size of the evangelical electorate, of course, even a modest response from average born-again voters can make a big impact. In sum, we can say that the new century presents both hopeful and cautionary signs for the faith-based movement.

4

PREPARE YE THE WAY

The story of Pastor Richard Wurmbrand, born in 1909 in Romania, captures in vivid detail the way totalitarian systems in the
twentieth century sought to eradicate religious faith, or at least its
salience and power. A former Jew and prominent Lutheran minister,
Wurmbrand was arrested and beaten several times by fascist authorities
during the Second World War. With the end of the war Wurmbrand
and his wife, Sabrina, evangelized among the Russian occupiers, and he
continued ministry even as the Communist dictatorship descended on
his homeland. For this he was arrested again and spent fourteen years in
prison (three of them in solitary confinement), was tortured relentlessly,
placed in a refrigerated "cold cell," had his teeth knocked out, suffered
numerous broken bones, and had holes burned all over his body. The
worst treatment, however, was meted out whenever he was caught
preaching the Gospel. Officials would tie his legs together and slowly
slam a rubber club into the bottoms of his feet. Because he refused to
stop preaching, the beatings were frequent. For the rest of his life he
could wear shoes only for the briefest time, and thus became known as
the "shoeless preacher," who would deliver his message to thousands sitting down, sometimes with his feet elevated by a pillow. Upon his death
in 2001, his followers poignantly recalled the words of scripture: "How
beautiful are the feet of those who bring good news" (Romans 10:15).[1]

Ransomed to freedom in 1965, Pastor Wurmbrand became, for a
time, "perhaps the most imposing orator on the Christian world stage."
Because of his visceral anti-Communism, he was viewed on the Left as
something of a lunatic, at one point famously taking off his shirt in a

*Romanian pastor Richard Wurmbrand, founder of Voice of the Martyrs.
Courtesy of Voice of the Martyrs.*

U.S. Senate committee hearing to show the scars of his torture. But he survived Romanian Communism and enjoyed the vindication of returning to his homeland a hero. He was eulogized as "a man who opened up the first hairline cracks" in the Iron Curtain, "cracks that would expand into fissures in the 1980s and become a contributory factor to the eventual collapse of the Soviet system itself."[2]

Wurmbrand's story furnishes a strand of corroboration to the thesis that Christians can serve as "canaries in the coal mine"—warning signals of the condition of human rights in particular regimes. Because of its putative independence from Moscow, for example, the Communist government of Romania had been treated benignly in American foreign policy—that is, until Christian advocates inside and outside of Congress began to spotlight its execrable human rights record.

What is especially important for our analysis is that Wurmbrand formed an organization devoted to providing succor to besieged Christians behind the Iron Curtain, linking the resources of the free churches in the West to the plight of fellow believers persecuted for their faith. That organization, Voice of the Martyrs (VOM), joined a constellation of other such groups that arose during the Cold War. This advocacy network laid the foundation for the movement against the persecution of Christians, which played a crucial role in forcing the foreign-policy community to attend to the wider issues of religious freedom and human rights abroad.

That story suggests the major theme of this chapter: how diverse activists and groups prepared the way for the new human rights movement in foreign policy, growing in number and confidence until a catalyst finally exploded their potential, channeled that energy, and linked them with a wider array of religious minorities and human rights groups. This chapter is about these disparate pioneers.

MISSIONARY ADVOCATES AND WATCHDOG GROUPS

With the Russian Revolution in 1917 a new force entered the world stage—an atheist ideology backed by totalitarian power. When the Iron Curtain descended across Eastern Europe at the end of the Second World War, followed by Communist victory in China, this force suddenly loomed large as a unique threat to Christendom. In response, an array of Christian missionary groups in the West arose to provide support to their besieged sisters and brothers behind the Iron or Bamboo Curtains, raising money and smuggling Bibles and supplies.

Heavily dependent on the initiative of visionaries, these efforts were sectarian, fragmented, and sometimes competing, reflecting pluralist divisions in the Christian world. There arose Catholic groups and Protestant ones, groups with global aspirations and others with laser focus on particular communities. Until the broader movement took off, there was little cooperation among such disparate organizations as the Egyptian Coptic Association, Iranian Christians International, and the Cardinal Kung Foundation, which supports underground Catholics in China loyal to the universal Church and the Vatican.

Of course, these efforts provided a source of vitality as well. This entrepreneurial energy is especially evident in the decentralized world of Protestant evangelism, which continues to produce a bountiful harvest of advocacy groups. One practically needs a scorecard to keep up, as new groups form and others split off from existing organizations (see appendix for a Who's Who). In a pattern reminiscent of the old Left, seemingly subtle theological disputes produce fierce tactical differences that proliferate advocacy voices. Some groups, like VOM and Open Doors with Brother Andrew, owe their origins to leaders from particular countries. Other groups, such as Christian Solidarity International (CSI), Christian Solidarity Worldwide, and International Christian Concern, represent competing branches from a common trunk. Each operates with a distinct philosophy, set of contacts, funding base, and leadership—though to outsiders they may seem redundant.

The flavor of this entrepreneurial vitality comes out in the stories of group formation. While VOM was the brainchild of Pastor Wurmbrand of Romania, for many years its operational leadership has been in the hands of Tom White, an early advocate for national legislation addressing persecution. A former teacher at a Christian high school on Grand Cayman island (south of Cuba), White became inspired by accounts of missionaries smuggling Bibles behind the Iron Curtain. After meeting Wurmbrand, White initiated an effort to penetrate Castro's "island of fear with the gospel of love" by undertaking daring if seemingly quixotic flying missions over Cuba, dropping Bibles and other religious literature from the air.[3] When his plane was forced down by authorities in 1979, White was arrested and spent seventeen months in Cuban prison, where he encountered and then helped nurture the subterranean Christian community that Castro failed to crush. Under his leadership VOM, headquartered in (of all places) Bartlesville, Oklahoma, expanded to encompass a worldwide ministry with offices in a dozen countries in Europe, Latin America, and the Pacific. Its mission is to "bring practical and spiritual assistance" to the persecuted of "Christ's body" and serve as "the voice of the underground church."[4] Its membership tripled to over 100,000 people when the campaign for national legislation publicized the cause and galvanized the broader movement.

Another Cold War product, Open Doors with Brother Andrew, is an international organization begun in 1955 as a support mechanism for the efforts of Holland pastor Andrew Vanderbijl, who smuggled Bibles and other Christian materials into Eastern Europe and the Soviet Union. With offices in seventeen countries, including the United States, its mission now focuses broadly on persecution of Christians in Communist, Islamic, and authoritarian governments. One of its most notable activities is to sponsor Compass Direct News Service, out of Santa Ana, California, whose credible monthly reports of incidents against Christians around the globe has become a major source of information for the advocacy network. Intriguingly, long before Christian-Muslim conflicts in Nigeria, Sudan, and Indonesia hit the pages of the elite press, they were a staple of reporting by Compass News Service.

Entrepreneurial leadership characterizes a cluster of Christian solidarity groups with similar names. The first of these to form was CSI, a Swiss-based group founded in 1977 by Reverend Hans Stuckelberger to demonstrate support for persecuted Christians and to serve as a watchdog on the activities of oppressive regimes. Less sectarian than VOM, the organization combines religious liberty advocacy with disaster relief and programs for victimized children.

The most prominent figure of CSI—and a pivotal leader in the faith-based movement—is John Eibner, director of the U.S. branch of the organization and assistant to Stuckelberger in Switzerland. Eibner embodies so many features of the evolving movement and its networks that it is useful to trace his story. An American whose grandparents emigrated from Hungary, Eibner grew up in a Baptist home[5] where talk about Communist oppression of the church in Eastern Europe was common fare. After graduating with a history degree from Barrington College, Rhode Island, he went on to receive his doctorate in international relations from the University of London. While at London he was associated with the Keston Institute, a widely respected organization that monitored and promoted religious freedom in the former Soviet Union and Eastern bloc. When Eibner joined CSI in 1990, he expected to work among the newly independent states of Eastern Europe, but with the collapse of the Iron Curtain new demands were arising elsewhere.

In 1992 Eibner was invited by the New Sudan Council of Churches to investigate slave raids and other atrocities against the African people there, making CSI the first advocacy group on the ground in Sudan. At the behest of local leaders, Eibner inaugurated in 1995 the somewhat controversial practice of slave redemption, which he continued to spearhead in the new century (see chapter 7).[6] Raising money in the West and operating through a complex network of local contacts, he documents redeeming over 80,000 slaves in 35 trips to Sudan between 1995 and 2003. The soft-spoken Eibner hardly seems swashbuckling, yet his trips involve dangerous zigzag flights to avoid ground fire and overland travel in primitive conditions. He has taken religious and congressional delegations to Sudan, testified frequently, and provided detailed information to Washington policymakers. Photographs of Eibner handing cash to an Arab trader to free a crowd of Africans, mostly women and children, circulate ubiquitously in church publications and secular outlets. Enormously respected in faith-based circles for his courage and resourcefulness, Eibner sees his work as a form of "prophetic ministry," a focus on justice and deliverance rooted in Hebrew and Christian scripture.[7]

Sometimes in pointed fashion, CSI distinguishes itself from spin-offs and competitors with similar titles. In its own website the organization issues a "caution" that suggests how much entrepreneurial "market competition" in advocacy has sprung up:

> Over the past few years, the dynamic growth and accomplishments of CHRISTIAN SOLIDARITY INTERNATIONAL (CSI) have given rise to other independent groups, organizations, and individuals using names and publicizing causes likely to be confused with those of CSI.

> The similarity in their use of words such as "Christian" and "Solidarity" may lead the public to believe these groups are affiliated with CSI and/or associated with CSI's administration, goals, causes and/or trustworthy reputation, when in fact, they are not.[8]

The above quote seems a bit uncharitable to other groups, but spin-off advocacy is often complementary to the cause of advocacy, because different groups fill separate niches.

One such spin-off, Christian Solidarity Worldwide, is led by Caroline Cox, a popular figure of Great Britain, who traveled with Eibner to Sudan on a number of occasions before starting her own organization. A grandmother, fervent Christian, and member of the House of Lords, Cox describes herself as "a nurse and social scientist by intention, and a Baroness by surprise." Using her prominence as Deputy Speaker of the House of Lords, Cox personally delivers help and documents the plight of believers in forsaken regions of southern Sudan, Burma, and the Armenian province of Nagorno Karabakh. As of 2001 she had traveled to Sudan twenty times, flying into unsecured landing strips, sleeping in tents, and hiking for miles

John Eibner of Christian Solidarity International pays an Arab trader to redeem Sudanese slaves, some of the thousands of African Christians and animists abducted by militias of National Islamic Front regime in Khartoum. Courtesy of Associated Press.

to redeem Sudanese slaves. She spotlighted the problem of state-generated famine in videos and frequent speeches in the United Kingdom and United States. She is said to have a price on her head by the Sudanese regime.[9]

Cox's star quality value has proven invaluable to the movement. She was the featured guest of churches in Midland, Texas, home of George and Laura Bush, for the 2001 International Day of Prayer for the Persecuted Church. The fact that she is a baroness made her a magnet for the country club set, while her Christian witness appealed to the evangelical and charismatic congregants in the community. Her message was a potent account of both heartrending suffering and inspiring faithfulness by people of faith in some of the world's dark corners.

Another spin-off from CSI is International Christian Concern, formerly headed by the late Steve Snyder, who saw the need for a Washington, D.C.-based watchdog group. He specialized in developing links to underground churches in such places as China, Pakistan, Saudi Arabia, and Algeria, highlighting the plight of Christian minorities there. Notably, he led some of the first congressional delegations that made explicit contact with these believers a matter of policy concern.

Though sectarian differences often characterize these disparate efforts, the growing sense of crisis for the suffering church, combined with the increasing engagement in the movement to redirect American foreign policy, has produced a modicum of ecumenical spirit. At a 1998 VOM conference, for example, a young man stood up during one session to lament the "threat" posed by Pope John Paul II's Jubilee 2000 campaign, the Catholic church's effort to reevangelize the Americas. The earnest evangelical asked this question: "Given the history of how the *Catholic church has persecuted Christians* [my emphasis], and how Catholics participated in Rwanda genocide, what should we do about this challenge from the *anti-Christ*?" Unruffled, Director Tom White answered that VOM in fact had worked with Catholic priests to distribute Bibles in Vietnam. "We didn't distribute the Catholic Bible, so I guess we defrocked the priests," he quipped. In a telling illustration of how movement alliances reduce sectarian insulation, White concluded simply, "We can't get into denominational battles."[10]

The priorities of these groups have also evolved over time. Though most were born in the Cold War and continue to operate in the remaining Communist regimes, their focus has broadened to encompass disparate countries where minority Christian communities are in jeopardy—from India where Hindu nationalism led to attacks on Christians, to Columbia where narco-guerrillas target ministers. An increasing focus is the Islamic world, where a network of local activists document the assault on religious freedom in countries under pressure from militant movements. This has spawned sensationalist stories of the "advancing jihad" and sometimes crude depictions that conflate the broader Islamic tradition with its current fundamentalist manifestations. In one VOM newsletter a Christian author from the Middle East charged that "the spirit of Islam is a spirit of fear, division, and violence."[11]

The documentation of the treatment of Christian minorities in Islamic countries, however, has served as a kind of early warning of the anti-Christian and anti-Western animus building in corners of the radical Islamic world—an animus that would spill out violently beyond national borders. Thus by spotlighting egregious persecution, religious groups may actually be working in the national strategic interest by exposing the character of regimes and signaling destabilizing regional or international threats. One dramatic example of this possibility was the witness of Bishop Gassis of Sudan. At a Washington, D.C., summit sponsored by Freedom House in 1999, which drew hundreds of activists from around the country, Gassis told the audience that the virulent "jihad" against his people would sweep across Africa and eventually be visited on America. Nina Shea recalls thinking, "No one's going to believe this."[12] Now Gassis seems prophetic.[13]

This same sentiment was expressed in the wake of the September 11 attack. Baroness Cox, for example, argued that years before the United States was targeted, "Jihad Warriors," inspired by the same ideology as Osama bin Laden, had targeted Christian communities in Sudan, Indonesia, and the Philippines.[14] Others pointed out that in his numerous communiques bin Laden had, in fact, declared war on Christianity, not just America.[15]

The mission focus clearly provides the linkage between disparate Christian communities around the world and potential advocates in the West, especially the United States. Take the example of the World Evangelical Fellowship (WEF), the major umbrella organization of global Protestant evangelization. As Director Dwight Gibson noted, the organization had not focused as much on religious freedom until local leaders voiced concerns at regional meetings about persecution and harassment of their communities. In one meeting in Prague, he recalls, the sentiment was "pray for us," raise our plight with officials, provide support for our cause. Because of what it was hearing, WEF conducted a survey of members in 1992 that helped invigorate initiatives of its Religious Liberty Commission. One of its ideas was an organized event of prayer and awareness. Though a modest undertaking, it was expanded dramatically when Michael Horowitz and other movement activists seized on the idea of a national day of prayer to raise awareness of the persecution of Christians.[16] Thus was born the International Day of Prayer for the Persecuted Church, which has become the signal annual event of the cause.

One advantage enjoyed by missionary and watchdog groups is that they are well-connected to the thriving grassroots reach of evangelical networks in the United States. This is why a variety of religious entrepreneurs, from James Dobson to Charles Colson to James Kennedy to Gary Bauer to Franklin Graham, have flooded the airwaves and mail with exhortation for action that reaches millions of followers. This fact has led some commentators to conflate the movement with the Christian Right.[17] But this is too simple an equation. John Eibner himself is critical of the way the "Christian Right likes to monopolize" the Sudan issue.[18] And some Christian Right groups actually eschewed early involvement with the faith-based movement because it invoked UN covenants.[19] What is clear is that more ecumenically oriented leaders in the Christian community are able to tap into existing religious networks to turn their constituents toward human rights engagement.

A POLISH POPE AND THE CATHOLIC CHURCH

Parallel movements on behalf of other besieged religious groups, such as Jews, Tibetan Buddhists, and Iranian Baha'i, did their own work in helping prepare the ground for a large religious freedom coalition. But no force loomed as large in preparing the way as the Catholic Church.

The 1978 election to the papacy of John Paul II, formerly Cardinal Karol Wojtyla of Cracow, was of momentous significance for the cause of religious freedom around the world. As an Eastern European cleric, Wojtyla experienced Nazi and Communist attempts to eradicate the Church as an independent force, and he helped lead the Church in resistance for a quarter century before his election as Pope. His tumultuous return to his homeland as pontiff in 1979 ignited the Polish people, buoyed their confidence against the Communist state, sparked the Solidarity labor movement, and ultimately helped bring down the Soviet empire in Poland and elsewhere.[20]

Looking back on the Pope's life, we can now see this episode as part of long and remarkably unbroken defense of free religious communities. As an active member of the Second Vatican Council (1962–1965), Bishop Wojtyla was one of the principal authors of the declaration on religious freedom, Dignitatis Humanae. This document profoundly altered Catholic teaching on church-state relations, linking human dignity and conscience to the right of peoples to form churches and practice their faith free of government coercion.[21] The future pontiff thus helped transform a Church that in the past had been an impediment to religious freedom into one of its most formidable global defenders.

One of the places where Vatican II made a dramatic difference was in Latin America, where a cadre of Church leaders increasingly championed human rights and promoted democratization in authoritarian regimes from the late 1960s onward. This placed them in harm's way, created martyrs, and established a credibility on human rights that would be pivotal to the campaign for religious freedom legislation.

As Pope, John Paul II placed religious freedom at the center of his vigorous defense of human rights. In a widely cited speech before the Vatican diplomatic corps in 1996, he sounded the clarion call against Communist and militant Islamic regimes that "practice discrimination against Jews, Christians, and other religious groups, going even so far as to refuse them the right to meet in private for prayer." Placing such maltreatment in context, the Pope declared that "this is an intolerable and unjustifiable violation not only of all the norms of current international law, but of the most fundamental human freedom, that of practicing one's faith openly, which for human beings is their reason for living."[22] Where possible the Pope acted himself, as when he named bishops for the Chinese Church operating underground and in opposition to the state-sanctioned body.

The Pope also championed ecumenical efforts to document modern martyrdom in his eloquent apostolic letter, Toward the Third Millennium (Tertio Millennio Adveniente). There he noted that on the eve of the next millennium "the church has once again become a Church of martyrs," now a "common inheritance of Catholics, Orthodox, Anglicans, and Protestants." Many of these martyrs, he lamented, are "unknown soldiers in God's great cause." As much as possible, "their witness should not be lost to the Church." Local churches, therefore, "should do everything possible to ensure that the memory of those who have suffered martyrdom should be safeguarded, gathering the necessary documentation, a gesture that cannot fail to have an ecumenical character and expression." Though he argued that this would serve as the same kind of faith inspiration as the "martyrologium" of the first centuries, John Paul's call for documentation dovetailed with strategies of human rights advocates to shine the light on abuses.[23] By placing the powerful imprimatur of the Catholic Church on the side of the cause of religious freedom, the Pope helped invite activism by his priests and bishops and smoothed their ecumenical alliances.

With the Pope preparing the way, veterans of human rights struggles at the U.S. Catholic Conference became pivotal players in the faith-based alliance in the 1990s, as did top Church leaders, such as Cardinal McCarrick of Washington, D.C. In testimony before Congress McCarrick echoed the Pope's view that religious liberty is the first freedom because it is rooted in the God-given dignity of the human person's free will and conscience. Because of this understanding, McCarrick noted how the Church not only spoke out on behalf of Catholics, but challenged persecution against Jews in the Soviet Union, Buddhists in Vietnam, Muslims in Bosnia, evangelicals in China, and adherents of traditional African faiths in Sudan.[24]

Part of the credibility of the Church flows from the fact that, under the leadership of John Paul II, its witness could not be put into a neat ideological box. The Pope criticized both right wing dictators and Marxist ones. In Latin America, for example, he steered the Church away from an uncritical embrace of Marxist insurgencies that some priests saw as allies in the cause of justice for the oppressed. In a famous incident at the Latin American bishops meeting in Puebla, Mexico, the Pope chastised Church leaders in Nicaragua who had allowed themselves to be co-opted by the Marxist Sandinista regime, even while affirming the social justice message of the faith. The Church of John Paul II, therefore, became one of the most consistent actors on human rights, helping to undermine both right-wing dictatorships and left-wing Communist regimes and acting to nurture and protect vulnerable democracies and the practice of religious freedom.

The fact that the United States came to embrace religious freedom as a foreign-policy aim seemed to bring the issue full circle, a fact not lost on the aging pontiff when he met with President George W. Bush. Unfortunately, when the head of the globe's largest religious institution met with the leader of its superpower on July 23, 2001, their discussion of religious freedom got submerged in press focus on the stem cell research controversy. But in fact the Pope had thanked the president for the nation's lead in making religious freedom a key foreign-policy goal: "It is significant that the promotion of religious freedom continues to be an important goal of American foreign policy in the international community. I gladly express the appreciation of the whole Catholic Church for America's commitment in this regard."[25]

THE PUBLICISTS: NINA SHEA AND PAUL MARSHALL

Nina Shea is one of the true pioneers in the faith-based movement. A human rights lawyer, she took up the cause of religious persecution when she noticed that it was slighted by the major international rights groups. For over a decade she was a lonely public voice, sometimes even shunned by supposed champions of human rights on the left. Her labors in the vineyard finally paid off, however, when the cause took off in the mid-1990s and her concerns were increasingly embraced by others, including secular groups. Her story illustrates

how social movements propel unsung activists (on shoestring budgets) into prominent national leaders with institutional heft.

Director of the Center for Religious Freedom at Freedom
House in Washington, D.C., three-term member of the U.S. Commission on International Religious Freedom, and frequent witness at
congressional hearings, Shea helped prepare the way for, and remains
a central player in, the ongoing movement.

A cradle Catholic, Shea attended parochial schools through high
school, to which she attributes a sensitivity to religious issues even
during early years in human rights work when she had become a
"lapsed Catholic." (Like so many of the people I got to know in this
research, Shea reconnected to her faith during the course of her advocacy of the religious freedom cause.) After receiving her law degree in 1979, Shea's ideological inclinations at the time (she was a liberal Democrat) drew her to work of the International League for
Human Rights, founded by the legendary Roger Baldwin as a global
counterpart to his American Civil Liberties Union (ACLU). Shea got
to know Baldwin, whom she views as a great American consistent in
his defense of civil liberties and therefore "anti-Communist."[26]

As program director for the International League, Shea gained
extraordinary exposure to the world of human rights advocacy. One
of her clients was the family of Andre Sakarov, the Soviet scientist and
celebrated dissident, whose case the League championed. She was
also involved in pivotal work documenting the atrocities of right-
wing death squads during the civil war in El Salvador in the early
1980s. Well-connected to liberal networks and human rights organizations, Shea found herself writing op-ed pieces in the *New York
Times*, getting invited to give guest lectures at Harvard, and the like.

That all changed when, upon hearing reports of human rights
abuses in Nicaragua, she turned her attention to the Marxist Sandinista government. Shea took numerous trips to Nicaragua and did the
main human rights reporting on the regime. As she notes, "I started
seeing the same things in Nicaragua that I saw in El Salvador," except
that "they were being done by the leftist regime and the leftist military, the Sandinistas."[27] So she published reports on the lack of due
process in Nicaragua and the killing of civilians in war zones by government troops.

For this she was blacklisted in ways reminiscent of the Mc-Carthy witch-hunts of the 1950s. Friends stopped talking to her, career opportunities dried up, and invitations to speak vanished as she became persona non grata on the Left.[28] The experience probably contributed to the sharp edge of her advocacy and rhetoric, but it also illustrates how leaders in the faith-based movement were driven by disillusionment with the perceived blinders or hypocrisy of secular human rights groups.

To be sure, leaders of secular groups dispute such depictions, either as wrong, exaggerated, or now dated.[29] But to Shea hypocrisy was clearly evident in the reaction to her reports from Nicaragua. "The whole human rights community was in an uproar about what I was writing," she recalls. Human Rights Watch went after Shea in the *New York Times*, calling her "a liar," and the left-wing magazine *Nation* published eight columns attacking her. This reaction was common to others who broke ranks with the Left. But as Shea recounts, "I never criticized the Left; I never criticized anybody but the Sandinistas."[30] But that was apparently a cardinal sin in certain circles.

Skeptics, of course, found reasons to suspect hidden motives in her work. After all, at the time she was writing on Nicaragua she had married Adam Meyerson, an editor and later vice president at the *conservative* Heritage Foundation. And critics charged her with sometimes making exaggerated or sensationalistic claims.[31] For example, Shea dramatically proclaimed that more Christians have been martyred for their faith in the twentieth century than in "the previous nineteen centuries combined," and that more are suffering today than at any time in history.[32] This assertion is based on systematic empirical research by demographers.[33] But as noted in chapter 2, such assertions may be somewhat less meaningful than they appear because "more Christians are also *not* suffering from religious persecution now."[34] Shea retorts that this qualification does not deny the basic fact that millions of Christians are persecuted for their faith. And her broader point is that comfortable Christians do not realize that they live in a time of great martyrdom, which is partly the fault of the Church. She recounts frustration with materials used to prepare Catholic Boy Scouts for their religious merit badges. Martyrdom was treated as something that happened in the past, such as against Japanese Christians suffering under the Shoguns, not a contemporary reality.[35]

Despite occasional criticism from secular organizations, Shea sees religious freedom advocacy as a continuation of her human rights career, which is evidenced by her continuing willingness to build alliances with labor unions, liberal groups, and religious minorities, and her frequent criticism of business conservatives who dismiss rights concerns.

Shea's actual turn to religious freedom was born out of a partnership with Humberto Belli, a Nicaraguan Catholic leader with close ties to the Pope, who served as an editor of his country's major newspaper, *La Prensa*. A former Marxist, Belli left Nicaragua in the early 1980s when the regime censored the newspaper and began clamping down on Church activities. In congressional testimony in 1982, he expressed concern about what he saw as a lack of appreciation, even in Catholic circles, of the inevitable threat Marxism posed to religious freedom.[36]

Belli ultimately proposed the idea to Nina Shea of founding a human rights organization. Shea had noticed that secular human rights groups were "defending everybody under the sun except the religious," so she agreed to work with Belli on the condition that the organization would have a *global* focus on religious persecution. Thus was born the Puebla Institute,[37] a "lay Catholic human rights group that defends religious freedom for all creeds in all parts of the world," that supports "democratization as the best means of ensuring religious and other human rights."[38] After several years of struggling to do both the human rights work and organizational maintenance, Shea merged with Freedom House, the well-established institute founded on the eve of the Second World War by Wendell Wilkie and Eleanor Roosevelt to promote human rights and democracy. Under the auspices of Freedom House, Shea directs the Center for Religious Freedom, carving a niche for herself as a leader of a key hub of religious freedom advocacy.

The story of Shea's growing prominence illustrates the way social movement mobilization both draws upon the efforts of activists and enhances them. Shea's fledgling organization helped prepare the way for the broader movement by building a documentary record and awareness in the policy community of the problem of religious persecution.

Nowhere was this more evident than on the human rights situation in China. As Shea recalls, "Nobody was doing reporting on China," particularly the regime's treatment of religious believers. In the wake of the Tiananmen Square crackdown in 1989, Shea and her staff began systematically to document the situation there. This effort was notable in probing actual policy edicts and official party statements on religion, which exposed the real fear authorities had of independent Christian churches as a "contagion" that had already undermined Communist regimes in Eastern Europe. Her office at Freedom House also developed some of the early western contacts with post-Tiananmen dissidents, such as Harry Wu, who documented the laogai system of labor camps.[39]

During the many debates in the 1990s over U.S. trade policy with China, Shea's organization published lists of hundreds of religious prisoners of the People's Republic to make the case against the unconditional granting of normalized trade status. She presented a detailed documentary case illuminating a number of "alarming trends" in China's "campaign to crush the underground churches."[40] This material figured in congressional debates and got picked up in news stories and received editorial comment in such outlets as the *Washington Post* and the *Wall Street Journal*.[41] This major focus on China continues. She continues to document arrests of religionists in China while pressing the American government to exercise leverage to get them released. Employing the soft power of publicity, her organization has given human rights awards to leaders of diverse religious communities in China, including the much persecuted (but to some cultlike) Falun Gong.

Though China was a major focus in the early years at Freedom House, Shea's organization ranged broadly, highlighting abuses against Christians and Buddhists in Vietnam and publicizing the religious dimension to atrocities committed by the Sudanese regime in Africa. As Shea's efforts gained traction, she began to develop more elite access. She not only had meetings with Reagan administration officials in the 1980s—including one with the president himself—but she was also appointed by President Clinton to lead the U.S. delegation to the UN Human Rights Commission in Geneva in 1993. By the mid-1990s, when the press needed a quote on religious freedom, she was often the one called.

Nina Shea, director of the Center for Religious Freedom at Freedom House. Courtesy of the Center for Religious Freedom at Freedom House.

But Shea also experienced the sectarian divisions that inhibited unified action—divisions that were only overcome, to a degree, when the more visible movement got rolling. Early on Shea detected a parochialism in the way her reports were picked up: "When I did Catholics it resonated with Catholics, and it didn't when I did Buddhists," while evangelicals would respond when she highlighted them, but not when she talked about Catholics. Shea was also surprised to find that it was considered "revolutionary" in the religious community to combine Catholics and Protestants in the same report, which her organization would do. "No one was looking at the fate of the entire Christian community"; instead there were a host of small advocacy groups with diverse sectarian bases.[42]

It would take the catalyst of movement mobilization to achieve this broader focus, and to catapult Shea into prominence beyond the Washington Beltway as the author of the popular book *In the Lion's Den*. How this happened offers intriguing lessons about how the emerging cause helped build a new domestic constituency for international concern and cement ecumenical alliances.

When Michael Horowitz teamed up with Shea to promote the cause of persecution against Christians, their first initiative was to organize a conference with prominent Christian leaders, mostly evangelicals but also some Catholics, which was held in January of 1996. This attracted press attention, and reporters started calling Shea for documentation, some of which she ferreted out of human rights reports.[43] She would send copies of various reports and testimony, and the response was, "Don't you have this in one place?" So Shea produced an extended booklet on the persecution of Christians, titled *In the Lion's Den*. That summer an official of the Southern Baptist Convention called Horowitz and invited him to write a book under its auspices. He suggested Shea instead, and she agreed to amplify the booklet and add dramatic photographs.

The success of *In the Lion's Den*, which sold over 50,000 copies by the turn of the decade and was excerpted extensively in religious presses, owed largely to the evangelical network and the formidable resources it had to get the word out. The book was actually published by the Southern Baptist Convention publishing house, Broadman and Holman, and contained endorsements by luminaries of the evangelical world, notable Catholics, a black church denominational leader, and such prominent politicians as Congressman Frank Wolf, former presidential candidate Steve Forbes, and past UN Ambassador Jeane Kirkpatrick. To promote the book Broadman & Holman booked Shea at conventions of evangelical broadcasters and home mission boards. Most crucially, since Shea's parental responsibilities limited travel, she was booked for numerous Christian radio interviews, which she could do from home. For "months and months," as Shea recalls, "all I did was Christian radio," perhaps a hundred interviews, where she got the word out. One cannot gainsay the impact of this effort. Christian radio reaches millions of people from over a thousand stations, and given the way syndication works, it is likely that Shea would have been heard more than once on some stations and in some markets.

An intriguing aspect of Shea's work has been the partnership with another key figure, Paul Marshall. A political theorist, human rights scholar, and former holder of a chair in religious studies at the University of Toronto, Marshall was approached by Christian advocates in the mid-1990s with a simple proposition: Would he do a study of the scope of persecution of Christians? The issue was beginning to percolate, and Marshall agreed to undertake the project, thinking that it would not take much time and would nicely complement his other work on human rights. But Marshall describes being astounded by the scope of the problem and how much he felt it was slighted by other human rights groups.[44] So he wrote *Their Blood Cries Out*.[45]

As a scholar Marshall placed the problem of persecution in a wider theoretical and philosophical context, and he offered a trenchant account of the reasons for the neglect of Christian persecution among mainstream scholars, journalists, and church leaders.[46] Marshall admits that his book is "deliberately popular, polemical, and pugnacious," but he also included over a hundred pages of notes and appendices to demonstrate his effort to be accurate.[47]

Though his audience overlapped somewhat with Shea's, Marshall's account helped take the issue into the scholarly and policy-making communities. It was frequently cited in journal articles and editorials, in congressional hearings and speeches on the floor of the House and Senate, and in subsequent scholarly books.[48] Even the substantive details of Marshall's work were employed in the policy debate. In defending language in the International Religious Freedom Act, for example, Senator Joseph Lieberman cited Marshall's definition of persecution. As the Senator put it: "Paul Marshall's seminal work *Their Blood Cries Out*, which has served as a manifesto for the recent movement against religious persecution, defines 'religious persecution' as 'in general, the denial of any of the rights of religious freedom.'"[49]

Marshall also tapped the networks of Christian radio, hit the lecture circuit, sold over 50,000 copies of his book, which is still on the market. As Shea summarized it, "together we got the word out."[50]

The message that Christians were suffering persecution abroad resonated in part because it appealed to the received worldview of American evangelicals, who often see themselves under siege in a hostile culture.[51] Moreover, by the time the two books came out, the efforts of missionary advocates and Christian solidarity organizations were percolating through religious circles, enhancing receptivity. Whatever the reasons, the positive response to these books had wider implications. It suggested the potential for a new constituency for international human rights, one that would dwarf anything the secular human rights community could muster.

The significance of that prospect was not lost on Shea, who witnessed what she describes as the "collapse" of the human rights movement in the early 1990s. In her analysis, up until then the human rights cause profited from diverse sources of grassroots support. Domestic ethnic groups, like the Lithuanians and Poles, pressed the plight of their counterparts behind the Iron Curtain, while Jews defended their brothers and sisters in the Soviet Union. On the left, mobilization in churches and liberal circles occurred over abuses by right-wing governments in Latin America. Meanwhile, African Americans and college students became the vanguard of a massive human rights campaign against apartheid in South Africa.

But as Shea recalls, "all that dissolved, almost overnight, with the collapse of the Soviet Union." Events converged rapidly, she noted, to take the sense of urgency out of human rights. "The Sandinistas had been voted out of office, the Soviet Union collapsed, Latin America was going democratic, and apartheid was gone." As Shea summarized it, "everybody thought it was over. Everybody thought there were no more problems." Grassroots support evaporated and even funding dried up as foundations, Left and Right, dropped out of human rights works. To Shea, therefore, the campaign for religious freedom provided a shot of adrenalin to the human rights cause at precisely the time when it was most desperately needed.[52]

Not only did publicists like Shea and Marshall help to fuel this new movement, they themselves were propelled by it into greater prominence and influence. Shea's operation grew and became better funded, and her policy role expanded as the movement took off. When the 1998 religious freedom legislation created an independent body to monitor government implementation of the law, Shea was selected as one of the first nine commissioners, and she was reappointed in 2001 and 2003. Her Center for Religious Freedom also became the focal point for coordinating efforts of the Sudan coalition in the late 1990s and into the next decade. She helped organized major events on religious freedom issues. In 2002, for example, the Center for Religious Freedom hosted a major conference on the growing threat to human rights of Islamist efforts to enact premodern Shari'a laws—a conference that featured moderate Islamic leaders who challenged the fidelity of militants to true Islam.

Paul Marshall, in turn, catapulted into a greater role. As foundation money flowed toward the cause, the Center for Religious Freedom was able to hire Marshall to undertake a major enterprise of scaling the status of religious freedom in countries around the world. Patterned after the Freedom House's general global freedom reports, this assessment, conducted by a cadre of regional experts applying formal criteria developed by Marshall, provided empirical country-by-country snapshots and credible comparisons by region and religion.[53] Ensconced in this position, Marshall had both resources at his fingertips and proximity to the center of policymaking, and he has become a familiar figure in the nation's capital and wider policy circles.

Marshall and Shea, in effect, illustrate the emergence of an advocacy infrastructure devoted to religious freedom. We can see how this operates with the vivid case of the U.S. State Department's 2001 country reports on religious freedom, which seemed to soft-pedal atrocities committed by the government of Sudan. In response, Shea worked inside the U.S. Commission on International Religious Freedom to help produce a more critical assessment, while Marshall provided an extended critique of the State Department's report on Sudan in balanced congressional testimony that lauded the department's efforts elsewhere.

JEWISH VOICES

A unique and tragic history has produced among Jews a kind of second sight about persecution and a commitment to international human rights, along with a hard-edged realism about protecting their own remnants from further threats. These attributes combine to make Jews among the most potent of allies of the emerging Christian solidarity constituency, a "strange bedfellows" alliance in light of frequent Jewish opposition to the domestic agenda of conservative Christian groups.

Jews helped prepare the way for the movement first by providing a model of international advocacy. For many Christian advocates, the campaign for Soviet Jewry in the 1970s would serve as an inspiration for their efforts to bend American foreign policy in the interest of their coreligionists abroad. Moreover, the relationships forged in that struggle facilitated ties when the concern about persecuted Christians became the focus. As early as the 1980s Jewish groups were taking up the plight of such groups as the Siberian Seven, the Russian Pentecostals who sought U.S. refuge from Soviet persecution.

These linkages developed into striking examples of Jewish leadership in the movement for persecuted Christians, as noted in the previous chapter. But in addition to lobby support, some Jews played a crucial role in publicizing the plight of believers abroad and thus preparing the way for the emergence of the full-fledged movement. One of those is Charles Jacobs, whose contribution to the Sudan cause is described in chapter 7. Jacobs founded the Boston-based American Anti-Slavery Group to combat various forms of chattel slavery around the world. From 1995 onward he publicized the enslavement of Christians and other non-Muslims in Sudan. One of his singular contributions involved sponsoring Sudanese exiles who have become well-known figures in Christian advocacy circles. Their stories received wide circulation in both religious publications and popular outlets, helping prepare the ground for policy initiatives.

One person who played a prominent role in publicizing the cause was Abe Rosenthal, former editor and columnist for the *New York Times*. The venerable journalist and human rights advocate became one of the most eloquent voices raising the specter of attacks against Christian communities in the Communist remnant and militant Islamic lands. And in doing so he helped prepare the way for the legislative campaign to follow.

Rosenthal's story illustrates how seemingly disparate threads can connect in meaningful and powerful ways. To understand his motivation we need to take what may seem like a detour to a pivotal moment in the reporter's life. After nearly a decade as a foreign correspondent for the *New York Times*, Rosenthal was called back to become metropolitan editor in 1964. Not long after taking the post, a story came across his desk that seemed all too routine but with a disturbing wrinkle. A young woman named Kitty Genovese was raped and murdered outside her Queens apartment, her attacker returning twice to complete the deed, and none of the thirty-eight neighbors who heard her screams called for help. Under Rosenthal's direction the *Times* broke the story that became a devastating parable of apathy in urban isolation and that sparked seminars and exposés across the nation. People asked themselves: Would they refuse to give help to a person they could hear crying out? In his writings and public statements, Rosenthal notes that he found himself asking a different question: "Would I ever refuse *again?*" Had he not walked past lepers and beggars "scores of times" in Asia? And suppose, he pondered, the screamer is not downstairs, or around the corner, but in a dungeon far away, and I know torture is taking place there right now; "how far away do you have to be to forgive yourself for not doing whatever is in your power to do?" The experience of writing *The Thirty-Eight Witnesses* seared Rosenthal's conscience and produced a fierce determination to do what he could to shine light into dark corners of world, to champion human rights.[54]

Rosenthal admits he had not paid much attention to the plight of Christian believers abroad, or religious persecution more generally, until Michael Horowitz "screamed me awake" on the issue. His formidable conscience piqued, Rosenthal used his perch at the *New York Times* to end "the journalistic silence" about the problem. From February of 1997 onward, Rosenthal penned no less than twenty columns on the persecution of Christians around the world.[55] Compelling and pointed, these columns challenged American policy toward such places as China and Saudi Arabia, exposed journalistic silence about the tragedy in Sudan, and publicized movement initiatives.

A few examples provide a flavor of Rosenthal's work. In "Persecuting the Christians," Rosenthal quoted liberally from passages of Nina Shea's book, *In the Lion's Den.* In "The Position of Worship," Rosenthal wrote of a form of torture designed to mock belief, in which Chinese Christians were forced to kneel as if in prayer while security guards "stomp on the backs of the heels until the heels are broken." In "Is This a Story?" Rosenthal chastised his fellow journalists for ignoring the National Day of Prayer for the Persecuted Church. In "The Well Poisoners," Rosenthal linked the fate of Christian minorities to that of Jews in the past. In several columns he spoke of slavery and genocide in Sudan, challenging elites to recognize the tragedy and respond.

These columns helped legitimate the cause among the literati. Equally important, they were widely syndicated in religious outlets, dramatically raising awareness within the Christian community and helping to persuade sometimes sheepish Christians that it was not selfish to act on behalf of their brothers and sisters abroad, that it was their duty both to the body of Christ and to the cause of human rights. Thus did Rosenthal, a New York Jew, become a central figure in publicizing the plight of foreign Christians among their coreligionists in the United States. And Christian leaders reciprocated by signing a letter, sponsored by Freedom House, to President George W. Bush recommending Rosenthal for the Presidential Medal of Freedom, the highest award given to civilians. In July of 2002, the president conferred the medal on Rosenthal, citing his work on behalf of persecuted believers.

Skeptics, of course, see a potential strategic dimension to the Jewish embrace of the Christian cause. Marshaling the Christian constituency could serve the "self-interest" of Jews, and of Israel, as a bulwark against the threat of militant Islam. Certainly the global war on terrorism revealed anti-Jewish and anti-Christian propaganda arising from the same militant Muslim organizations and governments, suggesting grounds for a sense of common threat. But extensive interviews and observation convinced me that much more than a narrow self-interest animated those involved, that the plight of persecuted Christians resonated in Jewish circles and produced potent allies and even leaders for the cause.

CONGRESSIONAL ADVOCATES

Presidents, their advisors, and the coterie of foreign policy commentariate who write for such influential journals as *Foreign Affairs* often complain about congressional "meddling" in foreign affairs.

They often see Congress as driven by ethnic constituencies or unaccountable moralism. An alternative view, which emerges below, demonstrates how Congress sometimes plays a key and valuable role in pressing human rights in American foreign policy. Certain members of Congress—by virtue of ties to religious constituencies, conviction, and location in the foreign-policy system—are inclined to assert a broader view of the national interest than narrow calculations of realpolitik or even business interests would allow.

We see this especially in the way that congressional members advanced the cause of religious rights, which percolated through Congress for several decades. Much of this effort initially focused on religious freedom in the Soviet system, whose reigning ideology treated transcendent faith as a reactionary force to be crushed. Beginning in the late 1960s disparate congressional initiatives built an edifice of statute, precedent, and testimony on religious persecution that helped prepare the ground for the broader movement to come.

Due to the campaign for Soviet Jewry in the 1970s, Congress passed, over President Nixon's objections, the Jackson-Vanik Act in 1974, which linked normal trade status to emigration policies of Communist countries. Even though historical circumstances have changed dramatically since then, the statute remains on the books, occasionally providing a lever for human rights demands against Communist governments. Indeed, its mechanisms required the annual vote to grant Most Favored Nation (MFN) status to China until such normal trade status was made permanent in 2000.

At the time of the campaign for Soviet Jewry, Russia had the third largest population of Jews in the world. As a small and often despised religious minority, Jews had suffered terribly, first under czars and then at the hands of Soviet authorities, who doubted their loyalty to the state. The Soviet government's antireligious campaign hit the small and marginalized Jewish community hard, and when the viability of the state of Israel was sealed in the Six Day War of 1967, "Jews from the Soviet bloc came increasingly to believe that a better life awaited them in Israel."[56] Because the Soviet government erected enormous bureaucratic barriers to emigration, the plight of the refuseniks became a cause célèbre of the American Jewish constituency and their Christian allies.

Whether the law resulted in greater Jewish emigration is still hotly debated.[57] But for other religious constituencies, Jewish success in extracting a price for dictatorial policies—of giving voice and leverage to vulnerable people—was an enormous boon and example. Indeed, some of the heroes of the movement against the persecution of Christians cut their eyeteeth in the earlier effort on behalf of Soviet Jews.[58]

A related effort involved the Helsinki Accords, adopted in 1975 by the Commission on Security and Cooperation in Europe, whose aim was to establish standards for human rights and the free flow of information as a bulwark for regional peace. The Accords contained provisions on religious freedom that signatories, including the Soviet Union, were supposed to honor. Though these provisions were grossly violated by the Communist bloc countries, they did highlight the situation and encouraged dissident movements. They also provided new levers for congressional critics of these regimes.

Notable for our purposes, numerous congressional hearings that investigated the implementation of the Helsinki Accords provided an early forum for human rights activists and accumulated a large corpus of congressional hearings and resolutions on the problem of religious persecution behind the Iron Curtain. Congressional members, in turn, built on this record throughout the 1980s and into the 1990s with initiatives that attempted to lever the release of particular religious prisoners or to spotlight the denial of religious freedom more generally, not just in the Communist orbit. In reviewing these documents we notice strands of the issues and themes that would emerge more visibly in the contemporary movement, and even some of the same players.

Though skeptics saw much of this congressional effort as symbolic—merely for domestic consumption—newly freed dissidents and pastors from prisons in Eastern Europe told a different story. Even in prison they became aware when congressional members took on their cause, heard through the grapevine when Communist authorities were being pressed on human rights. And it gave them heart and sometimes lessened their suffering.

Epochal trends around the globe in the early 1980s sparked a series of congressional initiatives on religious rights, which covered the plight of Jews in the Soviet Union, Baha'is in revolutionary Iran, Pentecostals and other Christians in the eastern bloc, Coptics in Egypt, the Church in Latin America, and persecution in Asia.[59] This effort presaged the themes of the movement to come, though its legacy lay dormant until circumstances would crystallize a more robust remedy to the problems noted.[60]

One reason Congress played such a pivotal role in promoting religious freedom is that many members themselves, and their staffs, are enmeshed in religious life and thus predisposed to sympathy for the cause. Cynics might be skeptical, but scholarly evidence suggests that religious commitments and worldviews do shape the work of many members.[61] My own exploration also confirms a thriving and influential religious life on the Hill, including weekly faith-sharing sessions among congressional members that cross party and denominational lines. Given the vibrancy of religious life in the United States, it should not surprise us that Congress reflects that cultural context to some extent.

Specifically, some members of Congress consciously linked their religious faith with work on behalf of international human rights and thus helped pave the way for the new faith-based movement against persecution. In the House, some of the most enduring leadership has come from three friends and Christian prayer partners—Tony Hall (D-OH), Frank Wolf (R-VA), and Chris Smith (R-NJ), who have been joined by a succession of others over time.[62] Elected between 1978 and 1980, these members brought to their work a passion born of years meeting with Jewish refuseniks, Chinese dissidents, imprisoned pastors, Sudanese refugees, tortured believers, famine sufferers, and victimized women. Together they "pressed for religious freedom in Romania, the East Bloc, Russia, the PRC, and in many Islamic nations since the early 1980s."[63] It was their publicity of the horrendous human rights abuses that ended MFN for Romania in the mid-1980s despite the fact that American diplomats viewed the Ceauescu regime as benign. In the late 1980s, after two years of negotiations, Wolf and Smith were the first legislators to get into the infamous Soviet gulag, Perm Camp 35, where they interviewed numerous religious prisoners and distributed Bibles. In the early 1990s they scored another coup by getting inside Beijing Prison No. 1, where they found gaunt, underfed Tiananmen Square prisoners working overtime to make socks and shoes for export to Western stores.[64] Not surprisingly, they voted against Permanent Normal Trade Relations for China in the summer of 2000. Their work built congressional credibility on human rights and provided ammunition for advocacy groups.

The Democrat of the trio was former representative Tony Hall, from working class Dayton, Ohio, a man who defies stereotypes; a devout born-again Christian, he participated for years in a weekly Bible study group on Capitol Hill. A strong union backer, he is renowned as a liberal crusader on international hunger issues, which he sees as flowing from his Christian calling. When informed that the Select Committee on Hunger was to be abolished in 1993, for example, he led a highly publicized hunger strike, citing scripture and shaming his colleagues into increasing their attention to the issue.[65] To Hall hunger and human rights are intertwined, as famines are created or exacerbated by the abuse of power. One of his most notable contributions to the cause of human rights may have been when he convinced his friend Frank Wolf to join him on a trip in 1984 to war-torn Ethiopia, where they personally witnessed the horror of a devastating famine. Wolf credits that searing trip with inspiring his sense of Christian mission to advance international justice and human rights.

Wolf, a Virginia Republican and devout Presbyterian, is known for intense conviction and passion, and he is revered as a giant among religious freedom advocates. The *Washington Post* profiled him as the Capitol's first "bleeding heart conservative," a human rights champion who "has traveled the world in search of famine, death and war, trying to find ways to help."[66] Described as saintly by many colleagues and friends, the evangelical legislator enjoys wide bipartisan respect (liberal San Francisco Democrat and House minority leader Nancy Pelosi referred to him as "my leader" on religious freedom issues). He sees his career in Congress as a response to the maxim, "To whom much is given, much is required," and he seems to care little for the blandishments of his office. "If you can't make a difference, why do this?" he says.[67]

As cochair of the Congressional Human Rights Caucus, Wolf has been "one of the House's leading crusaders for human rights."[68]

For years before sponsoring antipersecution legislation, Wolf was a passionate voice for international religious freedom, championing particular cases, conducting fact-finding trips, and firing off letters to foreign leaders and dissidents alike. One human rights activist recounted traveling through Eastern Europe (as Communism was breaking up) and meeting pastors who carried dog-eared letters from Congressman Wolf to use almost as a talisman when harassed by authorities. "Wolf was the name you heard of over there, when it came to religious liberty."[69] Wolf takes inspiration from the martyrdom of Dietrich Bonhoeffer, the German pastor who opposed the Nazis and ultimately was marched to the gallows just prior to the end of the Second World War. "There are Bonhoeffers all over the world," Wolf has thundered from the floor of the House and elsewhere. "We must defend them."[70]

Wolf's moralism is both endearing and frustrating for other politicians. He will tackle the most indelicate issues,[71] and he refuses to wheel and deal. As one activist put it, "Frank Wolf is a saint. I mean it in the most profound sense of the term. That sort of decency is so strong. I just love him." But Wolf is exasperating because "he won't trade votes" or use his position to demand quid pro quos when he has the leverage to do so. "He operates by example." The power of that example, to be sure, is fortified by seniority. In 2001 Wolf secured a coveted chairmanship of the Appropriations Subcommittee that oversees the State Department, giving him enormous leverage on human rights issues in U.S. foreign policy. Combined with his years of on-the-ground experience and clear religious convictions, Wolf looms large in the cause of international human rights.

If Wolf is the "saint" of the cause then Chris Smith is the tiger, feisty and tenacious in pursuit of legislative objectives. His rise to prominence demonstrates the power of religious commitments, but also how personality and events combined to fuel the emerging movement. Elected to Congress in 1980 when he was just twenty-seven, the New Jersey representative was catapulted into a pivotal chairmanship when the Republicans took control of Congress after the 1994 elections. Described as "a youthful-looking Republican with great seniority,"[72] Smith both paved the way for the movement and led the charge on key initiatives.

A devout Catholic, Smith traces his political convictions to his upbringing in the faith. As former director of New Jersey Right-to-Life, Smith entered Congress as a fierce opponent of abortion, which led some in the press to lump him into the new Christian Right movement. But throughout his career Smith has been supportive of labor unions, spending on poor children, international relief programs, and human rights, with a notably liberal voting record on a number of issues. In a sense he represents the distinct Roman Catholic political witness that combines more progressive economic ideas with traditional moral teachings.

Smith laments that the press "won't take you seriously if you are pro-life," and that his human rights work often gets interpreted as a "cover" for his antiabortion agenda. Instead, he sees his work flowing from Gospel injunctions, describing himself as a Matthew 25 Christian:

> The Gospel message has a very strong social justice component, especially Matthew 25 where Christ asked, "When I was hungry, did you give me food to eat? Visit me in prison?" And you know the bottom line to that is he says, "Whatsoever you do to the least of my brethren, you do to me." And that has been the core, the absolute bedrock of all right-to-life and human rights work that I've done.[73]

In public statements and committee work Smith freely elaborates on how his faith guides his view of the sacredness of life and the indivisibility of human rights: "Our Lord admonished us to care for the persecuted, the hungry, those in prison—the so-called least of our brethren. For me, this has meant inclusion of all people, regardless of race, sex, age or condition of dependency, including unborn babies. . . . Human rights are indivisible."[74] But Smith's pro-life stance does not deter him from building alliances with people that he fights "like cats and dogs" with over abortion policy. As we will see in chapter 8, he worked with feminists on sex trafficking legislation to rescue vulnerable women and children bought and sold on the international market. For him the religious mandate is the same.

Like Wolf, Smith sees his position in Congress as a sacred responsibility. "To have a strategic position like a member of Congress and not use it for the Kingdom of Heaven would be a dereliction of duty." A sense of a "positive burden" seems to characterize Smith, who seeks out accountability in weekly Bible study and devotional meetings with Christian colleagues.

Smith felt especially challenged to "walk the walk" of his faith when he made his first international foray of his congressional career. Shortly after taking office in 1981 he traveled to the Soviet Union for ten days with the National Conference on Soviet Jewry, where he "met a whole slew of refuseniks," along with the famed Siberian Seven, a group of Pentecostal Christians holed up in the American embassy seeking asylum from Soviet persecution. Smith felt a "total bond" with these Jews and Christians being "branded and ostracized," and he began to inform himself about the larger issue of persecution: "I read a book, *Tortured by Christ* by Richard Wurmbrand. Read it about five times. He makes a strong appeal for Christians in the West, in safe harbors, in a meaningful way to speak out on behalf of persecuted brethren. And I did my own inventory and said I better do a lot more. I want to live the gospel as faithfully as possible speaking on behalf of the disenfranchised." He concluded that "if somebody's being tortured and I'm trading [with the torturer] and acting as if that's not happening, shame on me, especially if I know about it and I don't make intercession on their behalf."[75]

To inform himself Smith has led numerous delegations abroad to investigate the status of religious freedom. Sometimes these trips provoked dramatic moments that served to highlight abuses. On one trip to China, Congressman Smith participated in a private mass officiated by Catholic Bishop Su Zhimin (a leading figure in the underground Church that maintains loyalty to the global Catholic Church) held in a run-down apartment in Beijing. Shortly thereafter Bishop Su was arrested by Chinese authorities and interrogated for ten days about his meeting with the congressman. The leader of the Cardinal Kung Foundation, which advocates for the Catholic Church in China, reported the arrest to Smith, who broke the news to the media and demanded action in a letter to his colleagues. This publicity led to Bishop Su's release, but his later rearrest highlights both the ongoing struggles of believers in China and the importance of keeping outside pressure on the regime.

In contrast to the image some have of meaningless posturing by members of Congress, Smith has thought a lot about how to make a real difference. Here, too, he finds inspiration in scripture: "We really have to be smart," to be "gentle as doves" but "wise as serpents." Thus the most important prayer of policymakers is Solomon's—to "pray for wisdom" about how to make the system work: "It's been an evolutionary thing. How to do it. Not just to make a floor speech . . . but to take the levers out there and use them in a way that's not counterproductive."[76]

Smith acknowledges that promoting human rights or religious freedom, to the exclusion of other economic and strategic objectives, is neither feasible nor wise. But he has seen numerous instances of how "pressure properly applied" can make a difference, and he believes that U.S. policymakers seldom if ever go too far using the levers of power to advance human rights. His analysis dovetails with the broader critique of foreign-policy "realism." He takes issue with "so-called professionals," especially those in his own party, whose mantra is "stability, stability, stability." "Dictatorships and lawless governments are unreliable trading partners, dangerous to their neighbors," and less stable than nations that respect human rights. Promotion of human rights, if done smartly, is indeed in the national interest. "If you get that right," he argues, "everything else follows."[77]

Smith got his chance to act on these convictions when the Republicans took control of the House after the 1994 elections, giving him the chairmanships of the International Relations Subcommittee on Human Rights and the Helsinki Commission. For the next six years the energetic Smith held over 150 hearings on human rights abuses, passed legislation on everything from support for victims of torture to sanctions against human trafficking, and pressed Democratic and Republican administrations and his own Republican colleagues to champion human rights in American foreign policy.[78]

This work was remarkable for its range. "You name a country and we've probably had a hearing on it."[79] Smith used his position to build a massive documentary record of the denial of religious freedom around the world, bringing together the disparate stories of Soviet Jews, Bosnian Muslims, Baha'is in Iran, or Buddhists of Tibet. What deserves special note is the role Smith's subcommittee played in the Christian solidarity movement and its alliances with other persecuted religionists. His was the first congressional committee to highlight the tragedy of slavery and potential genocide in Sudan. And it was Smith's subcommittee that held the first hearings devoted to the persecution of Christians, the findings of which were widely publicized in religious circles and sparked Congress to mandate a State Department review of the problem.[80]

Smith made the case for this new human rights focus by emphasizing the common bond many American Christians would have with the persecuted:

> In this age when human rights are always in danger of subordination to other objectives, whether it be the love of money, the fear of immigrants and refugees, or the desire to get along with governments and dictatorships that mistreat their own people, we need to be reminded that when people are persecuted in distant lands, it is often because they believe in God and seek to do His will "on earth, as it is in Heaven." The victims we so often ignore, whether the issue is refugee protection or most-favored-nation status for China, are usually the very people with whom we share values. We need to see their faces and be reminded that they are our brothers and our sisters.[81]

Making no effort to hide his own faith, and drawing upon his experiences abroad, Smith recounts stories of heroic sacrifice and fidelity by believers. In one such instance, Smith reported how Senator Bob Dole helped him and others secure the release of a Romanian pastor in 1984. Smith subsequently heard from the pastor how authorities had sent "two common thugs in his cell with instructions to end his life in exchange for reduced sentence," but that, in New Testament fashion, the pastor preached the Gospel to the men, who converted to "the truth that set them free."[82]

In this and many other instances Smith echoed what we hear often in Christian advocacy literature, that the crucial story is not about victims who deserve our support but heroes who fight our battles: "Today, millions of Christians endure torture and are humiliated for their faith. They are the 'least of our brethren' only in the circumstances in which they find themselves. For in reality, they are the moral giants, the unsung heroes whose faith and courage will be revealed in the life to come."[83]

Smith and Wolf were clearly pioneers in preparing the way for the very movement that would ultimately support their legislative initiatives. But they were not alone. A number of members of Congress worked quietly for years to secure the release of imprisoned pastors and religious leaders, writing to foreign heads of state, speaking to ambassadors, and the like. This form of international "constituent service" created a wealth of sympathetic experience and a receptivity to appeals of the emerging movement. In a way they were preparing themselves for the time of overt legislative action.

In the Senate such members were religiously diverse: Joseph Lieberman (D-CT), whose devout Jewish faith (and its link to his political convictions) became well-known in the 2000 presidential campaign; retired evangelical Dan Coats (R-IN), who ultimately viewed passage of the International Religious Freedom Act (IRFA) as his swan song; Methodist Richard Lugar (R-IN), whose office sponsored a full-time staff member to champion religious freedom cases; and Catholic Don Nickles (R-OK), who served as principal sponsor of religious freedom legislation. Nickles offers a particularly interesting case. He began his career in 1981 with a maiden Senate speech promoting religious freedom and announced his retirement in 2003 by citing sponsorship of IRFA as one of his proudest legislative accomplishments.[84] While his core conviction is that "personal, economic, and religious freedom" are "intertwined," it was casework on behalf of persecuted religionists abroad that taught the value of American pressure to address threats to religious liberty.[85]

In subsequent chapters we will encounter other congressional members whose rise to prominence serves as a lens into the nexus of social movement energy and elite power. This is especially the case since the 1990s brought to Washington successive groups of members who won with strong evangelical support, who maintain varying ties to conservative Christian networks, and have emerged as leaders in the ongoing faith-based human rights movement.

In the House these include Spencer Bachus (R-AL), who authored legislation to impose capital market sanctions against the government of Sudan; Joseph Pitts (R-PA), who created the religious prisoners congressional task force to magnify the impact of member intervention; and Tom Tancredo (R-CO), whose career demonstrates the role of church connections. He literally decided to go into politics when a guest speaker at his evangelical church in Denver piqued his conscience on Sudan.[86] Once Tancredo decided to run for national office he pledged that if elected he would strive to help bring justice and peace to the region.

In the Senate Sam Brownback (R–KS) has emerged as the pivotal leader in the faith-based movement, frequent speaker at religious conferences, author, and legislative sponsor of diverse initiatives. Intriguingly, he traces this activism to his roots in Pottawatomie County, the hotbed of evangelically inspired abolitionist agitation in the Kansas territory of the 1850s. Thus this heartland senator sees his work against Sudanese slavery, sex trafficking, and North Korean gulags as flowing from that same antislavery impulse that animated his forebearers. As we will see in later chapters, Brownback's engagement is not just rhetorical. He authored several key provisions on Sudan, including the Sudan Peace Act itself, sponsored the sex trafficking legislation, and is the leading congressional figure addressing the human rights catastrophe in North Korea. He hosts intimate dinners with human rights advocates, foreign exiles, scholars, and opinion makers to prepare the ground for policy initiatives. At one such event he featured Shaykh Kabbani and other Muslim moderates in a discussion of the abuse of Shari'a by militant Islam.

By this time some Democratic readers may be grinding their teeth, given the prominence of Republicans featured here. But a crucial aspect of this new movement is how concern for religious persecution is drawing conservatives with roots in faith communities into the kind of human rights engagement normally associated with the liberal spectrum. That said, the faith-based human rights movement gained genuinely bipartisan support. Not only were Hall, Lieberman, and Pelosi pacesetters in the campaign against persecution, but the late Paul Wellstone (D–MN) teamed up with Chris Smith on sex trafficking legislation, and Congressional Black Caucus members Donald Payne and Eleanor Holmes Norton worked closely with Congressman Bachus on the Sudan Peace Act.

Capitol Hill, of course, contains a thriving network of staff members who played their own roles in preparing the ground for the movement's political gains. Since the 1980s a number of congressional staff have quietly worked on religious freedom cases for their members. Some of these have been "fellows" who are sponsored and paid by religious groups to work in congressional offices. One such fellow was John Hanford, who worked for two decades on religious freedom cases for Senator Lugar (R–IN), before his appointment as Ambassador for International Religious Freedom.[87] Along with a cadre of other staff, he brought his experience in quiet diplomacy to bear in helping craft portions of the IRFA. Another pivotal staff member was Joseph Rees, Chris Smith's top aide on the Human Rights subcommittee. A law professor and former judge in American Samoa, Rees is a Catholic with deep connections to the international human rights networks. Starting in 1995 he orchestrated an elaborate set of hearings for Smith's subcommittee, which involved bringing people from around the world to testify. He also helped draft human rights legislation for the congressman, including the antipersecution bill and the human trafficking law. As a testament to his credibility, Rees was selected to become the first ambassador to Timor, in a ceremony attended by "an incredible array of liberals and conservatives."[88]

One lesson from this account of the congressional arena is that members and staff who are deeply enmeshed in religious networks are often leaders of the movement, not just responders to outside pressure. But this does not mean that they will always agree. As we will see in chapter 6, Hanford and Rees were vehement adversaries in the struggle to define the proper remedy for religious persecution abroad. Rees crafted tough language to expose persecuting countries in a House bill (Wolf-Specter), while Hanford built measures of quiet diplomacy into the Senate alternative (Nickles-Lieberman). They fought intense battles behind the scenes over these two visions. Ironically, both were subsequently appointed to ambassadorships by President George W. Bush, indicating both the legacy of their work and some enduring divisions in the faith-based community.

Conditions, as this chapter demonstrates, were ripe for social movement effulgence. In the next chapter we turn to the story of the man who served as catalyst in magnifying those nascent forces and channeling them toward government policy.

5

HE SENT A JEW

Two millennia ago "God sent a Jew into the world for the
Gentiles to know God and be at peace with God. . . . He sent
a Jew into our midst in 1996 to awaken us, a sleeping church."

—Charles Colson on Michael Horowitz[1]

To understand the new faith-based alliances on global human
rights one must appreciate not only the broad forces afoot, but
also individual human agency.[2] Indeed, throughout this book we will
encounter persons whose energetic efforts argue against determin-
ism, the view that individuals are largely irrelevant to historical
events.[3] Among the many activists, no one looms as large as Michael
Horowitz, who served as a kind of catalyst for the movement.

I use the term "catalyst" purposely. In chemistry, a catalyst is the
ingredient which, when mixed with other vital agents, produces a
chemical reaction that makes something different, or fundamentally
greater, than the constituent parts. This is analogous to the role
Horowitz played in helping to mobilize key religious constituencies,
especially evangelicals, on foreign policy. From religious persecution
to sex trafficking, the conditions were ripe for religious mobilization;
what was needed was someone to mix the ingredients. To extend the
metaphor, just as a catalyst must have unique properties to play its
role, Horowitz brought personal traits that enabled him to activate latent movement energies. These attributes include his Jewish identity,
government experience, elite connections, affinity for the Christian

community, polemical style, and strategic moxie that fit the imperatives of social movement mobilization.

This chapter examines these attributes, and it uses Horowitz's
story to understand the new politics of human rights and international relations. A sometimes polarizing figure, Horowitz is seen by
evangelical admirers as nothing less than a person appointed by God,[4]
and by critics as a hardball political operative with hidden agendas.
A kind of moral entrepreneur,[5] he is brash, blunt, bombastic,
supremely confident, relentless in political pursuit, and, critics charge,
given to hyperbole to dramatize his causes or exaggerate his role.[6] He
admits to being a difficult person to work with, that he "pounds the
table and demands things yesterday." With a salty tongue and profane
wit Horowitz does not suffer those he sees as fools, and some of the
people I interviewed for this book have felt bruised by his attacks.
But Horowitz also evokes a burning sense of personal responsibility,
and his heart pours out for victims—for persecuted believers, Sudanese slaves, trafficking victims, prisoners subject to rape—with a
sense of urgency that is infectious. "You can't fake that kind of passion," one critic acknowledged.[7]

Critics and admirers alike agree that Michael Horowitz's relentless efforts were crucial in catalyzing the new religious movement. Even traits that critics identified—his rhetorical hyperbole
and manic aggressiveness—helped sustain movement pressure. In
policy circles around Washington people talk about Horowitz in familiar, if not always charitable, terms ("I hope Mike will be
pleased"; or "Horowitz really ticked people off"). In some Christian communities beyond the Beltway he is almost renowned, as I
learned at a Voice of the Martyrs conference in Tulsa, Oklahoma,
where Horowitz was spoken of in almost reverent tones. Named
(along with Billy Graham and Mother Teresa) as one of the
"World's Top Ten Christians of 1997" by a (later embarrassed)
Southern Baptist Convention publication,[8] he is invited to speak at
evangelical colleges, profiled in religious publications, featured on
Christian television, feared by opponents, and lauded in the Congressional Record. What attributes and circumstances enabled him
to play his catalyst role? And what lessons about faith and politics
can we glean from this story?

THE JEWISH FACTOR

Crucial to Horowitz's ability to forge new alliances on global human rights is his Jewish identity. He grew up in a thriving Jewish community in the Bronx, enmeshed in the life of a synagogue, extended family at Shabbat dinners, and immigrant stories of garment sweatshops and upward mobility. The Horowitzes had relatives all across Europe to whom they sent letters and packages during the war, but few of them survived Hitler's terror. Attending yeshiva school in the 1940s Horowitz was often sent by the rabbi to solicit donations for the school, using a megaphone to call out, "Make sure Hitler never triumphs—keep the doors of the yeshiva open." Thus the Holocaust loomed large in the community and in Horowitz's experience. Horowitz considered becoming a rabbi, and he endured taunts and even a beating at the hands of gentile boys who chanted, "You killed our Christ."[9]

Horowitz used these experiences with devastating effectiveness to prod evangelical Christians to act on behalf of their own fellow religionists abroad, one of his singular contributions to the new movement. His mantra is that Christians should stop apologizing for the sins of their fathers and start championing the cause of their brothers and sisters abroad. "I would tell these Christian leaders that I got beat up and called a Christ killer, and they would become devastated and start apologizing. Then I would tell them to stop apologizing, because without the decency of Christians in this country I would be a lampshade."[10]

Like so many Jews of his generation, Horowitz's formative experiences inculcated a patriotic sense that America was a "blessed land," a refuge for Jews and the nation that defeated Hitler. He embraced American culture and seized opportunities with gusto, especially as provided by City College of New York (CCNY), that bastion of upward mobility for so many working-class kids in New York City. Elected student body president at CCNY in the late 1950s, Horowitz immersed in the ideological clashes of the time, developing a clear affinity with the anti-Communist "old Left" of Allard Lowenstein and Eleanor Roosevelt against varieties of "leftist anti-Americanism." He relished being "attacked by radical classmates for being a Cold

War liberal." This experience, a common baptism for many Jews who personified the neoconservative movement, provides a clue to Horowitz's worldview. He remains an American patriot and bleeding heart, who takes on injustice where he sees it. As former Reagan speech writer Peggy Noonan noted, "It's not a shock for anyone who knows Mike that he's worried about religious persecution, because persecuted Christians are undefended by the big people."[11] But Horowitz is also contemptuous of fuzzy utopianism and anti-Americanism, which he detects among those, especially on the Left, who resist vigorous American leadership abroad.

From City College Horowitz went on to Yale Law School, entering a class that would include numerous future luminaries in politics. One of those was Eleanor Holmes Norton (future D.C. representative to Congress and leader of the Congressional Black Caucus), who would work with Horowitz on the Sudan Peace Act. Like many liberal Jews of his generation he traveled south to join the battle for civil rights. On the faculty of the University of Mississippi Law School, he recruited students from black colleges and taught some of the first integrated classes in the history of Ole Miss. He was prominent enough that a candidate for lieutenant governor ran a campaign that called for firing "that Jew professor."[12]

After his stint in the South, Horowitz returned to New York City to practice labor law in the 1970s, a time of tumultuous battles over affirmative action and budgets. He describes experiencing an epiphany about certain "new class" American elites, especially what he viewed as their contempt for middle-class people—garbage workers, firemen, and police—who played by the rules but were being branded racist by "limousine liberals" with their Ivy League educations. This critique of the "smugness" of elites would endure in Horowitz's work with the religious community. If deracinated elites tended to see working-class people as benighted Archie Bunkers, they viewed evangelical Christians as "polyester bigots." This "sanctimonious arrogance" is rhetorical fodder for Horowitz, who inveighs against the secular biases that go unchallenged in the "faculty clubs, news rooms, Washington salons, and cocktail parties I no longer get invited to." Horowitz's political pilgrimage thus typified that of other Jews, who began as liberal Democrats before emerging as key voices in the Reagan era. Though Horowitz claims that he "didn't feel Jewish for six months" after changing his registration from Democrat to Republican, he continued to frame his commitments in the language of freedom and justice so characteristic of Jewish liberals. This aided his work with Democrats on a number of issues.

An article Horowitz wrote in 1980 about this political conversion caught the attention of Ronald Reagan's lieutenants, earning Horowitz a top position in the White House.[13] This gave him a chance to act on his emerging worldview and an opportunity to develop relationships with a new generation of evangelical leaders.

Horowitz's association with the Reagan administration gave him cachet when he prodded evangelical leaders to act against persecution of Christians abroad: "I'm a Jew; I'm interested in this. Why aren't you?" This prodding helped overcome the "uneasiness on the part of Christians who are conscious of being viewed as persecutors rather than the persecuted that promoting their cause is too chauvinistic."[14] Southern Baptist leader Richard Land said Horowitz's catalytic role was his ability "to shame Christian leaders" to action. Christian activist Gary Bauer described Horowitz as a "whirling dervish" able to "prick your conscience about what have you done *today?*" Because he is a Jewish American, "he gave the entire effort more credibility, that it wasn't some Religious Right hidden agenda."[15] Thus, as one reporter noted, the "Judaism that seemed the central paradox of Horowitz's sudden prominence quickly proved to be his central advantage."[16]

As a Jew, Horowitz especially helped legitimate the antipersecution cause by constantly drawing the link between lessons of the Holocaust and the new scourge of Christian persecution around the world. There was a time, he reminds listeners, when some Jews were sheepish about championing the cause of their own. In a letter to the directors of evangelical mission boards in 1995, Horowitz implored them to speak out against anti-Christian persecutions, to not repeat the shameful example he frequently cites: "When President Roosevelt was considering the appointment of the late Felix Frankfurter to the Supreme Court, he was visited by a delegation of leading American Jews who implored him not to make the appointment. Such an act, those 'leaders' said, would make matters worse, and they urged dealing with Hitler by making every effort not to provoke him to further anger."[17]

Horowitz also knows scripture and Christian argot well enough to speak in compelling terms. Alluding to the concept of the Church as the body of Christ, he reminds believers that "when one member suffers all suffer." In introducing his plan for a national day of prayer, he quoted Hebrews 13:3: "Remember those in prison as if you were their fellow prisoners, and those who are mistreated as if you yourselves were suffering."[18]

Horowitz's entreaties to join the movement extended to Catholics and mainline Protestants. But his special knack was bringing evangelicals into the faith-based coalition and connecting them with other partners in a wider human rights movement. As one activist put it, while evangelical leaders might feel issues of religious persecution or sex trafficking "burning in their hearts," Horowitz provided the vehicle for them to act.

This knack for speaking to the Christian conscience, combined with Horowitz's pertinacity, proved a tremendously effective combination. My conversations with evangelical leaders confirmed how Horowitz riveted their attention to religious persecution and other issues. Charles Colson lauded the fact that "Mike will not let you alone" on matters of conscience.[19] On religious persecution, for example, Colson cared deeply about the problem "but was not conscious of how pervasive it is" until Horowitz made his case.[20] Bill Armstrong, a prominent evangelical and former senator, echoed that he was "not fully aware of how much religious intolerance there is, how intense and ugly it is," until Horowitz pressed the issue: "I'm sure I would not have really focused on this issue if Michael Horowitz hadn't called me and insisted that I do so and in effect said, 'What's the matter with you evangelicals? I'm a Jew and here I'm trying to raise some public interest in what's happening to your brothers and sisters in Christ.'" Armstrong acknowledged that Horowitz is "abrasive," but he then observed how astonishing it was that "a Jew was responsible, almost single-handedly, for magnifying and focusing the nascent interest of the evangelical community."[21] Because they appreciate how Horowitz piqued their consciences on religious persecution, evangelical leaders are open to entreaties on other issues. Colson notes, for example, that "trafficking was not on the screen," until "Horowitz got us into it."

While it may seem at times that Horowitz was merely goading evangelical leaders into action, he sees it differently. He expresses deep admiration for the skill and energy of such figures as Charles Colson of Prison Fellowship, the late Bill Bright of Campus Crusade, James Dobson of Focus on the Family, Franklin Graham of Samaritan's Purse, and Ravi Zacharias of international missions. As religious entrepreneurs they have built huge ministries with global dimensions, leading Horowitz to quip that "if they were the heads of our major corporations, the economy would be humming." These are formidable but busy people who trust Horowitz when he presents an opportunity to make a political difference. As Charles Colson suggested, Horowitz "staffs" the evangelical elite, husbanding their valuable capital for strategic moments. In this Horowitz has been very effective, according to Colson, because invariably "when he suggested someone to call" or recommended some tactical action, "it was productive."[22]

A simple example illustrates how this works. With reports of virulent anti-Semitism mounting in the Middle East and Europe, Horowitz solicited evangelical leaders to sign a highly publicized letter to George W. Bush imploring the president to condemn publicly this threat to peace and civility (which he did). While several of these individuals had expressed concern about rising anti-Jewish sentiment abroad, Horowitz provided a vehicle for action that demonstrated evangelical solidarity with the Jewish community. [23]

Horowitz's knowledge of, and respect for, the born-again world also enables him to connect evangelical leaders with activists in the broader movement. When German physician Norbert Vollertson wrote exposés of the tormented people of North Korea, Horowitz activated his legendary fax list to get the word out to a receptive Christian community. Not only was Vollertson broadly featured on religious broadcasts and news outlets, but evangelical leaders responded with alacrity to appeals for action. Characteristic is this message from Sandy Rios, president of the conservative Concerned Women For America:

> Today I got a fax from the Jewish spearheader [Horowitz] of the international effort on North Korea. In the fax he stated the need to get Congressman Henry Hyde to plead for a full committee hearing. I called him immediately to tell him that the congressman is a personal friend and if I could help in any way, please let me know. He called back

immediately to say, "YES! Please!" I am in the process of arranging that meeting right now. Please pray for me, that I will present this to the congressman in such a way that he will act.[24]

Another advantage of Horowitz's Jewishness was that he could sidestep the doctrinal disputes and rivalries that undermine unity in the evangelical world. The image of evangelicals as the bulwark of a disciplined army masks bewildering theological diversity: Fundamentalists disdain Pentecostals; moderate evangelicals eschew association with the "Christian Right." As one activist put it, "The evangelical church in this country is very decentralized, and there's a lot of competition. By being a Jew, he transcended denominational differences."[25]

Horowitz was also able to capitalize on his Jewish identity, ironically, because he did not represent a Jewish organization. He was free to operate in freelance entrepreneurial fashion unencumbered by processes of organizational accountability. He had no board to report to, no constituency to be concerned with. Because of his high profile, a story line began appearing in the Christian press, and then in the broader media: "A Jew Battles Persecution of Christians."[26] Skilled at self-promotion, say his critics,[27] Horowitz nonetheless helped foster a sense that the broader Jewish community shared his passion and even his analysis, though that was by no means always the case. As one leader of a prominent Jewish organization notes, when Horowitz offers the refrain that he would be a lampshade without the goodness of the Christian community in America, "the implication is that he speaks for the Jewish community." This leads people to conclude that "even the Jewish community thinks not enough is being done on behalf of persecuted Christians," and perhaps even that "Jews have a responsibility to speak out more than everybody else." In politics appearances count.

Still, appearances are vulnerable if not backed by something more concrete. Here, too, Horowitz's Jewish roots, combined with his vast elite connections, served the faith-based movement well. Aware of how easily stereotyped a movement of evangelicals and Catholics could become, Horowitz assiduously enlisted prominent Jewish backers for the religious freedom campaign. He spoke to the Jewish community in the language of its historic commitment to human rights and its obligation to reciprocate for the support Christians provided during the campaign for Soviet Jewry.

Among those enlisted into the cause by Horowitz were former *New York Times* editor Abe Rosenthal, who did much to publicize atrocities against Christian minorities abroad, and fellow neoconservative Elliott Abrams, who became a pivotal leader as chair of the Commission on International Religious Freedom. But Horowitz also maintains ties to wider Jewish networks that have proved invaluable to the faith-based effort. He played a role in enlisting crucial support from such prominent liberals as Rabbi David Saperstein, the venerable lobbyist for Reform Judaism; Stacie Burdette, representative of the Anti-Defamation League; and others. Horowitz referred to Saperstein as a man "whom I love and with whom I agree on almost nothing."[28] Saperstein echoed Horowitz's view that support from Christians during the campaign for Soviet Jews in the 1970s commanded a response from Jews now that Christians are subject to persecution."[29] Saperstein went on to work with Horowitz and his evangelical friends on a number of subsequent initiatives.

Senator Joseph Lieberman (D-CT), who would cosponsor the final legislation on international religious freedom, also credited Horowitz, whom he referred to as a "tummler," a Yiddish term for "the hyperkinetic social directors of the Borscht Belt." Lieberman nicely summarized Horowitz's impact: "He has been relentless in forcing people to face the facts of worldwide persecution of Christians. It's not that he was the first, and it's not that Christian groups weren't involved. But when you talk to Mike, it is clear that this is not just another issue for him. It's inside his guts—or, should I say, his kishkes."[30]

Enlisting Jewish support for the antipersecution movement was crucial, because it helped inoculate a movement that could have been caricatured as a Christian Right front. But so was Horowitz's effort to draw the evangelical community into a strange bedfellows coalition with his Jewish friends. This points to another trait that Horowitz brought to the faith-based movement: chutzpah. This Yiddish term for a nervy, outrageous audacity is viewed as a trait cultivated by Jews to help them compete and thrive as a small minority in America. Chutzpah, the joke goes, is when a kid kills his parents and then pleads to the court for mercy on account of being an orphan. To critics it was no less outlandish for Horowitz to take upon himself the task of helping prod the evangelical community into a more mature international political engagement. But that is precisely what he attempted to do. His sympathy with, and understanding of, the evangelical community in America facilitated that act of chutzpah.

EVANGELICAL SYMPATHIES

It was at Ole Miss Law School that Horowitz first encountered evangelical Protestantism, and in spite of the "suffocating" hand of racism, he found many kindred spirits in this community who valued "faith, family, and tradition." Perhaps it was here that he discovered the knack for inspiring confidence among intelligent but "sheepish" religionists. Notably he found the white law students quick to apologize for themselves. "They would be stunned," when he, "a New York City Jew and Yale Law graduate" would tell them that they had something to teach the nation about race relations. Southern Protestants, he recalls, "reminded me of Jews . . . a part of the mainstream and yet separate from it."[31]

Horowitz's budding sympathies with evangelical Protestantism continued to grow when his work in the White House put him in contact with a cohort of well-educated evangelical Christians who had flocked to Washington during the Reagan era. Horowitz describes his surprise at meeting "smart young Ph.D.s, Supreme Court clerks, and Rhodes scholars" who happened to be Protestant evangelicals and obviously defied the stereotypes prominent in the elite, secular media (as in the infamous *Washington Post* story that depicted evangelicals as "largely poor, uneducated, and easy to command").[32] Moreover, he was struck by "the moral virtue and political courage" of these "reflective, caring young people who had been formed against the noisy, self-centered anarchies that were their campuses."[33]

One of those evangelicals, Michael McConnell, a prominent law professor and now a George W. Bush appointee to the federal bench, attended a church that opened its doors to a congregation of Christian Ethiopian exiles for Amharic language services. The plight of this community was Horowitz's first exposure to the cause of religious persecution abroad. McConnell enlisted his aid in opposing a State Department removal of blanket protection against deportation of Ethiopians back to a country run by a bitterly antireligious, Marxist dictatorship. Subsequently, Horowitz and his wife also sponsored many of them for asylum or citizenship. Horowitz describes his encounters with the Ethiopian Christians as powerful. Their decency and the power of their faith was so palpable that even his agnostic wife felt it.

After six years in the White House Horowitz left for private practice, then to one of the proliferating Washington think tanks that provide so many of the policy initiatives taken up by politicians. His work, mostly on tort reform, had little to do with his later cause. But Horowitz's continued involvement with the Ethiopian community, along with his experience working with evangelicals in the Reagan administration, crystallized his sense that the born-again community had a lot to offer American democracy, but that it was badly hampered by negative elite stereotypes and its own lack of political sophistication. He offered this analysis in a piece titled, "Bridges Crossed—and Yet to Cross: A Sympathetic Jewish Writer Speaks to Evangelicals" published in 1994, just a year before his foray into the religious persecution issue.[34] In this article Horowitz developed themes that would characterize his strategic approach to mobilizing the evangelical constituency on international human rights. It also suggests something of the sweep of Horowitz's vision and his chutzpah in offering it to evangelicals as a way *for them* to think about their own political witness.

Horowitz began the article with two reasons why evangelicals should resist the "hypocrisy of an American elite that now actively seeks to caricature and delegitimize" them and "deny them a place in the American mainstream." First, not only is such a denial "opportunistic," "venal," and "profoundly antidemocratic," it runs "counter to the sweep and spirit of American history." To develop that claim Horowitz cites historian Arthur Schlesinger's account of the fear and loathing New England elites felt "as they watched

Western frontiersmen participate in Andrew Jackson's inaugura-
tion." The spectacle of "farmers and settlers in Washington, not as
awed spectators but as men and women exuberantly celebrating at
a White House now felt to be operating in their interests," led the
elites to "describe the phenomenon as—gasp—the triumph of
KING MOB," spelled in capital letters. Evangelicals in politics,
Horowitz argued, are the current "King Mob," which, "after a few
fits and starts and with a few rough edges rounded, represents "an
essential chapter in America's continuing saga of democratization."
Because of this, Horowitz echoed the view that "the Bible belt is
America's safety belt," the center of "family-oriented, community-
minded, and religiously motivated Americans" who are the best
guarantors of a "civil and decent" nation.[35]

Horowitz went on to counsel the constituency on how to smooth
out its rough edges so its voice would be fully heard: don't whine, avoid
language that can alienate potential allies,[36] and acknowledge the sad
legacy of past anti-Semitism and racism. With respect to civil rights,
Horowitz argued that evangelicals should forthrightly admit "that it
was a good thing for the American Left to have succeeded, and good
for the American Right to have lost, in the historic struggles that gave
black Americans the right to vote and freed them from state-imposed
racism." Given the burden of "conservatism's past," Horowitz went so
far as to assert that "policies should be judged by the measure of hope
and opportunity they offer the poorest and most needful Americans."
Even though this is the "liberals' preferred frame of reference," conservatives should still win the policy debate, given how the "anything-
goes radical individualism" that the Left promotes has so undermined
poor and underclass Americans.

With respect to anti-Semitism, Horowitz's recommendation anticipated his efforts to forge an unlikely alliance of evangelicals and
Jews. Christians, Horowitz implored, must acknowledge their legacy
of religiously inspired intolerance, even if it lingers only in "fugitive,
anecdotal cases," because it is that history that "arms those who
would keep conservative Christians forever illegitimate and out of
power." To purge the community of that legacy, Horowitz called for
evangelicals to have an "intense dialogue with the American Jewish
community—if only to help ensure that they can no longer be eas-

ily used as a bloody-shirt symbol with which increasing numbers of Jewish waverers from liberal orthodoxy can be frightened into a return to the fold."

Read in retrospect, it is clear that this article presaged Horowitz's prodding of the Protestant evangelical community on the issue of worldwide religious persecution and other human rights abuses. As Horowitz repeatedly stressed, the movement was about nothing less than lifting the scales from the eyes of American elites and thereby reducing prejudice against Christian faith in the twenty-first century.

Central to that task was a rapprochement between Protestant evangelicals and Jews. To be sure, working relations between Jewish and evangelical leaders had been blossoming since the early 1990s, and not just owing to evangelical support for Israel. Tactical relationships emerged out of the battle to restore free exercise of religious protections narrowed by the Supreme Court in 1990.[37] Horowitz, however, sought to push this incipient rapprochement to a new level.

The scope of Horowitz's attempt to effect a Jewish-evangelical rapprochement is reflected in a battle, which he fought during the antipersecution campaign, over the content of the film on anti-Semitism featured at the United States Holocaust Memorial Museum. Horowitz watched the film with Christian evangelical friends, who were deeply offended by its depiction of Christianity's role in the history of anti-Semitism. As a consequence, Horowitz assembled Jews, including Elliott Abrams and film critic Michael Medved, to protest to the Museum. The *New York Times* carried the story with the headline, "Jewish Allies of Evangelicals Attack Film on Anti-Semitism," which suggested the potential broader consequence of the controversy. To Horowitz the film was inaccurate and patently anti-Christian, and he sought out Jewish historians to back his claim. He argued that the film did not fully account for the non-Christian and pagan sources of Nazi ideology. At a more strategic level, its "libels against Christianity" presented yet another barrier to "people of the book" working together.[38] The Holocaust Museum ultimately altered the film.

The lesson we can glean from Horowitz's background is that he was primed—by virtue of experience, inclination, and personal commitments—to nudge history when the moment could be seized. That moment presented itself, oddly, when the Horowitzes decided to hire a live-in housekeeper in 1995. Horowitz and his wife turned to the Ethiopians they knew through the exile church, and found one of them, an evangelist man named Getaneh, to take the job.

This hiring proved revealing in a number of ways. Horowitz's wife, Devra, detected racism in the reaction of some in the suburban community to Getaneh's presence in their home. But it was Getaneh's faith that so captivated Horowitz, who describes having long theological debates with his guest about God, Christianity, and the chance even for tyrants to be redeemed: "You mean if Mengistu became a Christian before he died, he'd go to heaven?"[39] Getaneh's forgiving spirit, which extended to those who tortured him, personified for Horowitz that modern Christians abroad really are "the lambs."

When Getaneh was threatened with deportation, Horowitz took on his case because he was outraged at the denial of asylum for Getaneh by the Immigration and Naturalization Service. What especially sparked his ire was that so little weight was given to the claim that Getaneh was threatened *as a Christian* if returned. Immigration attorneys told him it is "easier to pass a camel through a needle's eye than to get an asylum claim satisfied for a Christian who has escaped persecution."[40] Horowitz sprang into action, seeking out those, such as Nina Shea, who were documenting the broader problem of anti-Christian persecution that Getaneh's case exemplified. What Horowitz discovered was not only a burgeoning but unfocused cluster of disparate Christian organizations and activists, but a human rights issue being slighted. Here were all the ingredients he needed: an issue of fundamental justice, a huge problem ignored by elite prejudice, and the potential for alliances between Jews, evangelicals, Catholics, and others. The moment was ripe to alter the political landscape, and Horowitz found an issue into which he could pour his fierce energies and strategic vision. A review of his efforts suggests the extent to which his sympathies with the evangelical community continued to ramify in the enfolding drama.

Horowitz launched his crusade against persecution of Christians with a guest editorial in the *Wall Street Journal* in 1995.[41] The article elicited a minimal response from Christian groups, which puzzled Horowitz: "I knew that if I'd written about anti-Semitism in Muslim countries, Christian groups would have overwhelmed me with some sense of anguish and support and desire to do something about it." So he followed it up with a letter to the directors of 143 evangelical mission boards, imploring them to speak out against "today's anti-Christian persecutions." Breaking the silence surrounding these persecutions, he argued, would serve the broader human rights cause, a theme he echoed frequently: "Ironically, your voice also needs to be raised in the service of non-Christians seeking tolerance, democracy and religious freedom within their own countries. As with Jews during much of the twentieth century, Christian victims often 'merely' serve as pawns in struggles for the political souls of countries when evil and radical men seek to take them over."[42]

When this foray did not elicit much response, Horowitz brainstormed with Nina Shea and others about how to get the major Christian leaders involved in the issue. Horowitz recalled an early meeting in which the idea was floated of having a high profile conference on religious persecution. His response was, "Oh, that's a great idea, but who should we ask?" Instead of thinking in terms of staff directors of religious organizations, Horowitz immediately jumped to the highest level: "I said, give me the names of the ten most important leaders, give me their phone numbers." Horowitz then proceeded to make cold calls, making his passionate pitch that they had to act on behalf of the lambs, the fellow members of the body of Christ. Former Colorado senator Bill Armstrong described receiving one of those phone calls while at a conference:

> Michael Horowitz called and said, "Remember me? I used to know you when I was at OMB and you were in the Senate." Actually, I didn't remember, but I just took it for granted that he knew what he was talking about. And he told me what was on his mind. And I thought to myself, I'm in this beautiful mountain resort and this guy is calling me to ask me to think about one of the last things in the world that any person would ever wish to think about. But yet I found him so insistent and so compelling. . . . His appeal to conscience was, and remains, so strong that I just couldn't say, "Well, no, I haven't got time."[43]

This approach succeeded in getting a critical mass of key leaders on board for a major initiative. In rapid order Horowitz produced the first draft of what became the "Statement of Conscience" adopted by the National Association of Evangelicals; got Frank Wolf (R–VA), a leading evangelical congressman, to sponsor antipersecution legislation; and began assembling a coalition to push for its passage. Though the coalition included some of the most prominent and politically astute leaders in the evangelical community, they often deferred to Horowitz for strategic leadership.

Not only did his leadership earn Horowitz awards from evangelical organizations, it produced some remarkable ecumenical overtures. David Stravers, a self-confessing member of the "fundamentalist, Jesus-only, anti-liberal, anti-universalism wing of Christianity," wrote Horowitz about the frequently asked question of when he would "become a completed Jew." This phrase, which means accepting Jesus as the son of God, captures a sticking point in the Jewish-evangelical relationship. Jews, understandably, do not feel the need to be "completed" but devout evangelical Christians remain convinced of the need for all to accept Jesus Christ for salvation. On the basis of his interpretation of Matthew 25—"whoever helps a human representative of Jesus will be treated by God as if they helped Jesus"—Stravers said to Horowitz, "Brother, you qualify." Thus, Horowitz needed to do nothing "more to receive eternal life."[44]

A further testament to the special relationship Horowitz enjoys with born-again Christians was an award he received from the strongly evangelical Midland Ministerial Alliance, with whom he worked on Sudan. Wishing to show solidarity against escalating anti-Semitism in Europe and the Middle East, the Alliance presented Horowitz with a plaque that read simply: "We Are All Jews. In Honor of Michael Horowitz."[45]

WORLDVIEW

Central to this deep and remarkable bond with top evangelical leaders was a worldview—a withering critique of the secular age—that Horowitz shared with his Christian associates. A host of religious thinkers and conservative intellectuals have developed this critique for decades, but Horowitz explicitly made its link to faith-based mobilization. To Horowitz the international engagement of churches represented nothing less than the best chance to reverse the disastrous retreat of the transcendent in the twentieth century. Protecting "the lambs" abroad, in other words, offered hope for a world less bloody and totalitarian than the twentieth century dominated by the secular gods.

This reading of the twentieth century comes primarily from Paul Johnson, whose account of "modern times" Horowitz frequently cites. Johnson marks the beginning of the modern age with the vacuum created by the collapse of the religious impulse among educated and ruling classes in Europe. That vacuum would be filled, he showed, by politicians wielding totalitarian power under the banner of various secular ideologies. Johnson argues that this untrammeled "will to power" was presaged by Friedrich Nietzsche, who declared in 1886 that the "greatest event of recent times" was that "God is dead" among the literati, "that the Christian God is no long tenable."[46]

Horowitz frequently recurs to Nietzsche to dramatize the stakes of the struggle to carve out safe harbors for believers and to foster a new appreciation for the statutory role of Christianity in the coming century:

> Friedrich Nietzsche made a chilling prediction near the beginning of the twentieth century. He said that God was going to die in the eyes of enlightened man, but that there would be another god—politics—and this god would be a lot more bloody, a lot more efficient, and that the sins committed in the name of politics would dwarf by orders of magnitude all the sins committed in the name of religion. The bloody story of the twentieth century is simply a story of politics replacing faith. And this campaign to stop anti-Christian terrorism goes directly to the struggle to make the twenty-first century a century in which faith replaces politics as the basis of moral enthusiasm of young people.[47]

Horowitz echoed numerous encyclicals of John Paul II, which argue that human dignity is rooted in the conviction that each person is made in the image of God, and that this conviction is the only sure underpinning for international human rights. Christianity, Horowitz contends, is a force for "modernity and human rights," and therefore its surprising growth around the world should be recognized as a singularly hopeful sign:

> The world is witnessing the largest explosion of Christianity in all of its reported history. Christianity thus is doing for the Third World—in Africa and Asia and Latin America—exactly what it did in the West. It

is spreading the radical message of the equality of all before God and our accountability to Him for what we do. This is one of the truly hopeful signs for the next century, because it will help make the world's culture and politics far more caring, far less bloody than the twentieth century has been.[48]

Though sins have been committed in the name of Christianity, to Horowitz these pale in comparison to the "rivers of blood that flowed during a century when the world worshiped the God of politics." Thus "Christianity's present growth offers great protection against repressive, dark-age twenty-first-century forces."[49]

It is not hard to see how this message resonated with Christian leaders, especially such evangelical intellectuals as Charles Colson. In a colloquy published in his Prison Fellowship newsletter, Colson applauded Horowitz's analysis: "I don't believe I have ever heard it put more succinctly. Nietzsche became a prophet of the century with 100 million lives lost at the hands of governments. The question is: Now that we have seen politics replace faith, are we willing to bring back faith rather than the mailed fist as the cohesive force of our life?"[50]

To Colson, as to Horowitz, the very fate of Western civilization and democracy hinged on the answer to that question. Fighting religious persecution abroad and protecting vulnerable Christian communities, Horowitz argued, were vital means of promoting respect for human dignity and a democratic ethos. Despotic regimes recognize this if Western secularists do not always: "Our Judeo-Christian faith has taught the most radical political message of all times: the equality of all in the eyes of God. Thug regimes around the world know this and fear Christian Communities for being powerful deliverers and exemplars of that divine heresy." Christians are equally threatening to despots, Horowitz argues, because they are less easily manipulated by traditional motives: "A line in Handel's oratorio 'Solomon' describes the God we worship as one who seeks 'love unbought by price or fear.' What a subversive notion that is! If you are a regime that relies on bribes and threats to stay in power, brave believing communities prepared to risk all to worship Christ cannot be permitted to remain free."[51]

This latter point shows how Horowitz connects this worldview, which sees Christianity as a signal force for beating back the politics of barbarism, with the story of human rights. In Horowitz's vivid

Michael Horowitz with Charles Colson. Courtesy of Prison Fellowship.

riffs, "Christians are the Jews of the twenty-first century," the "victims of choice for thug regimes," "the canaries in the coal mine" that warn of other abuses.[52] These interrelated phrases, which linked traditional evangelicals and Catholics abroad with Jews, help sustain one of the more unusual political coalitions in recent times. Horowitz oversimplifies to make his point, but the metaphors he employed contained enough truth to gain traction.

In Horowitz's account of European history, treatment of the Jews was the best indicator of the general status of human rights in a society: "You could tell a country's level of democratic commitment by looking at how Jews were treated. Jews were the canaries in the coal mine." In other words, if the canaries died the mine was dangerous for other life. But today "too many Jews, my people, have by now been killed to be useful targets of evil, repressive regimes." Instead, "there are millions of vulnerable Third World Christians who are just right for that purpose, and they have become the scapegoats of choice for today's thugs," including "radical Islamic and remnant Communist regimes."[53] Consequently, vulnerable Christians have replaced Jews as the canaries: "The manner in which Christians are treated in many parts of the world is a litmus indicator of whether freedom exists not

only for them—but for all others in their societies. Christian villages
and churches have become the medium on which battles for freedom
in much of the Third World are waged."[54] Therefore, the moral authority of the Christian community "will be gravely tarnished if it fails
to exercise its growing political influence on behalf of people now
risking everything to engage in the 'simple' act of Christian worship
and witness."[55]

The good news, according to Horowitz, is that the campaign
against Soviet anti-Semitism in the 1970s–1980s demonstrated that
international efforts can make a difference in the outcome of those
battles:

> When seemingly all-powerful Soviet Communists had to bow to world-
> wide pressure to permit Jews to freely migrate, walls that the Commu-
> nists had built around churches and political dissidents began to crum-
> ble. They no longer seemed ten feet tall when they couldn't even gang
> up on a few Jews! Nor will the radical Islamists and Communist appa-
> ratchiks when they aren't even able to burn down a few churches. What
> is true today in the battle against anti-Christian pogroms in Asia and
> Africa was true in the battle against anti-Semitism during much of Eu-
> rope's history. Appease it, and thugs find the power to oppress all; stop it,
> and the same thugs lose much of their power to oppress anyone.[56]

As this review suggests, Horowitz sees the world in stark moral terms,
of clear good and evil. This trait resonated with his evangelical allies.
As historian Mark Noll observes, Protestant evangelicals have often
approached political issues as cosmic struggles between the godly and
the satanic.[57] Horowitz speaks that language.

STRATEGIC APPROACH

Horowitz acts on behalf of this vision through an enviable strategic
position that facilitates his catalytic role. With high-level government
experience and elite connections, he knows how to work the political system. But what also has made a difference is a strategic approach
that reflects the imperatives of social movement mobilization. To galvanize nascent forces into a unified effort requires that issues be
sharply drawn, enemies and heroes clearly identified, and activities fo-

cused on precise and obtainable goals. Horowitz's Manichaean tendency to see clear villains and victims, and his skills as a wordsmith in depicting them in vivid personal terms, provides a certain punch to the coalitions working against religious persecution and other human rights causes. Both his background and his instincts thus shaped how issues have been framed and fought, as we see below.

Horowitz entered the White House in 1981 as Chief Counsel for the Office of Management and Budget (OMB), which became the fulcrum of President Reagan's economic agenda. In that hothouse environment, where fierce battles were fought over a line in the State of the Union Address, Horowitz honed his skills as a strategist and political infighter. His years in the White House also crystallized his conviction that history does not march with some "inexorable Hegelian force," but that it turns on the decisions and choices of actors. As he mused, "I had been around, a fly on the wall" and thus had seen how "sea changes" happen, how "one shifts the terms of debate." Moreover, his White House years engendered in Horowitz a supreme confidence based on experience that he knew better than most how to do just that, including "how to create a buzz about an issue."[58]

Horowitz also had vital experience during the Reagan years in helping to pressure the Soviet Union to allow emigration for Jewish refuseniks who were denied requests to leave. As Southern Baptist leader Richard Land observed, this experience provided encouragement to evangelicals. Horowitz could "tell evangelical leaders how to do it, how they did it for refuseniks." Thus, Land concluded, if the United States could "get a response from the Soviet Union on Jews, we can do so on Christians."

Horowitz did not just bring experience and contacts to the faith-based movement. He also took maximum advantage of the think tank position he assumed upon leaving the White House. Serving as a "senior fellow" for the Hudson Institute, one of the proliferating think tanks that populate Washington, D.C., provided a nice perch for a policy entrepreneur like Horowitz. Staffed by a blend of scholars and well-connected former governmental officials, these organizations provide much of the policy initiative in the system, or as Horowitz quipped, they have "replaced the seven-thousand members of the American Political Science Association" for policy ideas.

Characteristically, Horowitz stretched his position to the limit. Originally hired to work on tort reform for the Washington office of the Hudson Institute, Horowitz undertook his initiative against religious persecution on a "freelance" basis. When the board members of the Institute became concerned that this work was diverting him from his main job, Horowitz refused to quit his antipersecution agitation. He was close to losing his job when a Christian foundation, which he had been prodding to support the initiatives of other organizations, offered out of the blue to fund his religious freedom work. This outcome confirmed for Charles Colson that Horowitz's work was indeed "providential."

As a result, Horowitz gained a new and rather incongruous title at the Hudson Institute: Senior Fellow and Director, Project on Civil Justice Reform and International Religious Liberty. Ever the entrepreneur, Horowitz began proposing legislation against international sex trafficking even before the International Religious Freedom Act passed Congress in 1998.

Horowitz likens his own strategic sense of how to advance a political cause with an understanding of how generals win military campaigns. A devotee of the Civil War, he loves to recount a vignette from Grant's autobiography about a crucial lesson the general learned early in the war. Approaching an enemy camp, Grant was filled with trepidation of a new commander, but that fear dissipated when he found the camp abandoned. Grant wrote that it suddenly occurred to him that the rebel commander "had been as much afraid of me as I had been of him. From that event to the close of the war I never forgot that the enemy had as much reason to fear my forces as I had to fear his."[59]

Horowitz takes a self-consciously similar view of political battle. If the issue is right, if people can be aroused, then a groundswell can be created that will move reelection-minded politicians to act. His motto is "never ask for a favor, never *have* to ask for a favor." Instead, offer politicians *opportunities*—to be on the right side of the issue, to be on the right side of history. Horowitz says he does not "hang around like a lobbyist," trying to line up cosponsors for a bill: "Too much effort is made to get some congressman to sponsor a bill." Instead, "you do the member a favor" by *allowing him* to sponsor the legislation: "Who gets my favor is the way it should be framed." The idea is to create a "gigantic parade and then ask if they want to be grand marshal." So you "never ask for a favor, only do them." And that goes for interest groups as well as politicians. "The train is leaving the station," he would tell groups. "We are *giving you* an opportunity to be on board, to take credit for the success of the legislation. If you don't, you will lose credibility. This is your chance."

From the moment he learned about the problem of persecution, and its neglect by elites, Horowitz says he never doubted that he could create a potent movement that would alter the political environment and force action. To overcome the timidity or fatalism of some Christian leaders, Horowitz's admonitions seemed ideally suited to building confidence and creating a sense of inevitability: "Don't try to join the establishment. Let them join you. Understand your own power and virtue." Tell those in power that you have help for them, an opportunity.

A tangible illustration of these principles involved press coverage of the campaign against persecution. Horowitz reassured his fellow advocates that they did not have to depend on the elite press, which underreported the story or treated it in patronizing fashion. "Our movement succeeded because we didn't care what was in the *New York Times*," he said. "We did care what was in denominational newsletters. We didn't want to be on Dan Rather; we wanted Christian radio networks." He sought to transform supplicants—who would "define success by getting a little story on page 47 of the *Times*"—into confident agitators. Tell reporters that *they* were missing the boat, he argued, show them that they were losing their credibility with a large swath of the American public.

FRAMING THE ISSUE

As the above strategic approach suggests, Horowitz knew that framing an issue is crucial to its success: "You've got to have focus to generate interest. You've got to frame the issue to make it a front line" concern. His controversial way of framing the persecution issue had ramifications beyond tactics because to a degree it has affected American foreign-policy choices and international perceptions. Tactics have policy consequences.

The key to the religious freedom alliance, Horowitz argued, was framing the issue as the need to defend victims of horrendous persecution—rather than framing it as combating discrimination or promoting some "utopian" goal of universal religious tolerance. The reason is simple: Elites could not ignore such patent human rights abuses as torture, murder, rape, abduction, enslavement, arrests, destruction of homes and churches, and forced conversions. "I knew," Horowitz mused, that focusing on persecution "would energize people, make it impossible" for people to ignore. "You had to frame it in terms of what happened to the Jews . . . in terms of Nazi Germany."

On the other hand, if the issue is cast in terms of mere discrimination, then the cause could be dismissed, because religion is viewed as problematic, and Christian proselytizing as provoking an "understandable" resistance. The central challenge for Horowitz was and is overcoming the mental roadblocks of elites in the opinion-shaping and policymaking communities. To him, these elites operate with distorted images in their minds about religion in general and Christianity in particular. To the "dinner party crowd, the liberal human rights crowd, the national media crowd," religious faith is part of the problem of human rights abuse, not part of the solution. Christians, to the elite crowd, are "persecutors, not victims themselves." They are "polyester bigots, retrogrades," not carriers of enlightened values. This is why a "liberal establishment community that generally cares about victims cared so little, affirmatively disbelieved what was in front of their eyes," when the subject turned to atrocities committed against Christian believers abroad.

For the movement to succeed, this mental picture had to be shattered. "The worldview is: Because Christians are out there proselytizing, that's why people are pissed off at them." The movement must not be defined in terms of the right to proselytize, consequently, because that would "play into the stereotypes elites have of them." The worst thing for the movement would be for it to be caricatured grossly as "dorky guys" who want to "pass out Bibles in Tiananmen Square or set up tent meetings in front of Mosques." Instead, the issue must be clear victims of injustice—"about the Chinese bishop getting his fingernails pulled out" or the holocaust against Sudanese

Christians. Moreover, the movement must vividly reflect unlikely alliances, the picture must be of evangelicals, Buddhists, Jews, Catholics, Baha'is, and Coptics working side by side for enlightened policies.

Horowitz had to battle his own evangelical friends about how to frame the issue, a dispute that endures among partisans of religious freedom. Evangelizing, or spreading the "good news" to all nations, is a central imperative of many Christians. Some in the community, therefore, felt that Horowitz did not fully appreciate this objective, that he viewed Christians, like Jews, as belonging to communities rather than as individuals who had been reached by evangelization. Horowitz recounts them saying, in effect: "You're not a Christian, you don't understand. Religious persecution is not the issue. The blood of the martyrs makes the church grow. The objective is to be free to evangelize." His response has been, "I agree with you. And I'm sitting here with a missionary understanding that the spread of Christianity is central to the well-being of the world for the twenty-first century. But if you are out there yammering for the right to hold a tent meeting in front of mosques, we'll go no place." Protecting the right to proselytize is in ultimate jeopardy, he argued, if evangelical leaders fail to "shatter the bigotry against Christian groups."

Horowitz also argued that focusing on hard-core persecution makes a more compelling lobby focus: "You mean the Chinese are out there murdering pastors, Congressman? And you want to do business as usual with them? What was your opponent's name?" On the other hand, if the issue got framed in "utopian" terms of preventing all discrimination, then it would "tie us up with scientologists" in Germany, "Catholic-Protestant tensions in Latin America and Ireland, Jewish-Evangelical tensions in Israel, and we'd go no place." The last thing one would want is for the State Department to act like some "international EEOC" (Equal Employment Opportunity Commission, which responds to discrimination claims).

Critics of Horowitz, as we see in chapter 6, charge that this focus on egregious persecution ignores a huge class of discriminatory human rights abuses and lets all but the worst regimes off the hook. Horowitz responds that the focus on hard-core persecution creates public consciousness that affects the atmosphere on discrimination. "When Netanyahu tried to cut a deal with the religious parties in

Israel to discriminate against evangelicals, it couldn't fly because we had created a movement against hard-core persecution. And when Russia tried to crack down, there was a reaction because of the public and elite consciousness." The focus on egregious persecution "affects discrimination," he contends, and promotes the broader goal of religious freedom.

Scholars note that when social movements galvanize and focus their nascent forces, the political system responds.[60] Horowitz's strategic approach reflected a scholarly insight that successful social movements depend on freeing people from the fatalistic view that they cannot move the political system.[61] To Horowitz, the campaign for international religious freedom legislation was primarily *a tool* to liberate the Christian community from its sheepishness and transform the way secular elites view devout faith in the twenty-first century. The drama of the legislative battle, moreover, would excite the partisans, provide a tangible goal for efforts, and draw diverse groups into its magnetic vortex. As the campaign waxed, in fact, group memberships mushroomed and new relationships were forged. Conservative evangelicals found themselves teaming up with Jews, Catholics, Episcopalians, Tibetan Buddhists, and Bahai's. Though the groups did not always agree on remedies, they created a formidable sense that *something* had to pass. As one evangelical leader wrote to Horowitz shortly after the new law went into effect: "When I came to Washington for that first consultation which you organized on the persecution issue, I was skeptical of your claim that this was the beginning of a sea change in the media regarding this issue. . . . So far you have been completely vindicated."[62]

SUDAN AS LITMUS

For years the human rights catastrophe in Sudan had been slighted in foreign-policy counsels. To pluck this tragedy from obscurity, as we will see in chapter 7, required extraordinarily diverse group efforts and individual initiatives, which in typical social movement fashion have sprung up in lots of parallel and loosely coordinated ways. Though

Horowitz's engagement followed in the pioneering steps of others,[63] what is instructive here is how Horowitz's attributes—his moral zeal and stark delineations, his polemical knack to simplify issues, his elite connections and chutzpah—helped serve that movement.

As with the persecution issue, Horowitz sought to marshal the moral and political capital of the religious community and focus it in laserlike fashion against the National Islamic Front regime in Khartoum. The defining moment for Horowitz's engagement came late in 1997. It was a time when activists were promoting religious persecution legislation, with Sudan often mentioned as one of the most egregious abusers. As one of the most visible activists, Horowitz got a call from a former associate in the Reagan administration, who invited him on a "trip to Khartoum" where he could see for himself that criticism of the regime was "off base." Horowitz recalls his reaction: "My blood ran so cold."[64] After the friend admitted that he was a hired lobbyist for the Sudanese regime, Horowitz provided this advice:

> Bruce, please, because you're a friend. You want to help your client. Here's how to do it: Hang up the phone, right this second. Because every second this conversation goes on my determination to deal with this murderous genocidal regime increases exponentially. . . . This conversation is devastating. It's the most counterproductive thing you could possibly be doing for your client.[65]

Staggered by "the thought that they were paying conservatives to lobby me," Horowitz reacted in typical unrestrained fashion: "The second he hangs up I go to the statute books and get the apartheid bill that was passed by Congress to deal with South Africa." Horowitz adapted the language for Sudan, and Frank Wolf gladly agreed to insert it in the Wolf-Specter bill. Involving severe trade sanctions, this provision was so controversial that House leaders ensured it would be stricken from the bill.[66] From that moment on, however, Horowitz believed that "we had to make Sudan central" to the cause, a conviction he shared with Nina Shea and a growing number of activists.

Sudan had to be central, Horowitz argued, both for moral and strategic reasons. The moral ground was obvious because Sudan was the "worst offender, the symbolic embodiment of all that we were fighting." As one who had toured the killing fields of Cambodia, Horowitz brought to the Sudan campaign a simple message: "You can't sit out a holocaust." To those who saw "complexity" in Sudan, Horowitz simplified it: "Sudan is the Hitler regime of our time." America's response to Sudan was also a strategic imperative, the "means of showing the world" that the new concern for religious freedom was "for real." If Sudan got off the hook, then how could other countries believe that the United States was serious about religious persecution? On the other hand, if massive international pressure led by the United States was brought to bear, then others would take notice. "The way to grow the movement, to make it ten feet tall," Horowitz argued, is to "create fear on the part of other regimes that you're next." Thus the way to "help house church Christians in China, evangelicals in Cuba, Catholics in Pakistan" is by making an example of the most evil of the regimes. Put in another context, Sudan could become a front line in the battle between the democracies and the regimes of despotism.

Among the unlikely allies Horowitz helped to bring together are Sudanese advocates and exiles outside of the D.C. Federal Courthouse. Front from left to right: Ken Starr, Walter Fauntroy, Joe Madison, Michael Horowitz, Johnnie Cochran, and Dick Gregory. Courtesy of Michael Horowitz, Hudson Institute.

Sudan, therefore, would become the "litmus test of America's seriousness on both human rights and religious persecution." The Sudanese regime must become a pariah state like apartheid South Africa. Ending the atrocities, or even "bringing down the regime," must become a "front line" issue engaged by the highest levels of U.S. government. This audacious vision, shared by a growing number of activists, achieved a diplomatic breakthrough for southern Sudan in 2004, as we see in chapter 7.

In attempting "to move Sudan out of the white noise category into an inescapable national priority," Horowitz early on drafted proposals, promoted the "right candidates" for executive positions, wrote articles, spun news stories, and blitzed Washington with faxes. As the ink was barely drying on the president's signature on the International Religious Freedom Act in 1998, Horowitz was on the phone with his congressional and religious contacts pressing particular names for the newly created independent commission. One of his arguments was that commissioners "call a spade a spade" and not temporize on Sudan. Thus he added his voice in support of such nominees as David Saperstein, Nina Shea, and Elliott Abrams, who took the lead in championing the cause on the commission.

THE CRITICS

Many of the attributes that make Horowitz an effective catalyst also render him a controversial and polarizing figure. Confidence can be seen as megalomania, persistence as bullying, media agitation as self-promotion. A number of activists complain that Horowitz is presumptuous, that he orders them around.[67] Others charge that he oversimplifies, engages in hyperbole, or wades into issues with rhetorical flourishes before fully understanding the complexities. One Sudan activist felt that Horowitz's rhetoric contributed to claims circulating among evangelicals that two million *Christians* had been killed in the civil war in Sudan, even though Christianity composes roughly 20 percent of southern Sudan. Such claims, the critic argued, undercut the credibility of the movement.[68]

Critics also sometimes take issue with Horowitz's essential vision and approach.[69] As we saw in chapter 3, profound differences exist within the religious and human rights communities about how best to fight religious persecution. Thus Horowitz's blunt policy remedies, especially on religious persecution, are viewed by some as counterproductive, likely to undermine quiet diplomatic efforts and bring reprisals against vulnerable religious minorities. Attitudes toward Horowitz, as I discovered in my interviews, thus reveal tensions within the religious community—regarding vision, tactics, and motives—that remain enduring aspects of the politics of international human rights.

A common criticism of Horowitz is that he is a shameless self-promoter, a "PR machine," someone who "exaggerates his own role." As one journalist wryly put it, "Michael Horowitz believes that one activist alone was responsible for moving the issue of Christian persecution into the mainstream: Michael Horowitz." This tendency caused tensions even with the closest of allies. It was the initial collaboration of Nina Shea and Horowitz that set into motion the National Association of Evangelicals "Statement of Conscience" and the ensuing legislative campaign. Their collaboration was mutually beneficial: Horowitz received education about the scope of the problem and Shea greater exposure for the cause. Yet bad publicity ensued when Horowitz told a reporter that Shea's Institute was dying until he came along. Prodded by a reporter, Shea's joking response—that "Michael would have died without this issue. . . . What did he have, tort reform?"—got magnified into a major tiff.[70] For some time there was little communication between them. But their vital collaboration ultimately was reestablished to the point that Horowitz vigorously backed Shea's appointment to a position on the U.S. Commission for International Religious Freedom.[71]

A frequent charge is that Horowitz operates with hidden agendas. Given that he served at the highest levels of the White House for six years, where people routinely operate with multiple agendas and egos become entangled in political motives, this should come as no surprise. But to some religious leaders, especially those not used to bare-knuckle politics, Horowitz appears too Machiavellian. In part this flows from the way he will appeal to political or partisan self-interest. The leader of one international Christian advocacy organization reported meeting with Horowitz late in 1995 when concern about persecution was just beginning to percolate. This evangelical Christian was aghast when the issue was put in partisan terms: "The whole discussion was that 'religious freedom is the Achilles heel in the Clinton administration. We can defeat Clinton in November 1996 using this.'" Such talk contributed to fear in the liberal Protestant community that Horowitz was setting up the issue as a stalking-horse for Christian Right attacks on Clinton, perhaps as a "line on a Christian Coalition" voter guide. But when Horowitz turned around and told Democrats how getting on board would gain them the support of evangelicals, some Christian conservatives expressed fear that this would enable Clinton to co-opt the evangelical community. Horowitz sought to gain support by whatever means possible.

A related criticism is that Horowitz has such confidence in his strategic acumen that he operates like a Lone Ranger at times, pursuing his own tactical agenda. During the Sudan battle, for example, Horowitz attempted to negotiate a compromise provision of the Sudan Peace Act while coalition partners were still lobbying to keep tougher language in the bill.[72]

Another common claim is that Horowitz's real agenda is to deploy the Christian community in the battle to contain militant Islam. His first salvo in the *Wall Street Journal*, after all, focused exclusively on the intolerance toward Christianity in the Islamic Crescent.[73] And some saw his success in enlisting Jewish allies in the antipersecution cause as evidence of this motive. For Horowitz, of course, this is not a hidden agenda at all; containing militant Islam is absolutely essential for the well-being of Jews, Christians, Baha'is, moderate Muslims, and freedom itself around the world. But he does not believe that his devotion to "the Christian lambs" is merely instrumental to this other cause.

Horowitz is a classic driven personality, impatient with those who do not see as many chess moves ahead as he does. Critics charge, however, that he is so sure of his own strategic vision that he can become ruthless and vindictive with those he perceives as barriers to his objectives. During the early phase of the antipersecution campaign, Horowitz wrote a conceptual plan and helped secure funding for the event known as the National Day of Prayer for the Persecuted Church.[74] Conceived as a way to educate local congregations in the plight of their suffering counterparts abroad, the event grew dramatically from its inception, in no small measure because of Horowitz's efforts. But Horowitz feuded bitterly with event organizers over the nature and extent of the political content in packets sent to local congregations. The evangelical leaders of the day wanted political content minimized, while Horowitz saw the event as an extension of the lobbying campaign. Horowitz maneuvered the first coordinator, Dwight Gibson, the North American Director for the World Evangelical Fellowship, out of his position by ways that, according to some accounts, were personal and hurtful. When Gibson's successor, Steve Haas, a former pastor for the famous Willow Creek Church in Chicago, refused to include an insert on the Wolf-Specter legislation in packets mailed to congregations, Horowitz faxed off plaintive memos. "You broke my heart," he wrote and charged that Haas had been manipulated by the opponents of the movement.[75]

Loath to get the Day of Prayer ensnared in competing legislative initiatives, Haas also resisted changing the date of the event from mid-November of each year. Horowitz remonstrated with Haas to change the date to before the 2000 elections. "Can you imagine," he mused, "what it would be like to have Joe Lieberman speaking at one church and George W. Bush at another and Al Gore at another?" Politicians would be "falling all over themselves" to demonstrate their sympathy for the suffering church, and "it would be front page news." Horowitz was incredulous that this dazzling opportunity to catapult the tragedy of persecution into the national spotlight would be squandered, and he did not shrink from hectoring, threatening, or otherwise making life difficult for Haas.

One lesson from this episode is that Horowitz sometimes operates with an agenda perceived as too worldly by some erstwhile evangelical allies. For Haas and other evangelicals involved in the day of prayer, expanding awareness of suffering was important but the essential point was to pray for the persecuted, to demonstrate the power of prayer.

Obviously, Horowitz is not one to shrink from a fight, which is both a powerful asset and a potential liability. The case of his battle with Human Rights Watch, the large and well-connected New York–based watchdog group, illustrates both realities. To Horowitz this liberal organization epitomized the blinders that have kept establishment human rights groups from attending to religious persecution.

In frequent speeches and conversations he used the Human Rights Watch annual report as a prop, to show how it highlighted special projects on women's rights, gay and lesbian rights, journalists' rights, and so on, but did not consider religious persecution.[76] To explain this omission Horowitz launches into a devastating riff on liberal or secular "bigotry" about believing Christians: "Aren't they bothersome? Don't they bring it on themselves? They are not our crowd. They are the people who burn people at the stake, don't they? They are not the victims."[77] But Horowitz did not merely try to get Human Rights Watch to improve its reporting, or even shame it to live up to its professed ideals. He turned the organization into the very embodiment of the barriers confronting people of faith.

When Kenneth Roth, Executive Director of Human Rights Watch, criticized the campaign against religious persecution as "special pleading" and "an effort to privilege certain classes of victims,"[78] Horowitz was outraged. And he responded in characteristic fashion: He tried to get Roth fired. He dashed off letters to board members of Human Rights Watch, faxed memos all over the place, and stepped up personal criticism of Roth.[79] Roth's evaluation of Horowitz is not surprising: "Under the guise of religious tolerance, he spreads divisiveness wherever he goes."[80] Even close allies of Horowitz thought he went too far. One of them explained that it was "not smart" for Horowitz to "pick fights" with Roth because Human Rights Watch, for all its flaws, was still an important potential resource for the religious rights movement.[81] And it ultimately did add a section on religious freedom in its focus on global issues.[82]

Horowitz tends to see the world in vivid moral terms, with clear good guys and bad. This ability to cut through "complexity" and white noise is an essential ingredient in Horowitz's catalytic role. But critics feel he tends to extend that Manichaean trait too far, that he is too quick to demonize. Indeed, even from allies I often heard the complaint that Horowitz interprets tactical disagreements or differences about proper remedies as opposition to the cause itself. One Catholic lobbyist criticized "this impugning of motives, this assumption that if you don't agree with every line of the bill as first drafted, every tactic, if you didn't come to every press conference, meant essentially you were an apologist for religious oppressors—this was both wrong on the merits and extremely unhelpful politically." Horowitz's "storm-the-barricade style," while useful at times, could be a liability:

> I told him he had to be quiet. He had to stop being the symbol, the voice of the movement. . . . And Michael's comment was, "You want me to be run over by a bus?" And I said not necessarily, but you have to stop impugning the motives of others, taking any criticism of the bill as disagreement with the importance of religious liberty. We were about trying to get something done, not settling old scores.[83]

A related complaint was arrogance. The very chutzpah that enabled Horowitz to shame Christian leaders into action and meld them into a concerted force could also be nettlesome. One congressional staff member, who even backed Horowitz's version of the persecution legislation, described Horowitz as a "Leninist," suggesting that Horowitz sees himself leading people where they *would want* to go *if only* they had the strategic insight he does: "With Mike it's either my way or the highway." Another congressional staffer said that some Christian group leaders felt "bullied" by Horowitz and frustrated that he was "driving the train": "He's smart and he knows it. And he wants you to know it. He always says, we did this before, or that, and we know how it works. Here's what needs to happen." Richard Cizik, director of the Washington office of the National Association of Evangelicals, characterized Horowitz's influence in this way: "By force of personality, intimidation, or moral suasion, he usually gets his way." This bare-knuckle approach sometimes disturbed Cizik, who has worked closely with Horowitz on both the religious freedom and sex trafficking legislation: "I know people who disagree with Mike who feel that they're the persecuted; they call me up and say, 'How can you assign this man this role?' And I say, 'I didn't. He took it, as an obligation of conscience.'"[84]

To critics Horowitz is a Svengali manipulating events and people. When Senate legislation seemed to be languishing in the office of Senator Don Nickles (R-OK) in the summer of 1998, a story "mysteriously" appeared in a Jewish weekly in New York charging that Nickles's "staff dithered while Christians die." When Senator Inhofe (R-OK) introduced an alternative bill to the one Horowitz backed, an editorial suddenly appeared in Oklahoma's largest news-paper cautioning Inhofe to adopt a different approach.[85]

Horowitz is certainly a devotee of hardball politics, and he seems to relish that he operates under no "Christian" compunction about turning the other cheek. As one journalist put it, "Horowitz has brought a confrontation style at odds with much New Testament theology. 'Hey,' he says, with the judgment and wrath of Jehovah in mind, 'I'm under no obligation to love my enemy.'"[86] It is clear that many of those engaged in the legislative battles over religious perse-cution were not prepared for this style: "He has a tendency to get in your face and get angry."

For reasons discussed in the next chapter, Horowitz's promotion of antipersecution legislation was particularly contentious. During the sometimes bitter battle over appropriate U.S. foreign-policy re-sponses to religious persecution, there were charges and counter-charges, bruised egos and recriminations, that had to be overcome to bring legislation to fruition. Some accused Horowitz of using unsa-vory tactics, even to the point of damaging the reputations of those he disagreed with. There was talk of being "slandered," "personally attacked," and "called names." Working for religious freedom legisla-tion, therefore, was no picnic: "It was hell," especially so for those staff members tasked with crafting a legislative alternative to the bill fa-vored by Horowitz. Several of them said they felt, ironically, "perse-cuted" by Horowitz.

SUMMARY

Michael Horowitz provided a kind of incendiary element that helped spark the new faith-based human rights movement. His blunt and ag-gressive style seemed well suited to focusing attention on gross hu-man rights atrocities abroad. Horowitz acknowledges his own impa-tience during these struggles, but he credits involvement with Christians and Jews in the cause of religious freedom with making him a better person, connecting him back to the rituals of his own faith, to synagogue attendance. After the religious freedom law was signed, he sought a kind of atonement for his political "sins" in a memo expressing gratitude to those whose "commitment to the interests of persecuted communities helped them overlook my abruptness, my many other failings."[87] To an extent he acknowledged as valid some criticism of his style, if not his motives.

Subsequent to passage of the International Religious Freedom Act, Horowitz helped press other human rights efforts—on sex trafficking, Sudan, and North Korea. To Horowitz these initiatives were subsequent acts of the grand drama of the new faith-based movement. In certain respects they were well suited to his blunt vision and style because they presented clear culprits unlikely to respond to the quiet diplomacy favored by some advocates of religious freedom.

To be sure, Horowitz was as relentless, insistent, and cocky as ever in those subsequent battles. Laura Lederer, who labored for years to document the problem of sex trafficking, quipped that some of her feminist colleagues called to complain that they would "never talk to him again," while she "only hung up on him once."[88] Still, she lauded Horowitz's "genius" in the trafficking campaign. Ultimately, I noticed little of the rancor in the sex trafficking battle that was evident in the religious persecution campaign. Indeed at receptions and events commemorating the passage of the Trafficking in Victims Protection Act (2000), there was a palpable sense of élan, accomplishment, and thankfulness among the tremendously diverse actors that Horowitz helped bring together.

A final example, noted in passing, illustrates Horowitz's role in pressing diverse human rights campaigns. In 2002–2003 Horowitz sparked an unusual effort to address the endemism of prison rape that savages the lives of hundreds of thousands of prisoners in the United States. To Horowitz the issue was another human rights tragedy that could be ameliorated if the conscience of religious America was mobilized. Though the Prison Rape Elimination Act, passed in 2003, dealt only with the domestic arena, in another sense the law's passage bears the Horowitz signature: a human rights problem ignored by policy elites, the mobilization of key religious activists (especially evangelicals), and passage of tough congressional legislation. The alliance Horowitz assembled for this legislation also bore his stamp. With Charles Colson anchoring evangelical participation, the coalition included Senator Ted Kennedy, the NAACP, La Raza, and the previously maligned Human Rights Watch.

Horowitz's role as a catalyst received broad recognition when he was featured in a front page article in the *Wall Street Journal* (May 26, 2004) on the international activism of evangelicals. This piece, no doubt, fed into his reputation for self-promotion. But equally telling was a prior incident. In the fall of 2003, when the impact of the faith-based movement began to reach elite consciousness, Horowitz helped promote a major story about the role of evangelicals in pressing human rights within the administration of George W. Bush. To help frame the story Horowitz doggedly conferred with the reporter, insisting on people she should interview, faxing background material, and the like. The resulting front page story in the *New York Times* provided an unusually favorable picture of the new politics of human rights and documented the pivotal role of evangelicals in forging unlikely alliances for global amelioration of abuses. Horowitz, the catalyst for this new politics, was not mentioned once in the article.[89]

Michael Horowitz provides a vivid illustration of the role of human agency, especially the way religious calling infuses the new global rights quest. But religious callings can differ, and being a "catalyst" does not mean directing the outcome of political struggles. As we will see in the next chapter, the multifarious expressions of the faith-based movement sprout in ways that, while sometimes competing, can also seem providential.

6

THE HAND OF PROVIDENCE
IN CONGRESS

In its continued effort to subjugate Tibet, the government of China
launched a "patriotic education" campaign in the mid-1990s, os-
tensibly designed to assimilate Tibetan Buddhists into Chinese culture. But those who refused to accept the teachings of the campaign
or to renounce the Dalai Lama faced imprisonment, beatings, torture,
and even death. Nearly three-quarters of Tibet's known political prisoners are Buddhist monks and nuns.[1]

The above report represents a small fraction of the massive documentary record that prompted Congress to pass the International
Religious Freedom Act (IRFA). In this chapter we explore the actual political struggle in Washington, D.C., that led to the passage of
the IRFA. Such an account is vital because the law is one of the
most sweeping human rights statutes on the books and the only one
of its kind in the world. It designates an ambassador-at-large for International Religious Freedom to head up a new office at the State
Department. It mandates that the State Department produce a comprehensive annual report on the status of religious freedom around
the world—which sets into motion presidential action against
violating countries. The law also authorizes an independent commission, with staff and budget, to recommend policies, monitor violations, and hold policymakers accountable for their response. It
reaches into the daily routines of foreign policy by providing better
training for diplomatic personnel and fostering their ongoing contacts with vulnerable religious communities on the ground. Finally,
it declares in ringing terms the intention of the United States to

183

stand "for liberty" and "with the persecuted."[2]   This law is drawing increasing attention from foreign capitals and embassies.[3] What are the Americans up to? Why did the law pass? Is it serious? The account below helps answer these questions, but it also provides a window into the changing dynamics of religious America, into new commitments and alliances that flow from the evolving international connections of church communities. In the ecology of human rights, the struggle for the IRFA shaped the environment for future initiatives. *Without IRFA there would be no Sudan Peace Act; without the religious advocacy coalition, there would be no human trafficking law.* The religious freedom campaign thus represents a kind of liminal moment in the politics of human rights.[4]

In understanding the lessons of this story we must move beyond the obvious point that Congress responds to constituent pressure, since the legislative campaign *itself* helped catalyze the nascent movement into a durable force. Indeed, the legislative campaign acted as a magnet drawing diverse groups into its field. Evangelical, Catholic, and Episcopalian groups were joined by those representing Jewish constituencies, Tibetan Buddhists, Iranian Baha'is, and other religious

Dalai Lama on the Mall in Washington, D.C. The Campaign for Tibet strongly backed international religious freedom legislation. Courtesy of Sonam Zoksang.

minorities in pressing for national legislation. Though the groups did not always agree on remedies, they created a formidable sense that *something* had to pass.

Viewed as something of a miracle by partisans, the legislation was the product of an intense and sometimes bitter lobby campaign. Not only were corporate lobbyists opposed to legislation that might upset business arrangements with foreign countries, but religious partisans themselves were divided over *how* the American government could best respond to persecution around the world. Some religious leaders sought tough and visible action against persecuting countries; others wanted to employ the quiet routines of diplomacy. Those calling for tough action were comfortable with vigorous (even unilateral) American leadership; those stressing quiet diplomacy tended to favor multilateral approaches. In all the twists and turns of the legislative process this divide was manifest. More significantly, it endures as a key feature of the continuing struggle over how America will respond to human rights abuses—from Sudan to North Korea. This legislative case study, therefore, exposes a persistent philosophical debate that will shape the politics of human rights for some time to come.

What makes the battle over religious freedom legislation instructive is that these competing visions did not correspond to the conventional ideological categories of liberal versus conservative. Indeed, the 1998 struggle over which approach to take was often a battle between *different camps* of evangelicals and their allies, complete with recrimination and claims of bad faith. When we view these events from a greater distance—when we "get up on the balcony" and look down—we can see that this *collective* struggle produced legislation that blended aspects of both visions, encompassing the diversity of the American religious landscape.

BACKGROUND

We have seen how a growing international Christian solidarity movement, linked to American religious networks, increasingly raised the specter of persecution against Christians around the world. We know that from the mid-1990s onward such activists as Nina Shea and Mike

Horowitz pressed for a more vigorous American government response. Their first foray in bringing systematic pressure was a major conference hosted by the National Association of Evangelicals (NAE), which catapulted the issue into wider consciousness. As one participant recounted, "You had Colson and everybody else, and that really awakened the evangelical conscience to this issue." Especially critical was that "you had the realization by folks in the pews that people just like them did not have the privileges they did." Participants at that conference (held on January 23, 1996), facilitated by Freedom House, issued a widely publicized "Statement of Conscience."[5]

The story behind that document illuminates the way partisans sometimes saw the hand of providence in the process. Working with Nina Shea and other activists, Michael Horowitz wrote a draft statement of principles, which he submitted to the NAE leadership for emendation and approval. Richard Cizik, director of government affairs for NAE, recounts how tense the situation was leading up to his organization's sponsorship of the statement. Some in the evangelical community voiced concern about reprisals against vulnerable Christian communities if persecuting countries were signaled out, an issue Cizik took seriously. With the deadline for the statement looming and the pressure mounting, Cizik's office kept getting calls from a "guy from Bangladesh" living in the Washington area. Cizik's initial response was "I don't have time right now, I've got to get this statement out." But the man was insistent, and Cizik finally invited him over. It turns out that the man was desperately concerned about the plight of the Christian minority in his country, and when Cizik showed him the NAE draft statement, the man wept tears of relief. "This is just what we need," he said. Reassured by what he judged was this providential sign, Cizik moved with confidence to secure his organization's imprimatur for the opening salvo of the movement.[6]

The Statement of Conscience identified the problem and articulated recommendations for government action. Those recommendations included the following: a major presidential address condemning anti-Christian persecution; appointment of a special advisor to the president for religious liberty; issuance of instructions to U.S. ambassadors and U.S. delegates to the United Nations to meet with religious dissidents and to press religious freedom; training of Immigration and

Naturalization Service (INS) officials on religious persecution issues; expedited religious asylum claims; and termination of nonhumanitarian foreign assistance to governments of countries that fail to take vigorous action to end anti-Christian or other religious persecution.[7]

Less than a month after the "Statement of Conscience," Congressman Chris Smith (R-NJ), Chairman of the Subcommittee on International Operations and Human Rights of the House International Relations Committee, responded with his own initiative. On February 15, 1996, Smith held hearings devoted exclusively to the persecution of Christians abroad.[8] These hearings provided a platform for a number of activists and religious leaders, but they were controversial. Muslim representatives felt that they unfairly singled out Muslim countries and represented a form of "Muslim-bashing." Some liberal Protestant and human rights leaders were similarly troubled by the focus on persecuted Christians and a questionable selectivity of the participants. Nonetheless, these hearings provided a documentary record that served as a crucial foundation for the legislative campaign that ensued, and often had other influences as well. One witness, David Forte, a professor of law at Cleveland State University, drew a sharp distinction between militant fundamentalists and mainstream Islam. In the wake of September 11 his testimony was circulated widely. Indeed, Horowitz faxed copies of Forte's testimony to Bush White House officials, resulting in press reports suggesting that Bush's rhetoric about militants "hijacking Islam" was drawn from Forte's important analysis.[9]

Spurred by Smith's hearings, Congress passed a resolution in the summer of 1996 requiring a report by the U.S. State Department on the persecution of Christians abroad, to include a catalog of U.S. policies in support of religious freedom. Secretary of State Madeleine Albright released that report on July 22, 1997,[10] and President Clinton followed by creating an advisory committee on religious freedom abroad. To Horowitz and others, the advisory committee was mere window dressing aimed at forestalling more serious action.

While early efforts prepared the way, the crucial strategic move was the decision to sponsor congressional legislation. As Horowitz envisioned it, a legislative campaign would focus the incipient movement, providing a tangible way for American Christians to exercise their citizenship on behalf of coreligionists. With a high profile victory, believers would discover their power.[11] The magnetic excitement of the campaign, in fact, drew diverse groups into the orbit of the cause, absorbing movement energies and sending them out in magnified form.

While Horowitz's strategic vision in many respects was vindicated by the process, his own legislative vehicle, the Wolf-Specter bill, was not what Congress passed in 1998. Moreover, his tenacity in pressing his favored remedy helped spark a bitter struggle among religious partisans that at times threatened to undermine the entire legislative campaign. It is not necessary here to catalog in infinite detail the strategies and conflicts that swirled around the competing religious persecution bills. But some analysis is instructive, because the two proposals that emerged in the House and Senate reflected two different visions of how the United States should respond to human rights abuses. One side envisioned tough and blunt American responses to nations that persecute religious believers. The other side favored a more calibrated diplomatic approach. The final legislation is, in certain respects, a blend of each of these two visions, reflecting either the genius of the Madisonian system or the Hand of Providence, depending on one's point of view.

The first legislative proposal to emerge was the one pressed by Horowitz and introduced by Congressman Frank Wolf (R-VA). In Frank Wolf, Horowitz found a kindred spirit—a fervent moralist who sees justice in stark terms. As one staffer put it, Wolf is "not a cautious person," but a visionary. Like Horowitz, Wolf is comfortable using the tools of U.S. power against countries that persecute religious minorities. Wolf was also a logical choice to sponsor the legislation because of his reputation—across the political spectrum—as a champion of human rights. Thus while some religious groups had concerns with his bill, they uniformly expressed deep respect for Wolf.[12] John Carr, of the U.S. Catholic Conference, echoed the common sentiment when he described Wolf as "my hero," the very embodiment of legislative campaign. Horowitz had only one concern, whether Wolf would be willing to play political "hardball" to get the legislation passed. Horowitz described meeting with Wolf and saying in effect, "Frank, you are my hero, but are you willing to do what it takes to win?"[13]

Congressman Frank Wolf. A well-known human rights activist, he authored House legislation on religious persecution. Courtesy of Prison Fellowship.

Because the 1970s Jackson-Vanik law was seen as facilitating Jewish emigration from the Soviet Union and its client states, Horowitz initially proposed legislation to deal just with persecution of Christians. But House staff members, particularly Joseph Rees, Chief Counsel for the Human Rights Subcommittee (working for Congressman Smith), insisted that the language had to be universal in scope. Rees noted that Jackson-Vanik, as written, was "not just about Jews." Thus the new law "can't be just about Christians."[14]

Working with a cadre of House staff members,[15] Rees drafted the legislation and negotiated amendment language. Recruited to the subcommittee in 1995 when Republicans took control of Congress, Rees had moved in the same Catholic international human rights circles as Congressman Smith. When Smith became chair after fifteen years in the congressional minority, he aggressively recruited Rees, persuading him to drop everything and come to D.C. immediately, to bring "one suit," and let his family join him later. Rees's background suggests why congressional staff can have such influence. A law school professor and former chief justice of Samoa, he had served in the Justice Department and as general counsel of the Immigration and Naturalization Service in the first Bush administration. He shares Smith's view that elite culture slights the persecution of believers. Persecution of Christians is the "biggest kind we don't do anything about," he observed in 1998. He attributed this to hostility about faith: "Elites don't like Christianity, perceive evangelicals and Catholics as forces of reaction."[16]

While the pent-up energy in the House helped crystallize backing for the new legislation, the atmosphere was different in the Senate. There Horowitz enlisted as cosponsor Senator Arlen Specter, a socially liberal Republican from Pennsylvania. Specter turned out to be a poor choice, as he failed to sign up more than a handful of cosponsors and did not really invest political capital in moving the legislation in the Senate. Instead, he apparently used his sponsorship to try to curry favor with conservative Christians, who had threatened to challenge him in the Republican primary. Specter also had so angered Senator Jesse Helms (R-NC) on a separate issue that the conservative icon pledged to block any "Specter bill" on foreign policy. With Specter's sponsorship largely symbolic, the legislation was really a House initiative jointly worked by Wolf as prime sponsor and Smith as floor manager. For over a year, however, the legislation was known as the Wolf-Specter bill.

Introduced in Congress in May 1997, Wolf-Specter was titled the Freedom From Religious Persecution Act. The title's emphasis on "persecution" reflected the strategic view that legislation should focus on the most egregious acts of abuse—acts that no one could excuse or justify. Part of the rationale for this approach was to avoid getting ensnared in debates about treatment of Scientologists in Germany, arguments about "aggressive proselytization" by Christians abroad, or disputes between Catholics and Protestants in Latin America.[17] Thus the bill focused on "widespread and ongoing persecution of persons on account of their personal beliefs," including "abduction, enslavement, killing, imprisonment, forced resettlement, rape, or crucifixion or other forms of torture." Countries practicing such atrocities were subject to automatic withdrawal of nonhumanitarian U.S. aid and an export ban on products that facilitate persecution. Horowitz vigorously denied that these provisions constituted a "sanction" as commonly understood in diplomatic circles, and he bristled whenever Wolf-Specter was criticized as a "sanctions bill." Real sanctions, he contended, moved beyond nonhumanitarian aid to such severe things as the denial of trade. Some allies acknowledged, however, that a few "trade promotion" programs were subject to cutoff in Wolf-Specter, thus intensifying business opposition.

The Wolf-Specter coalition was animated by the view that focusing on the worst acts of persecution would serve the broader aim of religious freedom. The argument was that the problem could not be as easily pushed under the rug when egregious and clearly indefensible acts were the target of U.S. action. Others disagreed, and this division drove much of the struggle over competing proposals. Will Inboden, who worked for Representative Tom DeLay (R-TX) and helped draft alternative legislation, observed that Wolf-Specter "proponents made a tactical decision to target only those regimes guilty of the most widespread, barbaric persecution." While acknowledging that there "may perhaps be some merit to this approach," Inboden echoed the common charge against Wolf-Specter that only one or two rogue nations, such as North Korea and Sudan, would cross the high threshold and come under its provisions.[18] Horowitz's retort was that even if that were true, which he did not acknowledge, it would send the powerful message to other despots that "you might be next."[19]

The main objective of the law, Horowitz contended, was *exposure* and *accountability*. To this end the law proposed an Office of Religious Persecution Monitoring, originally to be housed in the White House. This provision built on the "assumption," as one religious partisan noted, "that we would never get a straight scoop from the State Department, that fact finding would be highly massaged and diplomatically scrubbed." The Director of this Monitoring Office would determine which countries were found to be engaging in egregious persecution. Then mandatory sanctions would kick in, *unless* the president opted to waive them and publicly provide the reasons. The idea was to force the president to "opt out" of sanctions explicitly, ensuring accountability and publicity. Though the presidential waiver was greatly broadened in subsequent drafts, it still had to be a public act based on national security or a finding that it would promote the purposes of the act. This feature led some critics to suspect that the legislation was a partisan attempt to embarrass or hamstring President Clinton. Certainly there were tones of that among some of the religious partisans. As one Senate Republican staffer observed in the summer of 1998, "The Wolf-Specter premise is that the president can't be trusted, that he will fudge." Wolf backers acknowledged that there was "suspicion" that all they cared about was "impugning this administration." But backers argued that this kind of accountability was needed no matter who inhabited the Oval Office. And indeed, when George W. Bush assumed the presidency, many of the Wolf-Specter partisans, including Republicans such as Nina Shea, found themselves criticizing the administration for not taking more vigorous action with persecuting countries.

One of the more contentious provisions of the early bill would have changed U.S. immigration law by providing new grounds for asylum to those belonging to persecuted communities.[20] It would have extended to those fleeing persecution what is called "Lautenberg status," which is the most generous provision allowing entry into the United States. This provision was backed by liberal groups and Catholics, who viewed existing immigration law as restrictive and punitive.[21] Conservative advocates of tough immigration control, however, fought this feature, but so did some religious partisans who feared that "emptying" countries of their Christian populations would remove the Christian witness for saving souls.

A final provision, patterned on the legislation against apartheid in South Africa in the 1980s, would have imposed sanctions specifically against the government of Sudan. Since this affected trade policy, it was sent to the business-oriented Ways and Means Committee, where it was stripped from the bill. As we will see in the next chapter, partisans did not give up on the Sudan cause.

For the two years following the endorsement of the NAE "Statement of Conscience," Horowitz, Shea, and others built a coalition of groups to back legislation. From a growing fax list in Horowitz's office to Nina Shea's contacts at Freedom House, the coalition's steering committee reflected an ecumenical concern for ameliorating religious persecution. The committee sought to channel this concern toward passage of the Wolf-Specter bills. The February 1998 lobby campaign kickoff in Washington, D.C., included major evangelical leaders, such as Charles Colson, Gary Bauer, Rich Cizik, and Richard Land; representatives of the Catholic Church; heads of Jewish organizations; and Tibetan Buddhist advocates. Also in attendance were key congressional advocates, including Frank Wolf, Chris Smith, and Majority Leader Dick Armey, who assured the coalition members that he would guarantee floor action on the legislation. The bipartisan tenor of the event was reflected in the fact that liberal Democratic Congresswoman and future House Leader Nancy Pelosi also attended and endorsed Wolf-Specter, referring to Frank Wolf as "my leader" in the cause. Endorsements and testimonials for the movement also flowed in. Letters from courageous dissidents such as Natan Sharansky, Wei Jingsheng, and the Dalai Lama were read at the event. And *New York Times* columnist Abe Rosenthal was given an award—a plaque inscribed with a poignant passage from Isaiah 58— for his contribution to the cause.[22] Rosenthal spoke of how the event was like a luxurious soapy bath washing off the muck of Washington politics and scandal.[23]

As the House legislation went through the committee deliberations, the bill was modified to accommodate the concerns of different religious groups. Muslim representatives, for example, expressed the view that the legislation focused too heavily on persecution of Christians. They argued that it provided a kind of de facto preference, with Christians abroad automatically covered and others having to establish their case. In addition, the "findings section" of the bill (which described the problem) weighted Christian grievances heavily. Concerns about this imbalance were shared by others. Jewish leaders, such as Rabbi David Saperstein of the Union of American Hebrew Congregations, joined with Catholic and Muslim representatives in lobbying for more balance in the "findings" section of the legislation, which was ultimately broadened to encompass Tibetan Buddhists, Muslim Uyghurs of China, and Baha'is of Iran, among others. What was not negotiable to Horowitz and his allies was that some version of Wolf-Specter serve as a litmus test of America's response to global persecution.

Not surprisingly, a number of evangelical organizations lined up behind the legislation, including the National Association of Evangelicals, the Southern Baptist Convention, the National Religious Broadcasters, the Christian Coalition, the Family Research Council,

Congressman Chris Smith. As chairman of the Subcommittee on Human Rights of the House International Relations Committee, Smith was the point man for a number of interfaith initiatives. Courtesy of Prison Fellowship.

and Concerned Women for America. Through national radio, religious publications, and direct mail, evangelical luminaries, such as Charles Colson, Bill Bright, and James Dobson, spread the word that this was a priority of the Christian community.

How much actual grassroots mobilization occurred is subject to debate.[24] Dobson and Colson cut radio spots that reached millions, and news stories proliferated in Christian media outlets, such as *Christianity Today* and *World Magazine*. The Southern Baptist Convention sent packets to all of its 40,000 churches for the International Day of Prayer for the Persecuted Church and featured the campaign in its numerous publications. But some observers contend that the real impact on Congress stemmed less from average lay constituents than leaders. "It was a grass tops movement," said one congressional staffer, meaning that the energy came mostly from opinion leaders and organizations. Other observers contend that generalized constituent concern had indeed been picked up by the antenna of election-minded congressional members.[25] Senator Jesse Helms suggested this kind of force when he said that "the hearts and souls of the folks back home in churches and synagogues" had been stirred by "learning about the growing persistent torture and abuse of Christians, Jews and other religious minorities at the hands of foreign governments."[26]

Whatever the impact of evangelical mobilization, legislation would not have passed had its backers been restricted to the "Christian Right" constituency, and advocates knew that. Horowitz and others spent months in meetings with leaders of Catholic, Jewish, Buddhist, and Baha'i communities and were largely successful in enlisting support. Outreach to the "mainline" Protestant community, as we will see, was less so.

Absolutely crucial to the campaign was Catholic backing. Not only is the Roman Catholic Church the largest religious institution in the nation with vast international connections, but its lobbyists and bishops enjoyed access and credibility with key Democrats (this was before the sex abuse scandals broke). The Catholic Church is a large and complex organization, however, that moves slowly and deliberately, and a diversity of internal offices had to provide input and sign off before the bishops could formally endorse.

One advantage Wolf-Specter backers enjoyed was the long involvement of Catholic officials in international human rights and religious freedom work in Latin America, Eastern Europe, and elsewhere. Lobbyists for the bishops have long felt that U.S. foreign policy neglected religious freedom. Thus they were inclined to back legislation once certain concerns were addressed. When the U.S. Bishops Conference did endorse the legislation, as announced at the lobby kickoff meeting in February 1998, critics had a harder time impugning the legislation as a sop to the Christian Right. "My mantra," said John Carr, the Church's Secretary for Social Development and World Peace, was "get beyond the personalities, and let's focus on the people whose lives and rights are at risk."[27] Because of its international connections, the Church, as one lobbyist said, also "knew something," had useful information to present about the problem. Its concerns about religious persecution could not be ignored. Thus it is probably not an exaggeration to say, as one Catholic lobbyist did, that without Catholic Church backing, religious freedom legislation was doomed.

Also vital was support in the Jewish community. From the beginning Horowitz worked with Jewish leaders to back the legislation. Abe Rosenthal promoted the cause in several columns in the *New York Times*, especially after the February 1998 lobby kickoff. The Republican-oriented National Jewish Coalition lobbied for the legislation, and its director, Cheryl Halpern, was even featured in a *New York Times* photograph accompanying the story about Republican congressional leaders endorsing a cause of the "Christian Right."[28] Also notable was backing of the cause by the Anti-Defamation League (ADL). Its lobbyist, Stacie Burdette, had years before "started to notice a pattern of incidents of persecution against Christians." Thus as the campaign heated up, the need for ADL's engagement was clear: "That persecution was going on was undeniable; that the Jewish community had to get involved was undeniable; that the American government could and should be doing more was undeniable." Burdette participated in the steering committee Horowitz assembled, and she was successful in getting changes to the language of the legislation. The national director of ADL, Abraham Foxman, also joined with other religious leaders in signing a letter to Congress urging passage of the Wolf bill.

Especially notable was the effort of Rabbi David Saperstein, lobbyist for Reform Judaism and a veteran of over a quarter of a century of lobby battles in Washington. One of the most seasoned liberals in Washington, Saperstein was described by one religious insider as a "doer" with "lots of chutzpah and grace." Though he had problems with the original Wolf-Specter bill, he shared the goal of fighting religious persecution and agreed to participate in steering committee meetings, which he described as open, amicable, and amenable to input. At one point he worked with officials at the Catholic Conference and others in assembling half a dozen recommended changes to the bill. As Saperstein recounts it, when the coalition (and Frank Wolf) agreed to five of the six, "we decided to now endorse the new version of the bill" but still "fight for additional changes." The renowned liberal's endorsement of the final version of Wolf-Specter sent a powerful signal. The cause could hardly be viewed as sectarian if it was also backed by a man who had fought many battles against the Christian Right over the years.[29]

This latter point underscores a distinct feature of the antipersecution campaign: For months liberal Jews and conservative evangelicals on the steering committee met frequently over bagels to plan strategy together in a "ratty office" in a House office building.[30] In many ways this was a true strange-bedfellows alliance. As Stacie Burdette recounted, "There were days when you'd start off your morning sharing strategy" on the Wolf-Specter bill, and then "you'd spend the other part of your day working on a school prayer amendment" against some of the *very same people* you worked with in the morning.

Jews brought to this ecumenical table a distinct historical experience and results-oriented moxie. The legislative campaign for Soviet Jewry that started in the 1970s taught them that a focus on particular constituencies could play a role in the broader human rights cause. Though Jackson-Vanik focused only on the right to emigrate from Communist countries, it helped to liberalize the Soviet Union.[31] Thus, unlike some in the liberal Protestant community, who disdained the focus on persecuted Christians, Jewish leaders had no problem with that motivation. As one leader put it, "People used to say, well, this is the *Christian* bill. So what? If it is a good bill, so what?" Why should Jews refrain from helping in a good cause out of skepticism of the motives of conservative Christians? The question should simply be: "Are there or are there not Christians being persecuted, and are they or are they not getting enough attention?" At the same time, Jews pushed hard to broaden the findings section on strategic grounds, because the heavy focus on Christians would unnecessarily stigmatize the bill in the minds of outside skeptics.

The pragmatic toughness of Jewish engagement came out often. Stacie Burdette, for example, found the climate of hostility toward the State Department among some members of the Wolf-Specter steering committee alien, and she felt the bill needed revisions. Yet she saw her organization's backing of Wolf-Specter, which she knew would be altered in the Senate anyway, as a warning signal to a recalcitrant State Department: "We've told you over and over again that you need to get ahead of this issue a little bit and you haven't done a thing. Now there's this piece of legislation that's not perfect. You hate it. Its not exactly the way we would've written it, but we can't just let this issue dangle out there and not support it."[32]

A case of coalition building that moved beyond the Judeo-Christian nexus concerned the Tibetan Buddhist cause. The International Campaign for Tibet, with headquarters in Washington, acts on behalf of the exiled Dalai Lama and the Tibetan people living under harsh Chinese rule. The Tibetan cause enjoyed a certain cache among the Hollywood set (e.g., Richard Gere) that was of enormous benefit to the antipersecution movement, which otherwise might be typecast as a parochial Christian concern. But some activists were not newcomers to the cause. In 1997 Frank Wolf, concealing his identity as a member of Congress, traveled to Tibet and came back with a horrendous account of how China was "squeezing the life out of Tibet."[33] Given Wolf's credibility as the legislation's sponsor, it was not difficult for Horowitz to enlist Mary Beth Markey, a lobbyist for the Campaign for Tibet, to join the steering committee. Though she expressed occasional "uneasiness at the scarcity of referrals to non-Christian faiths in memos and meetings of our group,"[34] she embraced the cause and ultimately endorsed the legislation. She also worked to educate others *in the coalition* about the plight of the Tibetans, at one point asking them to watch and promote the movie *Kundun*, a dramatization of how the Chinese Communists treated the

Dalai Lama. Buddhist involvement extended beyond Washington representatives. The Dalai Lama himself sent a message of support to the lobby kickoff meeting, saying that he was "gratified by the efforts you are undertaking to draw attention to China's policies in my country which are increasingly focused on the eradication of the Tibetan Buddhist culture."[35]

The Tibetan cause, of course, dovetailed with the broader coalition on human rights in China. Since the early 1990s Nina Shea and others had been raising the issue of continuing oppression of religion in China, so that the "anti-PRC" coalition of religious groups, labor unions, and Chinese human rights activists flowed into, and fortified, the new alliance for religious freedom legislation. The China activists, however, continued to press issues beyond Wolf-Specter, and in 2000 fought an intense though unsuccessful effort to deny permanent normal trade status with China.

Horowitz, of course, trumpeted this ecumenical support. When critics charged that the Wolf-Specter bill was a Christian Right initiative, Horowitz responded with rhetorical flourish that the legislation was backed as vigorously by Jewish groups as by the Southern Baptist Convention, as much by the Tibetan Buddhists as the Catholic Church. The mounting endorsements by national groups also spurred religious presses to publicize the campaign among pastors and parishioners, generating grassroots support.

By the time the legislation was reported out of the committee in the spring of 1998, it had over 100 cosponsors in the House. Illustrating the bipartisan support for the bill, cosponsors included Tony Hall (D-OH) and Nancy Pelosi (D-CA), as well as Wolf (R-VA), Smith (R-NJ), Watts (R-OK), and Ben Gilman (R-NY). Nonetheless, there was a crucial Republican element to the politics behind Wolf-Specter. Christian evangelical groups were mobilizing for the legislation, with some making it one of their major legislative priorities. Republican staff members on the Hill admitted to me that there was a political need to "do something" for the conservative Christian community that helped the GOP seize control of the House after forty years of Democratic rule. For nearly two decades there had been grumbling among evangelical leaders that Republicans slight their social agenda after elections. In response, both Newt Gingrich

and Trent Lott endorsed religious freedom legislation in a widely reported meeting with activists, and they pledged to expedite its floor
consideration.[36] As it turned out these commitments were indeed
crucial to the process.

As we will see, there was considerable opposition to Wolf-
Specter, but backers of the legislation knew that few congressional
members would be willing to vote publicly against it. After all, who
wants to be known as "voting for persecution"? House leadership
commitment was pivotal, therefore, because it would determine
whether the bill would reach the floor for a vote and under what
conditions. It was Majority Leader Dick Armey who made sure that
the legislation would make it to the floor and under favorable rules
that would prevent "killer amendments"—changes that would frac-
ture delicately crafted compromises. It was convenient that Armey
had experienced a rather recent personal religious conversion. In
coalition meetings and on the floor of the House, Armey spoke with
considerable passion about how religious freedom is central to human dignity, that without it "little else matters." The floor leader,
Chris Smith, whose subcommittee had built a prodigious record of
abuses of religious freedom, was an equally passionate representative.
An often eloquent speaker, Smith combined a broad philosophical
commitment to human rights with detailed knowledge of conditions
in the many countries he had visited or featured in his hearings.

In many respects the House of Representatives operated just as
the framers of the Constitution envisioned. Responding to "public
passions," the House moved swiftly to pass what many viewed as
tough initial legislation. Those opposed were unable to block consideration in a body where the majority can exercise its will. After the
legislation was voted out of the International Relations Committee
by a 31–5 margin on March 25, 1998, House leaders brought it to
the floor on May 14, where it passed by a robust vote of 375–41. Numerous members rose to endorse the legislation before the vote, but
there was also genuine debate, with the opposition led by veteran
lawmaker and foreign-policy expert Lee Hamilton (D-IN), who took
the administration's position that the legislation would be counterproductive. (A number of his concerns over the lack of flexibility in
the bill would be incorporated in the Senate's alternative legislation.)

While some of the speeches on the floor of the House were predictable or perfunctory, nonetheless the tenor of the debate seemed to reflect genuine convictions that this issue embodied a core value of the American people, and that the legislation provided a needed response to a serious global problem.[37]

The floor debate also illustrated the impact of the broader social movement. Members of Congress referred to Horowitz by name, cited Nina Shea's and Paul Marshall's books, quoted literature of Voice of the Martyrs and other Christian solidarity groups, and mentioned how their constituents participated in the International Day of Prayer for the Persecuted Church. Letters from a wide array of religious leaders were read into the congressional record, including one from famed Soviet refusenik Natan Sharansky and another from the Dalai Lama lauding congressional action. The movement clearly had penetrated elite consciousness.

BUSINESS OPPOSITION

Who, then, opposed such a seemingly popular idea? The most vigorous opposition came from an alliance of corporate lobbies led by Frank Kittredge, president of the National Foreign Trade Council (NFTC), which represents the nation's 500 largest exporters. The NFTC had hired liberal consultant Ann Wexler to engineer a general antisanctions lobby campaign under the organizational rubric of USA★Engage. As Kittredge admitted to a reporter, USA★Engage was formed "because a lot of companies are not anxious to be spotlighted as supporters of countries like Iran or Burma," and the "way to avoid that is to band together in a coalition."[38] Though Wolf-Specter never dealt substantially with trade, an almost obsessive fear of alienating trading partners led USA★Engage to mount a lobby campaign against the religious freedom legislation, which congressional insiders described as "one of the most intense" they had seen in years.[39]

While well financed, this lobby effort was not always the most adroit. USA★Engage never really explained that its title meant that sanctions are bad and engagement is better. At one point, the organization distributed cardboard boomerangs to congressional offices as a way to convey that Wolf-Specter would boomerang against its backers and the United States. But as one staffer observed, the boomerang was "thin cardboard, flimsy, and does not fly, just like their arguments." Other tactics were more cunning. When the Wolf bill was introduced in the House in May 1997, USA★Engage moved quietly to solicit liberal churches to oppose the bill, even agreeing to "defray costs" of flying foreign religious leaders to Washington to testify against the legislation.[40] Internal documents of this campaign suggest that USA★Engage lobbyists understood that the best way to derail the legislation was to mobilize religious critics, which underscored the impact of the church-based campaign.[41]

Corporate opposition to an initiative so ardently backed by evangelicals "brought home," as one top GOP staffer noted, "the division within the Republican base between the business community and Christian conservatives." Evidence of this division came out in acid comments about business lobbies, as when one Republican staffer quipped that some corporations are willing to do business with countries that "boiled pastors in oil." Evangelical leaders, in turn, directed their ire at the corporate community. When business opposition threatened to derail the legislation, four of the "big guns" of the evangelical camp—James Dobson (Focus on the Family), Chuck Colson (Prison Fellowship), Gary Bauer (Family Research Council), and Randy Tate (Christian Coalition)—sent a pointed letter to then Senate Majority Leader Trent Lott. After expressing concern that the Senate might not act on legislation passed by the House, the four wrote this:

> We are particularly disturbed by the role of wealthy corporate interests in attempting to prevent these human rights issues from being addressed by Congress. Are our leaders willing to play hardball with China on Hollywood's pirated CD's and video tapes, but not with governments involved in persecuting people of faith? What a travesty if we as a nation subordinate our historical stand for freedom and human rights to the pursuit of profits.[42]

The fact that legislation ultimately passed Congress despite business opposition suggests that the religious community, especially evangelicalism, may be the principal grassroots resistance left to what Jacob Heilbrunn depicted as the "corporate takeover of foreign policy."[43] Or as Horowitz quipped, religious engagement is crucial because "there are more churches in America than Chambers of Commerce chapters." Perhaps one lesson for business is that engagement under some Sullivan-like principles (like those developed for South Africa under apartheid) might be a better long-run strategy on international trade than knee-jerk opposition to any human rights focus in American foreign policy.

OPPOSITION IN THE ADMINISTRATION

The Clinton administration also vigorously opposed the Wolf-Specter bill.[44] Secretary of State Madeleine Albright charged that the legislation did not "take into account the perspectives and values of others," and that it would create "an artificial hierarchy of human rights."[45] At one point she personally confronted Horowitz in a Washington restaurant, insisting that the legislation would create a mess in U.S. foreign policy by sanctioning so many countries with whom we have relations. And she pointedly charged that he wrote the legislation to "give Israel a free ride."[46] State Department officials, in turn, testified against the legislation, arguing that it would elevate religious freedom above other concerns, complicate trade and foreign relations, and add another automatic sanction to an already overburdened set of foreign-policy laws.[47]

One factor that bolstered administrative opposition was skepticism of the campaign among the traditional human rights groups, such as Human Rights Watch (as cataloged in chapter 3). Part of this skepticism came from the perception of some that evangelicals are neophytes to the rights cause who only care about fellow Christians. Noting that this mistrust affected legislative dynamics, one evangelical leader acknowledged that there are some "conservative Christians who will lose sleep over domestic religious freedom and saying the Lord's Prayer at a football game but will yawn when they read the little paragraph in the international column about X number of churches burned in Indonesia or X number of Falun Gong hauled off by their hair in Tiananmen Square." Thus it is not surprising that when "Johnny-come-lately" evangelicals had the audacity to mount a major legislative campaign, it provoked mistrust and perhaps some resentment.

The most telling, if unintended, contribution to the campaign by opponents came from President Clinton himself. Speaking to a group of some sixty evangelical leaders at the White House, Clinton attempted to persuade them to oppose Wolf-Specter. Unaware that a reporter was in attendance, Clinton argued that the rigid formula of automatic sanctions in the Wolf bill would lead officials in the "bowels of the bureaucracy to fudge the finding" to avoid creating diplomatic problems with strategic countries.[48] The admission that officials might "fudge the facts" about persecution—or lie—appeared on the front page of the *New York Times*, above the fold. The story created an instant sensation among religious partisans and unintentionally helped energize the effort to pass the House bill.

The event also influenced actual legislative give and take. In a memo to the office of Senator Lieberman (D-CT), Steve McFarland of the Christian Legal Society used as a rationale for expanding an independent commission's reporting function that it would "discourage 'fudging' of facts in the designation of violators."[49]

RELIGIOUS SKEPTICISM

While business opposition and diplomatic resistance were predictable, religious opposition to Wolf-Specter was a more complex matter. As we saw in chapter 3, mainline Protestant leaders expressed skepticism to the new campaign for persecuted Christians, and they reacted negatively to Wolf-Specter. In some cases, however, they offered substantive suggestions. Most influential early in the process was Oliver Thomas, chief counsel for the National Council of Churches (NCC), who offered a series of objections to the Wolf-Specter bill. These became the basis for congressional testimony and letters signed by denominational representatives against the bill. Thomas's critique was also echoed by State Department officials, such as Assistant Secretary of State for Human Rights John Shattuck. Realizing that the NCC would be an easy target, Thomas, who enjoys a reputation of reasonableness even among critics of the liberal churches, decided to articulate the systematic case against the bill only after "great prayer and angst." His objections were that the legislation privileged religious freedom over other rights, that its automatic sanctions were too blunt and could be counterproductive, that its definition of persecution was too narrow and unconnected with international declarations and covenants, that it represented a "one-size-fits-all" approach, that it favored Christians, that it shifted coordination of action on human rights outside the State Department, and that it emphasized unilateral American action rather than multilateral responses. House bill drafters, in fact, revised Wolf-Specter to accommodate some of these concerns, while the Senate incorporated still more of them. In key respects, however, the final legislation remained tougher than Thomas recommended.

Thomas's memo was the high point of NCC's influence in the process. Albert Pennybacker, Washington director of the NCC, merely opposed the legislation. Not only did he testify against the House legislation, but when the Senate alternative incorporated provisions addressing most of Thomas's concerns, he continued his opposition. More startling, he even agreed to accept money from the National Foreign Trade Council to support his efforts.[50] (In the fall of 1998 Pennybacker said the NCC had not yet received such payment but continued to welcome it.[51]) This willingness to "get in bed" with big business cries out for explanation, given how often the NCC has taken a left-wing posture against corporate interests. The explanation appears to be a general antipathy toward the antipersecution campaign. Though he saw the Senate bill as better than the House's, to Pennybacker it would have been better if there had been no bill at all. In part this conclusion stemmed from his belief that the problem of persecution is overblown, and that only by addressing global poverty can religious strife be overcome.[52] Part of this opposition probably flows from his organization's ongoing hostility toward the Christian Right, creating suspicion that the campaign is a Trojan horse for a conservative evangelical agenda. Part of it, as we saw in chapter 3, may stem from the fact that the NCC is "compromised" by its benign engagement with Communist countries and its continued links with state-sanctioned churches.

Though some mainline leaders may have been motivated by visible evangelical backing of Wolf-Specter, there were also evangelical opponents of the legislation. One group opposed Wolf-Specter because they felt it would involve "religious monitoring" by the federal government and "concentrated power" in the executive branch. The group feared that the legislation would allow the federal government to monitor religion "in the United States," raising the specter that some federal official would become a "powerful religious dictator." It quoted Herb Titus, a former law professor at Regent University (founded by Pat Robertson), who charged that the law was unconstitutional.[53]

Other evangelical leaders raised concerns about the immigration and asylum provisions of Wolf-Specter. Ironically, it was the very liberalized asylum provisions endorsed by Catholics that raised concern among some evangelicals. Under the legislation, if a refugee claimed membership in a community that was persecuted, asylum was to be expedited. While this seemed to provide a tremendous benefit to those fleeing persecution, some evangelical advocates argued that such liberalized asylum would lead to an emptying of the Christian population in the Middle East and elsewhere. Thus the legislation would unwittingly "undo the labor of Christian missionaries and martyrs over the centuries," said the late Steve Snyder of International Christian Concern, who backed Wolf-Specter but sought changes in its immigration provisions.[54] James Robb of Evangelicals for Immigration Reform echoed this concern in a letter to Congressman Henry Hyde:

> I predict many Middle Eastern nations will be effectively emptied of Christians within one or two decades if this measure passes. . . . I am concerned that tyrants such as Saddam Hussein could see in the combination of diplomatic pressure brought about by H.R. 2431 and the relaxed asylum provisions in the bill, an opportunity to pronounce a *pogrom.* They could use the bill as an excuse—and opportunity—to rid themselves of their Christian minorities.[55]

Some evangelical figures even went beyond these policy considerations to argue that, since the "blood of the martyrs is the seed of the church," Christians need to remain in such harsh environments. Upon hearing this assertion at one meeting, Michael Horowitz got so agitated that he snapped a pencil in his hands.[56]

Other evangelicals, such as Sam Ericsson of Advocates International, echoed concerns expressed by the NCC and State Department officials that the legislation was the wrong vehicle, too blunt a tool to work effectively. Ericsson argued that it was not connected to the routines of diplomacy, that its high threshold of egregious persecution left out a wide range of abuses, that only pariah states would be covered, and that the automatic sanction provision would lead to frequent presidential waivers and charges of hypocrisy. More comfortable with quiet diplomacy than confrontation, Ericsson also expressed concern that the legislation would invite reprisals against vulnerable Christian communities abroad and upset delicate arrangements local groups have with officials, something not to be taken lightly.[57] Thankfully, the record since passage of IRFA suggests that reprisals have not occurred because of public exposure of abuses.[58]

The evangelical community thus split on which approach to take in promoting religious freedom. One evangelical lobbyist summarized that split:

> There were multiple viewpoints. One camp believed that you attract a lot more through honey than vinegar, so forget about sanctions. You go to these countries and you say, "How can I help you promote religious freedom?" You don't waive sticks over their heads. Others said, "Look, this constructive engagement stuff has proven to be a dismal failure. Let's start leveraging our authority and throw our weight around."

The Jewish community was generally sympathetic toward religious freedom legislation, but it was not united either about the proper vehicle. Some Jewish organizations endorsed Wolf-Specter, while others saw fundamental problems in the legislation. The American Jewish Committee (AJC), while lauding the impulse behind the Wolf-Specter bill, recommended a series of major changes, several of which foreshadowed elements of the Senate's Nickles-Lieberman bill. For example, the AJC recommended that Congress substitute "a menu of calibrated and discretionary sanctions for the automatic but narrow sanctions proposed by the bill." It also called for broadening the definition of religious persecution that would trigger "the bill's sanctions so as to be consistent with the definition of religious persecution under international and U.S. law." Finally, the AJC recommended that offices created by the legislation be embedded in the machinery of the

State Department and National Security Council where policy is implemented. Here, the AJC suggested that by attempting to elevate the status of religious freedom through a White House office, it would unwittingly isolate promoting of religious rights from the information-gathering and diplomatic apparatus of the government.[59]

While the bill sailed through the House, things were different in the Senate. For one thing, senators guard their foreign-policy prerogatives and are loath to be pressured into "intemperate action." Second, the Senate is more critical of sanctions-based foreign policy than the House, making Wolf-Specter, which was cast as a "sanctions" bill, a harder sell in the upper chamber. Finally, the norms and rules of the Senate require supermajorities for action. Indeed, a single senator can hold up legislation, sometimes killing it when time runs out on the session. This places a premium on building the broadest consensus for success, which confirms to devotees of the Senate that it does indeed "check the passions" of the House with a more deliberate approach, just as the framers intended. For all these reasons, Wolf-Specter faced a perilous fate in the Senate, leading critics to charge that while Horowitz and his allies had an excellent strategy to get legislation through the House, they lacked a viable Senate strategy.

To understand how a Senate alternative to Wolf-Specter arose, it is necessary to take a journey into the internal politics of religion on Capitol Hill, particularly the role of staff.

A STAFF CADRE SEEKS AN ALTERNATIVE

One reason why the issue of religious freedom resonated in Congress is that many members and their staffs are enmeshed in religious communities themselves and thus predisposed to sympathy for the cause. An intriguing aspect of this faith life on Capitol Hill is the sponsorship by religious organizations of "congressional fellows" who work as staff for members of Congress but are paid by outside benefactors. To further the cause of religious freedom, for example, a number of evangelical groups have quietly sponsored such congressional fellows, some for years. A cadre of these evangelical fellows became central players in drafting an alternative to the Wolf-Specter legislation, sparking sometimes acrimonious conflict with other evangelicals allied with Horowitz. That evangelicals fought fiercely *among themselves* over which bill to back suggests a pluralism in the born-again world not always appreciated outside the community.

The key congressional Christian fellows involved in drafting what became Nickles-Lieberman included:

- John Hanford, nephew to Elizabeth Dole, who worked from 1987–2001 out of the office of Senator Richard Lugar (R-IN) on international religious freedom cases. He later was appointed by President George W. Bush to be ambassador for International Religious Freedom.
- William Inboden, who worked first for Sam Nunn (D-GA) and then out of the office of Representative Tom DeLay (R-TX).
- Laura Bryant Hanford, who worked out of the office of Representative Bob Clement (D-TN). Now married to Hanford, she crafted language for many provisions of the Senate's original IRFA.

It was not surprising that these individuals became engulfed in the issue, given their legislative specialization. Bryant and Inboden worked together in the mid-1990s on resolutions expressing the "sense of Congress" on religious persecution abroad. Of all the fellows John Hanford had the longest tenure, having spent a decade on religious freedom cases, laboring behind the scenes to gain the release of imprisoned pastors and believers. This experience gained him a considerable reputation on the Hill as the foremost proponent of quiet diplomacy with a passionate conviction about the proper way to approach the issue of religious freedom, and it wasn't the Wolf-Specter way. To some Wolf-Specter partisans Hanford's vehement opposition to the House bill suggested a sense of "proprietary ownership" of the cause, even an arrogance that would not brook interlopers on his turf. The whole constellation of aggressive new activists who demanded tough measures certainly challenged Hanford's approach.

Advocates of Wolf-Specter made contacts with Hanford, but could not come to a meeting of the minds, or even a modus operandi. There was simply too fundamental a divide: Wolf-Specter partisans demanded tough public measures; Hanford and his allies sought change through quiet diplomacy. As the lobby campaign heated up, the sides were increasingly personified by Horowitz and Hanford, who became bitter adversaries.[60] Insiders, in fact, referred to the Horowitz camp or the Hanford camp. To backers of Wolf-Specter, Hanford seemed obstructionist, objecting to any bill with teeth. To opponents of Wolf-Specter, Horowitz acted as if he could ramrod the bill through Congress without the normal give and take. Ultimately, the system absorbed the energies and perspectives of both sides.

Hanford, Bryant, and Inboden believed that Wolf-Specter was heavy-handed and needed major revisions.[61] To them it "rigidly" applied "one measure (sanctions) in one dimension (all or nothing, unless there's a waiver)" regardless of the "nature of the persecution, the particular circumstances in that country, or the status of that country's relationship with the United States." Thus Wolf-Specter offered the same remedy "for different problems in countries as diverse as North Korea, Egypt, Saudi Arabia, Cuba, China, Pakistan, Russia, and Morocco."[62] They also believed that Wolf-Specter was false toughness because so few countries would pass its threshold and thus require U.S. action. Moreover, the lack of calibrated responses would lead to routine waivers of action against strategically vital countries, such as Saudi Arabia, which would lead to a perception of hypocrisy.

The aides were spurred to come up with an alternative because of the momentum and excitement that had built in the religious community for the original legislation. Without Wolf-Specter, in other words, there would have been no Nickles-Lieberman. Initially the staff cadre spent hours working with Wolf and got what they saw as "some bad ideas" out of the original legislation, such as one provision that would have the CIA track persecution. But Horowitz, Wolf, and Smith resisted changes they thought would weaken the bill, setting up an inevitable struggle with those who saw the legislation as fundamentally flawed.

The trio of staffers began thinking seriously about drafting alternative legislation after a meeting that occurred on July 15, 1997. Wolf-Specter had been introduced in May 1997, but there were rumblings of concern in the Senate. Some evangelicals were not happy with the socially liberal Specter as the Senate sponsor and that, along with skepticism of the Wolf approach, led to a groping for an alternative. To that end Majority Leader Trent Lott created a task force to look into the issue and put Senator James Inhofe (R-OK) in charge. "It was intended to cut Specter out of the process and get a better policy approach," recounted one insider. Inhofe had Jim Jatras, a policy staffer (and an Eastern Orthodox Christian), consider alternative language. Jatras had his own objections to Wolf-Specter, and he drafted a bill that was presented at a meeting to which Inhofe invited a variety of religious and human rights leaders.

Horowitz was horrified by the proposal, sure that some of its provisions would have "split our movement apart." The bill focused exclusively on China and Sudan and contained a series of punitive measures against China, including barring visits by high-ranking officials and denying World Trade Organization membership. Even more problematic, the bill would fund a new religious liberty commission by defunding the Legal Services Corporation (LSC), which provides legal services to the poor.[63] This would, of course, cost the support of Jews, liberals, and probably Catholic organizations. Horowitz determined to shut down the Inhofe effort. At the meeting he fulminated, yelled, and even, according to some reports, threw things. So vehement were the objections raised by Horowitz and others that the meeting was described as "a food fight."[64] Spooked, Inhofe backed away, leaving a vacuum that the congressional fellows decided to fill.

Working with their "bosses' blessings and guidance," along with the "counsel of a number of experts," the trio of fellows took up where Inhofe left off, formulating language for an alternative bill.[65] Laura Bryant was the one who actually did most of the early research, leading her future spouse, John Hanford, to say that "there's more of Laura's genius in this bill than anyone's."[66] She spent months using the Congressional Research Service and overseas sources to investigate other foreign-policy laws, international human rights treaties, and the like, in an attempt to craft legislative language that would flow smoothly out of existing diplomatic practices and international norms: "We sought to build IRFA on existing mechanisms and to use the whole foreign policy toolbox. For example, we looked at the negotiation principles that help make sanctions effective in trade violations, and we sought to apply similar principles to this area of human rights."[67] Bryant also had the World Evangelical

Fellowship do a survey of some hundred of their field mission folk. The results were divided—with some opposing sanctions, some backing sanctions, and others primarily wanting exposure—but to Bryant the mixed reports fortified the assessment that Wolf-Specter was not the right approach.

Though Bryant and the others continued to negotiate with Wolf over changes to the original legislation, they also worked quietly with those seeking an alternative. One of the earliest of those contacts was with Senator Don Nickles's (R-OK) foreign-policy specialist, Steve Moffitt. He liked their approach better than Wolf-Specter and provided early detailed feedback—"I like this, I don't like that, why is this here?" As the legislation took shape, the trio "shopped it around" to congressional offices for possible sponsors. They had no luck until Moffitt presented his boss with a memo on the bill's high points.

Nickles was receptive because of his prior commitment to religious freedom, which he mentioned in his maiden speech on the floor of the Senate in 1981. As Moffitt recalled, whenever Nickles met with Chinese officials he told them the same thing. "If you want to improve relations with the United States there are three things you need to do: Get rid of your one child policy, improve democracy, and provide more religious freedom." Nickles agreed to serve as prime sponsor of the legislation. Moffitt thus joined the trio in the effort to refine the bill, which was introduced in March 1998 as the IRFA, cosponsored by Nickles and Senator Joseph Lieberman (D-CT). At this point Nickles's office became the focal point of fierce lobbying and contentious interreligious clashes. Steve Moffitt recounted what happened when Nickles-Lieberman was introduced:

> We were immediately bombarded by every group that you can possibly imagine. Some religious groups said of the bill, "It's too harsh, it's going to absolutely, positively harm our missionary efforts overseas." Other religious groups said, "This bill's not strong enough, we've got to do more." Business groups came and said, "This bill's too harsh, a sanctions bill. This is exactly like the bill we were opposing, the Wolf-Specter bill. You can't have sanctions."[68]

Everyone involved in this process described it as staggering in intensity. For six months the four staffers met in Nickles's office, for hours at a time several times a week, often starting sessions with a prayer, to refine language and negotiate changes with diverse stakeholders. What made the process so painful was what they described as an atmosphere of personal attacks from people who backed the House bill.

As envisioned by the drafters, Nickles-Lieberman sought to strengthen existing mechanisms of foreign policy by taking current standards on religious freedom in international human rights covenants and then calibrating presidential actions against violations of those standards. In the place of Wolf-Specter's automatic withdrawal of nonhumanitarian aid, the bill provided the president with a menu of responses of increasing severity, thirteen in all, from a private démarche to economic sanctions. The bill, in other words, employed a lower threshold for triggering actions than Wolf but provided more flexibility for the president to craft responses. It did embrace some of the spirit of the Wolf bill in that it required a designation of countries that practice gross violations of religious freedom. For serious persecution, the bill required the president to choose from among the more serious options, subject to a waiver.[69]

Central to the bill was a requirement that the State Department "designate" which countries fall into the category of gross persecutors. Bill drafters scoured other statutes as precedents and talked with such groups as Amnesty International.[70] They discovered that "there's a lot more diplomatic activity" when designations are required on an annual basis.[71] Incorporating such a mandate meant tougher language than that employed in the general human rights statute. Bill drafters felt this provision was underappreciated by the Wolf partisans.

Structurally, the law created a new office in the State Department and an ambassador-at-large for International Religious Freedom. It required enhanced reporting on religious freedom in the State Department's annual human rights report. The legislation also authorized "soft" initiatives designed to promote religious freedom (such as international exchanges and awards), mandated religious freedom training for foreign service and INS personnel, and guaranteed access by U.S. citizens to embassies for religious services (in response to the situation in Saudi Arabia). Several of these latter provisions, as Bryant noted, demonstrated how this new cause enhanced human rights more generally, in contrast to those who claimed that it fostered a hierarchy of rights: "We, in fact, carefully crafted provisions such as training, awards, and others to deal with human rights in general, including religious freedom."[72]

IRFA's drafters opposed the liberalized asylum and immigration provisions of Wolf-Specter, in part because they shared the concern of some evangelicals about the possible unintended emptying of Christians in some countries and in part because they knew senators were loath to revisit a recently passed law tightening immigration procedures. In response to the concern about persecuted believers being refused U.S. asylum by ignorant officials, they pointed to the training of asylum and immigration officers in Nickles-Lieberman. As a concession to Catholic lobbyists they also agreed to insert a study of the effects of the current immigration law, especially its provision of "expedited removal" of those seeking asylum, which the Church disliked.

Intriguingly, drafters also incorporated a watered-down version of a key aspect of the earlier Inhofe bill, the creation of a panel of distinguished citizens, modeled after the Civil Rights Commission, to assess facts about religious persecution and recommend policy responses to the president and Congress. As we will see, strengthening the role and independence of this commission became the focal point of efforts by activists to reconcile the spirit of Wolf-Specter with that of Nickles-Lieberman.

Backers of the IRFA, of course, gained a crucial cosponsor in Senator Joe Lieberman (D–CT), not only because he provided true bipartisan credentials but because of his stature. The Democratic nominee for vice president in 2000 had expressed deep concern about the problem of religious persecution abroad and conveyed to his staff his desire for legislative remedy. Thus although he had problems with the House bill, he was earnestly seeking an alternative to back. As the form of that alternative began to take shape, he had his staff work with the others to refine the draft for introduction.[73] Not only did Lieberman agree to become a principal sponsor, but later he listed that sponsorship on his website as one of his singular legislative accomplishments.

DUELING BILLS

Given that the involved religious community divided up in camps over the two bills, it is useful to note similarities. Both described religious persecution as a serious problem slighted in American foreign policy. Both invoked the centrality of religious freedom in America as providing a touchstone for the nation's actions abroad. Both cited Article 18 of the Universal Declaration of Human Rights and other United Nations and international covenants and called nations to live up to those ideals as embodied in the legislation. Both contained mechanisms to address severe religious persecution. Both envisioned religious training of State Department officials and new reports on the religious situation in countries around the world. Both mandated presidential actions.

But there were crucial differences between the two bills that reflected a philosophical divide. The shift in emphasis in the titles (from preventing "persecution" in Wolf-Specter to promoting "religious freedom" in Nickles-Lieberman) was more than symbolic. The House bill contemplated bluntly exposing and punishing egregious abuses. The Senate bill sought to prevent abuses from rising to that level through calibrated diplomatic measures addressing a broader array of violations in more countries.

Underlying the philosophical divide was the issue of trust in the regular foreign-policy system. Wolf-Specter partisans sought to provide less wiggle room because they distrusted the impulses of diplomacy. Said one Wolf partisan, "When millions are getting killed, then quiet diplomacy and constructive engagement are not enough." Backers of Nickles-Lieberman saw this kind of rhetoric as unhelpful, as they were seeking change by working through the diplomatic system. But working through the system presupposed, as one Wolf partisan argued, "that State and White House will do all they can," while "Wolf embodied distrust of those channels." To Nickles partisans this distrust of the president and the diplomatic corps led House drafters to produce an inflexible "sledgehammer" remedy, designed to make us feel better but which would be rarely used, and thus ineffective or counterproductive. "The goal," as Bryant put it, "is changing behavior. It's not punishment."[74] But what Nickles backers envisioned as carefully measured responses to persecution, Wolf partisans saw as giving too much room to substitute trivial actions for meaningful ones. Congressman Chris Smith said the Senate bill "stretches flexibility almost to the breaking point."[75] Give diplomats thirteen progressively less stringent options in response to persecution, Horowitz opined, and they will pick the lamest, most inconsequential ones. Horowitz felt vindicated on this score when both the Clinton and Bush administrations virtually ignored the menu by designating existing diplomatic actions as fulfilling the mandates of the new law.

Mistrust of the system also led some Wolf partisans to be skeptical about adding the new position of ambassador of International Religious Freedom to the Department of State bureaucracy. They feared that the ambassador might become mere window dressing, engaged in diversionary activities of little impact. One group of evangelical leaders even recommended dropping the position from the bill.[76]

The threshold question also divided the partisans. Critics of the House bill believed its extremely high threshold, which only triggered action against the worst regimes, would leave untouched serious violations of religious liberty. The problem with the House standard, as one Senate staffer argued, is that "our government will only really care if you have systematic, widespread, ongoing torture or imprisonment." Under this definition "the bar is so high that the administration would have an excuse for almost every country in the world, except Sudan, for not taking action. . . . I'm baffled why they defined it that way." The House bill, in other words, might unintentionally provide loopholes for administrative inaction against really bad actors. What if torture or imprisonment is concentrated in a particular region, or the capital city? That might not be interpreted as "widespread." The Wolf trigger might be limited to rogue regimes already under U.S. sanctions, and therefore relatively meaningless. Laura Bryant recounted how this possibility ultimately dawned on foes of action: "The Wolf-Specter definition constituted a much higher threshold of persecution. And in those furious, hectic last hours leading up to IRFA's passage, an interesting aspect of the legislative negotiations was that those who sought to weaken the bill were arguing for the higher threshold and definition to replace the definition that we have." Steve Moffitt echoed this: "The administration worked us over for weeks trying to get us to take the definition that Horowitz wrote in the Wolf bill. . . . They just loved to have that briar patch."[77] Thus, the supposedly more "moderate" Senate bill was actually tougher on serious persecution than the House version, according to its backers.

The Senate bill explicitly invoked international and UN covenants to define religious freedom, violations of which were then described as "religious persecution." Though the bill reserved serious sanctions for gross persecution, some action was required for any violation. Critics saw this expansive approach as utopian, getting the United States ensnared in minor charges of discrimination and interreligious squabbles. Horowitz castigated the bill as an attempt to make the United States an "international EEOC administered, God help us, by the State Department." The bill would "tie us up with Scientologists and get us caught up in battles again over Catholic-Protestant tensions in Latin America and Ireland, and Jewish-evangelical tensions in Israel," thus squandering the nation's moral authority and impact. Horowitz attributed this approach to "naive evangelicals" who never understood the strategic need to focus on egregious persecution.[78]

Nickles's partisans responded that invoking the UN charter and international covenants kept the new law from being seen as a superpower's attempt to "impose" its values on others. Rather, the United States was merely asking other countries to live up to their own agreements and professed principles. As Steve Moffitt observed, "Article 18 of the Universal Declaration of Human Rights says everyone has the right to freedom of thought, conscience, and religion. . . . This right includes freedom to change religion or belief, freedom either alone or in community with others or in public or private to manifest belief or religion in teaching, practice, worship, and observance." When countries sign the UN charter, they sign on to this principle: "We didn't put a gun to their head and say join the United Nations. They signed it." Where the House bill contemplated promoting religious freedom by making an example of egregious violators, the Senate bill sought to "catch" many violations before they rose to the level of the House standard. An added merit of the Senate definition, Bryant noted, was that it was "consistent with other parts of U.S. law." Thus when critics sought to weaken the bill by changing definitions, drafters were able to beat back such attempts: "We could say, 'No, this is consistent with stated and codified U.S. policy, and we're going to stick to it.'"[79]

Ironically, the State Department shared Horowitz's concern—if for different reasons—that the original Nickles-Lieberman language would ensnare the United States in nettlesome claims of discrimination and necessitate actions against numerous countries. Assistant Secretary of State John Shattuck testified that the broad definition of religious persecution—"any limitation on the right to religious freedom"—coupled with the requirement that the president take action against *all* violators, would require diplomatic actions against the majority of the world's countries. Even countries that generally ensure religious freedom, such as Austria or Belgium, might be found to practice some form of discrimination triggering a presidential response.[80]

Sharing this concern that the bill might undermine relations with decent nations were Senators Rod Grams (R-MN) and Chuck Hagel (R-NE), two members of the Foreign Relations Committee. Late in the process, they negotiated changes in Nickles-Lieberman so that "actions" by foreign governments, not the State Department reports, would serve as the triggering mechanism of U.S. law. This effectively eliminated the need for the president to take official action against *any* reported violation, however slight, that appeared in a State Department report. This shifted the weight of U.S. action toward greater violations, thus nudging the Senate bill in the direction of the House's philosophy.

This change in language also reduced leverage of groups like the Scientologists, who suffer discriminatory treatment in Germany. As one Senate staffer recalled, language in the bill that was removed would have created "more problems than it would resolve." This change was noticed: "After the bill was passed, we were more than forty-five minutes speaking to the Scientologists. . . . They were wondering why that language was removed. And I explained it to them and, of course, they weren't happy, but they understood."[81]

A different issue concerned whether the president had to "opt out" or "opt in" to sanctions. This seemingly subtle difference took on enormous weight in the debate between the two bills. In Wolf-Specter the president had to act *to prevent* automatic sanctions from kicking in. In other words the president had to "opt out" of sanctions—to take explicit action to prevent sanctions from going into effect. Advocates saw this as ensuring accountability and visibility. In Nickles-Lieberman the president had to choose which action to take, or had to "opt in" to a particular measure or sanction. This was designed to provide the necessary flexibility for the president to respond to complex strategic and on-the-ground contexts. To Wolf backers, however, this shift enabled the president to bury his choices in the bowels of the bureaucracy as well as choose the least consequential options. As Steve McFarland of the Christian Legal Society wrote in a memo to Senator Lieberman: "There is a significant political difference between the president intervening to stop an otherwise mandatory consequence and the president merely ignoring those sanctions and picking ineffective ones."[82] Several years after the bill passed, Nina Shea argued that events vindicated this concern because the U.S. Commission on which she served found itself continually pressing the president and the State Department to take more vigorous action.

Nickles's backers, however, responded that forcing the president to waive automatic sanctions would result in unhealthy patterns and charges of hypocrisy. One cited Saudi Arabia as an example: The United States has an "extremely important and necessary" relationship with the kingdom, so under Wolf-Specter the president would waive action "year after year after year, and our government would then have been silent on religious persecution."

In sum, Nickles-Lieberman advocates saw Wolf-Specter as a hasty and ill-thought-out bill, a "one-size-fits-all" approach to foreign policy. They viewed their alternative as a measured and flexible response to the complexities of situations around the world. Wolf-Specter partisans saw Nickles-Lieberman as having no bite, as utopian, mushy, and unwieldy. Horowitz described it as "Rube Goldberg" in its complexity.[83]

Reconciling these differing visions need not have been as acrimonious as it was; indeed the genius of the American legislative system is how it constantly seeks such consensus through compromise and accommodation. But several factors increased the acrimony of the process, which unintentionally, or "providentially," produced the remarkable endgame result.

The introduction of Nickles-Lieberman, literally just as the campaign for Wolf-Specter was culminating in the House, set up a confrontation between the two camps that divided the religious community. Given the perceived need to maintain unity and discipline in the face of business and administration opposition to Wolf-Specter, Horowitz saw the introduction of an alternative bill as a mortal threat to the very movement he helped to catalyze. Others shared this perception, including some key evangelical leaders, who had invested enormous energies in the Wolf approach.

Accentuating this divide, according to a wide array of insiders, was the personalities of the players. Some cited Michael Horowitz as using "unsavory tactics" and personally attacking those who took issue with his approach. "Anyone who criticized Wolf-Specter," one person claimed, "was demonized" by Horowitz. Some evangelical groups were "missing in action" in the final push to pass IRFA, another argued, "because they feared retaliatory defamation by Horowitz."

Even when Horowitz was not mentioned by name, he was invoked. As Moffitt wrote, "We got all kinds of abuse. I remember an article in the summer that appeared in a Jewish paper in New York that said that we were dawdling while Christians were dying." The article was directed explicitly at Senator Nickles's staff, and the suspicion of course was that it was planted by Horowitz. John Hanford also recalled the heated personal charges: "When Laura Bryant raised a couple of substantive questions about the Wolf-Specter bill, she was told by one leader that it was because of people like her that the Nazis succeeded in sending millions to the death camps, and she was standing in the way of larger numbers of religious believers being saved from a similar fate."[84]

On the other hand, John Hanford, a man of equally passionate convictions, also elicited strong reactions. To some Wolf-Specter partisans Hanford's sense of "proprietary ownership" made him stubborn and self-righteous. One House staffer involved in Wolf-Specter got so frustrated while attempting to work out differences with Hanford that he refused to meet further: "I will not sit in the same room with him."

This lack of trust made negotiations more difficult. One evangelical backer of Wolf-Specter described intense discussions as arising from mistrust about the goals of the other side: "Are they really interested in promoting religious liberty," or are they "lackeys of the administration?" Not only did this kind of suspicion prolong the consensus-building, it made the process insufferable to some participants. One insider described it as awful; another as the "most unpleasant experience of my life." Ironically, the fact that the partisans had to suffer through such a maddening process ended up contributing to the providential outcome at the end.

Another problem was the secrecy engendered by the acrimonious atmosphere. Wolf partisans complained about the closed process employed by the Nickles-Lieberman crafters. It was understandable that the Nickles group was gun-shy, but outsiders were exasperated about the "unbelievable secrecy of the process," that they were not even allowed to see drafts. For months, one Wolf backer said, "we couldn't see it." We would go time and again to sit down with Steve Moffitt, who had the best of intentions, and John Hanford, and would lay out six things we think are really important changes. And we kind of get very vague nods of the head. . . . But then you come back three months later and they'd say, 'Well we're working on that.'" Complaining about how close to the vest the Senate team operated, Horowitz claimed that "Bill Armstrong told me at one point he thought he could have had an easier time getting the formula for the H-Bomb than getting the copy of the draft" of Nickles-Lieberman. Another person summarized the experience of attempting to negotiate with the Nickles-Lieberman cadre, "Apart from pro-life litigation, in my experience, I've never been involved in a more acrimonious process."

Partisans of the Wolf approach felt they could not effectively press their case under these conditions. Very late in the process, a group of evangelical luminaries complained to Senator Nickles that their Washington representatives had "not had the opportunity to" see the latest draft of Nickles-Lieberman. Because of this, they wrote, "it is impossible for us to give our best advice—let alone to enthusiastically endorse the bill."[85] This problem helps account for the fact that grassroots mobilization was spotty or confused toward the end of the legislative session.[86]

RESURRECTION

With the religious community divided over what approach to employ, opposition by business lobbies and the administration threatened to kill the legislation, which was declared dead on the front page of the *New York Times*. That premature headline—"Measure Doomed by a Split among Republicans"[87]—was prompted by action of the Senate Foreign Relations Committee, which removed Nickles-Lieberman from its docket on July 22, 1998, thus keeping the bill from reaching the Senate floor. At the time Democrats on the panel planned to vote against the legislation, acceding to President Clinton's wishes, along with several business-oriented Republicans. Facing this defeat, backers pulled the bill from consideration. This action illuminated a Republican split between religious moralists and business interests. In announcing his planned negative vote, Senator Chuck Hagel (R–NE) reflected this latter perspective when he complained that the bill would alienate some of America's "most valuable diplomatic friends and economic partners."[88]

This was the bleakest moment for partisans of religious freedom legislation. Opponents were unified and aggressive; backers were splintering. As a *New York Times* reporter summarized the situation: "It is clear from the lineup in the Foreign Relations Committee today that no bill with teeth can pass the Senate. And almost certainly, too little time is left in this session of Congress to reconcile the differences between a watered-down Senate bill and the strict sanctions approved by the House."[89] Despite this assessment, a little more than two months later, on October 9, 1998, the IRFA passed the Senate by a vote of 98–0, and on the next day—the last of the session—it received unanimous approval in the House. It was signed into law by President Clinton on October 27. So what happened to turn things around?

There are many answers of course: constituency interest generated by the Christian solidarity movement, strategic decisions, converging events. But as I have pondered this question, a broader answer emerges. Despite misgivings about particular remedies, the idea of promoting religious freedom struck a broad chord in Washington and elsewhere. It contained an appeal to the deepest of American values and experience; it evoked passionate resolve across the theological and partisan spectrum; it resonated in the heartland. And so no one gave up. The diverse stakeholders cared enough to invest enormous energies, even while suffering through a confusing, frustrating, emotionally painful, and exhausting process. They continued to press new ideas and negotiate compromises, until a consensus finally emerged that most saw as stronger than either the initial House or Senate bills.

Staff Persistence

The persistence of the cadre of Hanford, Bryant, Inboden, and Moffitt illustrates their dedication to the cause of religious freedom. While they made mistakes and operated with excessive secrecy at times, this group invested enormous effort in crafting language and negotiating changes with diverse stakeholders, including a reluctant administration.

Because they were convinced that the Wolf bill was "dead" in the Senate, they sought to craft an alternative. For nearly a year, this cohort conducted research and crafted language for that alternative. When it was introduced in March 1998, the process intensified. For six months of strenuous negotiations, research, and revision, these in-dividuals did little else but attempt to gain passage of the legislation. As Steve Moffitt observed, "It seemed like every other day we were having a meeting in this conference room for about two or three hours with some group talking about something." In addition, enor-mous effort was invested in combing through human rights laws, trade regulations, and immigration statutes to insure that IRFA would mesh with existing law. As one participant recalled, "It was so many long hours of negotiating for weeks and months over page af-ter page, section after section with the time running out."[90]

Though the staff cadre was skittish about dealing with the Wolf-Specter coalition, they met with its members and many other stake-holders in the months leading up to the bill's passage. As Steve Mof-fitt observed, "We received criticism for talking to everybody that had different viewpoints on different sides of the aisle representing different interests, but our instructions were clear." Moffitt also con-tended that the staff cohort was open to changes: "If we felt it had merit and strengthened the bill and brought something that was good, we incorporated it into the bill."

One criticism was the staff's willingness to negotiate with the State Department and the Clinton administration. This criticism struck

Nickles partisans as reflecting a mistaken view that legislation could be rammed through Congress against the vehement opposition of the president. With the Senate nearing adjournment, a single senator acting on behalf of the administration could delay, and thus kill, the legislation. It was thus essential to negotiate with the president's people. On the other side, the president's advisors increasingly took the negotiations seriously when, late in the process, the bill refused to die. "The administration came to us with literally hundreds of items," one staffer recalled, requiring hours of negotiation to iron out differences. As momentum accelerated in the last week of the session, one of the president's top advisors, Stu Eisenstadt, showed up, and negotiations went late into the evening over pizza. While the group assumed that they "would have to fight tooth and nail with the Clinton administration to get this thing passed," the experience was not unpleasant. Apparently, once the Clinton people accepted the inevitability of legislation, they approached the negotiations in a "most professional" fashion.

Negotiations with key Senate critics were also crucial. Grams (R-MN) and Hagel (R-NE), who were concerned that the bill might upset international trade and American security interests, negotiated a series of changes. Ranking minority member Senator Joseph Biden also had to be accommodated. As one staffer recalled, the group worked "line by line" through Biden's concerns, "pages and pages and pages of it." All of this negotiation was crucial to insure that there would be no dissent from the "unanimous consent" request, under which a bill must come to the floor.[91]

One of the things the staff group was most proud of was holding fast on the requirement that the State Department must designate countries as serious violators of religious freedom. As one of them noted, "The State Department fought very hard against that particular thing." Because the language of designation was anchored in clear legal precedent, they were able to retain that provision of the bill, which they viewed as providing crucial leverage against persecutors.

Episcopal Support

As noted, mainline Protestant leaders not only opposed Wolf-Specter but remained cool to any legislation.[92] This opposition undercut what was otherwise a broad coalition that backed some kind of legislation and that included evangelicals, Catholics, Jews, Buddhists, Baha'is, and other religious minorities. Breaking ranks from the mainline Churches, however, was the Washington office of the Episcopal Church, headed by Tom Hart. His backing of Nickles-Lieberman provided an added boost to the cause. Indeed, a number of insiders, from Catholics, Jews, and evangelicals, to congressional staff, said that Tom Hart played an important role in enlisting support in the religious community for the Senate bill, particularly when it was declared dead in the summer of 1998. Characteristic is this assessment: "None of the groups were more active or strategic in pushing for IRFA than the Episcopal Church."

Why did Hart break ranks with his fellow liberal Protestants? One factor spurring Hart's engagement was the global transformation of the Anglican church, whose population has shifted dramatically to Africa and elsewhere outside of Europe and North America. With members in 164 countries, the Anglican Communion is, as Hart wrote in a letter endorsing the Senate bill, "the most geographically dispersed church in the world next to the Roman Catholic Church." It lives, therefore, in a number of unpleasant places. The fastest growing church, in fact, is in Sudan, where members, as Hart recounted, are herded into refugee camps, tortured, and enslaved. In Pakistan, "Anglicans are often beaten, their churches and villages raided, while women are raped and kidnapped." Because of this record, American Episcopal leaders "were hearing from our partners, from our people on the ground," as Hart observed. Especially moving was learning how some of these communions thrived amidst horrible conditions. "In the face of that sort of persecution where you have the choice between becoming a Muslim or having food or medicine," people are flocking to the Anglican Church, which "shamed us all into humility" and further motivated the search for a remedy.[93]

Hart also brought distinct political experience to the Episcopal office, which influenced his tactical approach and philosophy. Many leaders of the mainline Protestant community (and its umbrella the NCC) make their way to Washington through denominational social action ministries that tend to be long on resolutions but short on focus. Hart, on the other hand, came to the office from Capitol Hill, having worked for a Democratic senator.[94] This experience seemed to provide an appreciation for the tactical need to focus on key priorities and build alliances. Hart was also from a younger generation than those leaders in the mainline community who had received their political baptism in the 1960s. Where others in the mainline community were deeply skeptical or hostile to a movement infused with evangelical support, Hart did not seem to carry the same baggage.

When Wolf-Specter was introduced Hart had many of the same concerns as others: that automatic sanctions might cause reprisals against minority communities, that many abuses, such as church burnings, would not rise to its high threshold. These were outlined in a widely circulated letter that did not oppose the legislation outright. Because he believed that the foreign-policy establishment had "long ignored religious liberty concerns," he was receptive to a legislative remedy. When the alternative bill incorporated many of his concerns, "point by point," Hart responded quickly. In fact, his organization was the first to endorse Nickles-Lieberman. He saw the bill as a sophisticated foreign-policy instrument that addressed the issue of religious liberty in a helpful fashion.[95]

Hart did a number of things. He arranged dramatic testimony about the plight of Christians in certain Muslim nations by the Right Reverend Munawar Rumalshah Mano, Anglican Bishop of Peshawar, Pakistan, before the Senate Foreign Relations Committee. Bishop Mano was one of the few witnesses to actually endorse the approach of Nickles-Lieberman and link it to the context of his community around the world. In commenting on how the United States could most effectively respond to "the cry of the persecuted faithful," the Bishop said this:

> I understand the legislation passed in the House would mandate severe economic sanctions against countries that engage in religious persecution. This approach might have positive effects in certain circumstances, perhaps in Sudan, but I fear that in other circumstances severe sanctions could trigger reprisals against the religious minority for having caused the sanctions."[96]

The bishop argued that the Nickles-Lieberman approach would enable the United States to communicate to Pakistan that "we do not like what we see and hear," which would have a subtle yet "profoundly positive effect on the plight of the Christian community." The specifics of the Bishop's testimony suggest that he had consulted with Hart in crafting his comments.

Hart also participated intensively with the bill drafters and cosponsors, working on amendments, strategy, and communications. This effort in itself was notable in building bridges for subsequent faith-based initiatives. As Hart mused, "It was surprising to find myself in coalition with members of Congress who typically hold widely different ones than the churches take." This was especially true with the principal sponsor, and Hart was "totally, pleasantly surprised at both Senator Nickles, himself, and his staff's commitment from the get-go to be bipartisan."[97]

Hart took the initiative in assembling a religious coalition for the Nickles-Lieberman bill that included Catholic, Jewish, and various conservative evangelical groups. This meant that the liberal Hart made his case to groups like the Christian Coalition. And part of his pitch was that Nickles-Lieberman maintained the integrity and intent of Wolf-Specter, but was the only bill with a chance of passage.

Hart also drew upon the Episcopal office's close ties with liberal Democrats to lobby for their support, especially in the wake of the debacle in the Foreign Affairs Committee. As partisans regrouped for their final push, Hart went about building Democratic support for the bill in the waning days of the 105th Congress.

The Drive to Strengthen the Commission

Despite the above efforts, Nickles-Lieberman was still vulnerable to a splintering religious community, fierce corporate opposition, and administration intransigence. Thus a crucial question was whether Nickles-Lieberman could be revised to make it both more palatable to Wolf-Specter partisans and acceptable to Senate skeptics. One answer came in the form of a strengthened U.S. Commission on International Religious Freedom, which Horowitz championed. This effort to elevate the commission ran parallel to the work of the staff cadre negotiating changes to Nickles-Lieberman, and only toward the end of the session did these two initiatives merge.

As noted, drafters of Nickles-Lieberman had plucked the idea of creating a commission from the ill-fated Inhofe bill, incorporating it as a relatively minor provision of the Senate alternative. Once it became clear that the Senate bill was the only viable vehicle of responding to persecution, Wolf partisans mounted a campaign to fortify the role of the commission with Horowitz leading the charge.

The emergence of a strengthened commission as a central concern of the Wolf-Specter coalition reflected both the evolution of Michael Horowitz's thinking and a shift in the strategic milieu. When Horowitz first read through an early draft of the Nickles-Lieberman bill, he found himself crossing out section after section that he viewed as objectionable or ineffective. Then he came to a relatively minor clause creating a commission. He said that he liked the idea immediately, recalling the pivotal role of the Civil Rights Commission in advancing rights for African Americans in the 1950s and 1960s.[98]

By the summer of 1998 Horowitz began rallying his coalition to make a strengthened commission the centerpiece of antipersecution legislation, sometimes to the exclusion of other provisions. Indeed, Horowitz even suggested that the requirement for presidential action in Nickles-Lieberman could be dropped entirely in return for a more robust commission that would spotlight severe violations of religious freedom. To some this seemed an abrupt shift. Wolf partisans, after all, began by backing a bill with automatic sanctions and castigating Nickles-Lieberman as weak. But by the end of the summer they were, under the exhortation of Horowitz, saying that sanctions were less important than the "honest fact-finding" of a strengthened commission. This was absolutely mystifying to the Nickles-Lieberman cadre. Horowitz had been beating them over the heads about the weakness of sanctions in the Senate bill, then all of a sudden "he says he does not care" about sanctions. Even some of the original backers of Wolf-Specter saw this shift as puzzling. As one of them recounted: "I went to a million breakfast meetings that said we must have automatic sanctions, and the State Department was saying 'no automatic sanctions.' . . . One day I woke up and there was Michael saying no automatic sanctions." The abrupt shift led some to view Horowitz as acting erratically, especially in the chaotic weeks toward the end of the session.

In contrast, Horowitz perceived the shift as strategic "jujitsu." As the legislative process wore on, Horowitz recalled becoming painfully aware of a crucial flaw in the original Wolf-Specter. The provision for determining which countries were practicing persecution would be meaningless if an office in the State Department chose to "fudge the facts" about persecution to avoid embarrassing strategic nations. This would render moot any sanctions, whether mild or stringent. Since exposure and accountability were the original motivations, a high-profile commission might elevate the issue of religious persecution among policymakers. Moreover, the airing of abuses would allow the commission to sidestep the issue of sanctions, which was dividing the religious community and fostering fierce opposition from big business. Thus what seemed like a perplexing shift was actually a natural evolution.

Others in the coalition shared this sense. As one evangelical insider noted:

> When Wolf passed, we just hit a stone wall in the Senate. . . . The Steering Committee reassessed political realities, and took a second look at Nickles. . . . And the thinking kind of evolved, well, maybe what matters is that the American public get accurate fact-finding and information about the policy options that are available. . . . As long as everybody in Topeka and Seattle and Bakersfield can see what the president's menu looked like, the fact that he canceled the ping-pong tournament and a cultural exchange to Sudan, then, well, that will speak volumes to how little the administration is doing.

This emphasis on "honest fact-finding" demonstrates the line of logic from Wolf-Specter to the push for a strengthened commission. A common assumption, as one Wolf partisan observed, was that "we would never get a straight scoop from the State Department," that reports "would be highly massaged and diplomatically scrubbed." This skeptical view suggested the need for an independent and high-profile fact-finding entity, "not a low level functionary in the bowels in the Old Executive Offices." Needed was a body that "has subpoena authority, has a decent budget, has a staff, and has nonpartisan credentials to get this information as well as policy options laid out in front of the American religious public." To succeed, a commission must be truly independent "of Foggy Bottom and the White House," and it must have resources, "the wherewithal to do objective fact-finding."

These themes were echoed by a group of high-profile evangelical leaders recommending changes in the Senate bill that would enhance the commission's independence.[99] A commission that identifies and reports facts about "worldwide religious persecution," they wrote, "may bring the most direct and immediate relief" because of "the threat of exposure to global public opinion." Because "even tyrants modify their behavior to avoid being singled out as oppressive," the exposure of "honest and independent fact-finding" would be the key feature of effective legislation. The commission, therefore, should be "independent, with an independent chairman, and should be given a broad charter to investigate and report instances of religious persecution throughout the world." The chairman should not be "an appointed official of government, but rather a private citizen of great stature." The commission should have its own staff and budget, "so that it will not be dependent on the White House, State Department or other agency for support." Finally the commission should "not be dependent upon any process of referral from other agencies and officials." This latter point was in response to language in early drafts of Nickles-Lieberman that had the commission only responding to State Department reports.

This assessment guided lobbying efforts to change language in Nickles-Lieberman to ensure greater independence, support, and prominence for the commission. There was good reason for this effort, as the original commission would have been a creature of the government and with less high profile. Originally, the commission's staff and resources were to be detailed from the State Department and housed there. The ambassador would chair the commission and be a voting member. The prime responsibility of the commission would be to evaluate and make recommendations based on State Department reports. There was no explicit authority to hold independent hearings. The small number of outside individuals to serve (six), and the manner of their selection, also made it unlikely that the commission would have true bipartisan and multireligious credentials. Under these constraints, Horowitz charged, with characteristic acerbity, the commission would end up being "this rum-de-dum State Department advisory committee."

Former Senator Joins the Battle

As the summer wore on, the Nickles–Lieberman cadre accommodated some of these concerns, but Horowitz felt that features of the bill would not fly in the Senate and that "the principals" (the senators themselves) had not been engaged enough: "I knew that bill could not pass. It was all a bunch of staff guys talking with a bunch of staff guys." At the same time, Horowitz watched as his own coalition began to unravel, with some steering committee members, including Christian Right groups, switching sides and endorsing Nickles–Lieberman. Dismayed that they were endorsing a bill he saw as fundamentally flawed, Horowitz sought a way to regain the momentum. To this end, he called former Senator Bill Armstrong, a man with deep connections to the evangelical world. Horowitz implored Armstrong to get involved.

Armstrong agreed and played a role in strengthening the commission. The first thing he did was get a draft of Nickles–Lieberman, which members of the Horowitz coalition claimed was kept from them.[100] Armstrong then enlisted prominent leaders of the evangelical world to sign a letter to Senator Nickles, dated September 2, 1998, recommending changes that would enhance the role and independence of the commission.[101] Signing the letter were Bill Armstrong, Gary Bauer, Chuck Colson, Jim Dobson, Brant Gustavson, Don Hodel, Pat Nolan, and Pat Robertson. The impact of this letter remains in dispute. Staffers working on Nickles–Lieberman claim that several of the recommendations had already been incorporated in the bill,[102] and they viewed as modest those changes they made in response to the letter.

However it happened, the effort to transform the commission succeeded. Appointed commissioners were increased from six to nine, with the ambassador serving only as a nonvoting ex officio member. This allowed for a broader array of religious representatives on the commission. In place of the ambassador, the chair of the commission is now selected by the members themselves, thus enjoying true independence from the government. The selection procedure of commissioners was also changed to ensure that leaders of both parties and the White House select members, ensuring bipartisan credentials. The import of these changes can be seen in the caliber of commissioners. In the first four years of its operation, in fact, the commission comprised a broad cross section of prominent religious, civic, and human rights leaders with considerable political acumen (see appendix).[103]

Armstrong's intervention also made an impact on other senators, particularly fellow evangelical and retiring Senator Dan Coats (R–IN). Not only did Coats line up support from his colleagues for the legislation, he surprised partisans by securing an actual authorization of $3 million for the commission, an objective the Nickles-Lieberman cadre had dismissed as impossible in the waning days of the session.

This one action turned out to be pivotal because it gave the commission its own budget for staff and travel. A visit today to the Washington, D.C., headquarters of the U.S. Commission on International Religious Freedom shows how vital these resources are. Instead of borrowed space at the State Department, the commission has a suite of offices at 800 North Capitol Street. With its own independent budget the commission has hired an extensive administrative and research staff, complete with a press operation. A visit to the commission's website[104] reveals a prodigious amount of activity—frequent hearings, foreign travel and investigations by commissioners, and trenchant reports to government officials. Observers will also notice that the commission often takes tougher stands than others in the government, that its reports are refreshingly lucid, that it discloses inconvenient facts about American allies, and that it freely criticizes aspects of American foreign policy. While the commission has not been as aggressive or high profile as some hoped, it clearly is a more central player than the bill drafters originally envisioned and than some diplomats are comfortable with.[105]

The surprise of getting an actual appropriation attached to the bill, combined with other enhancements to the commission, gave Wolf partisans clear reasons to join in the emerging consensus behind the revised IRFA bill. Coats also let it be known among his colleagues that he saw the legislation as his swan song as a senator. And he threatened to use the vast parliamentary powers of a senator to keep the body in session (and senators away from their states in an election year) until the bill passed.

Enhancing the role of the commission also justified amendments that finessed some of the objections of the original Nickles-Lieberman by Senate critics. Senator Hagel, for example, was very concerned about the requirement of presidential action (however mild) against *any country* found to be practicing *any form* of discrimination or persecution: "It would be supremely arrogant for us to grade every country on earth."[106] With his colleague Grams, Hagel gained changes in Nickles-Lieberman that focused presidential actions on more serious violations, thus avoiding squandering the nation's moral capital on relatively trivial issues. Wolf partisans were happy with this change, in part because they felt the commission would provide accountability in identifying those serious violators.

Some of those favoring a strengthened commission went even further. The Armstrong letter suggested that with a properly strengthened commission the requirement for presidential actions in Nickles-Lieberman could be dropped entirely (if that "would enhance the bill's chances of passage"). Horowitz ran with this idea and drafted an alternative to Nickles-Lieberman that made the commission, not the State Department, responsible for leadership on religious freedom.[107] He floated this idea in a memo to steering committee members on September 23, 1998, just two weeks before the session would end, and sought unusual allies.[108] But this idea was never seriously considered because diverse stakeholders were rapidly coalescing around the amended version of Nickles-Lieberman.[109] With major objections accommodated and the commission strengthened, there was no groundswell for tampering with the legislation.

The final ingredient in sealing the compromise was Frank Wolf. If the Senate bill passed in the last days of the session, there would be no time for a conference committee to reconcile differences with the House (Wolf's bill). So the only chance for the new law would be if the House passed the Senate version without amendment. Wolf's blessing would make that happen. Senate negotiators had been in contact with Wolf, and when he assessed the final compromise bill and the strategic situation, he provided the pivotal signal.

The prodigious effort behind the IRFA blended diverse visions about how to promote religious freedom and prevent persecution. What is fascinating is how different visions among the partisans continue as the law is implemented. The U.S. Commission on International Religious Freedom has become the home of tougher and more visible initiatives. Early commissioners included a number of activists, such as Nina Shea, David Saperstein, Elliott Abrams, and Richard Land, who had been involved in the antipersecution movement, and the first executive director, Steve McFarland, was a Wolf-Specter advocate. The position of ambassador for International Religious Freedom, on the other hand, has been held by individuals hewing to the view that quiet diplomacy and positive approaches work best. The first ambassador, Robert Seiple, challenged the value of publicly identifying persecuting countries and expressed frustration with the commission for, in his words, working at cross-purposes with diplomacy. The second ambassador, appointed by George W. Bush, is none other than John Hanford, whose vision all along stressed less strident channels of activity.

A PROVIDENTIAL END

"It's a miracle this bill passed." Such was the common sentiment of actors in the arduous process that produced the International Religious Freedom Act of 1998. The messy ingredients of that miracle (the competing egos and acrimony) suggest the old adage that passing laws is a lot like sausage production—not meant for those with weak stomachs. As one partisan remarked about the IRFA: "It's true about the sausage thing . . . you shouldn't look too closely at how it's made."

Viewed in another way, however, the process looks providential, as if God were using the diverse perspectives, passions, egos, and pressures to create a unified and forceful outcome. Because it took so long to work out the compromises among the competing factions, the legislation had to be rushed through in the waning moments of the legislative session. Through a nifty parliamentary maneuver that bypassed the Foreign Affairs Committee,[110] Trent Lott was able to bring the compromise bill to the Senate floor on October 9, 1998. It passed by a vote of 98–0 in the final roll call of senators before the November elections. With no time for conference, and no one wanting to vote for persecution, the House moved swiftly the following day to pass the Senate bill by acclamation, thus ensuring, on the very last day of the 105th Congress, unanimous backing by both houses of the nation's representatives. Had the fighting among the factions been less intense, and the relations less acrimonious, the outcome would have been less dramatic. Had there been time for a conference committee between the two chambers, the resulting legislation might have produced dissenters and a mixed vote. Had the rival bills not enjoyed such vigorous advocates, there would not have been the groping for some blend of visions that produced what many—including Horowitz—viewed as better than either side began with.[111] Perhaps there is a theological lesson here: that partisans had to suffer through the process to ensure unanimity.

Many who gathered in front of the Capitol steps on October 10, 1998, to celebrate the passage of the IRFA saw this unanimity as indeed providential because it placed the government's unalloyed imprimatur on the cause of religious freedom around the world. Under a bright October sky there was a palpable sense of historic moment, as speaker after speaker directed often eloquent remarks to those abroad, to "tyrants who persecute" and "believers who suffer." After Senator Nickles described the bill as "one of the best accomplishments that we've made this Congress," Frank Wolf said that it "gives a voice to the voiceless." Speaking as one who had interviewed prisoners of conscience around the world, Wolf intoned: "The Catholic priests who are in jail in China today will know that this bill has passed. The evangelical pastors that are in jail will know it's passed." So, he observed, will Coptics in Egypt, Catholics in East Timor, Buddhists in Tibet, and other oppressed religious minorities. Wolf's friend, Congressman Chris Smith, displayed giant photographs of tortured believers—from a Tibetan monk to a Sudanese boy—to remind the audience of the stakes of the struggle. Chairman Gilman said that the legislation "sends a long overdue signal to repressive governments that their repressive behavior is no longer going to be tolerated." Persecuted believers will "learn that world opinion is awakening to their plight." Jeff Taylor of the Christian Coalition said that Congress had "taken the moral high ground . . . and served notice to the tyrants around the world that the spotlight will not be focused on them." Ari Storch of the National Jewish Coalition said that by shining the spotlight wherever "the darkness of persecution exists," the law would respond to the Holocaust admonition: "never again." Tom Hart called the legislation a fitting way to celebrate the fiftieth anniversary of the Universal Declaration of Human Rights. Will Dodson of the Southern Baptist Convention reassured those "who are living in fear around the world" that "we will work ceaselessly on your behalf." Rich Cizik of the National Association of Evangelicals spoke rhetorically to "the Chinese officials" he met who doubted congressional resolve: "To those whom I promised that this bill would pass, we have done it." Finally, Congressman Bob Clement reflected that God truly "reigned in this legislation," and he ended by quoting Isaiah 58: What is acceptable to God is to "undo the bands of the yoke and let the oppressed go free."[112]

Rhetorical flourishes, of course, do not predict the impact of the legislation, which will be addressed in the next two chapters. Here it is sufficient to note that its passage demonstrates how animated religious communities made a difference in American foreign policy. In spite of competing visions and fierce opposition, religious leaders and their followers shared the conviction that promoting religious freedom should be a key aim of America's global leadership. Because religious freedom legislation so appealed to a critical mass of Americans, and because it resonated with the nation's deepest traditions, it came to pass.

7

GENTLE AS DOVES, WISE AS SERPENTS IN THE SUDAN BATTLE[1]

Francis Bok cuts a striking figure. Six and a half feet tall but with the characteristic slimness of his Dinka tribe, he often leans down to speak, to utter simple words that seem biblical in their cadences and meaning: "I am telling my story to free my people in bondage. I will be their voice." In 1986, when he was seven years old, Bok was sent by his mother to the market some distance from his village in southern Sudan. Shortly after he left home, Arab militia, or *murahaliin*, swept through the village, killing Bok's parents[2] and most of the men, abducting many women and children, and burning the village down. Then they hit the market where Bok was: "I heard gunfire, then I saw killing. A twelve-year-old girl was crying, and they shot her in the head. Another girl they shot off her foot. I saw this happen." Captured by the militia, Bok was sold into slavery, to work for an Arab herder who called out his whole family to meet their new acquisition: "They all had sticks. They all beat me and laughed and called me '*abid, abid*,'" Arabic for slave.[3] He was made to sleep with the animals and eat scraps because, as his master told him, "You are an animal." He worked herding goats and cattle over miles of pasture and was beaten if any got lost. Isolated from his family and people, he tried to escape, but was caught, beaten, and told he would be killed if he tried again. After ten years in captivity he decided he "didn't care what happened" and escaped for good, fleeing to a refugee camp outside of Khartoum. But as word of his story circulated in the camp, he was arrested, tortured, and held in jail for months. Finally released, he sojourned to Cairo and then the United States, barely twenty years old, one of the "lost boys of Sudan."[4]

Bok is not simply a storyteller recounting the reality of modern slavery, riveting as that is. Rather, he has emerged as another powerful Christian witness to persecution and a new face in the struggle for religious freedom and human dignity. From Midland, Texas, where Sunday school children were drawn to him like a magnet, to Boston, where he carried the Olympic torch, to Washington, D.C., where he testified at congressional hearings—Francis Bok serves as an eloquent symbol of the faith-based movement that seeks to marshal American power on behalf of a distant people under siege. But if Bok and others in the exile community seem "gentle as doves," leaders of the Sudan campaign have to be "wise as serpents" to prevent decimation of the African peoples of Sudan.

The struggle over America's Sudan policy, which began in the early 1990s and accelerated after the passage of the International Religious Freedom Act of 1998 (IRFA), brings into sharp relief my argument about the role of the new faith-based human rights movement in American foreign policy. It illustrates how global religious developments penetrate American society, resulting in church-based activism that pours new energy into the human rights cause. The Sudan campaign also spotlights the role of religious conviction in the politics of human rights. Widespread atrocities committed by the regime in Khartoum went largely ignored in elite circles until Christian solidarity activists and their Jewish allies took up the cause of Sudan's ethnic and religious minorities. These activists tapped into domestic religious networks to generate a public groundswell for action, and they capitalized on the scaffolding created by the IRFA to bring pressure on the American government. In a sense, the faith-based community has plucked the tragedy in Sudan from obscurity and cast it into the light of international attention.

The Sudan campaign also illustrates how the faith-based drive against religious persecution forges unusual alliances. Sometimes miscast as a parochial cause of the Christian Right,[5] the Sudan cause weaves evangelicals into coalition with the Congressional Black Caucus, Catholic bishops, Jews, Episcopalians, and secular activists appalled by the indifference of the West toward this humanitarian tragedy. The Sudan alliance spans the cultural divide, with the liberal leaders of Reform Judaism working side by side with representatives of the Southern Baptist Convention.

With creativity and verve the Sudan activists employed a variety of tools—publicity, protest, grassroots mobilization, divestment pressure, direct humanitarian aid, and legislative sanctions—to alter the trajectory of Sudanese history. This campaign culminated in the passage of the Sudan Peace Act in 2002, which set the stage for a historic 2004 peace treaty ending civil war between the Khartoum regime and southern rebel groups. Thousands of former slaves have been manumitted, refugees are streaming back, and relief supplies now flow to famine-plagued areas once cut off by the regime, providing succor to a people long forsaken by the international community.[6]

In the wake of that stunning achievement, conflict erupted in the western province of Darfur, and Khartoum's response has been to unleash attacks on civilians that left thousands dead and over two million displaced. Not only could this action threaten the fragile peace in the south,[7] it created a humanitarian nightmare that the international community seems loath to address. Given an anemic UN response to date, United States action is the only thing averting further catastrophe. But sustaining and enhancing costly U.S. commitments to Darfur requires public backing. Thus, the fate of besieged people in Sudan, to a remarkable degree, continues to rest on the mobilization of American religious constituencies.

ROOTS AND NATURE OF THE SOUTHERN CONFLICT

In its 2002 report, the U.S. Commission on International Religious Freedom singled out the government of Sudan as "the world's most violent abuser of the right to freedom of religion and belief."[8] Colin Powell called Sudan "the worst human rights nightmare on the planet."[9] The regime in Khartoum earned this dubious distinction by its attempt to subdue or wipe out minority populations that resist its domination. Though periodic conflicts flare among the various peoples of Sudan, it was Khartoum's policy of forced Islamization, beginning in 1983, that sparked a twenty-year civil war. That conflict has claimed the lives of an estimated two million black African people, more fatalities than the conflicts "in Angola, Bosnia, Chechnya, Kosovo, Liberia, the Persian Gulf, Sierra Leone, Somalia, and Rwanda put together."[10] In addition, as many as five million southern Sudanese—out of a population of some 30 million—have been displaced, the largest percentage of the globe's internally displaced persons.

These figures come not from the religious advocacy community but from studies commissioned by the U.S. Committee on Refugees, a highly respected nonprofit organization. Millard Burr, a retired U.S. foreign service officer who coordinated aid operations in Sudan, sifted through thousands of pages of materials to come up with these figures on killed and displaced. In a chilling finding, Burr found that Sudan's own Statistics Bureau reported the dramatic shrinking of the southern African population,[11] which gives the lie to those who charge the faith-based movement with rhetorical excess in depicting the regime as genocidal.[12]

Despite this toll, and despite the fact that Khartoum's leaders declared the war as a means of spreading militant Islam into central Africa, the conflict in Sudan remained "Africa's forgotten war"[13]— until, that is, the American religious community engaged the cause.

The roots of the conflict can be traced as far back as the sixteenth century, when the Christian kingdoms of Sudan were defeated by Muslims advancing from Arabia, pushing the Dinkas and other tribes southward.[14] Since then, uneasy relations have existed between the dominant Arabic-speaking people of northern Sudan and African tribes of the south and the Nuba mountains. Though outsiders might sometimes see similarly dark-skinned people throughout the land, the country is divided both geographically and demographically. The north, which contains the capital of Khartoum, is home to a Muslim population similar to many other North African states. The south is home to various African peoples, the largest comprising the Dinka.[15]

The majority of these Africans are practitioners of traditional tribal faiths (often termed animists), though a substantial number (about 20 percent) are Christians who trace their roots as far back as the sixth century.[16] The central mountains contain the Nuba, a Nilotic people made up in roughly equal proportions of Christians, animists, and Muslims.

Though missionaries were expelled throughout Sudan in 1961, Christian churches have thrived in the south and probably constitute the most organized sector of the besieged African population. Catholics and Anglicans comprise the majority of this Christian population, though evangelical groups are notable. As we will see, church-based advocacy is shaped by these demographic patterns, as global Christian groups articulate concerns of the broader African population in Sudan, including non-Christians.

Long-standing rivalries in Sudan intensified when, in the wake of the Iranian revolution, militant fundamentalist movements spread among the Arab population. In response, Khartoum imposed a rigid form of Islamic law, or Shari'a, in 1983, which shattered the uneasy peace between the regions. Non-Muslims rebelled, joined even by some African Muslims who resisted the "contagion" of fundamentalism that Khartoum sought to spread.[17] Rebels coalesced in several sometimes competing groups, the most prominent being the Sudan People's Liberation Army (SPLA) and allied political movement (SPLM). Hopes for settlement were raised in 1989 when a newly elected government was scheduled to rescind Shari'a and grant greater autonomy to the south. Those hopes were dashed when General Omar al-Bashir seized power in a coup and redoubled the effort to unite the nation under the fundamentalist banner, forging an alliance with the militant National Islamic Front (NIF), which had never enjoyed electoral popularity but moved with alacrity to spread its severe version of the faith. The result: "Public floggings and amputations (including 'cross-amputation,' the cutting off of the right hand and left foot) returned to the stadium in Khartoum. Osama bin Laden was welcomed into the country, and Sudan strengthened its ties with Iran, Iraq (which it supported in the Persian Gulf War), and Libya—all countries that provided material and moral support for Sudan's war against the South."[18] Though Sudan has not received the same attention as regimes in Iran and Afghanistan, its attempt to Islamicize an unwilling people has been especially brutal.

Declaring its campaign a holy war, the regime has waged its jihad mostly against noncombatants, attacking undefended villages, burning huts and crops, indiscriminately killing civilians, especially men, and abducting women and children. To minimize threats to its own military, the regime has enlisted militias, or popular defense forces, from among the Arab herders, or Baggara, traditionally competitors with the Dinka for land. In lieu of pay, the government encouraged these militias to seize whatever loot they could capture, including human beings, thus rekindling the infamous Arab slave trade of generations past.

Calculations of the numbers of enslaved vary, with estimates from the tens of thousands to upwards of a hundred thousand.[19] Christian relief organizations provide crucial documentation of abductions in remote places, illustrating the unique role of faith-based networks in human rights advocacy. Through its extensive contacts on the ground, for example, Christian Solidarity International (CSI) reports that more than 25,000 children from the Sudan's Nuba Mountains have been kidnapped and sold as slaves. The UN Commission on Human Rights has received reports citing the locations of camps where people from northern Sudan and abroad came to purchase captured Christians and animists as slaves.[20] These ill-fated souls were often branded to identify them as property and maimed to prevent their escape. Often they are given new Muslim names and subjected to other forms of "acculturation" to the dominant north (Islamization and Arabization). UN Special Rapporteur for Human Rights Gaspar Biro, who began documenting the growing slave trade in 1994, noted the brutal extremes this practice could take. He reported one instance in which twelve adults and children were executed for refusing to convert.[21]

The Sudanese military facilitated slaving by providing slow-moving trains on which the militia can load their human cargo for shipment to markets in the north. In a haunting echo of the European Holocaust, some Sudanese advocates have demanded that these train lines be bombed to inhibit the traffic to slave markets.

Among the thousands abducted, women and girls are often raped and forced to undergo ritual genital mutilation and become concubines. African slaves are commonly branded, beaten, given Muslim names, and forced to renounce their faith. Horrendous abuses, from the cutting of Achilles tendons to crucifixions, have been documented.[22] Here again, Christian watchdog groups ensured that abuses would not go unreported by providing meticulous documentation. Field researchers for CSI conducted over a thousand face-to-face interviews with recently freed slaves for a report issued in July 2003 (see table 7.1).

Table 7.1.   Survey of Freed Sudanese Slaves

Among total respondents:

> 96% said they were forced laborers
> 96% said they were beaten frequently
> 60% said they were forced to convert to Islam

Among women and girls:

> 70% said they had been raped
> 60% said they had been gang-raped

N = 1,306

Source: Christian Solidarity International Survey, released by
Freedom House, July 7, 2003.

The regime also has employed scorched earth policies to manufacture famine, burning crops, killing livestock, and scattering people,
many of whom starve or die of exposure. It has manipulated the UN
famine relief effort, Operation Lifeline Sudan (OLS), by denying the
United Nations access to the very regions most threatened by mass
starvation. Massive population displacements have resulted from military campaigns aimed at terrorizing the population. Hundreds of
thousands of refugees have been herded into Orwellian "peace
camps," fetid places where many have died. In some cases refugees are
told to convert to Islam or starve. Emaciated women have sold their
babies in the hope of preserving their progeny, who are then raised as
Muslims. Summarizing the situation, Congressman Spencer Bachus
(R-AL) notes that many Sudanese are given a simple choice: "They
are either told to embrace the state-sponsored faith or die."[23]

Though the regime targets animists and Muslims who resist its
fundamentalism, it has literally attempted to wipe out Christianity,
which historically provided the cultural glue for the south. Though
underreported in the elite press, which often depicted the struggle as
"ethnic" strife, this story of religious persecution has been prodigiously
documented by a succession of UN rapporteurs, the U.S. Committee
on Refugees, congressional hearings, and the Commission on International Religious Freedom.[24] It has also been widely publicized in
Christian and Jewish circles, galvanizing a movement from the pews of
the American heartland demanding a vigorous American response.

The regime in Khartoum, beset by economic and political
problems, has also exploited a latent sentiment of racial and religious

superiority among Muslim Arabs and fueled it into a full-fledge ideology that justifies subjugation of the less developed and supposedly inferior African people.[25] When northerners contemptuously refer to Africans—whether Christian, Muslim, or animist—as *abeed*, the term is used interchangeably for "blacks" and "slaves." Osama bin Laden, who was a guest of the regime for several years, himself reportedly used the epithet and employed slaves, suggesting that racism was incorporated into his militant fundamentalist ideology.[26]

This regime's terror has also spilled out of Sudan. Khartoum has armed and financed the notorious Lord's Resistance Army, which conducts raids against southern Sudanese from its base in Uganda. This bizarre paramilitary cult has wreaked havoc in northern Uganda, abducting thousands of children to fill its army and rendering the region almost ungovernable.[27]

There is a word for a campaign of massacres, terror, manufactured famine, concentration camps, enslavement, abduction of children, and forced conversions: It is *genocidal*. Some take issue with activists' use of the term.[28] But it was meticulous documentation that led the U.S. Committee on Refugees to produce reports "Quantifying Genocide," the U.S. Holocaust Museum's Committee of Conscience to issue a "genocide alert" on Sudan, and the Commission on International Religious Freedom to depict regime actions as genocidal.[29]

To be sure, rebel abuses and factional fighting among the tribes in the south have also contributed to the misery of the Sudanese people, leading some commentators to equate atrocities committed by both sides of the conflict. The liberal Washington Office on Africa, for example, once reported that factional fighting in the south was responsible for more deaths than direct clashes between Sudanese government forces and southern rebels.[30] This could only conceivably be the case if restricted to *combat* deaths as opposed to the vast majority killed through manufactured famine, ethnic cleansing, and exposure. Moreover, as the Committee of Conscience reported, the government of Khartoum bears the lion's share of responsibility for the many fatalities in the south because it has used a "divide-to-destroy strategy to pit ethnic groups against each other."[31] As Sudanese Catholic Bishop Macram Gassis observed, while rebel forces may commit atrocities, only Khartoum has demanded that his people renounce their African heritage: "If we will not change, it will kill us or starve us to death or put us in chains."[32]

THE SILENCE OF THE WEST

"Why is the destruction of a black civilization unimportant to us?"[33] Variations of that plaintive question echo often among Sudanese activists. Given the staggering dimensions of the Sudan tragedy, one might expect blistering press exposés, numerous broadcast stories, and human rights protests from the West. Instead, a "deadly silence" for years characterized the Western response. To be sure, human rights groups did report on abuses, but we saw no hew and cry comparable to the antiapartheid cause in South Africa, nothing akin even to criticism of Israeli treatment of Palestinians.[34] News coverage, even after the faith-based movement took up the cause, remained amazingly spotty until atrocities in Darfur sparked international attention.

As noted in chapter 3, Charles Jacobs offers an explanation for this "silence." He argues that a syndrome afflicts the progressive human rights community and their media allies in which the depth of outrage has everything to do with *who* the victimizer is, rather than *what* is being done against the victimized.[35] Thus people of southern Sudan are abandoned in the worst circumstances "because they don't have the good luck to have the right oppressor."[36] If such widespread atrocities against a black African population were committed by a white government, instead of an Arab Muslim one, there would be massive international outcry and mobilization against the economic and military foundations of the regime. But because the raison d'être of traditional human rights groups is expiation for the sins of the West, he argues, many rights violations go undisturbed.[37]

While rights groups dispute this analysis, their most vigorous and worthy exposure of Sudanese atrocities came when Khartoum ravaged the Muslim population of Darfur. Thus, while the Sudan coalition was depicted as parochial because some of its members stress sufferings of the Christian population, the movement actually operated with a more universal human rights vision because it focused mostly on *what* was being done to the oppressed.

CHRISTIAN SOLIDARITY CONNECTIONS

The plight of the southern Sudanese people would have remained in the backwater of American concern had not the Christian solidarity movement picked up the case. Such groups as CSI, Christian Solidarity Worldwide, Samaritan's Purse, Servant's Heart, and Safe Harbor International highlighted abuses and facilitated ties between Sudanese religious leaders and American church networks.

From the mid-1990s onward, for example, Catholic and Anglican bishops from Sudan have been feted in American tours of church networks. The work of Faith McDonnell, a conservative Episcopalian raised in the Salvation Army, illustrates how these connections operate. She has been the frequent host of such Anglican bishops as Bullen Dolli and Henry Riak, taking them on American tours and enabling them to share harrowing stories of the persecution of their African people. McDonnell evokes the unique blend of the spiritual and political in the movement. An earnest Christian, she speaks in personal terms about the suffering of her brothers and sisters in Sudan. But her soft-spoken voice belies a steely determination to hold the regime to account, as McDonnell organizes routine protests with exiles in front of the Sudanese Embassy.[38]

McDonnell's effort in the Episcopal community also illustrates how the Sudan cause unites an otherwise divided church. She works for the Institute on Religion and Democracy, a Washington, D.C., think tank that frequently criticizes the liberal stands taken by the American Episcopal hierarchy. But on Sudan she and Tom Hart, the director of the Washington Episcopal office, shared similar positions. Taking his cues from the Sudanese Anglican community, Hart was a strong backer of the Sudan Peace Act and helped enlist fellow mainline leaders to join a coalition they previously eschewed.[39]

The most vivid illustration of how international church linkages propel the movement is the work of Sudanese Catholic Bishop Macram Gassis of El Obeid, who has gained an international platform to champion his besieged people. Like Bishop Tutu in South Africa, Gassis moves between worlds, serving as a religious leader of his flock and as an international spokesman for their plight. His diocese is larger than Italy, covering a good portion of south and central

Sudan, the very area afflicted by the devastation. He is particularly formidable because he grew up in Khartoum as an Arabic speaker, one who "should identify" with the north. Instead he has become, next to SPLA leader John Garang, the most visible opponent of the fundamentalist regime. A passionate, articulate, and sophisticated spokesman, Gassis draws upon religious linkages in Europe and the United States to generate pressure on the Bashir regime and to raise monetary support for relief and development. On his pastoral trips to Sudan he has taken religious leaders, human rights activists, and congressional staff members, flying into unsecured areas under threat from attack by Khartoum military.

In a crucial way Gassis is a channel between his African people and the global Catholic Church. In one of many vignettes, Gassis issued a blistering statement when he learned of the apparently intentional bombing of a Catholic school and other civilian sites in the Nuba Mountains in February 2000:

> With deep grief and dismay I have learned from my diocesan staff that the Islamic fundamentalist regime of Khartoum has once again unleashed its deadly bombers on the innocent civilian population of the Nuba Mountains. . . . I have time and time again told the world that the National Islamic Front regime in Khartoum has been, and is, conducting a campaign of genocide aimed at exterminating the Christian, African, and non-Arab populations of Sudan in order to establish a uniform Arab-Islamic fundamentalist state in the heart of Africa. . . . We cannot bring back the fourteen children martyred under the trees of Kauda. There are many Rachels there today, weeping for their children. What we can do is call upon the international community to refuse to stand idly by while the African and Christian peoples of Sudan are exterminated.[40]

This kind of eloquent witness helped spur condemnation of the regime by Pope John Paul II, along with action by leaders of the U.S. Catholic bishops, who sent delegations to Sudan, testified before Congress, and publicized their findings in local Catholic publications around the country.[41]

Gassis also moves in lay religious circles, which led to the creation of his American relief foundation. From the mid-1990s onward, Nina Shea, one of his key American compatriots, introduced him to a wide network of activists. Among those was William Saunders, an attorney then with the liberal Lawyers Committee on Human Rights. The meeting changed Saunders's life and provided a way for him to respond to a deepening sense of religious calling. A devout Roman Catholic, Saunders ultimately left the Lawyers Committee and joined the evangelically based Family Research Council to work on the Sudan cause. Here we see another illustration of how an "ecumenism of suffering" emerged in the nascent movement, with Catholics working comfortably with evangelicals to advance religious freedom. Bishop Gassis asked Saunders to set up a foundation—the Bishop Gassis Sudan Relief Fund—designed to channel supplies to the besieged Nuba Mountains. Saunders also promoted Bishop Gassis's work in numerous outlets, writing articles from the battle zone with such titles as "The Slaughter of the Innocents," "Christmas in Sudan," and "Grace Still More Abounds."[42]

By the late 1990s, the growing advocacy infrastructure in Washington created a ready audience for Bishop Gassis and other Sudanese advocates. Bishop Gassis was the first individual to testify before the U.S. Commission on International Religious Freedom. He spoke at the U.S. Holocaust Museum, met with senior administration officials and members of Congress, and traveled extensively around the country to promote his cause. What makes his story compelling is that, according to Saunders, Bishop Gassis is under criminal indictment by Khartoum and because of death threats travels under heavy guard when ministering to his flock. Indeed, he is now located in Nairobi, Kenya, having been forced from the country. Described as tireless and inspiring by numerous activists, he was given the Wilberforce Award by Charles Colson's Prison Fellowship International for promoting religious freedom in his country.[43] A powerful video documentary about his work in the Nuba Mountains is now commonly featured at numerous events around the United States spotlighting the plight of the persecuted church. It highlights the fact that the Muslim, Christian, and animist Nuba people had lived in reasonable harmony with one another before the war and now suffer equally under attacks from the north.[44]

As Gassis's story illustrates, one of the crucial contributions of the new movement in the American religious community was to

Bishop Gassis with two parishioners in the Nuba Mountains, Sudan. Courtesy of William Saunders, Family Research Council.

spotlight the religious dimension to the war in Sudan. Some secular human rights groups had reported on aspects of the tragedy the war was producing, and State Department reports highlighted human rights abuses. But as Nina Shea observed, what was missing was an appreciation for the *religious* basis of the conflict. To Sudanese in the south and the Nuba Mountains, the religious dimension was clear: Khartoum intended to eradicate the non-Muslim presence in the country. Yet this was not appreciated in the West.

A pivotal moment that crystallized this realization (and sparked the emergence of the Sudan coalition) occurred in 1998. A famine was spreading across southern Sudan, and the response of the government in Khartoum was to ban international relief flights, in effect seizing the opportunity to manufacture starvation as a tool of war. As Shea recounts, Khartoum's ban on relief flights to famine-stricken areas in 1998 brought "two and half million to the brink of starvation," and the "UN didn't raise a word of protest." It was clear to her that the government of Sudan saw the famine as a means of subjugating religious minorities as part of its "jihad," but others did not understand this awful reality: "The more I looked at it, I was astonished. It was about *religion*, and no one was saying that at the time. Nobody but nobody was saying that."[45] Instead, others were describing the conflict as ethnic, or as a battle over pastureland or water rights—concerns that would fail to elicit as much of a reaction from policy-makers as religious genocide.

In response, Shea wrote a guest editorial in the *Wall Street Journal* in the summer of 1998 titled "A War on Religion," which traced the tragedy to the military leaders' attempts at forced Islamization. Shea argued that if the religious freedom coalition "is to remain a se-rious force, it must now take up the challenge of seeking an end to the genocide in Sudan." "Nowhere in today's world," she concluded, "is religious persecution more appalling."[46] This conclusion ulti-mately would be echoed in government and commission reports and news stories, a vindication of the efforts by the religious community to clarify the stakes of the conflict.

SLAVE REDEMPTION TO FREE GOD'S CHILDREN

One linkage between Western groups and Sudanese people involved slave redemption as a response to the slave trade that emerged over the course of the civil war. The effort began as African family mem-bers "journeyed across porous front lines or engaged go-betweens" to buy their relatives' freedom.[47] They ultimately appealed to Bishop Gassis and other local leaders to try to find and return their relatives held captive. These leaders enlisted Arab middlemen to redeem slaves for payment. Among the slaves, of course, were many Christians.

Shocked by this brutal system of modern slavery, some Christ-ian advocacy groups inaugurated their own effort to free these "children of God" by systematic redemption efforts. The most aggressive has been Swiss-based CSI.[48] Heading the effort is John Eibner, an American with considerable academic credentials in in-ternational affairs,[49] who at the invitation of the New Sudan Coun-cil of Churches established the first Western-organized presence in 1992. Implored by local people seeking to secure freedom for fam-ily members in bondage, Eibner began redemption initiatives in 1995. Raising money in the West and operating through a complex network of local contacts, Eibner traveled thirty-five times to Sudan between 1995 and 2003, often dodging enemy fire and enduring harsh conditions. He documents redeeming over 80,000 Sudanese slaves during that time, and evocative photographs of these transactions circulate widely.[50] His evident courage and resourcefulness have earned Eibner enormous respect in religious circles and in the wider movement. Charles Jacobs says that Eibner makes him think of the Jewish legend of a few "undiscovered holy men who hold up the world."[51]

The practice of slave redemption has sparked controversy. UNICEF head Carol Bellamy denounced the practice, arguing that no organization should take part in any such transaction. UNICEF's credibility on the issue, however, was undermined by its complicity with Khartoum's manipulation of food aid and its silence on slavery.[52] More devastating were press exposés, which claimed that this infusion of western money led to corruption and even scams where rebel officials arrange for people to pose as abductees to inflate the number of slaves for redemption.[53] Even sympathetic Christian advocates acknowledge the potential for problems: "Anytime you have tens of thousands of American dollars coming into an area you've got potential problems of corruption."[54] Other activists noted that slave redemption "won't save Sudan," implying that it might siphon energies from more long-term solutions.[55]

In the wake of negative press reports, a number of Sudanese leaders and activists rushed to defend the work of John Eibner, noting that he undertakes extensive safeguards against abuse[56] and that many of the redeemed slaves have been held for years and show manifest signs of abuse.[57] Bishop Gassis pointedly criticized news organizations for failing to interview redeemed slaves and slave retrievers, or to report the research by Arab and Dinka scholars who regularly witness the redemption efforts of CSI.[58]

Eibner feels vindicated by events on the ground. Between 2001–2003, slave redemptions accelerated even as slave raids diminished with cease-fire agreements. Rather than fuel a "market" for slaves, therefore, Eibner believes that redemption made slaving more "politically expensive" by embarrassing the Sudanese government and shaming slave owners with exposure.[59] When the peace process created a window of opportunity, his organization was able to gain the voluntary manumission of 6,000 slaves in March of 2003.[60] After this Eibner declared the time "ripe for a mass exodus of slaves,"[61] and he gained the participation of UNICEF in identifying and repatriating those freed.[62]

Slave redemption also personalized the issue by providing the pictures. "Without slave redemption," Jacobs argues, "there would not have been the Sudan movement."[63] A great example is the case of Barbara Vogel, a Colorado grade school teacher who saw a photograph in a local newspaper of "a beautiful black girl who had been freed after seven years of slavery." The next day, Vogel read the story to her fifth-grade class, and "many began to cry," and they asked, "What are we going to do about this?" She investigated possibilities and found out about CSI's slave redemption effort. In a widely reported story, Vogel's students raised over $50,000 for CSI, which reported redeeming over 1,000 slaves with the money.[64] Vogel's students also created an organization, sent letters to political leaders and celebrities, and became featured guests at national events designed to raise public awareness about the crisis in Sudan. Their initiative sparked similar efforts around the country, leading Vogel to estimate that her kids helped redeem over 9,000 slaves.[65] A resolution passed by Congress praised Vogel's students as America's "little abolitionists," and a flag was raised over the Capitol in their honor on February 25, 1999.[66]

The cause of Sudanese slaves was especially publicized through Christian networks. A staff member for Senator Sam Brownback put Sudan coalition members in contact with the makers of the popular television program *Touched by an Angel*.[67] This led to a Washington meeting in which Nina Shea and other advocates provided producer Chris Williamson and star Roma Downey with background for a planned episode on slavery in Sudan. Shea helped write the script, which included numerous themes of the coalition's struggle. In one of the most watched episodes of 1999, the drama featured a plot about a female United States senator whose son becomes involved in a school fund-raising effort (like Vogel's class) to purchase freedom for Sudanese slaves. Graphic descriptions of civil war atrocities, slave beatings, and sexual chattel were interspersed in the episode with depictions of the insider world of power politics in Washington. Morally challenged by the angel, the senator ultimately overcomes lobby pressure and travels to Sudan to personally redeem slaves and thereby expose the horror of such practice. In the climax actual Sudanese exiles were featured as redeemed slaves returning to their homes.[68]

One of the most powerful impacts of the slave issue, not surprisingly, involves the black community. In the early phases of the Sudan campaign black support was limited to disparate leaders, such as anti-slavery activist Samuel Cotton, Congressman Donald Payne (D-NJ), and Chuck Singleton, pastor of the largest African American congregation in Southern California. Beyond these voices the plight of black Africans in Southern Sudan received scant attention by the American Civil Rights establishment and major black political leaders. Critics charged that such figures as the Reverend Jesse Jackson remained silent on atrocities in Sudan for fear of offending Muslim allies.[69]

But as faith-based advocacy groups kept documenting slave trading and other atrocities of the regime, black preachers with huge

Faith McDonnell of the Institute on Religion and Democracy with Rt. Reverend Peter Munde, Bishop of Yambio, Southern Sudan; a young activist; Rt. Reverend Enock Drati, Bishop of Madi and West Nile; and Rt. Reverend Henry Orombi, Bishop of Nebbi, Uganda at the time of the photo, now Archbishop of Uganda. Courtesy of Faith McDonnell, the Institute on Religion and Democracy.

congregations and broadcast ministries increasingly mobilized their followers to join the cause and prodded others into action. At a May 2000 rally Pastor Singleton joined an illustrious assembly of black clergy to kick off a publicity campaign for stock divestment and congressional legislation. At the rally and press conference, the Reverend T. D. Jakes, a prominent broadcast preacher from Dallas, chided black political leaders by proclaiming that "the silence of the righteous is fuel of the wicked." The Reverend Marvin Williams, head of an alliance of fifty black churches in Atlanta, explicitly challenged Jesse Jackson with the pointed rhetorical query: "Where is Action Jackson?" And Reverend Marvin Faulkner of New York City announced a forty-day hunger strike to pique the conscience of his black brothers and sisters.[70]

Pressure on established black leaders mounted as, in characteristic social movement fashion, new leaders emerged, fired by fresh energy and passion. One such figure is Reverend Gloria White Hammond of the Bethel African Methodist Episcopal Church of Boston, who was enlisted into the cause by Charles Jacobs of the American Anti-Slavery Group (AASG). She took a series of trips sponsored by CSI to Sudan—trips that received coverage in such national outlets as NBC and the *Today Show*. Her story was especially compelling because Hammond, a pediatrician, gave medical attention to ex-slaves disfigured by abuse, such as an eleven-year-old boy who had his nose cut off for losing a cow.[71]

The odyssey of Joe Madison, a popular radio personality in Washington, D.C. (known as the "Black Eagle"),[72] also illustrates how faith-based networks operate to expand awareness. Madison knew little about Sudan until he saw an interview with Charles Jacobs on a weekly PBS program devoted to African American issues.[73] Stunned to hear of slavery in Sudan and Mauritania, Madison began attending Capitol Hill briefings organized by the Sudan coalition. What immediately attracted him to the movement was its bipartisan flavor, especially at the time when President Bill Clinton's impeachment produced a poisonous partisanship atmosphere in Washington, D.C.[74]

At one such meeting John Eibner approached Madison to ask, "Would you like to go to the war zone?" In a life-altering move,

Madison traveled with Eibner to Sudan in the fall of 2001, then returned on a second trip in the spring of 2002 with former congressman and civil rights legend Walter Fauntroy.[75] The experience of personally witnessing the redemption of over 7,000 slaves "shook" Madison "to the marrow" of his "bones." Trying not to sound melodramatic, he describes how he literally fell to his knees when he first beheld the sight of so many black Africans huddled under trees in the bush waiting to be freed. Watching the emotional reunions with family members, he recalls seeing the face of a man who, looking for his wife and daughter, discovered his mother, too.[76]

Madison's return from these trips produced moments of high drama in the nation's capital, beginning with testimony before the Congressional Caucus on Human Rights on April 26, 2001. With his deep baritone radio voice resounding through the room, Madison captured the experience:

> After trekking through mud, heat, flies, mosquitoes, my eyes saw a scene that could have been staged for the movie *Roots*, except it was real. It was as if someone had placed me in a time machine and sent me back four hundred years to an African slave trade and I was witnessing the slavery of my ancestors. It was surreal. Thousands of human souls, Black Africans, citizens of their own country, dirty, sick, and hungry in the scorching sun, waiting under the branches of a huge tree to be liberated.[77]

Madison described gruesome evidence of atrocities committed against these people, many of whom he interviewed, and he then closed with the words of Frederick Douglass: "Slavery is the common enemy of all mankind. The slave is part of the human family. Slavery is a system of such gigantic evil that no one nation is equal to its removal. It requires the humanity of all of us and the morality of the world to remove it." As soon as Madison finished speaking, a Dinka woman stood up in the hearing room and sang a liberation song in her African tongue to a stunned and silent audience.[78]

Madison acknowledges the obvious racial dimension to his involvement, the sense of solidarity with black Africans, but he also points to his Christian convictions. He is very much a part of the faith-based constituency in the Sudan campaign. And his credibility helped overcome reticence in black circles to join a coalition that included

"Christian Right" figures. Black leaders would say to Madison, in effect, "If you say it is so, we believe. What should we do?"[79]

Crucial to the Sudan campaign was the engagement of the African American elite at the NAACP, the Urban League, and the Congressional Black Caucus. In classic social movement fashion the black leadership had to hear from multiple sources—from black clergy, antislavery activists, a handful of congressional leaders, and prominent Sudan activists. Thus, Charles Jacobs booked Francis Bok at black churches, Joe Madison personally enlisted colleagues, and Rabbi David Saperstein, who sat on the Board of the NAACP, vigorously made the case for that organization to embrace the struggle. When Kweisi Mfume, head of the NAACP, publicly criticized Sudan, that sent a signal that the movement was achieving a critical mass.[80]

The growing engagement of African American leaders, of course, produced one of the most striking "strange bedfellows" coalitions in recent history, as such figures as Kweisi Mfume, Eleanor Holmes Norton, Walter Fauntroy, and Reverend Al Sharpton joined evangelical leaders and staunch conservatives in Congress[81] in calling for tough U.S. action against the National Islamic Front regime. Reverend Sharpton, who had taken a trip to Sudan at Madison's urging, announced that the thought of running for president occurred to him while on a trip to Sudan, sparking Jesse Jackson to break his "deafening silence."[82] An astonished Michael Horowitz mused, "Who would have thought that Al Sharpton would be challenging Jesse Jackson for the leadership role in the American black community over the issue of Sudan?"[83]

This alliance was embodied in specific tactics. To challenge "indifferent administration policies toward the victims of a Holocaust in Sudan," Madison and Fauntroy joined Horowitz in a Good Friday 2001 protest at the Sudanese embassy, where they chained themselves to a fence post and were arrested. While waiting in the detention cell Madison and Horowitz began engaging in a bit of competitive braggadocio about who they could get to represent them, with Horowitz saying he knew Ken Starr and Madison responding that he knew Johnnie Cochran. Then it dawned on them that this would be a legal "dream team," and to their delight both Starr and Cochran jumped at the opportunity to serve as cocounsels. In a public relations twist, the trio decided that Starr would represent Madison and Fauntroy and Johnnie Cochran would represent Horowitz. Though the *New York Times* ignored the story, it did receive major play in the Washington papers and in religious presses that highlighted the emerging coalition of black leaders and conservative Christians demanding U.S. action against Sudanese atrocities. Photographs of the three chained to the embassy and then surrounded by counsels and Sudanese exiles outside of D.C. district court circulated widely.[84] "It's not going to be these three gentlemen on trial," Johnnie Cochran promised in announcing the legal strategy. "It's going to be the Sudanese government."[85] Fearing a show trial, prosecutors dropped charges against the three. But other arrests and demonstrations followed, including one in which Congressman Donald Payne (D-NJ) and Pentecostal minister and journalist Barbara Reynolds were "handcuffed and pushed into the paddy wagon" after their protest at the Sudanese embassy.[86]

RAISING PUBLIC AWARENESS

As the above vignettes indicate, a major goal of the movement was raising the profile of the cause. One of the earliest and most effective efforts at publicizing the Sudan tragedy was undertaken by the Boston-based AASG, the human rights organization founded by Charles Jacobs and devoted to fighting global slavery in its diverse forms.[87]

Jacobs, who is Jewish, came to the cause in 1994 when he read a small item in *The Economist* magazine about the purchase of slaves in Sudan. Appalled by this report of modern slavery, his first response was to call his congressman, Barney Frank, a liberal Democrat from Massachusetts, and Nat Hentoff, the civil liberties columnist for *Village Voice*. Both said they would investigate but encouraged him to take up the cause. So he "started making phone calls, met people from Sudan and Mauritania, did research," and wrote a piece on slavery in North Africa in the *New York Times*.[88] Surprised when his op-ed piece failed to arouse other human rights and civil rights organizations, he founded the AASG in 1995, which he has directed ever since, expanding the mission far beyond Africa.[89]

Though not overtly religious in orientation, the focus of AASG naturally drew Jacobs into the Sudan coalition. He has taken delegations to Sudan, written op-ed pieces for Boston newspapers, and enlisted others to the cause through nationwide e-mail blitzes. From the start he attempted to get around the "ideological blindness and obstinacy" of secular human rights groups by appealing to "the decent left," especially as represented in African American and Jewish circles. Jacob's singular contribution involved putting a human face to the tragedy by sponsoring Sudanese exiles to share their stories. Echoing nineteenth-century slave narratives, these testimonials resonated powerfully in American religious circles, but they were also aired in congressional hearings and news outlets. His success was recognized when Coretta Scott King, widow of Dr. Martin Luther King Jr., presented Jacobs with the Boston Freedom Award in 2000.[90]

The saga of Francis Bok illustrates how Jacobs capitalized on faith-based networks to magnify the voices of ex-slaves. After Bok left Cairo as a "UN refugee," he was resettled in North Dakota by Lutheran Social Services, and he later moved to Iowa. Out of the blue Bok got a call requesting that he come to Boston. It turns out that the man who filled out Bok's UN forms in Cairo was now working for Lutheran Social Services in Boston and had passed along his name to staff at the AASG.[91] With great reluctance Bok finally agreed to meet with officials of the organization, a decision that transformed his life.

In Boston, Bok was overwhelmed to discover offices teeming with activity on Sudan, photographs of Dinka people on the walls, Americans who understood. Bok agreed to move to Boston and work for the AASG by sharing his story. Understanding the power of Bok's testimonial, Jacobs arranged for his first speech at a large African American congregation in Boston, which was packed because of publicity that an ex-slave would be speaking. When the nervous Bok finished, the crowd roared and wept and "laid hands" on him.[92] Though Bok spoke in diverse settings from then on, Jacobs noticed that the greatest impact was in Jewish congregations and black churches. "People weep," observed Jacobs, when Bok implores them to "free my people," when he reminds them that God "opened the Red Sea" for the Hebrews but has yet to "open it for my people."[93] Bok went on to speak at congressional hearings, activist events, rock concerts, and even the Kennedy School of Government at Harvard, at which an official of the Clinton administration found herself grilled about "the president's silence" on Sudan.[94]

Jacobs also sponsored Abuk Bak, who was featured in the February 2002 issue of *Ladies Home Journal*, a magazine with a circulation of 30 million. Millions of potential readers saw the photograph of this delicate young woman and read her riveting account of how in 1987, at age twelve, she witnessed the killing of her kinfolk in the "Christian village of Achuru" and suffered abduction. She described how troops "threw ropes around our necks and began dragging us along like animals," perhaps more than a hundred women and children on a long journey to a stockade, a holding pen for the slave market. She was then sold into a life of unrelenting misery:

> I lived the life of a slave. Ahmed would wake me up before sunrise, and if I rose too slowly he'd hit me with a stick. I was given a little food and then sent to the fields to herd cows and goats all day. At sunset, I was allowed to come back but was only given the family's leftovers for dinner. After I finished, I'd have to wash clothes. Sometimes Ahmed made me work for 24 hours straight. I was so lonely. There were no other slaves nearby, so I didn't know anyone who spoke my language.[95]

In an echo of Francis Bok, she spoke "on behalf of those who cannot escape. I know I am one of the lucky ones."[96]

The growing publicity about the Sudan tragedy brought into the coalition activists who propelled the cause in different ways. One of the most fascinating is a seemingly unlikely activist, a professor of English literature at Smith College, Eric Reeves. The unusual turn of events that led him to raise public awareness on Sudan illustrates how activists largely outside of the religious world joined the faith-based coalition.[97]

A child of the sixties and "conscientious objector" during the Vietnam War, Reeves still proudly carries his draft card designation. Oddly, it was a hobby that turned his conscience to Sudan. When he wasn't teaching Shakespeare or Milton, Reeves developed such skill as a master wood turner that his works sell in major galleries. He donates the proceeds to Doctors Without Borders to build cholera hospitals in Africa. In 1998 that organization reported to contributors that the "invisible tragedy" of Sudan was the most

A professor of English Literature at Smith College, Eric Reeves relentlessly documented human rights abuses by the government of Sudan. In riveting prose, Reeves warned of looming ethnic cleansing in the western region of Darfur a year before the issue received wide international attention in 2004. Courtesy of Eric Reeves.

underreported humanitarian crisis of the year, and something "clicked" for Reeves. Here was "the greatest humanitarian crisis of the last half-century," as Reeves recalls thinking, a "morally unambiguous situation" that cried out for response.[98]

Riveted by the human rights tragedy taking place and disturbed by the lack of response in elite intellectual circles, Reeves decided to devote his 1999 sabbatical leave[99] to seeing what he could do. He did research, met with other activists and Sudanese exiles, and discovered a flair for writing opinion and analyses. Unwilling to give up his full-time commitment to the Sudan cause, he took another year's leave from academe's ivy walls by mortgaging his house. As he quipped, "What are home equity loans for."[100] Even when he returned to teaching, Reeves continued working intensely to raise awareness of the Sudan tragedy, in effect working two jobs.

Reeves saw meticulous documentation of facts as his stock-in-trade, a way to buoy the legitimacy of the movement.[101] This leads him to caution against loose activist claims, such as the assertion that sometimes circulated among evangelicals that the two million killed in Sudan were all *Christians*. But Reeves was not shy from employing potent rhetoric himself. Particularly drawn to the economic aspects of the conflict, he mastered the complexities of capital markets and Sudanese politics to produce trenchant reports that accused corporations with complicity in genocide (see box 7.1). As of 2003 he had penned over eighty op-ed pieces in such outlets as the *Washington Post*, the *Wall Street Journal*, and the *Los Angeles Times*, along with major newspapers in Canada and Europe. He also uses a system of e-mail broadsides, twice a week, that go out directly to hundreds of journalists, nongovernmental organizations, religious leaders, politicians, governmental officials, and human rights groups. Circulated widely through the networks of Freedom House, the AASG, and religious organizations, these reports not only raise awareness but link conditions in Sudan with recommendations for tough economic and

---

Box 7.1.   Eric Reeves: Intellectual Advocate

"Genocidal Ambition on the New York Stock Exchange," *Intellectual Capital*, November 11, 1999.

"Don't Let Oil Revenues in Sudan Fuel Genocide," *Globe and Mail* (Canada), May 4, 1999.

"Sudan's Genocidal Oil: It's Time to Divest," *Los Angeles Times*, August 30, 1999.

"The Netherlands to Ship Genocidal Oil," *Trouw* (The Netherlands), September 4, 1999.

"Mr. Clinton's Broken Promise on African Genocide," *Sunday Tribune*, November 28, 1999.

"Goldman Sachs, China National Petroleum Corp, and the Destruction of Sudan," *Newark Star-Ledger*, April 27, 2000.

"A UN Seat for Genocide," *Washington Post*, August 15, 2000.

"Oil and Human Destruction in Sudan," *Los Angeles Times*, June 4, 2001.

"Capital Crime in Sudan," *Washington Post*, August 20, 2001.

"The Terror in Sudan," *Washington Post*, July 6, 2002.

"A Brutal Regime Persists in a Distracted World," *International Herald Tribune* (United Kingdom), April 2, 2003.

"Sudan: The Unsung Evils are Rewarded," *Philadelphia Inquirer*, May 27, 2003.

These are a sample of the eighty-plus editorials penned by Eric Reeves, Smith College professor of seventeenth-century English Literature, who uses his academic flair for research and writing to highlight the plight of African Sudanese and to promote tough measures against the regime.

political action that would undermine the regime's incentive to continue the war.

Reeves works with a wide array of religious leaders, from liberal to conservative, so he thinks the "strange bedfellows" aspect of the coalition is overdrawn. But his research naturally connects him with those evangelical Christian groups that operate in Sudan because they provide essential on-the-ground information. One of his closest contacts is the field director of Samaritan's Purse, Ken Isaacs, an evangelical whose credibility and enduring commitment Reeves found compelling.

A telling pattern emerges in the stories of activists like Jacobs and Reeves. Both have become close allies with Christian figures in the Sudan cause—Reeves with Ken Isaacs, and Jacobs with John Eibner. Once again we see how the American religious constituency helps fill a void in a way that other activists gratefully acknowledge.

The successful publicizing efforts of Jacobs and Reeves also shine as exceptions to the limited national media coverage on southern Sudan. In contrast to the sustained, almost daily coverage of the antiapartheid campaign, reporting on the Sudan struggle was scanty, especially in prestige outlets.[102] Thus the activation of church networks played a crucial role in expanding grassroots activism, at least among certain sectors of the religious community. Such evangelical luminaries as Charles Colson, Franklin Graham, and Richard Land wrote and spoke about the crisis in Sudan, and their articles were picked up in numerous religious presses. The nation's largest Protestant denomination, the Southern Baptist Convention (SBC), became especially engaged in the issue. It is perhaps not coincidental that *on the same day* that the U.S. House of Representatives passed legislation in 2001 restricting oil investment in Sudan, the delegates of the 15-million-member SBC passed a resolution condemning the regime in Khartoum for its genocide and calling for direct aid to the victims.[103]

Religious presses were central to this public awareness campaign. *World Magazine*, an evangelical publication with a circulation of well over 100,000, featured Sudanese stories based upon trips by their reporter, Mindy Belz. She produced half a dozen major reports between 2000 and 2001 alone. Her reportage was facilitated by the missionary and relief activism of such groups as Servant's Heart, Samaritan's Purse, and the Bishop Gassis Organization.[104] She provided detailed accounts of attacks against specific villages, relief efforts by Christian organizations, political developments in the area, and overt appeals to Washington policymakers. Mindy Belz, to some activists, represented a courageous contrast to the lack of coverage by the secular media loath to take the risks involved in covering the remote war. As one advocate put it, "The major networks won't send reporters into southern Sudan because it is supposedly too dangerous, but Mindy Belz goes in." As of 2003 she remained virtually the sole journalist offering on-the-ground reports there, much to the chagrin of those who have been unsuccessful in prodding secular media coverage.[105]

Activists also raised awareness through college networks. In the spring of 1999 some 400 Christian college students, from Wheaton and Calvin to Harvard and Berkeley, many driving all night, landed with backpacks and sleeping backs at Georgetown University for a conference on Sudan sponsored by Freedom House and supported by the Coalition for Christian Colleges and Universities. The format was distinctly 1960s, with rousing speakers, such as the Baroness Caroline Cox of Christian Solidarity Worldwide, slide shows highlighting the brutality of the regime, testimonies by escaped Sudanese Christians, and breakout sessions on organizing strategies for an e-mail campaign by techno-friendly students. But for those who might have experienced time warp, there were also moments that suggested an evangelical flavor to the meeting, as when a young man stood up to implore his fellow students to join him in prayer. Creative tactics ensued, as when students at Southern Wesleyan University constructed a mock slave pit on Lincoln's birthday, while on another campus a student braved the cold in a makeshift slave pen for several days until at least 75 percent of his peers had contacted Congress.[106] The effort generated over 15,000 e-mails to Congress, which Nina Shea assembled and delivered to the House International Relations Committee.[107]

Another example of how Christian networks facilitated public awareness is the case of Christian rock musician Ken Tamplin. A well-connected recording artist and songwriter, Tamplin has produced music for major Hollywood movies and television programs and is a three-time winner of the Dove Award, the Christian version of the Grammy. After attending a benefit dinner for Christians in Sudan sponsored by his church, Calvary Chapel Costa Mesa, which featured Baroness Cox, Tamplin decided to commit himself to the cause: "I just thought, oh my God, what can I do?" What he did was pull together other Christian artists and produce an album titled "Make Me Your Voice," in which all the royalties went to Sudanese relief efforts. The title song of the album served as an anthem for the movement, and the pony-tailed songwriter was a peripatetic presence, attending congressional hearings, participating in Sudan coalition strategy sessions, and, of course, offering concerts.[108]

Tamplin was featured at a signal event called "Rock the Desert," a Christian music festival that in August 2001 drew more than 30,000 youth to the Midland, Texas, hometown of George W. and Laura Bush. This event was organized by Marcy Tull, a homemaker and mother who had developed an outreach to teens in the Midland area through Christian music, skateboarding, and other activities. Because she was friends with local activists on the Sudan issue, she tied the cause to the concert, which featured a mock slave cell and promotional material on the Sudan Peace Act. The concert was one of a series of events that catapulted Midland activists into a surprising role in the Sudan peace process, first lobbying for the Sudan Peace Act and then directly pressing all sides in Sudan to negotiate an end to the civil war. The pivotal moment turned on the selection of Midland to host the "national service" for International Day of Prayer for the Persecuted Church (IDOP), held on the weekend of November 3 (and repeated in 2002). In previous years, the IDOP always held its premier church service in a major congregation in a prominent city on the East or West Coast, but in 2001 organizers chose Midland, Texas, a community of 96,000 in population. In part the decision was strategic since Midland was the home of the Bushes. More importantly, the Midland community demonstrated extraordinary ecumenical élan rooted in its history. A deeply church-based culture marks this oil capital of west Texas, where Baptists, Catholics, Methodists, Presbyterians, and Pentecostals mix with a certain affability. When the oil bust shook the community in the 1980s, many Midlanders became engulfed in what locals describe as a genuine religious revival, with oil executives, homemakers, and a future president participating in Bible studies and prayer groups.[109]

As concern for the persecuted church bubbled up, Midland clergy and laity seized an opportunity to present the IDOP with an innovative plan. Rather than a single church service, the Midland Ministerial Alliance (which lists 200 affiliated churches)[110] proposed a weekend-long, community-wide event for maximum impact. Spearheading the effort was Deborah Fikes, who brought distinct experience to the task. An ardent evangelical, she had worked to foster ministerial ties across Midland's racial and ethnic divides. Plus, she and her husband had already taken the initiative to found an organization called Brothers and Sisters in Christ (BASIC), which supports the ministry of sister churches in Sudan. Hosting the IDOP literally launched this "self-described 'housewife' and 'rancher's daughter'"[111] into national and international prominence as a key Sudan activist, mobilizer, and citizen-diplomat.

During that November event, national and international speakers descended upon Midland, and on Sunday they fanned out to some forty participating congregations, ensuring that multitudes of Midland residents, including Laura Bush's mother, heard the message. Speakers focused on a number of persecuting countries, but Sudan dominated the discussion. For example, Baroness Cox spoke at the First Presbyterian Church about how her numerous trips to the Sudanese bush left her inspired and humbled by the faith and fidelity of Sudanese Christians in the face of horrific suffering. Down the street at the First Baptist Church, Kevin Turner of Strategic World Impact offered a fiery sermon, in a televised service broadcast throughout the region, about touring devastated villages where buzzards feasted on human flesh. But he echoed Cox's theme that the story is not only about tragedy but Christian triumph. He described standing in a crowd of 500 women and children when they were attacked by a helicopter gunship, which scattered the crowd and resulted in a ninety-mile track across the desert "with the body of Christ." In characteristic evangelic argot, Turner described how God delivered him when relief kits that he had distributed days earlier ended up being shared with their group by local Christians. Meanwhile, the Catholic church hosted a speech and video presentation by Gabe Meyer of the Bishop Gassis Sudan Relief Fund on the work of the bishop among the Nuba people facing extinction. Ex-slave Francis Bok was featured at numerous events, including at a local Hispanic church. And through-out the weekend Tamplin was ubiquitous, going from church to church offering music and singing his Sudan anthem.[112]

This experienced galvanized the west Texas community into be-coming ground zero in the grassroots campaign on Sudan and, as we will see, a strategic player in high-level negotiations leading toward a peace treaty.[113]

In 2002, as the battle for the Sudan Peace Act entered its decisive phase, the Midland Ministerial Alliance intensified its efforts and more explicitly tied them to the political situation in Washington, by invit-ing Sudanese bishops and other Sudanese speakers to the community. The repeat of "Rock the Desert," held in August during President Bush's Texas 2002 vacation, was bigger than the previous year, with 90,000 in attendance, and more focused on Sudan.[114] For two months prior to the concert, a team of some 200 Sudan exiles designed a live-in Sudanese village in the concert park, which they built side by side with Teen Challenge volunteers. Understanding the import of the po-litical moment, volunteers raised money so the village could be recon-structed in Washington, D.C., during demonstration vigils for the Su-dan Peace Act. Taking a page from the left's use of street theater, organizers for the Midland concert staged a raid by Arab militia, who scorched parts of the village area to show the devastation of the attacks. A group of sturdy souls even "fled" on a trek through the Texas desert. Dennis Bennett, founder of Servant's Heart, advertised the event be-forehand: "We understand that at some point, there may be a raid on the Sudanese village by Murahaleen (Muslim holy warriors) during the weekend event, so we will have our 'go packs' ready if we need to evac-uate quickly. Anyone care to join us for a 10–20 mile hike?"[115]

Initiatives in Midland and elsewhere, which received wide cover-age in religious outlets, raised public concern, especially among lead-ers and attentive lay activists in the evangelical world. A 2002 survey of evangelical elites—prominent pastors, denominational heads, entre-preneurs in broadcast ministries, and leaders of the array of charitable, development, and advocacy organizations—found high awareness of the tragedy in Sudan. Some 70 percent of respondents had "heard a lot" about the Sudan situation, while over 40 percent had actually contributed to an organization working in that troubled land.[116]

The threat of genocide, defined in international law as "a crime against humanity," also drew distinctive support in Jewish circles for the cause. How that happened is instructive. In 1995 Elie Wiesel, Nobel Prize winner and Holocaust survivor, prodded President Clinton to act against genocide in Bosnia at a public event sponsored by the U.S. Holocaust Memorial Museum. Out of that event came the establishment of the Committee of Conscience, an outreach and advocacy arm of the museum. Jerry Fowler, director of the Committee of Conscience, noted that this action flowed logically from the mandate of the museum to prevent future genocide through remembrance and action. Spurred by reports coming out of Sudan, the Committee of Conscience issued an unprecedented "genocide warning" for Sudan early in 2001.

Here was an organization with extraordinary credibility designating that genocide was in fact threatened in Sudan, a major coup for the cause. But activists like Mike Horowitz and Nina Shea found the museum's follow-up deficient. As Horowitz recounted the events, instead of announcing the designation at a public session with invited speakers such as "Frank Wolf, Don Payne, John McCain, and the President of the United States," the staff sent out a mere news release. Then the museum sponsored a series of panels featuring the Council for Strategic and International Studies (CSIS),[117] a think tank that Horowitz characterized as the "constructive engagement crowd" whose report on the "complexities" of the problem represented no threat to the Khartoum regime. Horowitz was livid that the Holocaust Museum would end up "just flacking the constructive engagement crowd." That would never have happened "in the context of South Africa."

Horowitz was not sheepish in his response: "Nina and I had the most knock-down-drag-out session at the Holocaust Museum with Sarah Blumfield," the director. "You're the Holocaust Museum," he remonstrated, "you can make it happen alone." Instead, the first big program was to "puff up the CSIS report." The fight focused on Jerry Fowler, who had organized the program on Sudan. With Fowler in the room Horowitz told Blumfield to "fire this guy" because he was "costing you an opportunity to establish the moral credibility of the Holocaust Museum." Fowler later responded with a certain equanimity to this roughing-up, noting that "getting along with people" is not one of "Mike's" strong points.[118]

After Horowitz's outburst, David Saperstein worked to calm the situation with the museum staff and to quietly make the case for them to tackle the issue aggressively. As the leader of the only national Jewish organization deeply engaged in the Sudan issue,[119] Saperstein had enormous credibility, and he probably helped the museum staff respond positively to the criticism by Horowitz and Shea. Saperstein also engineered a stunning grassroots outreach, which distributed an insert on Sudan to synagogues throughout America for use in Passover Seders.[120]

Ultimately the Holocaust Museum moved assertively. Fowler developed a powerful exhibit at the museum (with a companion brochure) on the atrocities committed by the National Islamic Front regime. Not only did this action raise awareness among the hundreds of thousands of tourists who visited the museum, it also signaled to Jewish leaders the importance of the cause. When President George W. Bush met with Jewish leaders in April 2001 for the Day of Remembrance at the Capitol, he was admonished to do something about Sudan's crimes against humanity. A month later he chose to address Sudan in a hard-hitting speech before the American Jewish Committee, in which he accused Sudan of "crimes so monstrous that the American conscience had to assert itself" and proclaimed that "my administration will continue to speak and act for as long as persecution and atrocities in Sudan last."[121]

SCAFFOLDING FOR ADVOCACY

The Sudan cause gained greater traction because prior efforts had erected a scaffolding for religious freedom advocacy. The processes of the 1998 religious freedom legislation provided hooks for Sudan action and publicity, and the U.S. Commission on International Religious Freedom featured Sudan in its various hearings and reports. Moreover, the campaign for legislation forged religious alliances and trust relationships among activists that served as resources for the Sudan initiatives. Thus, the advocacy infrastructure was quite robust and poised to respond to emerging developments. When the State Department produced a human rights report that seemed to temporize the tragedy in

Sudan, it was critiqued by Paul Marshall at Freedom House and by the U.S. Commission on International Religious Freedom.

To illustrate how this scaffolding operated, we can consider the role of Elliott Abrams in the cause. A former staff member for Senator Daniel Patrick Moynihan, Abrams served in the Reagan administration as Assistant Secretary of State for Human Rights and Humanitarian Affairs. He is best remembered as the point man for Ronald Reagan's Central American policies. Viewed by critics at the time as cocky, contemptuous of Congress, and tolerant of right-wing death squads in El Salvador and Contra rebels in Nicaragua, Abrams ultimately pleaded guilty to two misdemeanor charges of withholding information from Congress in the Iran Contra affair. This record led some on the Left to question his commitment to human rights, arguing that he had "blood on his hands" for his Central American role.[122] Diplomats inside the government, however, paint a picture of a person who aggressively pressed human rights against dictatorships of the Right and Left.[123]

After he left government Abrams went on to write a book about Jews in America, making the case for a renewal of faith as the only sure means of preserving the community.[124] His interest in faith and human rights helped lead him to the presidency of the Ethics and Public Policy Center, a religiously based D.C. think tank, where he hosted conferences on religion and foreign policy and authored hard-hitting articles making the case for the use of American power in promoting human rights. In particular, he argued against the highjacking of foreign policy by big business, suggesting instead that American leadership must transcend commercial interests. Abrams also linked the promotion of human rights and religious freedom with the nation's national security. As he put it in one essay, "It is wrong to suggest that human-rights goals are at odds with our national-security goals. We should have learned from our victory in the Cold War that the assertion of American ideals is essential to the advancement of our security interests."[125] Finally, he made the case for the deployment of U.S. power in defense of international human rights. To Abrams the unique opportunity of the times was rooted in a single fact: "For the first time in history, a democratic society is the dominant world power." Abrams pondered the prospect that the nation's power, combined with that of like-minded allies, could "be used to eliminate or at least reduce abuses of the rights of man."[126]

The passage of the International Religious Freedom Act of 1998 provided an opportunity for Abrams to act on these convictions. He sought and gained appointment as a member of the bipartisan U.S. Commission on International Religious Freedom, and in 2000 was selected chairman by his fellow commissioners. As a commissioner Abrams traveled to Sudan, where he heard from leaders of the be-sieged communities of the south and was stunned to witness the dev-astating impact of the extended conflict on the region. Abrams said he had never seen a land so bereft of infrastructure.[127] He joined with other commissioners in fashioning tough and creative policy propos-als, such as denying capital market access for oil companies doing busi-ness in the Sudan, which horrified market purists and officials of both the Clinton and Bush administrations. In a May 2001 article he out-lined that and other steps that the Bush administration could take "against one of the world's most brutal regimes."[128] Less than a month after publishing this article, Abrams became an advocate inside the Bush administration when he was tapped to become a top deputy to Condoleezza Rice, President Bush's National Security Advisor.[129]

We also see how the movement infrastructure operated among members of Congress. Religious freedom stalwarts Frank Wolf and Chris Smith took on the Sudan cause and were joined by Tom Tan-credo (R–CO), whose district included Barbara Vogel, Spencer Bachus (R–AL), and Donald Payne (D–MD). Tancredo describes his local church in Denver as his "window on the world" because that's where he learned about the Sudan situation. After House leaders granted his "odd" request to serve on the African Subcommittee, Tancredo traveled to Sudan. While visiting one congregation there he realized that his human rights journey "started in my church" in Denver and "ended in a church" in the Sudanese bush.[130]

In the Senate Sam Brownback (R–KS) emerged as one of the most important leaders of the faith-based Sudan coalition. He has trav-eled to Sudan, spoken at coalition events, and sponsored congressional initiatives, including an amendment allowing food aid to rebel areas that he has pressed the executive branch to use vigorously. He literally sees his work on Sudan as rooted in his Kansas forebearers agitation against American slavery. Brownback's colleague Bill Frist (R–TN) is a physician who not only traveled to Sudan to document the situation there, but under the auspices of Samaritan's Purse "performed surgery in a bush hospital bombed by planes from Khartoum."[131]

Elite access can be crucial to social movement success, and the growing advocacy infrastructure facilitated it. As Christian solidarity networks coalesced, evangelical elites increasingly paid attention to the crisis in Sudan and raised the issue with political leaders. Thus, even if the issue did not reach pervasively into the pews, concern was waxing among pastors, denominational heads, relief directors, national evangelists, and parachurch organizations. This was especially crucial in the presidency of George W. Bush, whose electoral base was heavily evangelical and who maintained personal relationships with such figures as Charles Colson and Franklin Graham. This kind of access was precisely what some insiders hoped would turn the day at crucial moments. One activist mused about a "dream scenario" in which Colin Powell and others at the State Department would advise the president to stay out of Sudan, and then the president would have lunch with Charles Colson and Franklin Graham, who would demand that he act.

Senator Sam Brownback at Sudan Rally. Courtesy of Prison Fellowship.

To a remarkable degree, something like this happened. Graham, who offered prayer at Bush's inaugural, personally pressed the new president on the need for American involvement in Sudan.[132] And a short time later a delegation of religious leaders met with Karl Rove, the President's top advisor, pressing the case for the President's intercession in the Sudanese conflict. The meeting illustrated both the access of evangelicals and their unlikely alliances because it included, as the *New York Times* reported, "Colson, the born-again Christian who spent seven months in jail for his role in Watergate, and David Saperstein, a Reform rabbi and longtime lobbyist for liberal causes in Washington."[133] Because of this pressure, some in the administration got nudged beyond their comfort zone on Sudan.

COMPASSIONATE AND CUNNING

For a number of activists, compassion for the people of Sudan first manifested itself in direct humanitarian relief. As noted, the UN relief program (Operation Sudan Lifeline) often failed to deliver aid to areas of greatest need because Khartoum banned flights to war-torn or rebel-held areas. While such secular groups as UNICEF refused to violate Sudan's restrictions, Christian groups moved with considerable daring to meet the challenge, violating Sudanese airspace and avoiding military patrols to bring tangible help to suffering people of southern Sudan and the central Nuba Mountains. For a growing number of Christian solidarity activists, traveling into war-torn areas of Sudan has become a crucial sign of discipleship, akin to the badge of honor that leftists gained in the 1930s battling fascists in the Spanish civil war. And the analogy is more than rhetorical, as those who personally joined in the people's struggle in Sudan witnessed attacks, viewed scorched villages and mutilated bodies, and dodged enemy fire as they delivered relief supplies in unsecured areas. They provided crucial information not available through conventional news or diplomatic circles. They are treated with awe in religious circles.

One of the most prominent of these is Franklin Graham, heir of the vast Billy Graham ministries. For a quarter of a century he has directed Samaritan's Purse, a highly respected organization that goes into some of the most desperate and dangerous places on earth. Ranked as the most efficient religious charity by *Smart Money* magazine, the organization delivered relief supplies and established clinics and schools in the midst of the civil war in Sudan. Graham brings a certain swashbuckling style to this work, taking delight in "personally piloting the group's small planes through airspace prone to artillery attacks and sniper fire."[134]

While such activists may lack a Hemingway to popularize their exploits, their initiative provides crucial information for the policy debate in Washington. Epitomizing this blend of field daring and policy sophistication is Dennis Bennett of Servant's Heart. A former banker with twenty years of experience in international risk management, he seems an unlikely advocate for persecuted Christians. But he got drawn into concern for fellow believers through his church in Renton, Washington. When he retired from the banking business he and his wife founded Servant's Heart Ministries to provide support to besieged believers abroad. Like many other advocates in the 1990s, he heard stories of atrocities committed in Sudan, and so he decided to develop a ministry there.

Bennett, who comes across as a hardheaded financial type, has taken numerous harrowing flights into war-torn areas of Sudan to deliver relief supplies. As of this writing his organization employs sixty people in the Eastern Upper Nile and Southern Blue Nile regions of Sudan, providing medical, educational, agricultural, relief, and spiritual assistance in the war zone. Through instantaneous global communication Bennett's network furnishes vital information to advocacy groups in the West. His on-the-ground reports of atrocities in oil concession areas, for example, gave ammunition to those highlighting the complicity of the oil industry in ethnic cleansing.[135] Later, when cease-fire agreements promised an end to the war, Bennett cautioned advocates to watch if Khartoum withdraws troops from the "garrison towns of Juba, Wau, Torit" as the litmus test of its seriousness.[136] Armed with this kind of information, activists signaled U.S. agencies and the Sudanese government of their highly specific lobby demands.

Occasionally Bennett's passion led him to pass along second-hand reports of atrocities that later turned out to be exaggerated.[137]

Such exaggerations provide ammunition to apologists of Sudan, suggesting the importance of maintaining discipline in the movement.[138]

Of course, this same passion led Bennett and others to circum-
vent the co-opted UN system that failed to deliver relief supplies to
areas of greatest need. Their heroic example prompted Congress to
appropriate more money for American relief to be delivered outside
of Khartoum's control. In turn, President Bush's relief and development team, USAID director Andrew Natsios, who was deeply embedded in the religious community, and his deputy Roger Winter,
who had been one of the key documenters of the humanitarian
tragedy in Sudan, worked to ensure that more aid was actually delivered to people in the war zone.

This kind of strategic realism was evident among the activists
who organized the political side of the campaign in Washington,
D.C. From 1999 onward a group met regularly to hash out strategies.
Most of the meetings were hosted by Nina Shea and held in the conference room of the stately Freedom House building near Dupont
Circle. Those who couldn't travel participated by phone hookups.
This group built upon the coalition that emerged during the campaign for religious freedom legislation, but it attracted a variety of
new activists, both in the religious community and beyond.[139]

What is striking in these strategy sessions is the blend of moral
zeal and hardheaded political calculation. Discussions focused on how
to frame arguments to avoid getting bogged down in side battles that
were hard to understand or justify, such as the nature of the SPLA.[140]
Instead, the group focused on framing cogent aims, such as getting
food to starving people, busting the flight ban imposed by Sudan, ending its manipulation of food aid as a weapon of war, scaring away investment in oil companies profiting from "blood money." Discussion
also turned on who could get to what senator, when to mobilize publicity in religious outlets. The group moved from pressing the Brownback amendment, which provided for U.S. food aid to be distributed
outside the flawed UN system, to the Bachus provision denying capital market access to oil companies doing business in Sudan, to a divestment campaign against such oil companies. The group also
mounted pressure on the Securities and Exchange Commission, the
State Department, and the White House to take action against Sudan.

Formidable bureaucratic obstacles had to be shattered for such action to occur. In a telling meeting with President Clinton's Secretary of State Madeline Albright, a group of coalition activists pressed her to charge Sudan with genocide. Albright reportedly turned to her assistant, who responded that the State Department couldn't do that because such a designation of "crimes against humanity," according to international law, would require serious action by the American government.[141] Because the human rights situation in Sudan was "not marketable to the American people,"[142] such serious action was not possible.

Such thinking, Horowitz argued, was guilty of the "sin of static political analysis." When social movements reach critical mass they "change everything." Thus presidential attention and international media coverage would expose Sudan as a pariah state, threaten its oil investment, and shame European nations for their acquiescence to atrocities. As the campaign waxed, in fact, religious and political leaders in the United Kingdom and Australia, among other countries, took up the cause.[143]

Sudan activists pressed on a variety of policy fronts, using incremental victories as windows to more bold initiatives. For example, the coalition promoted monitoring teams to investigate atrocities on the ground in Sudan. Eric Reeves made a particularly compelling case for such teams. Reeves pointed to a specific case in the Western Upper Nile town of Lare where monitors discovered that the "formerly thriving area of over 9,000 inhabitants" was virtually vacant. He then chastised the State Department's Africa bureau for its failure to renew the mandate for the Civilian Monitoring Team.[144] Because the coalition helped keep monitoring teams on the ground, information on fresh atrocities kept pressure for more dramatic policies.

Forging unusual alliances was crucial to the campaign's successes. The coalition included diverse religious groups, the Congressional Black Caucus, national security hawks, and antislavery organizations. One of the intriguing episodes in the struggle has involved a linkage with the formidable pro-Israel lobby, the American Israel Public Affairs Committee (AIPAC). As various Sudan initiatives were gaining prominence on the political agenda, the Iran-Libya Sanctions Act was coming up for renewal in 2001. The legislation, strongly backed by AIPAC, levied sanctions against Iran and Libya for their support of international terrorism (often aimed at Israel). The act provided an opportunity for the Sudan coalition to piggyback on the renewal by adding Sudan to the legislation. This was precisely what Nina Shea and others sought, but AIPAC wanted a "clean bill" without such an addition. This strategic reality provided an opportunity for a deal that Horowitz helped broker, in which AIPAC agreed to back capital market sanctions legislation against Sudan in return for the coalition not attempting to attach Sudan to the Iran-Libya Act. When AIPAC faltered in its follow-though, Horowitz apparently let the word out, and a major story appeared that described AIPAC as "reneging" on its commitment.[145] This was but one of numerous skirmishes in the most audacious campaign of the Sudan coalition—the drive to deny oil revenue to the regime in Khartoum.

CONTENDING WITH MAMMON

In the 1999 episode of *Touched by an Angel*, the fictional female senator is confronted by a lobbyist for the confectionary industry who demands that she not raise the issue of slavery in Sudan. The reason: Sudan is the globe's largest exporter of gum arabic, an essential ingredient in soft drinks and candies. Though simplified for dramatic effect, the episode captured one of the peculiar features of the Sudan story. Under heavy sanctions by the United States for its support of international terrorism, Sudan nonetheless was able, in varying ways, to continue selling its gum arabic to U.S. companies. At one point, the industry gained passage of an obscure trade bill provision that suspended sanctions on gum arabic, which produced a stinging *Washington Post* editorial rebuke that such action would drain any "virtuous diplomacy" of its authority.[146] Partisans found attacking this monied interest difficult, however, because at least some southern Sudanese arguably benefit from the export of gum arabic, and because Europeans would merely pick up the market after U.S. sanctions.

Wrangling over gum arabic quickly receded, however, as another more powerful economic interest loomed over the conflict in Sudan: oil. Spurred by billions of dollars of international investment, Sudan's oil fields, most located in the south, became linked by pipeline to northern ports by the late 1990s. While the issue of gum arabic seemed ambiguous, the implication of the new oil development to African Sudanese was clear: It imperiled their survival. Millions in oil revenue enabled Sudan to buy advanced weaponry, and it spurred brutal ethnic cleansing in areas surrounding the oil fields.[147] But contending with mammon meant contending with multinational oil companies and their powerful investors.

As an innovative response to this challenge the Sudan movement turned to capital market strategies as a tool of human rights advocacy. When it became clear that oil revenue was fueling the war, activists initiated efforts to deny international capital to companies developing Sudan's oil industry. Strategies included divestment campaigns, disclosure rules to scare away potential investors, and the denial of access to U.S. capital markets. This audacious campaign reveals how the movement blends religious passion with the expertise and connections of diverse actors drawn to the cause.

One of the early voices in this campaign was Dennis Bennett, whose banking experience drew him into researching the economic aspects of the conflict. His investigation in 1996 led him to conclude that the government of Sudan was essentially broke, leading him to ponder the question: "How could a country so heavily in debt spend a million dollars a day on this civil war?" He concluded that "it was by the promise of future revenues of oil."[148]

By 1998 that oil began flowing, enabling Khartoum to purchase up-to-date weaponry. Because of U.S. sanctions, no American companies were involved in Sudan's oil industry at the time, but firms from Canada, China, Malaysia, and Indonesia operated under concessions from the Sudanese government.

From the manufactured famine in 1998 onward, developments on the ground provided corroboration that oil revenue might enable Khartoum to break the tenuous hold of southern tribes against its military advances. This ominous prospect emerged from documentation by both religious groups and independent nongovernmental organizations.[149] In a presentation in April 1999 Roger Winter, then director of the U.S. Committee on Refugees, explicitly highlighted the role of Talisman Energy of Canada in developing Sudan's new oil industry. It was this briefing that led Eric Reeves to publish a series of articles on the link between oil revenue and atrocities, which helped spark the divestment campaign against Talisman.[150]

Talisman Energy of Canada, which purchased concessions in 1998, emerged as a crucial target of the Sudan campaign for two reasons: (1) it was building some of the largest and most sophisticated oil infrastructure in Sudan, and (2) as a company based in an open society it was more vulnerable to divestment efforts. This became apparent in 1999 when Eric Reeves fired off the first of his editorial salvos. His piece, "Don't Let Oil Revenues in Sudan Fuel Genocide," published in a leading Canada newspaper, "hit like a bombshell in the investment community."[151] Reeves followed up with an article in the *Los Angeles Times* that for the first time called for divestment of Talisman stock. Activists quickly seized on divestment as a key strategy in their campaign. In classic social movement style, loosely coordinated initiatives sprouted in diverse places. Letters to fund managers went out from the movement's amalgam of Christian solidarity groups, antislavery activists, Jewish leaders, and black pastors, calling for a selloff of Talisman stock. Students organized divestment initiatives with their college funds. These efforts helped spread incendiary publicity about Talisman's "complicity" with genocide.

The anti–Talisman campaign illustrates the ways movement effervescence sprouts diverse initiatives and tactics.[152] In one instance Tommy Calvert, a Tufts University student recruited by the American Anti-Slavery Group, joined with Reeves and others in the successful effort to convince the huge college professors pension fund, TIAA-CREFF, to sell its sizable Talisman holdings. Reeves describes a first meeting with pension managers, who said in effect, "We don't do divestment." But confronted with the damaging case against Talisman, and faced with a coalition that included the Congressional Black Caucus, Jewish groups, evangelical leaders, and college students, the managers divested within three weeks. Oddly, Reeves viewed the battle as a mismatch, arguing that the company "didn't have a chance," that it could not take such public scrutiny.[153]

Reeves was right, as the divestment campaign was devastating to Talisman. Indeed, after TIAA-CREFF liquidated Talisman stock, the coalition "ran the tables" on major fund managers from Canada and the United States. Cities, states, and national church denominations all sold Talisman stock. New Jersey alone liquidated 800,000 shares of Talisman under pressure from numerous sides, including intervention by two of its most prominent congressional members, Donald Payne, a Democrat, and Chris Smith, a Republican. Activists cheered the news when Talisman's stock plummeted, but Talisman's problems did not end there.

From 1998 onward Christian relief organizations and human rights monitors on the ground documented the decimation of southern villages, massacres, and abductions in oil concession areas, suggesting a calculated military campaign by the Sudanese government to remove populations in the way of its exploitation of oil located in the south. This led to charges that multinational companies, aware of ethnic cleansing of villages near oil fields and pipelines, were complicit in the atrocities.[154] Hard evidence surfaced when the AASG secured an internal memo which suggested that Talisman officials knew and were working with Sudanese armed forces as they conducted operations.[155]

Armed with this information a coalition of American and Canadian activists filed a multimillion dollar civil lawsuit against Talisman on November 11, 2001. The class action suit was filed on behalf of non-Muslims and African Sudanese living within fifty miles of Talisman's oil production concessions areas. Drawing upon documentation by religious relief organizations of ethnic cleansing around oil fields and pipelines, the suit filed "accused the company of collaborating with Sudan" to commit war crimes, including murder, forced displacement, destruction of property, rape, and enslavement. In a move with potentially far-reaching human rights implications, a U.S. District Judge refused to dismiss the suit and ruled in March 2003 that Talisman could be held liable for genocide if the facts warranted. The suit is pending trial.[156]

Even as the movement mounted its campaign against Talisman, a new target loomed on the horizon. Word leaked out that the investment firm of Goldman Sachs was planning to manage an Initial Public Offering (IPO) for China National Petroleum Company (CNPC), which hoped to raise $8–10 billion to develop its stake in Sudan. In yet another example of the role of movement connections,

Eric Reeves, who wrote one of the first pieces on the implications of the IPO, credits Dennis Bennett for giving him the "heads-up" on the sale. The threat posed by this massive infusion of investment money sparked efforts by Sudan activists to scare away potential investors. From late 1999 into 2000, articles blossomed in evangelical publications and advocacy outlets, letters went out to large investors, and sympathetic political leaders weighed in with charges that this stock offering would be "blood money" for Sudan's attempt to eradicate a people.[157] Critics of the Chinese government, from labor unions to Tibetan advocates, jumped on board the campaign.

Though estimates vary, the effort "hammered" CNPC, denying a large portion of the hoped-for capital. Reeves claimed that CNPC raised only $3 billion of its $10 billion goal. This "$7 billion haircut," especially since it represented the first wave of such capital-raising by Chinese industry, sent shock waves through the investment community. Not only did this episode signal that the movement was a force to be reckoned with, but it affected the situation on the ground. As Bennett quipped, "If China had raised all the money it wanted, the SPLA would have been toast" because with such an infusion Khartoum would overrun rebel opposition.[158]

The success in scaring away capital for Sudan's oil industry suggests that sovereign nations cannot always assume that investors will be able to ignore human rights abuses. It also buoyed those who have other complaints with the actions of global corporations. One such figure is Roger Robinson, a former official of the National Security Council in the Reagan administration. As chairman of the William Casey Institute, a national security think tank, Robinson spotlights the dangers posed by companies selling advanced technology (suitable for weapons) to rogue regimes and other potential adversaries of the United States. For several years Robinson has been advancing creative proposals for greater disclosure of these practices with the Securities and Exchange Commission (SEC). The idea was to let investors know the "material risk" they faced buying shares of companies doing business with "bad actors," some of them under U.S. sanction.

The story of how Roger Robinson was drawn into the coalition suggests the magnetic power of movements to foster diverse coalitions. As the Sudan campaign heated up, a natural alliance emerged between Christian advocates concerned about religious persecution and national security hawks. Robinson, for example, became enlisted in the Sudan cause after a lunch meeting in 1999 with Nina Shea, in which she outlined how the same regime that provided haven to Osama bin Laden was engaged in a "jihad" against its own people and hoping to spread that fundamentalist movement into Africa. This alliance, as one activist noted, "was a marriage made in heaven." Each gained allies in the other's cause, but the benefits went beyond that. The religious community gained the expertise of the Casey Institute on capital markets, while the Casey Institute got the tangible case of Sudan to test its policy approach.

This alliance produced a striking convergence of national security, human rights, and religious freedom concerns, which led groups and key members of Congress to press the SEC to strengthen disclosure and transparency requirements with respect to global "bad actors" seeking to raise funds in bond and equity markets. In a letter to Congressman Frank Wolf, SEC's Acting Chair, Laura Unger, acknowledged the role of the Casey Institute, the U.S. Commission on International Religious Freedom, and the State Department Office of International Religious Freedom in making the case for action by the SEC.[159] Then in a move that achieved international business coverage in May 2001, the SEC in effect announced that "national security, human rights, and religious freedom will be viewed by the SEC as potentially material risks to U.S. and other investors, thereby requiring new echelons of disclosure and transparency."[160] Translated, this means that pension fund managers will have information on massive human rights abuses so that they can avoid such risky ventures. The energy behind the faith-based Sudan movement, in this case, led to policy innovations that may provide new levers for subsequent human rights causes.

The blending of concerns for religious freedom, human rights, and national security also produced what activists themselves viewed as wonderfully quirky relationships. Roger Robinson, the Reaganite hawk, worked closely with Eric Reeves, the wood-turning child of the sixties, who worked with Ken Isaacs, the evangelical relief director.

CAPITAL MARKET STRATEGIES IN THE
SUDAN PEACE ACT

Scaring away investors could only go so far in maintaining pressure on the Khartoum regime to cease attacks on civilians. This reality led the coalition to press Congress for an even more ambitious hammer. Once again, we observe how the movement acted as a magnet, drawing together disparate groups in the legislative battle, this time for a law denying access to U.S. capital markets for all oil companies doing business in Sudan.

The first major organization to advance this concept was the U.S. Commission on International Religious Freedom. Backed by the work of Robinson, Reeves, and Jacobs, Nina Shea took a proposal to the commission to back capital market sanctions against Sudan. Two of the commissioners, Elliott Abrams and Chair David Saperstein, were already involved in the Sudan campaign and advanced the proposal. But ultimately all members of the commission embraced the idea as a way to fulfill the spirit of the commission's legislative charter to promote policies aimed at addressing religious persecution. In its March 2001 report on Sudan, the commission declared that oil revenue was exacerbating atrocities, and it recommended that foreign oil companies be denied access to U.S. capital markets while Sudan prosecuted the war against its own people.[161]

This idea of delisting certain companies from U.S. stock markets was bold but plausibly efficacious: Check Khartoum's aggression by restricting dollars for its oil development. And commissioners advanced this case in numerous forums. Elliott Abrams made the case that U.S. policy should force foreign companies to choose: "Be in Sudan, or be in our capital markets."[162] His colleague, Michael Young (a Mormon), testified to Congress that the "only way to get Khartoum's attention is to curtail its oil revenues."[163]

The commission's idea was ultimately picked up by Congressman Spencer Bachus (R–AL), a soft-spoken Alabaman with an uncanny sense of moral clarity. "When you have to make a choice between dollars and lives," he told evangelical leaders at one forum, "you choose lives."[164] In the summer of 2001, Bachus successfully attached an amendment to the proposed Sudan Peace Act that would deny access to American stock exchanges for oil companies doing business in Sudan. That legislation passed the House of Representatives by a stunning vote of 422–2.[165] In attempting to convince their Senate colleagues to back the legislation, House members argued that it merely closed a loophole: "Why do we allow foreign companies that obtain Sudanese oil to trade on our capital markets when American companies are prohibited from doing so?"[166] But to Washington insiders the Bachus Amendment suggested a new strategic boldness in the faith-based movement.

Ironically, the Bush administration's "ham-handed"[167] effort to appoint a special envoy to Sudan helped produce the Bachus Amendment. Barely a month after the president's dramatic condemnation of Sudan before the American Jewish Committee (in May 2001), Secretary of State Colin Powell chose as special envoy Chester Crocker, a previous advocate of "constructive engagement" with apartheid in South Africa. To Sudan advocates, Crocker would have temporized the evil of the regime, as indicated by his stated opinion that policy should not "tilt toward the Christians" in Sudan. When his views were made public, Sudan activists, from members of the Congressional Black Caucus to Jewish groups to Christian organizations, criticized the appointment, and Crocker withdrew his name from consideration.[168] Crocker's derisive statements angered activists and united them behind the "radical" approach embraced by Bachus later that summer.

The House success of the Bachus Amendment caused apoplexy in the investment community. Alan Greenspan testified against the Bachus Amendment, and the big guns on Wall Street weighed in to lobby against Senate passage. One lobbyist for Goldman Sachs said that every PAC dollar coming out of Wall Street would have "Bachus written all over it."[169] This opposition led some in the coalition to predict that such shortsightedness would come back to haunt the business community. Indeed, in a bizarre twist Charles Jacobs was prepared to deliver a line in his press conference speech on the morning of September 11 pointedly challenging Alan Greenspan's opposition to capital market leverage: "Alan, don't you realize that this kind of terrorism will find you on Wall Street?"[170] The speech was never delivered.

Not only Wall Street leaders, but officials of the Bush administration opposed the Bachus Amendment's radical departure from free market capitalism. As one insider quipped, "These are Republicans." Together, the Bush administration and the investment lobby convinced the Senate to omit the provision in its version of the Sudan Peace Act. Even such Sudanese advocates as Senator Bill Frist resisted the capital market tool.

The battle over the Bachus Amendment reflected the willingness of the interfaith coalition to take on entrenched economic interests. But it also pointed toward a growing foreign-policy divide in the GOP between religious moralists and market purists. As Republican Congressman Chris Smith put it, "I'm a free market guy," but "when it comes to a country that has killed two million people," exceptional sanctions are justified.[171] This divide simmered within the Bush administration itself. While the president accused Sudan of "crimes so monstrous that the American conscience had to assert itself," his economic advisers vehemently opposed acting on that conviction.

The main argument against the Bachus Amendment was that cutting access to U.S. capital markets would be ineffective because it would just drive companies elsewhere. But James Buckee, CEO of Talisman Energy, said his company would pull out of Sudan rather than risk losing access to American stock exchanges.[172] In other words, the Bachus Amendment threatened to bring real pressure on Sudan's oil interests. Indeed, the mere threat of it probably contributed to Khartoum's decision to sign a protocol for peace negotiations in the summer of 2002.[173] Despite the setback in the Senate, activists had not given up on exercising financial leverage against the regime in Sudan.

THE CHALLENGE OF REALPOLITIK

By the fall of 2001 the Sudan coalition had reasons for optimism. President Bush had denounced the government of Sudan and eloquently declared that the "monstrous crimes" committed by the regime required an American response. He appointed Andrew Natsios, former head of the Christian relief organization World Vision, as his humanitarian coordinator for aid to the southern Sudanese, with a charge to ensure that relief supplies not be subject to manipulation by Khartoum. And more supplies, in fact, were bypassing the compromised UN system and getting through to besieged areas.

Activists also had reason to hope that some form of capital market sanction might remain in the Sudan Peace Act when House and Senate conferees met to iron out their differences. Deliberation over the Sudan Peace Act, indeed, had become a high-stakes drama in Washington. With rising confidence a group of coalition members, led by Nina Shea, assembled for a press conference in the Capitol building on the morning of September 11, 2001, to announce the beginning of a national mobilization campaign for the Sudan Peace Act *with* the Bachus Amendment. Before the conference could begin, Capitol police rushed in.

When the world changed on September 11, 2001, the Sudan coalition found itself in a new strategic environment in which human rights concerns might be pushed aside in the nation's War on Terror. The government of Sudan quickly seized the opportunity to "get America off its back" by offering some cooperation in the War on Terror. Because Sudan had originally given haven to bin Laden through the mid-1990s and sponsored other terrorist organizations, U.S. officials were keenly interested in obtaining information and cooperation from Khartoum. In return for this information, a number of State Department officials heaped fulsome praise on the regime's cooperation. "Their cooperation was really terrific," said Deputy of State Richard Armitage.[174] Another official was quoted as saying that "the United States doesn't have time for human rights anymore."[175] The Bush administration pressed Congress to suspend its consideration of the Sudan Peace Act and acceded to the lifting of UN sanctions, which had been in place for Sudan's support of international terrorism.

The value of Sudan's cooperation is a matter of great debate. But to activists, what happened (at least in the short run) is that "appeasers" in the State Department saw an opportunity to gain the upper hand from human rights critics. As Michael Horowitz put it, "The bad guys at State seized the opportunity." The Bush administration, therefore, became the target of a major lobby effort by the coalition.

Tensions between the Sudan coalition and the State Department especially surfaced over the work of Walter Kansteiner, who as Assistant Secretary of State for African Affairs was the chief diplomatic spokesman for U.S.-Sudan policy. Kansteiner had articulated the administration's opposition to the Bachus Amendment and lauded the regime for its cooperation in the War on Terror. He also tended to put the most positive spin on actions of the regime during cease-fire talks and agreements, even while activists on the ground were reporting on egregious violations. And he was the administration's main proponent of normalizing relations with Khartoum.

Kansteiner represented to the coalition the voice of capitulation on Sudan, and his prominence suggested the need to provide outside pressure on the administration. Reeves wrote blistering accounts of Kansteiner's "shallow and ineffectual" leadership in the State Department, which produced the "deepest shame for the Africa Bureau."[176] "There is no grade low enough" for Kansteiner, Reeves opined.[177] Horowitz debated Kansteiner on National Public Radio, charging at one point that he was hurting his own cause and his president's. Kansteiner was also raked over the coals by congressional representatives. At a June 2002 hearing of the House International Relations Committee, Rep. Tom Tancredo (R-CO) cataloged the litany of atrocities committed by the regime and then asked Kansteiner "isn't there some point where we say this has gone far enough" and support capital market sanctions. Kansteiner's reply was, "I'm sure there is, but this isn't it."[178] The quote got wide circulation in religious networks around the country.

Kansteiner's response contrasted with others in the Bush administration who advanced a more aggressive posture. This internal struggle epitomizes the wider battle over how central human rights considerations should be in American foreign policy—a debate that spans presidential administrations. After 9-11 this debate sharpened between advisors who believe the United States should aggressively promote democratization and human rights and those who interpret the national interest more in economic and geopolitical terms. This divide resulted in mixed signals from the administration. Elliott Abrams, Andrew Natsios, and Roger Winter (the latter two at USAID) pushed an assertive Sudan posture, while

Kansteiner and others backed a more accommodating policy toward the regime.

The Sudan coalition was initially thrown off balance by Khartoum's adroit exploitation of the antiterror initiative. As coalition members groped for an appropriate strategic response, a blizzard of e-mails and faxes began to flow from religious organizations stressing the fact that Sudan promoted the same ideology that built al Qaeda. Haltingly at first, religious activists began to give voice to a new understanding of the significance of the struggle in Sudan. As Baroness Cox emphasized in her speeches in Midland, Texas, the Christian and animist communities in Sudan had been the first victims of "jihad warriors" inspired by the same militant ideology as bin Laden's. Southern Sudanese leaders, in turn, were quoted in religious presses as expressing sympathy but not surprise that the terror they experience on a daily basis is finally reaching American shores. Bishop Gassis told a Washington, D.C., audience in June 2002 that for years he had been warning that the jihad against his people would ultimately be turned against the West.[179]

This understanding helped provide strategic focus, but it also lent itself to casting the conflict in ways that could stereotype the movement as only interested in Christians. Indeed, stories began appearing that suggested a "clash of civilizations"[180] was underway, with the southern Sudanese representing a kind of outpost of Christian (or Western) civilization holding out against the tide of aggressive Islam. That was a subtext of the treatment of John Garang, controversial leader of the SPLA rebels, who was featured in positive profiles by *World Magazine* as the defender of the Christian people of Sudan.[181]

Given the situation in Sudan a plausible case could be made for such a depiction. More problematically, lurid stories of Islam's putatively violent or polygamous history began sprouting in evangelical magazines and newsletters. In appealing on behalf of "victims of jihad-terrorism," Voice of the Martyrs referred to "Islamic hatred," making little distinction between the broad Islamic tradition and its radical expression.[182] Franklin Graham echoed this sentiment when he said that "the God of Islam is not the same God" as that worshiped by Christians or Jews, that Islam "is a very evil and wicked religion."[183] Though denounced by a wide array of other evangelical leaders,[184] such intemperate remarks about Islam fed into a perception within Muslim circles that the Sudan campaign was anti-Muslim or anti-Arab. This intensified defensiveness about the regime among American Muslim organizations, which sometimes hosted speakers who downplayed atrocities or even claimed that "slavery is a sham in Sudan."[185]

Despite the intemperate rhetoric of some in the Christian community, the main Sudan activists drew a sharp distinction between the "radical" regime in Sudan and the Muslim faith. They embraced the position, articulated by Cleveland law professor David Forte and later echoed by President Bush, that militant Islam represents a heresy, an attempt to hijack a sister faith home to a great civilization.[186]

Still, there were doubters. Charles Jacobs wrote that he was "perplexed" about the coalition's posture toward Islam: "We have been saying, guided by David Forte and others, that Islamism or Radical Islam is a twentieth-century distortion of the religion of the Prophet Mohammed," but Jacobs then cited recent articles by historian Paul Johnson arguing against drawing such a distinction and suggesting that Islam itself is a militant faith inhospitable to religious freedom. Jacobs then posed this question: "Is the Forte position taken by us because it is the only feasible political position?—or do we say it because we believe it?"[187]

While this internal debate about Islam was taking place, organizations in Washington, D.C., were struggling to keep pressure on the administration, which they feared might go soft. Led by Nina Shea at Freedom House and Diane Knippers at the Institute on Religion and Democracy, a group of over 100 religious leaders sent a letter to President Bush in November 2001, urging him not to compromise his commitment to religious freedom in the War on Terror. The letter was signed by a number of evangelical luminaries, such as Charles Colson, but also by notable Jewish, Catholic, Episcopal, and African American leaders. The hard-hitting letter began by quoting Bush's own words before the American Jewish Committee that "my administration will continue to speak and act for as long as the persecution and atrocities in the Sudan last." But then the letter charged that "your administration may have inadvertently signaled that the United States will overlook terrorism within Sudan's borders in exchange for gestures and promises from Khartoum not to export it to our shores." The letter went on to catalog continued attacks on civilians in Sudan subsequent to September 11, 2001. It continued, "By rewarding and praising Khartoum at the very moment it is stepping up its bombing, starvation, and literal enslavement of religious minorities, the United States appears to be willing to tolerate religiously-based internal terrorism."[188] Independently, activists from Midland, Texas, employed their own unique back channels to convey their implacable commitment to the Sudan cause.

These efforts helped maintain the administration's focus on Sudan. Condoleezza Rice wrote that the "pariah status of the government of Sudan" will not end until it ceases "the enslavement, oppression, violence, and terror that have become its hallmarks." And she reassured the coalition that cooperation in the campaign against terrorism "is not a commodity to be traded among other national security or foreign policy imperatives, including respect for basic human rights."[189] Bush followed up by appointing former senator and Episcopal priest John Danforth as his special envoy on Sudan. Danforth negotiated the creation of the Civilian Protection Monitoring Team (CPMT) to monitor military attacks on civilians,[190] which provided some of the "most authoritative" information on the impact of military operations on the ground.[191] Danforth later helped bring Khartoum into serious peace negotiations with rebel groups of the south.

AMENDED SUDAN PEACE ACT PREVAILS

The Sudan coalition did not give up on capital market leverage against the regime. The problem was that Bachus opponents capitalized on the new strategic environment to halt creation of a conference committee to iron out differences between House and Senate versions of the Sudan Peace Act. Taking the lead in this effort was free market purist Senator Phil Gramm (R-TX), who threatened to filibuster against the Sudan Peace Act if the House insisted on bringing forward the Bachus Amendment. Fearing that some form of capital market sanctions might pass a House-Senate conference committee, Gramm in effect put a "hold" on appointment of Senate conferees unless the House dropped the Bachus language.

The fact that Gramm was the obstructionist sparked initiatives by some of his west Texas constituents. Constant e-mail traffic had been flowing between Washington and the Midland Ministerial Alliance, enabling the local group to focus its mobilization at strategic moments. Thus packets went out to the independent Texas oil producers who had coalesced previously during the Day of Prayer for the Persecuted Church.[192] This conjured the striking aspect of Texas oilmen exercising their "Christian discipleship" by lobbying a senator on behalf of an African people half a world away.

The Midland folks were also linked to groups reporting on atrocities on the ground in Sudan, which buoyed their confidence in pressing their own beloved president. In a letter to Bush on July 10, 2002, a broad array of Midland church representatives reminded the president that "some of our group are in communication (by satellite phone, e-mails, and digital photos) on a weekly basis with Sudanese along the frontlines." The religious leaders also expressed the view that the president was "not getting the full picture" from his advisors, and that unless the president acted forcefully the issue might be used in a partisan manner. That would be unfortunate, but, the leaders concluded, "we feel we must fulfill the call of God on our lives and stand with our persecuted brothers and sisters in Sudan, however God leads us."[193] There was a subtle threat in these words—more to executive branch and White House officials than the president himself—that at some point his Midland friends might be compelled to take actions that could embarrass the president. An intriguing dimension of this fierce commitment, as Deborah Fikes observed, was a sense of solidarity with black pastors in Midland, who felt a special kinship with their Sudanese brethren

The government of Sudan helped bolster the case for action by a series of attacks in the spring of 2002 on civilian villages around the oil fields, effectively "cleansing" them of their population. In response, a bipartisan group of some two dozen House members, frustrated with Senate inaction, wrote Tom Daschle and Trent Lott in June 2002, urging them to stop blocking the Sudan Peace Act and arguing that without the House's capital market provision "the Government of Sudan will continue to pay for oil with the blood of its people."[194] This was followed by a letter delivered to Daschle signed by all thirty-nine members of the Congressional Black Caucus, stating that they considered action against Sudan "the same way as the struggle against the apartheid regime of South Africa."[195]

With this high-profile pressure most coalition activists still hoped for passage of the Sudan Peace Act *with* the Bachus Amendment.[196] But by the mid-summer of 2002 time was running short, giving Senate opponents ample leverage to employ delaying tactics. Coalition leaders finally conceded that pressing Bachus might derail the entire bill before adjournment. So they made a strategic decision to offer compromise language, in lieu of the Bachus Amendment, that would still provide leverage against Khartoum. On July 30, 2002, Michael Horowitz, Nina Shea, and Shannon Royce of the SBC presented Senator Brownback with provisions that would: (1) authorize $100 million of aid per year to areas of Sudan not controlled by the government, (2) require the parties to engage in good faith negotiations to end the civil war, (3) establish a timetable for such negotiations, and (4) authorize the president to deny oil revenue to the regime if it failed to comply within the timetable.[197] Brownback secured Senate approval of these amendments to replace the Bachus provision, thus breaking the logjam for the Sudan Peace Act. In one sense, this compromise reflected the movement's tactical flexibility in seeking the long-term goal: real change in Sudan. In another sense it was a concession that the coalition could not overcome combined opposition from Wall Street and foreign-policy realists who saw the Bachus Amendment as too radical.

Sudan advocates differed in their assessment of the final bill, which seemed less muscular than the one that passed the House. Eleanor Holmes Norton (D-DC) expressed deep disappointment that the Bachus Amendment—"the engine that drove the bill that passed overwhelmingly in this House"—was removed.[198] Others accentuated the positive, pointing to the remarkable U.S. financial commitment to the people of southern Sudan and the latent threat to the regime's oil revenue.

Even with compromises secured, however, Sudan advocates feared that Congress might fail to act before adjournment. So they organized a series of church-based vigils at the State Department to ensure that Congress acted on the legislation in time. Sponsored by

Church Alliance for a New Sudan, the September 2002 vigil represented a true collaborative effort between Washington figures, such as
Faith McDonnell, Director of the Church Alliance, and such Texas
activists as Deborah Fikes of Midland and Donna Ballard from Dallas. The idea was that "the hot breath of the vigil" would be breathing down the necks of members of Congress as they deliberated on
the Sudan Peace Act. The moving witness of the vigil, which attracted a diverse array of African American pastors, lay citizens, members of Congress, and Sudanese exiles, made manifest the biblical in-
junction to be "gentle as doves and wise as serpents." Prayer and
hymns were matched with strategic analysis and pivotal timing to
keep the issue alive at the very moment that debate over congressional authorization of war against Iraq could have crowded Sudan
off the agenda.[199]

In an amazing echo of the IRFA story, the Sudan Peace Act
was given up for dead on a number of occasions, passing on the
very eve of congressional adjournment in October. Like IRFA, it
passed because of grassroots mobilization, activist tenacity, and persistent shepherding by key members of Congress. The government
of Sudan also played a role. Despite its cease-fire agreements, the
regime intensified attacks in the summer and into the fall of 2002,
displacing thousands and killing numerous civilians who lived
nowhere near rebel fighters.[200] Because of the advocacy infrastructure in Sudan and its links to Washington groups, the regime's
brazenness immediately became part of the backdrop of continued
agitation for action.

The passage of the Sudan Peace Act represented a major triumph of the movement, producing a Hollywood-like bill signing
ceremony at the Roosevelt Room in the White House on October
21, 2002. In the presence of Colin Powell, Condoleezza Rice, Sudan coalition members, and Sudanese exiles, President Bush signed
the act. Though scantily reported by the elite press,[201] word of the
signing went forth from the religious presses and advocacy e-mail,
buoying confidence for the inevitable battles to come, as the coalition sought to turn the symbolism of the moment into a reality on
the ground.[202] In his remarks at the ceremony, Bush acknowledged
the power of the faith-based movement. "I will not forget Sudan,"

he pledged, then added dryly, "And if I do, I know that you will prod me."[203]

In that he was correct, as Nina Shea later promised that her organization would vigilantly monitor Khartoum's "good faith" compliance with the act, viewing as "prima facie evidence of bad faith continued bombing of civilians, slave raids, and bans on relief flights." If bad faith was determined, she pledged that the coalition would press to obtain capital market sanctions as provided in the act.[204]

Immediately following the bill signing, Bush was approached by Yar Kang, a statuesque Sudanese model from South Dakota. Nervous and overcome with emotion, she exclaimed, "Thank you, thank you, President Bush. God bless you. I am so happy I don't know what to say!" To which the President replied, "I think you're doing a good job."[205]

Attending the signing ceremony were a number of luminaries of the IRFA battle, such as Michael Horowitz, Nina Shea, Faith McDonnell, David Saperstein, Stacie Burdette, and Tom Hart.[206] The

Francis Bok and other Sudanese exiles with President Bush after the signing of the Sudan Peace Act.

White House gathering also featured new movement cadres: African American leaders such as Joe Madison, Walter Fauntroy, Donald Payne, and Eleanor Holmes Norton; Midlanders Deborah Fikes and Fran Boyle; and diverse other advocates, such as Charles Jacobs, Shannon Royce of the SBC, Felice Gaer (Jewish human rights activist and member of the U.S. Commission), and Smith College Professor Eric Reeves.

Also witnessing the event was Francis Bok, capping a remarkable journey that took him from slavery in the Sudanese bush to the White House. The young man who spoke to church groups about his desire to "free his people in bondage," now stood in the center of American power as the president signaled the nation's resolve to help achieve that very aim. After Bush greeted Bok, the ex-slave expressed his thanks to the President: "On behalf of the people of southern Sudan and on behalf of those still in bondage, I thank you." Bok went on to say that if "the boys and girls still in slavery could know that today you signed a law to help set them free, their faces would light up in hope."[207] Bush spoke to Bok for several minutes, telling him that it was *his* honor to help. The poignancy of the moment was captured by Charles Jacobs: "This may be the first time, since the nineteenth century, an American president has met with a former slave."[208]

A BREAKTHROUGH FOR PEACE?

While this dramatic signing did not immediately end the struggle, it propelled a breakthrough. By the fall of 2003 a security pact had been signed between the government of Sudan and rebel groups, producing a cease-fire that held across most of the south. With U.S. prodding, negotiations then produced a peace treaty by the spring of 2004.[209]

This breakthrough did not come without fierce lobbying by Sudan coalition members, including back-channel communications from the Midland Ministerial Alliance directly to President Bush, the government of Sudan, and rebel leaders. The story of that final campaign illustrates the unique way faith-based networks enhance human rights advocacy.

Despite ongoing peace negotiations and putative cease-fire agreements, Khartoum continued to launch military operations against civilians, especially in oil concession areas.[210] This flouting of the Sudan Peace Act evoked only perfunctory criticism by the State Department, in part because of Khartoum's adroit exploitation of the War on Terror. Throughout the spring of 2003 the State Department presented an upbeat assessment of the regime's cooperation in the War on Terror, leading activists to charge American officials with soft-pedaling Sudan's human rights record. Foreign service officers, it was claimed, "sat on" their own information on cease-fire violations, issuing only tepid criticism when civilian killings, displacement, and abductions were publicized.[211] The Civilian Protection Monitoring Team was "grounded" by Khartoum's military at crucial moments, and the State Department issued "no public protest."[212] Activists also expressed horror at the prospect that the State Department might remove Sudan from its list of countries sponsoring terrorism.[213]

Khartoum's international rehabilitation was furthered when the UN Commission on Human Rights, chaired by autocratic Libya, voted in April 2003 to upgrade Sudan's status (removing its designation as a country "with special problems"). Related action removed from Sudan the special UN rapporteurs whose reports had been instrumental in spotlighting the regime's responsibility for massive human suffering.[214]

Further evidence of a premature "rehabilitation" of Sudan came when the Bush administration issued its mandated report six months from the signing of the Sudan Peace Act.[215] Acting on the basis of the State Department assessment, President Bush certified in April 2003 that the government of Sudan was "negotiating in good faith."

This provoked howls of denunciation. Activists depicted the designation as a "whitewash," "tragic," "catastrophic," and just plain inaccurate.[216] While most of the ire was leveled against the State Department, some vented their fury at the president himself. Referring to a May massacre of Christian villagers, Dennis Bennett charged that President Bush was "complicit in these murders" because of his "refusal to investigate these atrocities and to hold the Government of Sudan accountable."[217] Such tough talk indicated the willingness of some evangelicals in the coalition to play "hardball" with the administration to prevent it from letting the Bashir regime "off the hook." Collectively, a drumbeat of exposés flooded religious publications and networks, keeping the heat on the administration to take a tougher line with Khartoum.

A secret weapon of this final lobby campaign turned out to be citizen diplomacy by the Midland religious community. Galvanized by back-to-back national events for the persecuted church, scores of community activists with the Midland Ministerial Alliance literally committed themselves to ending the war in Sudan. With a keen appreciation of Midland's unique position as the president's hometown, they approached this ambitious goal with a combination of moral zeal and strategic moxie. Anchoring this effort were Jerry Hilton, pastor of the First Presbyterian Church (which President Bush attended as a youth), and Deborah Fikes, the stay-at-home mom whose skills as an organizer were acknowledged far and wide. Because of her personal connections to the Sudanese Christian community and by virtue of her contacts with national advocates, Fikes timed the alliance's lobbying to match strategic situations.

When cease-fire violations mounted in the spring of 2003, the Midland Ministers Alliance delivered a sharp letter to the Sudanese embassy. Under the letterhead banner "Hometown of President and First Lady Laura Bush," the letter was signed by the mayor, city councilmen, oil company executives, homemakers, the Catholic bishop, and pastors and laity representing the entire Protestant community— Methodist, Baptist, Lutheran, Presbyterian, and Episcopalian. "Over the past five years," the signatories wrote, "we have documented, exposed, and rallied against the bombing of civilians, slave raids, ethnic cleansing and other forms of terror." Since the passage of the Sudan Peace Act, "a team of our coalition partners has documented massive atrocities against civilians. Fields littered with human remains, mass graves, and empty villages are testament to the deliberate policies of genocide and ethnic cleansing." Such flouting of the law will have devastating consequences for the regime, leading the signatories to invoke the oil sanction provision of the law. The letter stated, "We strongly urge you not to test our resolve."[218]

This missive got the attention of the government of Sudan and sparked a remarkable flow of direct communication between the Alliance and Sudanese diplomats. Spurring this communication was a sense that Midland Christians were tied to the president "on a deeper level" than official Washington. The foreign minister of Sudan, for example, encouraged his ambassador to the United States, Khidir H. Ahmed, to contact Christians from the "*village of George Bush.*" Midland leaders, in turn, conveyed back-channel communication to the government of Sudan that probably helped induce seriousness in peace negotiations.[219] From that point onward Deborah Fikes and her compatriots maintained contact with Sudanese officials, presenting their views in a tough but respectful fashion. Thus while some activists demonstrated outside the Sudanese embassy, the Midland folks were conveying a similar, if softer, message from the inside.[220]

Being from the President's "village" also facilitated access by Midlanders to the highest levels of American government. A wide array of U.S. government officials acknowledged prodding by the Midland Alliance. This prodding included the president himself. When Sudan coalition leaders were personally urging the president to "press hard for peace in Sudan," Laura Bush herself chimed in about how "horrible" situation in Sudan was.[221]

Ultimately, the Midland Alliance developed contacts with all the parties to peace negotiations—the Khartoum regime, the SPLM, the U.S. government, and the negotiators in Kenya. John Garang, SPLM leader, maintained close e-mail contact with Fikes, providing her with information and asking for prayers. But sympathy with rebel groups did not prevent the Alliance from prodding them. Concerned that the SPLM might interpret the clout of the "president's village" as an excuse to press for unrealistic demands, the Ministerial Alliance sent a blunt message to the rebels: "If the SPLM leaves itself open to blame for the failure of peace negotiations, our ability to ensure immediate invocation of the Sudan Peace Act or to take other steps to hold the government of Sudan accountable or to cause the United States to take the side of the SPLM in any resumed military conflict will be enormously, perhaps impossibly compromised."

"Don't mess with Midland" became the refrain in a variety of circles. At critical moments in peace negotiations all parties heard that failure would cause serious political fallout for the president. This was backed by the resolve of activists to descend on Washington for public action, perhaps even arrests, if their quieter pressure did not yield results. "Failure of effort," therefore, meant that officials would have to explain to the president why his friends were getting arrested in front of the White House.[222]

Beyond this strategic level, the Midland folks also boosted the morale of others in the Sudan coalition. Nina Shea reported that at the exact moment she was meeting with President Bush on Sudanese human rights, a "hundred or so" Midlanders met to pray for her. Senator Brownback, after meeting for hours with these citizen-diplomats, described them as "beautiful and humble people"—the spiritual descendants of the abolitionists of the nineteenth century. Michael Horowitz said he was stunned by the decency and moral convictions of these people and noted how they buoyed his spirits in the struggle.

We can never know the full impact of this citizen diplomacy, but the collective effort of the Sudan alliance achieved striking results. After a historic meeting between Sudan President Omar Bashir and SPLM leader John Garang in April 2003, President Bush moved that summer to dispatch special envoy Danforth back to Sudan to "make clear that the only option on the table is peace." By the fall the sides had moved swiftly toward a peace treaty guaranteeing greater autonomy for the south.[223] Throughout most of the south the guns were quiet and slave raids had ceased.[224]

A huge task remains, and some coalition activists have shifted focus to rebuilding southern Sudan. Unfortunately, to deal with another insurgency, this time by African Muslims in the western province of Darfur, the government of Sudan unleashed so-called Janjaweed militias and employed scorched earth strategies, killing civilians and sending refugees fleeing without sustenance. This act showed how Khartoum's radical Islamist policies imperil other Muslims (in this case Sufis). The swiftness of the horror captured world attention and was widely documented by secular human rights groups and the elite press.[225] By the spring of 2004 some one million people had been displaced and another million war-affected, all of whom face a dire fate unless massive aid flows into the region. But because of Khartoum's success in scattering people into inaccessible places and in impeding aid shipments, Andrew Natsios of USAID declared on June 3, 2004, that even if relief gets in "we'll lose a third of a million people" by the end of the year, "and if we don't . . . a million."[226]

Despite such a staggering assessment on the ten-year anniversary of the Rwanda genocide, international response has been abysmal. The United Nations failed at the crucial moment to condemn the Sudan government or authorize early action to stem the inexorable catastrophe. Astonishingly, the African nations elected Sudan to a seat on the UN Human Rights Commission about the same time, and the European Union continued normal relations with Khartoum.

Though belatedly, the United States took the lead in condemning the ethnic cleansing, sustaining economic sanctions on Sudan, and getting relief supplies into the region. By the summer of 2004 the Bush administration had designated $285 million in direct aid to Darfur, compared to $12 million total for the twenty-five member nations of the EU,[227] and Natsios was mobilizing U.S. logistical resources to move the aid. Staving off further mass death will involve bolder moves. Though the Bush Administration designated the attacks on Darfur a "genocide," follow-up has failed to stem the tragedy. Indeed, some activists believe it would involve mounting a non-UN-sponsored humanitarian intervention, with military escorts, to stop Khartoum from blocking shipments and to protect refugees from continued militia attacks. At this point in time it is unlikely that an American president could undertake such a radical military step without strong public pressure. But even maintaining the current U.S. commitment will require the kind of public backing faith-based networks uniquely can foster. Sustaining public interest remains a key challenge of the drive for a new Sudan.

The faith-based movement has bent the arc of Sudanese history, though it is too early to say how much. Even if a fragile peace holds in the south and genocide is forestalled in Darfur, it will take immense outside resources to repair the shattered lands of the Dinka, Nuba, and other African peoples. But if the ravaged people of Sudan do gain a modicum of peace and stability, historians will point to an unlikely alliance that moved the American government to intervene in a conflict that many foreign-policy elites viewed as unimportant to the national interest.

Ironically, this intervention may turn out to better serve America's national security than the hands-off approach urged by "tough-minded realists." It has already checked Khartoum's effort to spread its radical version of Islam into other African countries, which would have aggravated the religious and ethnic strife already afflicting that continent and created more safe havens for terrorists. As Bishop Gassis predicted, we ignore massive human rights abuses at our own peril.

8

GO FORTH

It shall be the policy of the United States . . . to condemn violations of religious freedom, and to promote, and to assist
other governments in the promotion of, the fundamental right
to freedom of religion.

—International Religious Freedom Act[1]

In February 2002 President George W. Bush, visiting China on the
thirtieth anniversary of President Nixon's historic trip, surprised
the Chinese leaders by the vigor of his advocacy for religious freedom. In public appearances and private meetings, "Mr. Bush repeatedly pressed his theme that religious and political freedom would not
lead to chaos, using words that were both a forceful projection of his
own religious faith and a subtle criticism of what he sees as the op-
pressiveness of President Jiang Zemin's regime." In an uncensored
speech broadcast throughout the country, Bush challenged Chinese
leaders to end all persecution, "so that all in China are free to gather
and worship as they wish." Bush lauded the fact that tens of millions
of Chinese were reconnecting with various religious traditions.[2]
Bush's aggressive posture on religious freedom suggested how much
circumstances had changed since the mid-1990s, when a new American ambassador to China was completely unaware of the persecution
of house church Christians.[3]

The faith–based movement is filling a void in international affairs. As the signal grassroots effort of our time on human rights, it is
the major force in pressing for U.S. leadership against global religious

persecution, especially highlighting abuses in such "inconvenient" places as China, Sudan, and Saudi Arabia. But it has "gone forth" from this foundation to address other human rights issues, from gulags in North Korea to human trafficking, bringing a blend of conscience and constituency to slighted abuses.

This chapter begins by examining the impact of movement initiatives, then moves to some reflections on what the faith-based effort has to teach us.

A NEW ARCHITECTURE FOR HUMAN RIGHTS

The architecture built by the International Religious Freedom Act (IRFA) has enhanced human rights attention in American foreign policy. A new State Department office, a vast reporting enterprise, and an external watchdog commission not only highlight violations of religious freedom but also expose broader patterns of human rights abuse.

Heading up the Office of International Religious Freedom at the State Department is the world's first ambassador-at-large for International Religious Freedom, who communicates American policy to foreign leaders and oversees reporting on the status of religious rights around the world. The first ambassador was Robert Seiple, former head of the Christian relief agency World Vision. He brought to his job a fervent desire to enhance the profile of religious rights within the foreign service and around the world. During his tenure he traveled to almost every problem country listed in the State Department annual report (around forty), meeting with officials and intervening on behalf of specific people or concerns. He was succeeded by John Hanford, whose religious freedom case work in Congress provided a clear foundation for his leadership of the State Department program.

The work of this office is changing the culture of the foreign service, which was often indifferent or hostile to religion.[4] We now see sometimes eloquent pronouncements coming out of the "stodgy" State Department. The introduction to the 2001 Annual Report expressed this understanding of the link between religion and human rights:

America's founders made religious freedom the first freedom of the Constitution—giving it pride of place among those liberties enumerated in the Bill of Rights—because they believed that guaranteeing the right to search for transcendent truths and ultimate human purpose was a critical component of a durable democracy. The founders believed in the universality of human dignity—that all human beings are endowed by the Creator with certain rights that are theirs by virtue of their existence. These rights were inalienable because they were understood to exist prior to societies and governments, and were granted by neither.[5]

The document asserted that the "inviolable and universal dignity of the human person" is "at the core of U.S. human rights policy abroad, including the policy of advocating religious freedom."[6] Governments that respect religious freedom, the report argued, are "more likely to protect other fundamental human rights" and be stable democracies. Thus promoting religious freedom serves the national interest because the spread of democracy promotes good neighbors, economic prosperity, and peace. The report also takes pains to catalog the numerous UN and international covenants that enshrine religious freedom as a fundamental right,[7] giving the lie to criticisms that the law represents merely a U.S. attempt to impose its view on the world.[8]

The Office of International Religious Freedom has made religious concerns "part of the wallpaper" of Foggy Bottom and provides new leverage to career diplomats devoted to the cause.[9] The Office provides recommendations and discussion points for the secretary of state, ambassadors, and undersecretaries when they meet with foreign officials. It coordinates training of foreign service personnel and immigration officials on religious freedom issues. It raises religious freedom issues in international forums, and supports the efforts of nongovernmental organizations (NGOs) working to ease religious strife.[10]

The central task of the State Department office is to produce an annual report on the status of religious freedom *in every nation* on Earth (except the United States), a prodigious effort that requires officials to maintain contacts with diverse religious communities to investigate abuses. David Saperstein, who served as first chair of the U.S. Commission on International Religious Freedom, lauded the impact of this effort: "I think that nothing—nothing—IRFA did has had a greater impact on the ground than the fact that in every embassy there are now foreign service officials who immerse themselves in these issues to prepare the report; who build relations with local religious leaders who are able to turn to them for help and intervention when problems arise."[11] Not only do leaders of religious communities abroad cite the positive impact of this effort, but foreign governments pay attention. According to one senior foreign service officer, the annual report on religious freedom is one of the two most sought after documents by foreign embassies, who attentively read it to find out what is being said about their country.[12] In addition, Western governments that cannot afford to undertake such an effort are sending U.S. reports out to their own foreign service officers as a blueprint for concerns to be addressed.[13]

This report significantly expands overall human rights chronicling. Indeed, its very comprehensiveness provides a benchmark, a point of departure for advocacy groups. Thus when early reports by the State Department seemed to soft-pedal certain abuses for strategic reasons, institutions such as Freedom House or the U.S. Commission provided a critique and drew tougher conclusions. Such scrutiny by outside groups has led to improvements in the report, with later issues containing robust thematic overviews that clearly identify the main sources of violations and avoid mincing words.

The report prompts a series of diplomatic communiqués, especially to governments in "countries of particular concern"—those designated as engaging in or tolerating "particularly severe violations" of freedom of religion. The publishing of this list is valuable for the advocacy community, which agitates for the inclusion of other countries on the basis of the law's criteria.

Because of the need to produce the annual report, American diplomats all over the world now must develop contacts with religious communities and convey to foreign governments why the United States is acting on their behalf. The range and depth of this activity is conveyed annually.[14] While dramatic changes are not expected from this activity, incremental advances can occur: one country loosening up restrictions on worship, another releasing some religious prisoners, another ceasing raids upon house churches. When American officials informed Uzbekistan that the United States was leaning toward labeling it one of the "countries of particular concern," it freed its known Christian prisoners and broadened the range of acceptable practice.[15] After intense negotiations with American officials and other international organizations, the government of Kazakhstan avoided passing restrictive religious laws, initiated dialogue among religions, and reduced harassment of religious minorities.[16] As events in the past have taught us, such incremental victories may stimulate far more dramatic advances.

Ironically, a feature of the law that involved intense lobby struggles—the menu of actions against persecuting countries—has not really come into play. The State Department has merely designated existing actions (imposed for other reasons) as fulfilling the requirements of the law. This diplomatic skittishness about making the law bite harder has heightened the importance of outside pressure and public exposure, as we see below.

SPEAKING TRUTH TO POWER: THE U.S. COMMISSION

A key part of the new architecture of human rights is the U.S. Commission on International Religious Freedom. Created as a watchdog and policy advocate, the commission provides an independent assessment of the status of religious freedom, critiques the State Department report, and offers detailed policy recommendations. Designed to produce "honest fact-finding," the commission is less constrained by diplomatic considerations than the State Department. It can "speak truth to power," not temporizing on the record of countries of strategic importance. Its reports on such places as Sudan, Saudi Arabia, Vietnam, and North Korea, therefore, often read more cogently than official government documents.

A "strengthened" commission, as we saw in chapter 6, was backed by those seeking a high profile and tough focus on religious freedom. From the beginning commissioners have taken seriously that charge. Indeed, one of the first battles commissioners fought was for greater autonomy from what they saw as "micromanagement" by certain congressional staffers.[17] More recently the commission has sought to enhance its capacity to get recommendations adopted by various branches of government.[18] Backed by a research staff of over a dozen personnel, the commission's work is generally lauded by the activist community.

The nine commissioners, selected through a bipartisan formula,[19] serve two-year terms. The prominence and credentials of commissioners give the body a certain heft in Washington and abroad (see appendix). Equally important, because the commission itself embodies religious pluralism—with members from Jewish, Catholic, evangelical, mainline Protestant, Muslim, Mormon, and Baha'i communities—its actions carry moral weight. In a sense, the commission manifests the nation's religious heritage in international councils.

The commission conducts hearings, takes delegations to foreign countries, consults with religious leaders, and meets with top officials. Its reports provide some of the most cogent accounts of the status of religious freedom available.[20] Policy recommendations target flagrant abuse (Sudan, North Korea), emerging problems (anticult laws in Europe), or opportunities (to guarantee religious freedom in the new Afghanistan and Iraq).[21]

President Bush and Condoleezza Rice with members of the U.S. Commission on International Religious Freedom. Courtesy of the U.S. Commission on International Religious Freedom, photographed by White House photographer Tina Hager.

The keen attention of foreign governments to the commission testify to its clout. In 2003 Chinese authorities engaged in months of negotiations with the commission over a proposed delegation trip to the People's Republic. When China imposed last-minute restrictions on the commissioners' itinerary in Hong Kong, the commission canceled the trip. Not only did this action receive extensive news coverage, but it exposed looming threats to freedom in the province. As Commission Chair Michael Young commented, "This action on the part of the Chinese government suggests a degree of Chinese control over foreign access to Hong Kong that is unprecedented and in contradiction to the concept of 'one country, two systems.'"[22] The commission thus signaled that cordial relations with the United States may depend on Chinese authorities providing greater access for American officials to local religious leaders.

One of the ways the commission makes an impact is by concentrating on specific policy details often slighted by other entities. The commission criticized China's 1999 "evil cult" law, for example, noting how it was used to prosecute individuals for importing Bibles. The commission also chastised Chinese authorities for refusing refugee status to North Korean asylum seekers who flee from a totalitarian state, "the least free on earth." Recognizing how religious freedom is intertwined with broader human rights advances, the commission promoted the idea of U.S. distribution of radios in Afghanistan "with the aim of ensuring that each village has at least one radio for communal listening." In specifying how lax police enforcement fueled mob violence against religious minorities, the commission asserted that the U.S. government earmark "funds for training of Indonesian police and prosecutors in human rights."[23]

A key way the commission "speaks truth to power" involves the designation of Countries of Particular Concern (CPC)—those nations in which "particularly severe violations" occur. While the State Department designated only six such countries in 2003—Burma, China, Iran, Iraq, North Korea, and Sudan—the commission pressed for the additional designations of Laos, Pakistan, Saudi Arabia, Turkmenistan, Vietnam, and India.[24] Because of the commission's high profile, these recommendations are sometimes confused with actual designations by the State Department, which understandably upsets some U.S. diplomats. But such exposure also keeps the heat on offending nations.

These recommended designations serve several purposes. They highlight the denial of religious freedom in places that receive scant attention, such as Turkmenistan. They also single out countries of strategic import that the State Department is loath to offend. Saudi Arabia is such a case, and the U.S. Commission has been insistent that the kingdom be included on the list since it prohibits all nonstate-sponsored religious expression and subjects Shi'a clerics and Christian foreign workers to imprisonment and torture. The 2003 report pointedly reminded the State Department that by law it must "take into account any findings or recommendations by the Commission," which have consistently called for the CPC designation.[25]

The lengths to which diplomats go in not offending the Saudis was illustrated by former Ambassador Seiple, who claimed that the State Department had "decided that there was not religious persecution in Saudi Arabia." Seiple went on to admit that *if* religious persecution were acknowledged "we would have been obliged by the legislation to designate the country as a country of particular concern and look at various lists of sanctions that could be applied." Playing its watchdog role, the commission took Seiple to task for these statements, calling them "inexplicable" given that State Department's own report admits that "freedom of religion does not exist" in the Kingdom. Seiple's successor, John Hanford, responded that a CPC designation would have to be seriously considered for Saudi Arabia.[26]

In addition to these CPC recommendations, the commission also creates a "Watch List" of countries where serious problems loom. In particular, the commission has criticized the tendency of certain authorities to acquiesce to mob violence against religious minorities: in India, where a Hindu nationalist government inflamed religious attacks against Muslims and Christians; in Indonesia, where jihad fighters slaughter whole villages of Christians; and Nigeria, where Islamic vigilantes enforce their interpretation of Shari'a on non-Muslim people.[27] In this sense, the commission has been attempting to provide an early warning of looming threats to human rights and civil peace.

One of those early warnings involved the state-building process in Afghanistan. The commission repeatedly cautioned American officials to pay more attention to the religious situation there, noting emerging threats posed by Islamic militancy to women's rights and the freedom of ethnic and religious minorities. To highlight this concern, a delegation of commissioners traveled to Afghanistan to meet with officials of the Karzai government, along with civil society organizations. On the eve of this trip Chairman Michael Young summarized the commission's concern: "There are troubling indications that Afghanistan is being reconstructed, without serious U.S. opposition, as a state in which an extreme interpretation of Sharia would be enforced by a government which the United States supports and with which our nation is closely identified."[28] The commission's actions illustrate how promoting religious freedom enhances overall rights. In both Afghanistan and Iraq, the commission's work vividly highlighted the threat to women's rights posed by the imposition of rigid Shari'a in the newly formed constitutions, a complaint echoed by local women's advocates.

While the commission feels free to criticize U.S. diplomacy, it actually works closely with the State Department, and commissioners argue that if there is tension at times, it is healthy. As one commission official observed, "The State Department has acknowledged how our critique of their work has been very helpful to them."[29] By serving as a watchdog over the State Department process, the commission provides a counterweight to the inevitable pressures on diplomats to soften their responses to particular persecuting countries. Moreover, the commission's more aggressive "bad cop" approach allows U.S. officials to take a more soothing "good cop" role. Thus the secretary of state can communicate to foreign leaders the "pressures" he or she is under, informing them "sadly" of the looming threat of bad publicity or sanctions if situations do not improve. And while former ambassador Seiple chastised the commission for creating confusion, his own efforts at quiet diplomacy were likely aided by the commission's action.[30]

At the urging of David Saperstein, the first chair of the commission, members have striven for consensus. Given the religious and political diversity on the body, it was felt that unanimous approval would provide legitimacy and cachet to controversial recommendations. The commission attained a remarkable success in this approach. When disagreements cannot be ironed out, individual commissioners write dissents included in the commission's annual report. These few dissents have been understandable. Laila Al-Marayati, past president of the Muslim Women's League, penned a critique of the commission's decision to refrain from commenting on the situation in Israel and the occupied territories. In particular, she raised a number of issues with respect to the denial of religious rights to non-Jews, and she offered her own policy descriptions.[31] In addition, Dr. Al-Marayati dissented from recommendations in the 2000 and 2001 annual reports for U.S. aid to the Sudan People's Liberation Army and other opposition groups in southern Sudan. Other commissioners dissented from designating India as a "country of concern," arguing that the abuses were concentrated in a few regions.

What is striking, however, is the limited number of such dissents. Indeed, Al-Marayati agreed to a number of recommendations opposed by representatives of the American Muslim community. There were even instances in which Al-Marayati signed onto a recommendation that was denounced by her husband, himself a prominent American Muslim leader.[32] Because a norm operates to ensure Muslim representation on the body, the commission thus plays a modest role in fostering debate within the Muslim community about the status of religious freedom in Muslim countries.

A leitmotiv of the commission's work is its judgment that "U.S. policy does not appear to be commensurate with the gravity of religious freedom problems or where conditions of religious freedom have deteriorated." To bridge that gap the commission has advanced policy proposals adopted by the State Department, Congress, the president, and foreign authorities. A catalog of the achievements of the U.S. Commission illustrates how the new architecture for religious freedom advances human rights in American foreign policy:

- **Afghanistan**. Pressed for incorporation of human rights provisions in the Afghanistan Freedom Support Act, signed into law December 4, 2002. These provisions included constitutional guarantees of religious freedom, the rights of women and girls, and promotion of religious freedom in school curricula.

- **China**. Successfully recommended that President Bush condition a state visit to China on the opportunity to make an uncensored speech on religious freedom, delivered on February 21, 2002.
- **Europe**. Successfully pressed the French government to promulgate significant policy changes regarding "anticult" treatment of religious minorities. Drew attention to the rise of anti-Semitic violence in France and Belgium, sparking Congress to pass resolutions condemning it. Successfully urged members of the Organization for Security and Cooperation in Europe to hold meetings focused on religious freedom and anti-Semitism.
- **North Korea**. Successfully urged the State Department to add North Korea to its list of countries of concern in 2001. Pressed both the U.S. and Chinese governments to recognize and protect North Korean refugees, and gained Senate resolution incorporating these recommendations. Successfully urged passage of a resolution addressing human rights abuses in North Korea at the 59th Human Rights Convention in Geneva.
- **Pakistan**. Highlighted the undemocratic nature of the separate-electorate system for religious minorities, which the Pakistani government abolished in 2002. Successfully prompted the U.S. government to urge Pakistan to curtail religious schools that promote violence and to appropriate U.S. funds to assist Pakistan in that effort.
- **Sudan**. Successfully called for a special envoy, helped insure humanitarian assistance to worst hit areas, and raised awareness of a link between the oil industry and atrocities.
- **Turkmenistan**. Urged U.S. government to sponsor a resolution on human rights in Turkmenistan, adopted in the 59th session of the Human Rights Commission in Geneva.
- **Uzbekistan**. Successfully recommended that congressional assistance to Uzbekistan be contingent on that government's effort to improve conditions of religious freedom.

- **Vietnam**. Successfully advised the U.S. House of Representatives to pass legislation on human rights in Vietnam prior to approving a bilateral trade agreement.
- **War on Terror**. One of first groups calling for protection of religious freedom during the war against terrorism, it successfully recommended that President Bush highlight religious freedom in a UN General Assembly speech on November 10, 2001.[33]

While these impacts cannot be solely attributed to the commission, its role looms pretty large in the new architecture of human rights. How the broader advocacy infrastructure boosts humanitarian concerns is highlighted in the emerging North Korean struggle.

NORTH KOREA

The unfolding North Korean story presents another example of the role of the faith-based constituency on human rights. In the spring of 2003, revelations about the horrific nature of the Stalinist regime made a splash in national news stories.[34] The timing and detail of these revelations owes a debt to the religious community. First, because of their on-the-ground operations among refugees, Christian groups provided crucial documentation of concentration camps, executions, torture, and starvation. Some courageous souls even penetrated North Korea itself, bringing back fresh accounts of conditions in the most closed society on Earth.[35] Second, religious advocates highlighted the ideology behind the regime's brutality—a kind of state religion in which Kim Il Sung and Kim Jong Il are viewed as gods and those that do not pay homage are treated as heretics.[36] Third, popular Christian outlets widely featured accounts of the humanitarian catastrophe in North Korea before their secular counterparts followed suit. Readers of the evangelical magazine *World*, for example, learned of the story a full year before it was picked up by *Time* and *U.S. News and World Report*.[37] Fourth, the infrastructure created by IRFA brought the issue more deeply into foreign-policy councils. The U.S. Commission on International Religious Freedom collected testimony from North Korean refugees, widely publicized their plight, and pressed governments in the region to provide help. It backed legislation sponsored by Senator Sam Brownback to allow refugees to gain asylum.[38] In turn, the State Department, in its 2003 report, declared North Korea the globe's worst abuser of religious freedom.[39]

Most dramatically, the faith-based movement helped vault a new human rights champion into international prominence. The story of Norbert Vollertsen illustrates how religiously called leaders connect vulnerable people abroad with advocacy networks at home. Vollertsen, a German doctor, spent eighteen months in North Korea providing medical aid under the auspices of a German aid group.[40] While treating a burn victim, Vollertsen stripped skin from his own thigh for a graft. For this act he was awarded a prestigious "Freedom Medal" from the government, which gave him VIP treatment and the ability to travel freely around the country. This turned out to be a blunder by the government of Kim Jong Il because Vollertsen secretly videotaped what he saw and returned to the West committed to exposing what he described as the genocidal policies of the regime.[41]

Vollertsen found children in hospitals who looked like Nazi concentration camp victims, their growth stunted, their eyes hollow.[42] He saw evidence of extensive famine, and refugees told him stories of mass executions, baby killings, and gruesome medical experiments. But what stunned him was the Orwellian nightmare of it all: of starving children "forced to engage in daily, two-hour songfests idolizing the 'Dear Leader'" while the party elite enjoyed a sumptuous lifestyle of gourmet banquets, posh hotels, casinos, and luxury cars.[43] Haunted by the Jewish Holocaust, Vollertsen is driven by parallels to speak out: "I am a German. You know about our history, that we kept silent, that we failed to act."[44] When faced with "something going on like in Nazi Germany," he explained, "I have to intervene."[45]

Vollertsen's exposé was met with indifference throughout Europe.[46] But from the moment he landed in the United States he has been embraced in American faith-based circles, featured in religious publications, interviewed on Christian radio, feted at religious conferences, and consulted by policymakers.[47] Michael Horowitz, who helped connect Vollertsen to evangelical leaders, said he had never seen "anybody who has become a hero to so many people so quickly."[48]

Vollertsen's work led to a personal transformation that embedded him even more deeply in the faith-based movement. He describes being moved by the faith and courage of Christian refugees he interviewed in China and by the commitment of believers in the United States to ameliorate their suffering. And as he shared his story, he kept hearing from Christian leaders, such as Charles Colson, that he was being "called" to this work. This rang true, and in response to that sense of calling Vollertsen experienced a Christian conversion. Word of this commitment to Christ only enhanced the response of the evangelical community to his campaign.[49]

What characterizes the work of Vollertsen and others in the emerging North Korean coalition is the same blend of passion and strategic analysis characteristic of the other faith-based struggles treated in this book. Through exposure and diplomatic action, the coalition first sought to provide tangible relief for the hundreds of thousands of refugees in China, who are often exploited by traffickers or sent back to the hell they left. Vollertsen staged actions at embassies in Beijing with refugees demanding asylum.[50] In turn, Senator Brownback (R-KS), chair of the East Asian and Pacific Affairs Subcommittee in the House, wrote a lengthy piece on refugees to accompany legislation he sponsored to facilitate asylum for North Korean refugees and defectors.[51] The U.S. Commission on International Religious Freedom backed this initiative, but also recommended funding human rights organizations, activities, and monitors, expanding broadcasts to the people of the north, and creating a congressional caucus on human rights in North Korea.[52]

This collective effort is but one component of a broader strategy that seeks to undermine the very regime itself. The aim flows from the conviction that only the overthrow of the regime will end the suffering of the people and provide regional security. Though bold and certainly controversial, this effort illustrates the sophistication of the movement because it would use the lever of human rights in the same way it was employed against another nuclear-armed Communist power— the Soviet Union. As outlined in a "statement of principles" signed by a group of religious freedom advocates and political figures, the idea would be to condition any negotiations between the regime and the United States on including human rights in the discussions. This was precisely what the United States did with the Soviet Union in 1972 in the Helsinki Agreement, which set in motion a process that cracked open spaces for human rights, encouraged defectors, and ultimately helped undermine the legitimacy of the regime. To implement this vision, Senator Brownback introduced and Congress passed the North Korean Human Rights Act of 2004, which requires the U.S. government to incorporate human rights considerations in policy actions aimed at the regime. While fear of North Korean military reprisals has led some political leaders to ignore the human rights tragedy, interfaith advocates see peace and security intimately tied to human rights.[53]

Though we cannot know what ramifications this law will have, what can be said is that without the faith-based movement the humanitarian catastrophe in North Korea would be receiving far less attention. A serious void is partly being filled.

TRAFFICKING INTO SLAVERY: THE NEW ABOLITIONIST MOVEMENT

A young woman in Veracruz, Mexico, is lured by an offer to work in a restaurant in Florida, only to discover when she arrived that her "job" was to work in a brothel as a prostitute. Enslaved by a combination of debt bondage, coercion, and violence, she was forced to work twelve hours a day for six days a week, and when she resisted she was repeatedly raped.[54] But this is not even the most horrific instance of chattel brutality in the global human trafficking "industry." Donna Hughes, professor of women's studies at the University of Rhode Island, documents that in some countries, girls as young as five years old are sold to pimps to perform oral sex, with penetration occurring by age ten.[55] While prostitution is probably as old as humanity, what we see today in the world is the underside of globalization: "The growth of sex slavery with millions of victims and billions of dollars for international organized crime."[56] The industry forces a staggering number of women and children into brutal forms of exploitation that one federal judge called the "most base, most vile, most despicable, most reprehensible crimes" he had ever seen.[57]

The response to this grotesque trade by some international NGOs and AIDS prevention programs *has not included* attempting to set the victims free. Instead, young girls have been treated as "sex workers," given "assertiveness and self-esteem" training, encouraged to develop "solidarity" with each other and better relations with their pimps, and taught how to "negotiate" condom use with foreign customers. Astonishingly, some of these programs were funded or promoted by agencies of the U.S. government, a practice that began in the Clinton administration but lingered into 2003, when activists calling themselves "New Abolitionists" against slavery finally quashed it.[58] An alternative approach is now emerging in the United States and abroad. Cambodian authorities, for example, under pressure by faith-based activists and the U.S. government, arrested traffickers, closed down the brothels, freed the women and girls, and provided succor to those in need.[59]

The campaign against human trafficking has all the hallmarks of other accounts in this book: (1) a massive and slighted humanitarian tragedy, (2) engagement by the faith-based movement in alliance with others (in this case women's groups), and (3) pressure on the U.S. government to exercise more international leadership to stem abuses. The result has been tough congressional legislation, robust executive action, and new international cooperation against global crime syndicates.

This story deserves extended discussion because it illustrates how the faith-based movement is "going forth" in attempting to "free God's children." While skeptics see parochial motives in the movement's focus on religious freedom, the same cannot be said about this initiative. Moreover, the Trafficking Victims Protection Act,[60] passed by Congress in October of 2000, may turn out to be among the most consequential initiatives of America's human rights leadership. The act strengthens laws against the trafficking, mostly of women and children, for the purposes of forced prostitution, bonded labor, and other forms of involuntary servitude. It sanctions countries that fail to criminalize and punish offenders, and it provides protection for victims.

This initiative shows how the religious community brings distinct moral and grassroots resources to bear in filling some of the dark voids of human rights protection. But it also illustrates the way social movements can build political capital for forays beyond their original focus. Without the advocacy networks galvanized by the campaign against religious persecution, it is unlikely trafficking legislation would have been passed or vigorously applied. Ironically, then, feminist activists against this exploitation of women find their best allies among evangelicals and other religionists in the new faith-based constituency.

Though human trafficking has long been a problem, it metastasized in the freewheeling global environment of the 1990s. Organized crime syndicates moved into the vacuum created by the collapse of the Soviet Union and exploited the booming international sex trade in Asia. As many as a million women and children each year are trafficked into forced prostitution, many bought and sold until they die young of disease and abuse.[61] Impoverished young women and girls from Asia, Russia, Eastern Europe, and Latin America are either targeted with misleading appeals or are sold outright by families, ending up virtual slaves of their pimps.[62] This is a lucrative business, according to Laura Lederer, a leading expert, because "unlike drugs, which are sold only once, a human being can be sold over and over again."[63]

John Busby, head of the Salvation Army of the United States, led his organization's support for human trafficking legislation. Courtesy of the Salvation Army.

Inadequate attention to this humanitarian catastrophe is attributable to several factors. Its rapid growth caught many off guard. National laws were largely inadequate to deal with the sophistication of the crime syndicates involved, whose vast profits enabled them to bribe officials and avoid prosecution. Also, as trafficking grew in the 1990s, human rights organizations paid insufficient attention, in part because they focused narrowly on *government* violations of rights, while trafficking was a commercial enterprise.[64] Some secular groups and countries also slighted trafficking out of ambivalence about how to treat prostitution. An ideology of radical autonomy on sexual matters, embraced in certain western European nations, affirms the right of women to be "sex workers" and seeks only health and safety regulation of legalized prostitution. Those adhering to this position draw a sharp distinction between "forced" prostitution and that chosen as a career. The problem with this position, according to legal advocates and the majority of the feminist organizations, is that vulnerable women are hardly able to give meaningful consent to their own sexual exploitation.[65] Watered-down laws shield traffickers—even those who sell children into forced prostitution—from prosecution.

Until the interfaith coalition entered the scene, those battling human trafficking often engaged in lonely struggles to highlight the problem. To understand the significance of the faith-based contribution, therefore, it is helpful to trace these early struggles.

A pioneering figure is Laura Lederer, whose odyssey is revealing in itself. Lederer's feminist credentials go back a quarter of a century, when she was one of the founders of the "Take Back the Night" movement against rape and hard-core pornography, and she has worked since then against what she describes as the vast commercial exploitation of women and children.[66] In her last year of law school at the University of Minnesota, Lederer was asked to do a presentation on trafficking at the Beijing Conference on Women in 1995. To research her presentation she dialed up ministries of justice in numerous countries and gathered police arrest records and journalistic reports. This enabled her to provide elementary outlines of the link between trafficking laws and routes ("this is the point of origin, here is the transit, here's the point of destination"). Women from the developing world reacted enthusiastically to her presentation, saying such things as, "This is a terrible problem in our country, and no-body's doing anything."[67]

Propelled by this response, Lederer secured a small grant to create the Protection Project, which began as a "sleepy little research project" to expand on her Beijing presentation. That project blossomed when officials of the International Narcotics and Law Enforcement Division, which oversaw trafficking issues at the Department of State, heard of her work. The office provided major funding for the Protection Project, which Lederer took to Harvard University at the invitation of the Women's Division of the JFK School of Government.[68]

As head of the Protection Project, Lederer produced prodigious documentation of worldwide trafficking routes, laws from nearly 200 countries, and survivor stories.[69] This record buoyed the case for harsher penalties on traffickers, sanctions against countries that fail to prosecute them, and better treatment of victims.[70]

Parallel to Lederer's efforts was the work of another human rights pioneer, Gary Haugen, founder and president of the Christian-based International Justice Mission (IJM). A former Justice Department lawyer, Haugen directed the UN genocide investigation in Rwanda. The searing experience of investigating the killing fields of Africa led Haugen, an evangelical, to a new understanding of the biblical mandate to fight against injustice. As he wrote in a book for fellow believers, the "good news about injustice" is that "God is against it."[71] Through direct case intervention, speaking, and writing, Haugen strives to reclaim the vocabulary of justice for the evangelical community. A generation ago, he notes, evangelicals shied away from what they saw as "liberal social gospel" concerns. Such theological obstacles are receding, he argues, especially for "those under thirty" who understand that "you can still be orthodox and traditional and take action." When confronted with stories of forced labor, abductions, detentions, and torture, the response is "What can we do?"[72]

Haugen founded the IJM in 1997 to provide a practical response to that question. Working with other human rights groups,[73] his organization takes on real cases and employs the underappreciated tool of law enforcement on behalf of victims of oppression. Many violations occur because of broken or corrupt legal systems, so IJM intervenes with authorities to provide legal protections for the vulnerable and succor to victims. Its cases involve forced prostitution, bonded servitude of children, unprosecuted sex assaults, seizures of land from widows, and other forms of exploitation. Employing teams of investigators and lawyers, the organization provides resources and pressure on local police and courts to enforce existing laws.[74]

In this way lay members of IJM see the difference they can make in the lives of real people. Haugen believes that this approach is one of the best ways to "take a community historically disengaged" in international affairs and get them engaged. Rather than ask the evangelical laity to respond to the "most intractable and contentious issues," the IJM provides examples of clear moral abuses that are stoppable.

The philosophy of IJM led to a major emphasis against trafficking. After hearing from Christian mission groups about abductions and sales of children for prostitution, IJM began deploying undercover investigators throughout Asia. This produced thousands of hours of experience from the inside of the trafficking industry, experience that proved pivotal as trafficking legislation made its way through Congress. To remind himself of the stakes involved—and of how intervention can make a difference—Haugen keeps a broken padlock on his desk. It came from a delegation he led to investigate forced prostitution of young girls in Asia. After marching with authorities to an infamous brothel, Haugen found the door padlocked, which he personally cut with a bolt cutter, finding horribly suffering girls inside who had literally been locked in. The impact of Haugen's obvious energy and eloquence, as we will see, were magnified as the legislative campaign connected him to the interfaith advocacy infrastructure.

Something similar occurred with another person, Jessica Neuwirth, who labored against trafficking within the feminist community. Working for Amnesty International in the early 1990s, she noticed that human rights groups at that time tended to slight such cultural or "commercial" abuses as female genital mutilation and sex trafficking.[75] So in 1992 Neuwirth founded Equality Now, an international women's rights organization designed to fill this void in human rights advocacy.

Neuwirth parts company with those secular human rights leaders who promote legalization of prostitution. Her investigations lead her to doubt the "voluntary" nature of much prostitution, and she concludes that legalization, as provided in Denmark and the Netherlands, just contributes to more trafficking of vulnerable women and girls. Moreover, at numerous UN forums devoted to the elimination of discrimination against women, Neuwirth found pro-prostitution interests working to water down definitions and laws, leaving women open to continued exploitation. She was thus disposed to support American action when the issue emerged.

The formative efforts of Lederer, Haugen, and Neuwirth, notable as they were, did not gain major policy traction in Washington, D.C., until the issue was engaged by the new faith-based coalition. Here again, Michael Horowitz served as a catalyst in connecting these activists with religious leaders who could mobilize constituent pressure. In January of 1998, even as the movement was gearing up for the final push for IRFA, Horowitz was thinking about a similar effort on sex trafficking.[76] He had read a *New York Times* story detailing how vulnerable Slavic women were trafficked into virtual slavery in brothels of western Europe, Israel, and the United States, and he expressed particular disgust with how Israel was acquiescing in such abuse.[77] Horowitz decided that something had to be done and the faith-based coalition was the perfect vehicle to do it. As he talked up the issue, one of the most receptive religious activists was Mariam Bell of Prison Fellowship. Bell had actually worked with Lederer years earlier on child pornography issues.[78] So when Horowitz began promoting legislation Bell told Lederer, "You have to go and introduce yourself to Michael Horowitz."[79]

This partnership between Horowitz and Lederer turned out to be pivotal in helping to set the agenda on international trafficking. Lederer brought to bear her voluminous documentation of the problem, and Horowitz connected her to the advocacy community in Washington. Lederer especially appreciated Horowitz's "genius" in the ways of Washington politics, in how to keep the ball moving forward.[80]

One of the things Horowitz pressed upon Lederer was the need to get women's groups behind the effort. He told her, in effect, "I've got these religious groups, and they are really interested in this; this is the human rights issue of our times. What about the women's groups?" She conveyed that the major feminist leaders would be wary of an alliance with the conservative religious community and skittish about its agenda on trafficking. She also noted tension within feminist ranks over how to treat prostitution. But she had known Jessica Neuwirth for years and admired the way she would sometimes "go out on a limb" on certain issues, so Lederer saw Equality Now as a prime organization to enlist in the cause. Moreover, leaders at Equality Now were well connected to Gloria Steinem, and with her "celebrity" backing, the other feminist leaders might come on board. That is, in fact, what happened.

What helped make the trafficking campaign work was the scaffolding and relationships forged in the religious freedom effort. Congressman Chris Smith responded with enthusiasm to the emerging cause by spearheading the legislative initiative. He had his top aide, Joseph Rees, compose a human trafficking bill, which he introduced in 1999. Rees had written the initial draft of Wolf-Specter, and his trafficking language involved a similar withdrawal of nonhumanitarian aid as a way to induce countries to change practices. While critics of Wolf-Specter took issue with this approach on religious freedom, the trafficking issue was less ambiguous. Dealing with powerful crime syndicates warranted the kind of tough measures contained in Smith's bill.

Just as we saw in other movement initiatives, the campaign for legislation acted as a magnet, drawing activists into common cause. The detailed recommendations of Lederer and Haugen, for example, toughened the legislation.[81] The lobbying campaign also featured victims themselves—trafficked women—who provided the most dramatic moments in the process, riveting hushed audiences with the brutality of their accounts and the dignity of their mien. Their testimony, which received wide play in religious magazines, palpably affected members of Congress, energized the coalition, and fortified provisions of the legislation dealing with treatment of victims—who often suffer further victimization by host countries when freed from traffickers.

The collective weight of this testimony suggested several things. First, victims must not be treated as criminals, and provision must be

Jessica Neuwirth of Equality Now, a key leader in the antitrafficking campaign. Courtesy of Equality Now.

made for their health and rehabilitation. Second, there must be "consequences for governments that don't deal with the problems." Threatening the withdrawal of nonhumanitarian aid moved the fight against trafficking from "a good idea to an urgent priority."[82] As Haugen stated in congressional testimony: "U.S. policy toward a country can have a very powerful effect upon the priorities of a nation's most senior authorities," and if "the goodies that flow from a country's relationship with the world's only remaining superpower" are jeopardized, then it will respond. Finally, there must be a way to measure whether a government is meeting a minimal standard to maintain good relations with the United States. Based on his organization's work, Haugen suggested such measurable criteria as the number of arrests of traffickers and the police in complicity with them. If governments had to report on this, then the word would quickly filter down to local officials, undercutting the cozy environment of police complicity upon which trafficking rests.[83]

Both the spirit of the law and its specific provisions reflect the movement's impact. Declaring that "trafficking in persons is a modern form of slavery" and a "degrading institution," the legislation makes detailed changes in laws to protect and rehabilitate victims, especially exploited women and girls. Noting how minimal sentences provide little deterrent to crime syndicates, it treats sex traffickers as rapists and imposes severe penalties. Finding that government policies enable trafficking, it requires that countries be designated according to trafficking practices. Countries must be designated as Tier I (where governments fully comply with standards), Tier II (where governments do not yet comply but are making significant efforts), and Tier III (where governments do not comply and are not making significant efforts). Tier III designees face the withdrawal of nonhumanitarian aid (subject to presidential waiver), along with embarrassing exposure.[84] As we will see, this lever is achieving measurable change.

The legislative campaign built upon the earlier alliance against persecution. This feature was captured at a strategy meeting that occurred on May 11, 1999, in a hideaway room in the U.S. Capitol with a dozen or so in attendance. Charles Colson thanked Michael Horowitz for convening the meeting, then opened it with an ecumenical prayer (to the "God of Abraham, Isaac, and Jacob"). Colson set the tone by declaring that the nation must use its economic power and moral authority to protect the vulnerable and that for him abolition of trafficking is a Christian mandate. Laura Lederer then presented a report on the dimensions and horrors of the problem, which clearly moved the delegation of religious leaders. Congressman Chris Smith summarized his legislation, and House Majority Leader Dick Armey pledged to ensure the bill would get to the floor. In addition to Colson, the conservative religious community was represented by such luminaries as Richard Cizik of the National Association of Evangelicals (NAE), William Bennett, and Richard Land of the Southern Baptist Convention (SBC). Though less well-known than Colson, Dr. Land brings formidable credentials (degrees from Princeton and Oxford) that enable him to move comfortably in the policy milieu. The group also included the redoubtable liberal David Saperstein. Horowitz quipped that "David's constituency pays him to right the Christian Right, but with considerable political courage he took on the persecution issue."[85]

The congenial discussion focused on strategy. All agreed that Smith's bill was superior to the competing one sponsored by the late

Paul Wellstone (D–MN), which was described as lacking an enforcement mechanism and muddling sex trafficking with low-wage sweatshop issues (for which remedies were less clear). It was agreed that Senator Brownback would be a good Senate sponsor. Saperstein pledged to build support among Democrats in Congress. Or as one person quipped, he could "kosher it" for the Democrats. Saperstein also noted that mainline religious leaders realized they had mishandled the persecution issue and could be brought on board this time. Horowitz was skeptical, but Richard Cizik agreed with Saperstein and even pledged to make the pitch to them. Horowitz spoke of the need to convey to business groups that they do not want to "wage war with the churches." Rees cautioned that reasonable people disagree with the kind of sanctions included in the Smith bill, and Saperstein suggested keeping an open mind to fears about the impact of a cutoff of nonhumanitarian aid. Colson thought this "wise counsel." When Congressman Smith castigated the Clinton administration, Colson responded that the issue is not between the "bad administration and the good Congress," but that "most Republicans are economically driven and powerful economic interests will oppose this legislation." A key strategic concern was recruiting feminist support. Lederer and Saperstein pledged to work with women's groups. To generate grassroots support the evangelical leaders agreed to plan a major event featuring born–again leaders from around the country (working around Colson's schedule as the draw). Cizik pledged to secure the signatures of a wide array of religious leaders endorsing the bill. Saperstein expressed optimism about the prospects of the bill, in part because of its backing by the "gold star" group of evangelical leaders in the room.

After the meeting, the top leadership of the evangelical world swiftly mobilized their networks in support of the legislation. The SBC and the NAE passed resolutions; Colson and Land went on the air; the Salvation Army made trafficking a key priority;[86] and religious presses featured victims of modern slavery. Some leaders saw this as a logical follow–up to their work on the religious freedom legislation. Richard Cizik argued that evangelicals must "live up to" the promise that they care about more than their coreligionists abroad. John Busby of the Salvation Army traced his engagement to the legacy of the founders of Army, the Booths, who fought trafficking in the nineteenth century. Charles Colson compared modern trafficking to the slave trade fought by great religious leaders of the past. Because no other human rights group can approach the potential of evangelical leaders to reach average citizens, Colson argued, evangelicals have a special obligation in shaping America's response.[87] Laura Lederer noticed this commitment: "It was an easy segue for many of the religious groups to say, 'We've been working on Sudan—here's another form of human slavery.'" She also observed that religious advocates brought moral clarity: "We're made in the image of God; you don't do this."[88]

Enlisting feminist groups, on the other hand, turned out to be more dicey. Not only was the feminist community split over such issues as pornography and prostitution, but there was hesitancy to back legislation sponsored by pro-life Republican Chris Smith. As one person put it, "It's just a bad PR thing for us." Before they joined the Smith coalition, Neuwirth and her associate Pamela Shifman engaged in negotiation for months with Wellstone, hoping to make his bill tougher. Meanwhile, Lederer entreated her feminist colleagues, in effect saying, "Come on over to this side . . . the water's fine." Revisions in the Smith bill facilitated their decision to join the alliance. As Neuwirth noted, the problem with the Wellstone bill was that it completely merged labor issues with sex trafficking, undercutting aggressive enforcement against prostitution syndicates. On the other hand, the original Smith bill focused mostly on sex trafficking. Equality Now "advocated that both" forced labor and sex trafficking be included, but wanted to "keep them separate" so that sex trafficking enforcement retained its teeth.[89] As the Smith bill incorporated more labor provisions, Neuwirth found more reasons to join the coalition. This process shows how advancing one cause can aid the broader human rights quest.

With Equality Now on board, Gloria Steinem was recruited.[90] And with Gloria Steinem's endorsement other major feminist leaders joined the alliance behind the Smith bill. Neuwirth, consequently, was "a dream come true" because she helped bring prominent feminist leaders into the faith-based coalition.

The key members of the trafficking coalition were sometimes depicted as a triumvirate of evangelicals, Jews, and feminists. Though oversimplified (Chris Smith is a Catholic), this depiction captures the political dynamic. The kickoff briefing on September 13, 1999, for example, was hosted by the NAE (Cizik), the Religious Action Center of Reform Judaism (Saperstein), and the Protection Project (Lederer). Jessica Neuwirth was also billed as a featured speaker. Cizik was unabashed in inviting his members to "join with" Saperstein, Neuwirth, and Lederer, ending the letter, without irony, by declaring that "Together we can make history for the cause of Christ."[91] The event, held in a Senate office building in Washington, D.C., did make history by signaling to policymakers the breadth of the emerging coalition.

The budding alliance between feminists and evangelicals was not without strain, even though they shared the same positions. In early 2000 the State Department sought to approve language in a UN treaty that would exclude "voluntary prostitution" from its definition of trafficking. Major feminist and evangelical leaders opposed this move, arguing that it would undercut efforts to deal with crime syndicates that trap women and girls. When Charles Colson and William Bennett used the issue to criticize Hillary Clinton's role on a women's task force, however, feminist leaders cried foul. Neuwirth blasted Colson and Bennett for "an outrageous, cynical exploitation of the serious issue of sex trafficking and an attempted manipulation of feminist leaders as a political ploy to attack Hillary Clinton."[92] The tiff probably refocused members on the central legislative objective; the coalition held.

The most vociferous opposition to the alliance came from State Department officials and the Clinton administration, which castigated the Smith bill as the "son of Wolf-Specter"[93] and touted the Wellstone bill as a better alternative. Opposition from the human rights community was more subtle. In defending the idea that women should have the right to do whatever they wish with their bodies, some groups saw a pro-choice position on prostitution as akin to their stance on abortion rights. Thus while they never officially opposed trafficking legislation, "they were," as one activist put it, "arrayed against us behind the scenes."[94] Feminist backers of the Smith bill responded that the idea of trafficking into "voluntary prostitution" plays right into the hands of the organized crime syndicates that prey on the economic desperation of women, children, and their families.

The legislative campaign exposed what many viewed as unhealthy relationships between State Department officials and those who took the pro-prostitution position. While a battle in the bowels of the bureaucracy may not seem the stuff of social movements, grantmaking by the State Department came under coalition scrutiny. With international activists funneling information about activities of U.S. officials, Laura Lederer led the way in exposing extensive State Department support for groups that promote legalized prostitution.[95] Characteristic of this process was a December 1999 memo from Pamela Shifman recounting how, at an international conference, a U.S. Justice Department official publicly declared that he favored legalization of prostitution.[96]

As the human trafficking legislation worked its way through Congress in 2000, State Department policies took heat from virtually all of the major feminist groups, which attacked the administration's refusal to define "prostitution of others" as a form of sexual exploitation. In a letter to Secretary of State Madeleine Albright, in January of 2000, ten leaders of women's organizations charged that the "administration's current position on the definition of trafficking is extremely detrimental to women." The signatories included Jessica Neuwirth of Equality Now, Gloria Feldt of Planned Parenthood Federation of America, Patricia Ireland of National Organization for Women, Eleanor Smeal of The Feminist Majority, and Gloria Steinem of *Ms. Magazine.* In particular, women's leaders took to task State Department opposition to the provision of the new law that included under the definition of traffickers, "the purchase, sale, recruitment, harboring, transportation, transfer or receipt of a person for the purpose of a commercial sex act." By taking this position, they argued, the administration was serving the interests of the trafficking industry. In addition, the feminist leaders took issue with the State Department's position at UN negotiations on a convention against transnational organized crime: "To our chagrin, the United States strongly supports the use of the term 'forced prostitution' rather than 'prostitution' in the definition of 'sexual exploitation.'" This definition, they argued, would not "cover some of the most common methods" by which traffickers prey on the victims.[97]

Notably, the position taken by the feminist leaders was identical to that voiced by the evangelical luminaries involved in the campaign. And both were voicing principles articulated in the 1949 United Nations Convention, which recognized that "the traffic in persons for the purpose of prostitution is incompatible with the dignity and worth of the human person and endangers the welfare of the individual, the family and the community."[98]

Lederer's work exposing questionable State Department policies and grants, which precipitated the stinging rebuke of the government by feminist leaders, also earned her a lesson in hardball politics. In May 2000, on the eve of House passage of trafficking legislation, Lederer was informed that the State Department was ending funding for the Protection Project and that she had to vacate her office at the Kennedy School of Government by the end of the month. Though she had been anticipating a transition, the latter blow was viewed as reflecting pressure by the administration on the Kennedy School.[99]

Outraged antitrafficking activists swung into action, providing a lesson of their own in the clout of the advocacy infrastructure. Memos flew around Washington and stories appeared in religious outlets. Horowitz called the action a tale of "no-good-deed-in-Washington-goes-unpunished" and pledged that it would be reversed. Seizing on an upcoming House vote, he activated coalition networks to encourage House members to cite Lederer's work during floor debate—sufficient to "make Laura's mother blush."[100] Congressional members called upon the State Department to renew funding of the Protection Project, even as they moved to earmark such funds if State failed to act.[101] In turn, high-profile efforts ensured a new home for the Protection Project. Former CIA director James Woolsey, a partner in a prominent Washington law firm,[102] provided pro bono legal work to facilitate transfer of the project to the Johns Hopkins School for Advanced International Studies, whose then dean, Paul Wolfowitz, welcomed Lederer's project. As a result of this action the Johns Hopkins name is affixed to the landmark report Lederer produced less than a year later.[103]

The breadth of the trafficking coalition and its momentum helped Smith enlist bipartisan support for his bill, including his liberal colleague Sam Gejdenson, who agreed to cosponsor it. Meanwhile, Sam Brownback was aggressively moving similar legislation in the Senate. This put Paul Wellstone in a tough position because groups close to him—such as Human Rights Watch—were cool to Smith-Gejdenson. But feminists leaders, such as Neuwirth, Steinem, and Smeal, ultimately convinced him to embrace the Smith-Gejdenson formula. In one of the last legislative actions before his untimely death, Wellstone ended up cosponsoring the Senate bill with Brownback.

Even in Washington, which is known for strange bedfellows, the groups that coalesced for the final legislation offered a sight to behold. At a pivotal last stage of the legislative campaign, members of Congress received a letter from Gloria Steinem and other feminist leaders at the very moment that they were being lobbied by such figures as Charles Colson of Prison Fellowship, Richard Land of the SBC, Kevin Mannoia and Richard Cizik of the NAE, and John Busby of the Salvation Army. As Lederer recounts, a conference was held in the Senate caucus room in which "Bill Bennett got up and gave a speech and then after that we read Gloria's statement." The gist of the conference was "Bill Bennett and Gloria Steinem and Chuck Colson and Gloria Feldt all are saying the same thing."[104]

With the passage of the law in October 2000 a palpable sense of historic moment charged participants. Before a packed audience celebrating the bill's passage in a Capitol Hill room, Brownback and Wellstone lauded each other, with Wellstone saying that Brownback was "a joy to work with." Brownback recounted hearing Thai children sing the refrain of a song, "You can sell my body but you can't sell my soul." Chris Smith responded that "we want to make sure they can't have your body." Senator Barbara Mikulski boomed her greeting to "fellow abolitionists." Laura Lederer and Pamela Shifman lauded the "incredible heroes" and "knights" of the struggle, which included Gary Haugen and James Woolsey, who said that "the lowest circle of hell is not hot enough" for those who traffic people into slavery. Haugen offered an impassioned address in which he challenged himself and others to do more. "God takes attendance," he said, and will ask of the struggle against global slavery, "Where were you?"[105]

This excitement, however, festered into anger as the lack of enforcement by the State Department threatened to undo these arduous efforts. Activists hoped the new law would serve as a lever against complicit governments; instead they charged that it was being treated as a mere paperwork exercise with minimal impact on foreign relations. The State Department's annual "Trafficking in Persons" (TIP) reports in 2001 and 2002, activists charged, represented a "literal whitewash" of countries "where trafficking of women and children into sexual and slave bondage by criminal syndicates and corrupt public officials remained largely unaddressed."[106] Indeed, countries with vast child prostitution rings were not designated as flagrant abusers.[107] In testimony before Congress, Gary Haugen provided a detailed critique of the weaknesses of the reports.

Equally distressing was that the State Department continued to make grants to groups opposed to vigorous enforcement of the law and otherwise sent signals to foreign governments and crime syndicates that they had little to fear from the new law. Some grants even went to groups that provided tacit approval of child prostitution, including NGOs involved in an infamous collaboration with child prostituting pimps in Cambodia.[108] By the summer of 2002 activists were increasingly pointed in their criticism, referring to the Bush administration's enforcement of the Trafficking Act as "comic mishandling," "one and one half years of drift," and "a debacle of missed opportunities." There was serious talk among evangelicals about the need to embarrass their president to get action.[109] Horowitz was incredulous that the administration would allow itself to become vulnerable to *60 Minutes*-type exposés about government grantees that "teach seven-year-old girls how to get their customers to wear condoms and to use techniques that make sexual penetration less painful."[110]

Much of the movement's ire was directed against then director of the TIP Office, Nancy Ely-Raphael, who was viewed by coalition members as naive, out of her depth, or a captive of staff hostile to the law. Horowitz called her an "irretrievably disastrous choice" because she had become the vessel for pro-prostitution interests.[111] Beyond personal attributes, Ely-Raphael simply represented bureaucratic inertia. After intense pressure from the faith-based community, the administration intervened to relieve her of the post.[112]

This episode set the stage for the pivotal search for a new director—a person to provide the leadership envisioned by the advocates. Aware of the passionate concerns of the antitrafficking activists, Paula Dobriansky, Undersecretary of State for Global Affairs, met with Frank Wolf and Mike Horowitz in the summer of 2002 to discuss possible candidates. During that meeting she mentioned the name of John Miller, a former member of Congress from Seattle with whom she had worked on human rights issues in Eastern Europe. As the story is told, Wolf raved about his former colleague, retorting that Miller "is either a saint or a fool" because Miller stood up to Boeing, his district's largest employer, on human rights in China.[113]

The saga of John Miller, appointed by President Bush in 2003 to direct the antitrafficking office, illustrates how social movements draw out new leaders and magnify their work. Miller's vigorous enforcement of the trafficking law, as we will see, is transforming the laws and practices of numerous countries. At the center of one of the most consequential human rights initiatives of a generation, his words and actions are intensely followed in capitals around the world. Yet less than a year before agreeing to lead the nation's quest "to abolish modern slavery," the unassuming Miller was living in Seattle, teaching at a yeshiva high school. He is both a product and exemplar of the new faith-based movement.

Miller had served in Congress from 1985–1993, where he developed a keen interest in international affairs. A moderate Republican and member of the human rights caucus, he joined Nancy Pelosi (D-CA) on the first congressional delegation to China after Tiananmen square. He admits not having heard much at all about the sex trafficking problem until Horowitz and Wolf called him to consider taking the director's job. After reading through materials they provided, he was "blown away by the issue." And he recalls thinking, "This was the great human rights cause today, and if I could make a little difference, that would be great."[114]

To movement activists Miller was an ideal candidate for the job. He combines political experience with a fervent commitment to the cause and a willingness to employ U.S. power to get results. Plus his own Jewish faith resonates with faith-based grounding of the cause. He cites the famous passage in Exodus in which God instructs Moses to "go tell Pharaoh to let my people go." But Miller likes to complete the famous line, which reads, "Let my people go *that they may serve me.*" (Miller's emphasis). As he summarized the meaning, "If that doesn't capsulize the connection between God and freedom, I don't know what does."[115]

This religious understanding seems the wellspring of Miller's moral clarity on the issue, and helps explain his ability to break through the white noise of Washington policy pronouncements. In a speech at Georgetown University in February 2003, Miller could not have sounded less like a government functionary. After quoting the fiery words of nineteenth-century abolitionists, Miller told listeners that he had "accepted the invitation of the President and Secretary of State . . . to lead this effort *to abolish modern day slavery.*" He demanded an end of euphemistic language: "We are talking about 'slaves,' not 'laborers.' We are talking about 'victims,' not 'sex workers.'" On behalf of the U.S. government, he declared war on the global crime syndicates that rape and enslave women and children, and he put foreign governments on notice that they would be held accountable for their responses.[116]

In responding to critics, Miller frequently evokes historic parallels between the efforts of his office with those of William Wilberforce, who fought the slave trade in his day: "The question that always gets asked is the same question Wilberforce got asked in 1798, when he explained his initiative to end the slave trade. And the question was, and this is literally a quote: 'What right do you have to impose British moral values on the world?' The same question gets asked today."[117] One response to that question is that UN covenants and protocols clearly condemn human trafficking. But to the question of why the United States should be taking action, Miller's answer is simple: "If not us, who? Who else is going to do it?"[118]

Clearly John Miller is a major new voice in the faith-based human rights movement. A telling part of his saga is that it took concerted action by movement leaders to secure his nomination over the objections of President's Bush's senior political adviser, Karl Rove. Despite backing by Dobriansky, members of Congress, antitrafficking activists, and faith-based leaders, Miller's nomination was blocked by Rove because Miller had been a McCain supporter in the 2000 presidential elections.[119] This precipitated a flurry of efforts to communicate the gravity of the situation to Rove and others at the White House, that the "President's religious base was not happy." In internal memos there was even talk about the possible need to "embarrass Karl Rove" to get Miller appointed.

This turn to hardheaded politics illustrates how the faith-based movement provides a counterweight to political calculation. Rove probably thought that blocking a nominee for a "mere" office at the State Department was a low-risk affair. But because of their international engagement, the nation's major evangelical leaders saw this as emblematic of the administration's lack of leadership on trafficking. In a pointed letter to Rove, drafted by Horowitz, these leaders championed Miller's nomination as a way the administration could signal the president's resolve. Among those signing the letter were Sandy Rios (Concerned Women for America), Gary Bauer, John Busby, Charles Colson, and Richard Cizik.[120] This initiative created a real problem for the White House, because these are the very leaders capable of reaching millions of citizens through church networks, broadcast programs, and publications. Rove ultimately backed down.

Miller was sworn into office in the spring of 2003 and in a few months had transformed the TIP Office at the State Department. In place of the dull and drab photocopied TIP report of year's past, the 2003 issue was a polished book with color photographs, dramatic victims stories, box inserts with best practices from around the world, and forceful prose. Its country reports do not pull punches in identifying complicity in trafficking. A rarity in diplomatic administration, it is also an eloquent and passionate document, a summons to the world's nations to cooperate in ending modern servitude.[121]

In anticipation of the report, the word went out to embassies around the world that tier designations would not be softened for allies and that aid cutoffs would ensue unless measurable changes occurred. Miller notified specific governments that they would be placed on the Tier III list (the most flagrant abusers subject to the loss of U.S. aid), leading in some cases to immediate action. In a remarkable example of American leverage, governments began to clamp down on the crime syndicates that ran trafficking operations and to arrest corrupt local officials.

This outcome is precisely what bill drafters envisioned: not that sanctions would be leveled but that the *threat* of sanctions or exposure would foster changes in behavior. As Miller described the process, in the two months *preceding* the issuance of the TIP report in June 2003, "there were more changes than in the previous several years."[122] Antitrafficking laws passed in the Philippines, Haiti, Burkina Faso, and Georgia. Scores of arrests occurred in Serbia and Cambodia, with the freeing of hundreds of women and girls. Cambodia in fact moved so aggressively that Miller's office had to upgrade its status to Tier II. The United Arab Emirates banned underage and underfed camel jockeys and repatriated the boys. After Miller informed Indian officials that normal relations with the United States were dependent on the crackdown of its vast child prostitution industry, authorities moved to break up rings and free children. In addition to legal changes, a number of countries also initiated awareness campaigns, mobilized civic groups, created vigilance committees, and engaged in moral suasion of businesses as a means of reducing the exploitation of vulnerable women and children. Because of a cunning feature of the legislation that gives countries in Tier III several months to respond before aid cutoffs occur, American diplomats expect ongoing actions.[123]

This striking global response on trafficking provides a certain vindication for faith-based activists who pressed for greater American leadership on human rights. What, then, are the lessons of the new alliance?

THE FAITH-BASED HUMAN RIGHTS QUEST: ASSESSING THE LESSONS AND CHALLENGES

Bolstering American leadership on international human rights—and thus altering the global environment—is no mean feat. This achievement suggests a number of lessons. First, it should be clear that one cannot understand America's role in the world without understanding

American religion. The pluralist vibrancy, rich social networks, and international connections of American churches constitute a pivotal resource for social movement mobilization on foreign affairs.

A wellspring of this influence is the trinity of connections between religious communities around the world, American churches, and the faith-based advocacy infrastructure. These linkages encompass a wide array of religionists—from Jews to Baha'is, Tibetan Buddhists to Sufi Muslims—which join in coalitions pressing diverse human rights concerns. But because Christianity is the most global of all faiths—with a presence in virtually every country—it looms large in the movement.[124] And because born-again Christians sport the most prolific social networks in the United States, their leaders play a pivotal role in generating constituent support for movement initiatives.

Implicit in this analysis—but not yet explicitly developed—is the role of *religious calling* as a motivator of human rights activism. Of course, human motivation is extraordinarily complex, but my immersion in this movement led me to conclude that religious conscience plays a significant role in the work of advocates—whether in Washington, in the American heartland, or abroad. Not only are many human rights activists driven by faith convictions, but a number shared how their personal faith was reawakened by involvement in the movement.

Religious callings helped stitch together relationships pivotal to the movement. In numerous meetings I saw diverse religionists working comfortably together, bonded by a shared sense of the *ecumenism of suffering* involved in religious persecution, human trafficking, and other abuses. I also saw victims—of persecution, torture, rape, forced prostitution, and bonded servitude—moving seamlessly among American church representatives, advocates, and government officials. What I witnessed is the process by which vulnerable people abroad are being connected by church networks to policy councils in the United States.

The faith-based human rights movement thus demonstrates the impact of individual altruism and choice in politics. Repeatedly we have seen how the fervency of individuals, or the strategic decisions of activists and policymakers, shaped political outcomes. This finding runs counter to much political science scholarship, which so focuses on "forces" and "factors" that individual agency gets lost. Yet it is hard to imagine IRFA, the Sudan Peace Act, or sex trafficking legislation being enacted without the efforts of the *particular* people featured in this book. Real people not only invested energy in the cause, but chose strategies that could have been different.

These findings suggest that in comprehending American politics, cynicism is not realism. To be sure, skepticism about motives is always warranted, but the cynical assumption of the basest motives of political actors is rarely an accurate depiction. Observations of the activists and members of Congress involved in the movement underlined their genuine commitment to justice and human dignity, however differently they interpreted those obligations. Politics, in other words, is not just about money and cozy relationships. Passionate social movement mobilization can alter the calculus of politics.

The new international mobilization also has much to teach us about the role of churches in social movements. As we saw in this book, church-based networks and fervency provided crucial resources to the new human rights movement—resources that activists exploited when windows of opportunity opened. What makes this new faith-based movement distinct is that it is focused on humanitarian concerns beyond our borders, *not on domestic grievances* that have typically driven social movements of the past. Driving this process is a globalization that knits churches and fellow believers across the planet, as vividly illustrated by growing ties between Sudanese congregations and local American fellowships.

The new faith-based quest may help reduce prejudice against, or ignorance of, religion. In numerous instances the movement exposed pockets of secular myopia, which trivialize religious devotion or discount its positive contributions. Such bias against faith can lead to real world blunders. As one scholar observed, "Some of worst foreign policy mistakes in the last thirty years have resulted from the absolute faith of the elites who make the major decisions in American society that religion ought not to matter and that, therefore, it does not matter." This "learned repugnance for religion" had permeated graduate school training of our foreign-policy decision makers for a generation. Dismissing religion in this way, unfortunately, blinds American policymakers to religious ferment, as when the CIA ignored the activities of Islamic clerics on the eve of the Iranian Revolution.[125] To reject the religious dimension, in other words, renders "incomprehensible some of the key issues and crises in the world today."[126] Ironically, the American architecture created to promote religious freedom ensures that officials will be in better touch with religious developments on the ground that may impinge on U.S. interests.

Ignoring religion also cuts diplomats off from a positive resource. One of the emerging themes of foreign-policy research is the unheralded church role in mediation and reconciliation of international conflicts and civil wars.[127] American church groups, as an example, are poised to cement the fragile peace in southern Sudan by rebuilding civil society and promoting reconciliation. Given the pivotal role of churches in the peace process, American diplomats are likely to welcome such aid.

Related to this new appreciation for religion is a nascent understanding of the potential role of Christianity in the twenty-first century. While some secular elites in the past tended to view Christian adherence as a retrograde phenomenon, its emerging global presence suggests its role as a potentially democratizing force.[128] Because it is the most widely dispersed religious faith around the world, Christianity can serve as a barometer of human rights, an early warning signal of broader global threats. Long before the militant Islamic movement attacked the United States, for example, jihad warriors were assaulting Christian populations in the Philippines, Sudan, Indonesia, and elsewhere. In a different vein, the treatment of house churches in China and Vietnam, or of Christians in North Korea, provides a vital gauge of the extent to which these societies are prepared to enter the community of nations.

This brings us to the signal feature in the politics of human rights: the new international engagement of evangelicals. As Robert Putnam has observed, in the past three decades evangelicals have created the most robust social networks in the nation. But Putnam also argues that this contribution has been limited, mostly replenishing "bonding social capital" *within* the community rather than "bridging social capital" *outward*.[129] Concern with the suffering of brothers and sisters abroad, however, appears to have drawn segments of the evangelical population outside of their enclaves and into public action. Alliances with Catholics, Jews, Episcopalians, Mormons, Baha'is, Buddhists, Sufi Muslims, and Chinese Falun Gong practitioners suggest the extent to which the evangelical community has begun to embody more of the "bridging social capital" than Putnam originally found.

International humanitarian activism, by its very nature, serves as a crucial "bridge" between evangelicals and broader communities. Indeed, an anthropologist might have noticed a kind of "we feeling" among the diverse activists working for IRFA, the Sudan Peace Act, the trafficking law, and North Korean refugee legislation. The movement, in other words, appears to be building social capital—networks of reciprocity and trust—that will be available for other political struggles.

Given that the relationship between Christianity and Islam may help define the twenty-first century, a crucial question arises: does that "we feeling" extend to Muslims struggling for the soul of their own faith? Here we can note a tension among evangelicals. Inflammatory remarks about Islam by a few prominent evangelists obviously undercuts alliances with moderate Muslims. And beyond these rhetorical excesses, we also see a broader theme in religious outlets of an inevitable "clash of civilizations" between the two proselytizing faiths.[130] In certain respects the threat of Islam is replacing the threat of Communism in the imagination of evangelicals.

But this impulse is not the only one. Because human rights engagement fosters exposure to people of different faiths, it can break down stereotypes. The faith-based alliance, for example, stressed the sharp distinction between Islamic civilization and militants who have "hijacked" its symbols for political ends. Moreover, leaders of the interfaith movement, including evangelicals, have described moderate Muslims as among the most numerous victims of the militant fundamentalists. The imposition of rigid Shari'a law, which bears little resemblance to Islamic civilizations of the past, increasingly constitutes a threat to human rights and civil peace in a number of countries. Because of this threat, evangelicals have joined in common cause with Muslim moderates and dissenters who are victimized by radical fundamentalism.[131] At a Washington, D.C., conference on abuse of Shari'a, held in the summer of 2002, many of the same figures involved in previous faith-based campaigns joined with Muhammad Hisham

Kabbani, a Sufi Muslim and head of the Islamic Supreme Council of America, and Azar Nafisi, a noted Iranian feminist.[132] Even among Christian activists in the heartland there is fresh thinking about their relation to Islam. Speaking on behalf of the Ministerial Alliance in Midland, Texas, Deborah Fikes said they feel strongly about the "need to build relationships with Muslims here in the United States and abroad." Acknowledging the hesitancy of evangelical Christians to "work side by side with Muslims," she observed that the Midland folks concluded that "Christ wants us to love our Muslim contacts."[133]

International religious engagement thus is not only influencing American politics, but appears to be changing the way some evangelicals view themselves and their place in the world. Notable achievements flowed from an unusual combination of ardent commitment and strategic realism. On a number of occasions I discerned an astute tactical grasp of politics, an understanding that it requires not just good intentions but shrewd analysis.[134]

Given that born-again voters represent a quarter of the electorate and a major voting bloc within the Republican Party, their considerable engagement has profound political implications.[135] Iron-

Gary Haugen with some of the children he champions.
Courtesy of International Justice Mission.

ically, while the common perception is that evangelical activism pushes the GOP to the Right on domestic issues, on a series of international issues the opposite has been the case, something even "bicoastal elites" have noticed.[136] *New York Times* columnist Nicholas Kristof, for example, notes that evangelicals have become the nation's "newest internationalists," saving lives "in some of the most forgotten parts of the world."[137] *New York Times* reporter Elisabeth Bumiller documented how evangelical influence in the Bush administration resulted in surprising human rights achievements.[138]

Evangelicals thus provide one of the few significant counterweights to the domination of foreign policy by corporate interests or strategic calculation. Indeed, concern about the "hijacking" of American foreign policy by big business has become a staple of emerging evangelical rhetoric. And on a number of issues evangelical leaders have joined with Catholics, Jews, and others in alliance against the corporate wing of the Republican Party. This has helped broaden foreign-policy calculations beyond dollars and cozy relationships. When such evangelical figures as Charles Colson, Richard Land, Franklin Graham, Gary Haugen, Diane Knippers, and others press for a higher priority for human rights, they embody what to many liberals and secularists might seem like a mind-bending prospect: *evangelicals as a foreign-policy conscience of conservatism.*

The challenge is to sustain this effort. Otherwise, "business as usual" will push human rights onto an island, cut off from real levers of power. Keeping that from happening may require even deeper constituency mobilization than the movement has achieved so far. To be sure, ardent lay engagement is a striking feature of the new politics of human rights, and surveys do show that evangelicals now support the promotion of human rights abroad more than the general public.[139] But beyond energetic work among national religious leaders, prominent pastors, and certain local activists, the movement sprouts only "pockets" of deep grassroots awareness and mobilization.[140] Some lay activists themselves lament that their fellow evangelicals have not grasped the biblical mandate to use their influence and wealth on behalf of the oppressed and poor of the world.

One possible indication of the outer limits of evangelical mobilization concerns the evolving Sudan story. Religious constituencies helped achieve the triumph of a peace treaty for southern Sudan. But then a new humanitarian catastrophe loomed with Khartoum's brutal ethnic cleansing of African Muslims in the western province of Darfur, leaving two million imperiled.[141] It is not clear that church leaders will be successful in mobilizing public support to sustain the kind of major, ongoing U.S. commitment necessary to stem further tragedy.

A continuing barrier to vigorous evangelical engagement remains the dearth of clear theological reflection on politics. Evangelical scholars themselves have lamented the anti–intellectual and individualist strain of pietism that inhibits coherent public witness.[142] Despite the efforts of Charles Colson, Gary Haugen, Richard Land, and Richard Cizik to connect evangelical theology with social justice, it is unclear how much of this has penetrated the lay level. Consequently, born-again activism on international issues could wane or be siphoned off by other concerns. In particular, a recrudescence of the culture war—this time over gay marriage—could swallow evangelical energies and undermine the strange-bedfellow alliances so essential to the faith-based movement. Will evangelicals be loath to work with those they see as mortal adversaries on marriage or abortion, or will they continue to forge uncomfortable alliances on behalf of the millions enslaved and suffering around the world? Given the strategic position of evangelicalism in American politics, its leaders bear an enormous responsibility to equip adherents with a sophisticated theological grasp of how and why to pursue justice and human rights, even while defending their position on traditional values.

The continuing theological ambivalence of evangelicals toward worldly engagement helps explain the importance of Jews in buoying evangelical activism. Far more than mainline Protestants or even Catholics, Jews have been mainstays in all of the initiatives charted in this book, sometimes prodding their evangelical allies. We see this with Horowitz, of course, but also with David Saperstein, who was a pivotal player in legislation on religious freedom, Sudan, and sex trafficking, and who remains active on such emerging issues as North Korea. But the list includes other national leaders, such as Abe Rosenthal, Stacie Burdette, Elliott Abrams, Charles Jacobs, Cheryl Halpern, and Abraham Foxman. The historic Jewish concern for human rights, along with a sense of common concerns in a dangerous world, has sealed this unusual alliance with born-again Protestants. To be sure, suspicion lingers, as when one evangelical leader conveyed concern about Saperstein's prominent role in the faith-based movement because "he fights us on everything else." Still, it is a testament to profoundly changing perceptions that such figures as Horowitz and Rosenthal would become literal heroes of Bible-believing Christians in the heartland.

One reason for these alliances is that diverse leaders are recognizing their stake in the direction of the evangelical movement in politics. Through a profound demographic revolution, upward of 70 percent of the estimated 650 million "Great Commission" Christians in the world now live in developing nations.[143] Because so many of these believers struggle amidst poverty and exploitation, aid workers and church leaders increasingly channel their concerns to affluent sister churches in the West. Thus the same globalization of the faith that helps fuel the new human rights movement also generates constituent support for humanitarian international initiatives, such as debt relief and AIDS funding for Africa.

This phenomenon emerged in the campaign to relieve debts burdening impoverished nations. Long a cause of international development organizations, debt relief enlists such diverse actors as Pope John Paul II and Irish rock singer Bono of U2. In 2000 this campaign gained a U.S. congressional appropriation of over $400 million, which leveraged much more from international financial institutions and other nations. In support of this effort evangelical aid organizations testified to the impact of debt on impoverished nations and pressed the cause with conservative legislators normally skeptical of foreign aid. And even the most conservative networks were mobilized for the cause. When tightfisted Republican Senator Phil Gramm (R–TX) threatened to filibuster the legislation, Pat Robertson, who had been contacted by Tom Hart of the Episcopal office, went on *The 700 Club* and asked viewers to contact Gramm (whose number was flashed on the screen) and demand that he remove his hold on the legislation, which he promptly did.[144]

Whether the issue is Third World debt, religious persecution, or slavery, Americans have been thrust into a historic moment in which their country is the world's unparalleled superpower. This reality creates a special stewardship role for religious leaders, who have the capacity to reach fellow citizens and shape their awareness of this global responsibility. The extent to which this happens depends on how American religionists interpret their own past, and which models they draw upon for inspiration.

THE LEGACY OF WILBERFORCE

It is fascinating how a historic personage can come to symbolize a new quest. William Wilberforce is such a figure in the faith-based movement. Charles Colson's Prison Fellowship created the Wilberforce Forum for its policy advocacy and gives an annual Wilberforce Award to individuals whose faith leads them to advance the cause of religious freedom and human dignity. John Miller frequently adverts to Wilberforce as his model.

William Wilberforce indeed represents a model of theologically rooted activism on behalf of human dignity that modern religionists would do well to emulate. A great English parliamentarian of two centuries ago, Wilberforce was known for eloquence and extraordinary gifts of leadership, which marked him for greatness. Indeed, he probably could have been prime minister, had he played his cards right. Yet a profound Christian conversion led him to understand how transitory are the blandishments of this world, so he never became prime minister. All he did was end the slave trade, and in the process help lay the foundations for the great moral revival of the Victorian period.

Wilberforce believed that whatever power he enjoyed as a member of Parliament was worthless unless it was used to advance human dignity and justice. And thus when he gazed at the moral cancer of his nation's slave trade, he introduced legislation in 1787 to abolish it. It failed. Undaunted, he continued to teach, to organize, to fight parliamentary maneuvers—*for two decades*—before the historic law passed.

Out of this crucible Wilberforce emerged as a shining symbol of faith-based statesmanship. Indeed, so great was his standing in the aftermath of this victory that he was able to help lead the renovation of his society, reforming manners and, it was said, making goodness fashionable in England.

Two facets of the Wilberforce lesson stand out. First is his persistence. To follow the Wilberforce model means to dedicate efforts for the long haul, for decades if necessary. If the British Parliament was slow to move in Wilberforce's time, the American political system, with its Madisonian checks, can be frustratingly glacial. Temporary setbacks and bureaucratic resistance are to be expected, and activists must prepare for years of halting steps to untie the yokes oppressing so many around the world.

The second lesson from Wilberforce concerns the potential salutary societal impact of this outward humanitarian focus. The parliamentary law Wilberforce pressed not only ended England's participation in the slave trade; it also turned the British navy into a righteous instrument enforcing the new international regime, lending a greater moral legitimacy to British leadership at the time. Moreover, it was by fighting slavery as a fundamental affront to human dignity that Wilberforce was simultaneously able to address the moral laxity in his own society.

We see parallels in our own time. Critics of America's presence in the world see the nation as materialistic, hedonistic, hypocritical, or concerned only with its own power. By elevating human rights in U.S. foreign policy, evangelical activists and their allies promote the nation's better side abroad, blunt charges of hypocrisy, and enhance the moral credibility of America's global leadership.

Similarly, success in renovating society at home may hinge, ironically, on a more global humanitarian focus. While this may seem paradoxical, the Christian faith itself is nothing if not paradoxical. For three decades now evangelicals and religious allies have fought frustrating battles, with limited success, against what they see as the coarsening of the culture, family breakdown, and secular hostility toward faith. Now we see how international engagement has not only achieved some notable successes, but has simultaneously begun to break down negative secular stereotypes of born-again Christians. New relationships forged in the international crucible are now available to address social and moral renovation at home.

But the link between international and domestic rights may go deeper. It is through commitments "outside of ourselves" that we discover our better angels. Thus, as I observed, the élan created by people passionately working on behalf of those halfway around the world seemed to make them more generous, charitable, morally clear, and confident among themselves—resources that can be applied to domestic renovation. Fighting for human dignity abroad helps to clarify the stakes at home, helps people to see what is good about the nation and worth fortifying, versus what is shallow or transitory.

The stewardship responsibility of American religionists is suggested by a study showing that the advanced nations of the world have the means to end the global scourge of slavery, which engulfs as many as 27 million people.[145] For those of us who believe that all people are made in the image of God—that they share such inherent dignity—this cause is nothing less than divine mandate.

Perhaps one way to understand the stakes is to consider the story of a single Cambodian girl, Laneh, age six. A grainy video filmed by undercover investigators for the IJM captured the sickening sight of her being offered by a pimp to a customer for sex.[146] IJM had heard reports from Christian workers in Cambodia of a "lawless village outside Phnom Penh [Svay Pak] composed almost entirely of brothels" where young girls were "being sold on the open market to be raped and molested by sex tourists."[147] After pressing unsuccessfully to get Cambodian authorities to investigate, IJM decided to run its own undercover operation, at considerable risk to detectives in a violent place where corrupt police officials protected brothel operators. Armed with the documentation, Gary Haugen mounted a campaign to expose and bring down Svay Pak and Cambodia's other child prostitution rings. He showed the undercover video to ambassadors, members of Congress, and Cambodian authorities. He got American news networks to air major stories based on his documentation.[148]

Haugen's relentless pressure on Cambodia finally gained bite when the State Department's trafficking office, under the leadership of John Miller, notified Cambodia in the spring of 2003 that it would be designated as a Tier III nation. Finally moved to action, Cambodian authorities joined IJM investigators in a raid of brothels in Svay Pak, arresting a dozen perpetrators and freeing some forty girls, ages six to twelve, including Laneh. This action sparked a broader crack-down of the child prostitution industry in Cambodia.[149]

Laneh and the other girls were placed in the care of a Christian organization committed to their long-term healing. In place of the grim video the IJM now features a photograph of Laneh and a group of her friends laughing at a party, soft drinks in hand.[150] Ending the horror of Svay Pak would not have happened without the work of IJM. It would not have happened without those who fought for congressional trafficking legislation and then pressed the American government to aggressively apply it. It would not have happened without the initiative of the State Department's Office of Human Trafficking. But in a broader sense, ending the horror of Svay Pak would not have happened without the campaign for religious free-dom, which galvanized church leaders and focused their mobilization on human rights as a key aim of America's global leadership.

Because of the faith-based movement Laneh, a child of God, was set free.

NOTES

CHAPTER 1

1. Even though Ethiopia is not an Islamic country, its Islamic regions gained relative autonomy in the wake of the Communist regime's collapse.

2. See Samuel Freedman, "Horowitz's List," *New York Magazine*, March 31, 1997. I interviewed both Getaneh and Horowitz about Getaneh's story, read numerous accounts in religious publications, and observed his participation and testimony at faith-based conferences.

3. John D. McCarthy and Mayer N. Zald, *The Trend of Social Movements in America: Professionalization and Resource Mobilization* (Morristown, NJ: General Learning Press, 1973); John D. McCarthy and Mayer N. Zald, "Resource Mobilization and Social Movements: A Partial Theory," *American Journal of Sociology* 82 (1977): 1212–41; Doug McAdam, *Political Process and the Development of Black Insurgency, 1930–1970* (Chicago: University of Chicago Press, 1985); Sidney Tarrow, *Power in Movement* (New York: Cambridge University Press, 1994).

4. One of the exceptions to dismissive reporting of the new international role of evangelicals is Nicholas Kristof of the *New York Times.* He described evangelicals as the "newest internationalists," not only providing extensive relief and development aid but fighting against human rights abuses in numerous places around the globe. See Nicholas D. Kristof, "Following God Abroad," *New York Times*, May 21, 2002.

5. Phillip Jenkins, who has captured this momentous development, uses the term "global south" to depict the developing countries of Latin America, Africa, and Asia, even though some are not technically south of the equator. See Phillip Jenkins, *The Next Christendom: The Coming of Global Christianity* (New York: Oxford University Press, 2002).

6. See especially James Davison Hunter, *Culture Wars: The Struggle to Define America* (New York: Basic Books, 1991).

7. Edward Luttwak, "The Missing Dimension," in *Religion: The Missing Dimension of Statecraft*, ed. Douglas Johnston and Cynthia Sampson (New York: Oxford University Press, 1994), chapter 2.

8. I take up this proposition more fully in chapter 2 and elsewhere. There is a lot of scholarly debate about the correlates of democratization; Samuel Huntington has offered the most compelling case so far for the pivotal role of global Christianity as a democratizing force. See Huntington, *The Third Wave: Democratization in the Late Twentieth Century* (Norman: University of Oklahoma Press, 1991).

9. Gary Haugen, *Good News about Injustice* (Downers Grove, IL: InterVarsity Press, 1999).

10. Kristof, "Following God Abroad."

11. The nature of this research presented a challenge in determining how to cite some of this material. In a single passage there may be multiple quotes by the same person from different conversations at different times. To keep my narrative uncluttered, therefore, I have not included an endnote for every quote, and I generally cite quotes where they provide signposts to the reader, such as at the beginning of a section. Where quotations have no citation, the reader can assume they were taken from interviews, informal conversations, or meetings. I do, of course, cite all published material.

12. This is the phrase that congressional scholar Richard Fenno uses to describe his method of research. See Richard Fenno, *Home Style* (Boston: Little Brown, 1978).

13. See especially Allen Hertzke, "Genocide Fueled by Oil," *Weekly Standard*, July 22, 2002; and Allen Hertzke and Daniel Philpott, "Defending the Faiths," *National Interest*, Fall 2000, and "On This They Do Agree," *Wall Street Journal*, October 10, 2003.

14. Scholars call this approach phenomenological, which is often related to the ethnographic method of research.

15. Alliances forged in the human rights movement have facilitated ecumenical work on such issues as poverty, underdevelopment, and debt relief, but they are beyond the main purview of my research. Other scholars are concerned with interreligious conflict, religious tolerance, model laws, and problems associated with proselytizing. My work touches on these but not as directly as others.

16. The conference, held in Washington, D.C., was sponsored by the Ethics and Public Policy Conference and chaired by its then-president, Elliott Abrams.

17. From a 1992 story in an official Chinese state-run organ, cited in Paul Marshall, *Their Blood Cries Out* (Dallas, TX: Word, 1997), 10–11; originally found in the report *China: Religious Freedom Denied* (Washington, DC: Puebla Institute, 1994), 13.

18. Terrorism, Russian weakness, Iraqi aggression, Balkan instability, and the rise of China were all on the radar of foreign-policy specialists as emerging issues with the end of the Cold War.

19. Tarrow, *Power in Movement.*

20. Movement scholars see three factors that come together to create a social movement: grievances, resources, and opportunity structures. Many accounts emphasize how much movements rely on windows of opportunity opening up and on political changes or events that create the right moment for mobilization. In this book, I emphasize both opportunities and resources but also the strategic choices of leaders—in other words, human agency.

21. An excellent catalogue of how this paradigm guided and misguided generations of social scientists is provided by Rodney Stark, "Religious Effects: In Praise of 'Ideological Humbug,'" *Review of Religious Research* 41 (March 2000): 289–310.

22. Gilles Kepel, *The Revenge of God: The Resurgence of Islam, Christianity, and Judaism in the Modern World,* trans. Alan Braley (University Park: Pennsylvania State Press, 1994), 1.

23. Edward Luttwak, "The Missing Dimension," in *Religion, The Missing Dimension of Statecraft*, ed. Douglas Johnston and Cynthia Sampson (New York: Oxford University Press, 1994).

24. What is striking about the current era is that we see so-called fundamentalist movements in virtually all the major faiths—Islam, Judaism, Christianity, Hinduism, and even Buddhism—though of varying intensity and breadth.

25. Samuel P. Huntington, *The Clash of Civilizations and the Remaking of World Order* (New York: Touchstone, 1996), 96.

26. Paul Johnson, *Modern Times*, rev. ed. (New York: HarperPerennial, 1991), 700. Among those intellectuals who predicted the demise of religious faith were "Feuerbach and Marx, Durkheim and Frazer, Lenin, Wells, Shaw, Gide, Sartre and many others."

27. George Weigel, "Religion and Peace: An Argument Complexified," *Washington Quarterly* 14 (spring 1991): 27; Kepel, *Revenge of God*.

28. Huntington, *Clash of Civilizations*, 96.

29. On the revivals of German Pentecostal evangelist Reinhard Bonnke in Nigeria, see Corrie Cutrer, "Come and Receive Your Miracle," *Christianity Today*, February 5, 2001. On Pope John Paul II, see George Weigel, *Witness to Hope* (New York: HarperCollins, 1999).

30. Kepel, *Revenge of God*, 2.

31. Johnson, *Modern Times*, 704–5.

32. Samuel Huntington, "Religious Persecution and Religious Relevance in Today's World," in *The Influence of Faith: Religious Groups and U.S. Foreign Policy*, ed. Elliott Abrams (Lanham, MD: Rowman & Littlefield, 2001), 58.

33. Kevin Boyle and Juliet Sheen, eds., *Freedom of Religion and Belief: A World Report* (London: Routledge, 1997).

34. Freedom House, "Religious Freedom 'Deteriorating' New Freedom House Survey Finds," news release, October 26, 2000. This news release summarized findings of the Freedom House publication by Paul Marshall, ed., *Religious Freedom in the World: A Global Report on Freedom and Persecution* (Nashville, TN: Broadman & Holman, 2000).

35. Huntington, *Clash of Civilizations*.

36. Huntington, *Clash of Civilizations*.

37. Pope John Paul II, "Tertio Millennio Adveniente: Toward the Third Millennium," Apostolic Letter, November 10, 1994.

38. Phillip Jenkins, *The Next Christendom*.

39. Evangelical leaders now routinely cite Article 18 of the UN Declaration of Human Rights as embodying their vision of religious freedom.

40. At a conference sponsored by Freedom House in 2002, a number of evangelical leaders conferred with moderate Muslim leaders about the threat of fundamentalist interpretations of Shari'a.

41. U.S. Commission on International Religious Freedom, March 2001 report.

42. Andrew F. Walls, "Eusebius Tries Again: Reconceiving the Study of Christian History," *International Bulletin of Missionary Research* 24 (July 2000).

43. Marshall, *Their Blood Cries Out*, 7.

44. Because categories employed by demographers have changed over time, precise comparisons cannot be made. For example, the categories in 1950 were North America versus South America with Central America attached to the North; by 1995 the more descriptive categories of Northern America and Latin America were used. Problems dealing with the former Soviet Union also muddy the analysis. For example, the entire Soviet Union was included in Europe, but after its breakup, the Central Asian republics were included in Asia. Moreover, with the collapse of Communism, the counted population of Orthodox in Russia mushroomed. Nonetheless, the basic pattern remains unmistakable. Thus, even when Northern America, Europe (including Russia), and Oceania (including Australia and New Zealand) are combined, their proportion of the globe's Christian population is only 41 percent. The percentage is even lower for the non-Orthodox Western branches of Christianity, with only 37 percent from North America and Europe. Figures from 1999 are from *Britannica Book of the Year 2000*; 1950 figures are from *Britannica Book of the Year 1950*.

45. Barrett, David B., George T. Kurian, and Todd M. Johnson, eds., *World Christian Encyclopedia*, 2nd ed. (New York: Oxford University Press, 2001). Forty-six percent of all Africans are Christians, compared to 40 percent who are Muslims. In sub-Saharan regions Christians are the majority.

46. Walls, "Eusebius Tries Again."

47. Jenkins, *The Next Christendom*; "The Next Christianity," *Atlantic Monthly* (October 2002): 53–68.

48. Marshall, *Their Blood Cries Out*, 8.

49. This information is based on the mammoth *World Christian Encyclopedia*, 2001. The specific quote is from a review of that two-volume set by Mark Noll, "Who Would Have Thought," *Books & Culture*, (November/December 2001).

50. Diane Knippers, "Sex and the Anglicans," *Weekly Standard*, September 7, 1998, 29.

51. "Lutherans by the Numbers," *Christian Century*, March 4, 1998.

52. Barrett et al., *World Christian Encyclopedia*. See also "Annual Statistical Table on Global Mission, 1996," *International Bulletin of Missionary Research*, January 1996; "A Century of Growth," *Christianity Today*, (November 16, 1998).

53. Mormons, of course, are not viewed as orthodox in their Christianity, but their unique system of mandated service for young people produces thousands of missionaries and will accelerate the globalization of the church.

54. Paul E. Pierson, "The Rise of Christian Mission and Relief Agencies," in *The Influence of Faith: Religious Groups and U.S. Foreign Policy*, ed. Elliott Abrams (Lanham, MD: Rowman & Littlefield, 2001).

55. Gustav Niebuhr of the *New York Times*, "Crossroads for Evangelism," *Denver Post*, July 30, 2000.

56. The most graphic instance concerned the Rwanda civil war, in which Catholic Hutus, including some priests and religious leaders, participated in the genocide against the Tutsis. Some priests, in fact, allowed atrocities to occur in parishes where Tutsis had sought refuge. The Vatican, of course, condemned this complicity and approved the convictions of these priests in war crimes trials.

57. Walls, "Eusebius Tries Again."

58. Ann Motley Hallum, *Beyond Missionaries: Toward an Understanding of the Protestant Movement in Central America* (Lanham, MD: Rowman & Littlefield Publishers, 1996).

59. Huntington, *Clash of Civilizations*, 99. While 20 percent of Brazil's population is Protestant (versus 70 percent Catholic), total Sunday attendance in Protestant churches is over 20 million versus 12 million in Catholic parishes.

60. Marshall, *Their Blood Cries Out*, 254.

61. This distinction is also crucial because demographers often include Orthodox Russia as part of Europe, which dramatically increases the overall European Christian population and masks the decline of Christian adherents in Western Europe.

62. Orthodoxy did not experience the same crucial encounter with the Enlightenment that purged Western churches of their medieval vestiges, and its continued melding of church and state make democratization more difficult in Orthodox lands. See Huntington, *Clash of Civilizations*.

63. Andrew F. Walls, "On the Road with Christianity: A Conversation with Missiologist Andrew Walls," interview by Donald A. Yerxa, *Books & Culture* (May/June 2001): 9.

64. Huntington, *Clash of Civilizations*, 65.

65. Goodstein, "A Move to Fight the 'Persecution' Facing Christians," *New York Times*, November 9, 1998.

66. Marshall, *Their Blood Cries Out*. Marshall's estimates are based on reasonable assumptions, according to Samuel Huntington. Huntington adds that it is conceivable that more Muslims than Christians suffer religious persecution; the difference is that they suffer it largely at the hands of Muslim governments. Huntington, "Religious Persecution," 61.

67. See Bassam Tibi, *The Challenge of Fundamentalism: Political Islam and the New World Disorder* (Berkeley: University of California Press, 1998); and Samuel Huntington, *The Clash of Civilizations*.

68. These included Franco-German reconciliation after the Second World War and the resolution of the Nigerian Civil War and conflicts in Nicaragua and Rhodesia. See Douglas Johnston and Cynthia Sampson, eds., *Religion: The Missing Dimension of Statecraft* (New York: Oxford University Press, 1994).

69. Elliott Abrams, ed., *The Influence of Faith: Religious Groups & U.S. Foreign Policy* (Lanham, MD: Rowman & Littlefield, 2001).

70. Johnson introduces this as a major theme of his book *Modern Times*.

71. T. S. Eliot, *The Idea of a Christian Society* (San Diego, CA: Harvest, 1948), 50.

72. The National Commission on Civic Renewal, "A Nation of Spectators: How Civic Disengagement Weakens America and What We Can Do About It" (College Park, MD: 1998); E. J. Dionne Jr. and John J. DiIulio Jr., eds., *What's God Got to Do with the American Experiment?* (Washington, DC: Brookings, 2000).

73. Robert Putnam, *Bowling Alone: The Collapse and Revival of American Community* (New York: Simon & Schuster, 2000), chapter 4.

74. The scholars documenting the civic role of religion include Putnam, *Bowling Alone*; Theda Skocpol, "How Americans Became Civic," in *Civic Engagement in American Democracy*, ed. Theda Skocpol and Morris P. Fiorina (Washington, DC: Brookings, 1999); Sidney Verba, Kay Lehman Schlozman, and Henry E. Brady, *Voice and Equality: Civic Voluntarism in American Society* (Cambridge: Harvard University Press, 1995); and Dionne and DiIulio, *What's God Got to Do with the American Experiment?*

75. Pope John Paul II, "World Peace Day Message," *Origins* 17 (1987): 494; as cited by J. Bryan Hehir, "Religious Freedom and U.S. Foreign Policy: Categories and Choices," in *The Influence of Faith: Religious Groups & U.S. Foreign Policy*, ed. Elliott Abrams (Lanham, MD: Rowman & Littlefield, 2001).

76. A prolific author, columnist, and radio commentator, Colson is enormously influential in the evangelical world and beyond. His most recent book with Nancy Pearcey is *How Now Shall We Live?* (Wheaton, IL: Tyndale House, 1999).

77. Haugen, *Good News about Injustice*.

78. In *Oregon v. Smith* (1990), the Supreme Court struck down the so-called compelling state interest test that had provided leverage for claimants seeking exemption from secular laws that burden their religious practice. Congress responded by passing the Religious Freedom Restoration Act, which the Supreme Court struck down as unconstitutional, leading Congress to pass a narrower law attempting to provide relief for religious claimants. The cause united Jewish, Catholic, evangelical, mainline Protestant, Mormon, and Muslim leaders. David Saperstein suggested to me that this struggle helped forge the relationships that blossomed further in the international battles.

79. The extraordinary diversity of colonial religious sects, often the outgrowth of persecution in Europe, eventually led the founders of the new nation to guarantee the autonomy of church institutions, creating a "free market" in religion, which funneled creedal divisions into generally peaceful competition for the faithful and provided all sects with a stake in the pluralist system.

See Roger Finke and Rodney Stark, *The Churching of America, 1776–1990: Winners and Losers in Our Religious Economy* (New Brunswick, NJ: Rutgers University Press, 1992).

80. Steven Rickard, former director of Amnesty International and currently director of the Nuremberg Legacy Project, has aggressively promoted religious freedom in testimony before Congress and in written articles. While taking issue with some proposals of the faith-based movement, he has expressed strong support for the cause and has defended Christians who advocate on behalf of fellow believers. See Stephen Rickard, "United against Persecution," *Washington Times*, December 11, 1997; "Religion and Global Affairs: Repression and Response," Symposium on Religion and Global Affairs, *SAIS Review*, summer-fall 1998; Testimony before the Committee on International Relations, U.S. House of Representatives, September 10, 1997; Testimony before the Subcommittee on International Operations and Human Rights, Committee on International Relations, U.S. House of Representatives, October 6, 1999.

81. Mary Ann Glendon, *A World Made New: Eleanor Roosevelt and the Universal Declaration of Human Rights* (New York: Random House, 2001).

82. See statement of Winnifred Fallers Sullivan, as quoted in *Religious Persecution as a U.S. Policy Issue*, ed. Rosalind I. J. Hackett, Mark Silk, and Dennis Hoover (Hartford, CT: Center for the Study of Religion in Public Life, 2000), 52, 54. See also Kevin Boyle and Juliet Sheen, eds., *Freedom of Religion and Belief: A World Report* (London: Routledge, 1997), which emphasizes the problematic aspects of religion and seems to underplay the central role of autocratic regimes in repressing religious practice.

83. Upon his release from a Chinese prison, Wei Jingshen joined the religious freedom coalition, writing a letter of support for the February 4, 1998, kickoff campaign for legislation. During the debate over granting permanent normal trade relations, in fact, Wei worked out of the offices of the Family Research Council, where I met him.

84. Samuel Huntington, *The Third Wave*. Seymour Martin Lipset summarized his work on democracy in "Excerpts from Three Lectures on Democracy," *Extensions*, Carl Albert Congressional Research Center (spring 1998). Other scholars remain skeptical of this relationship, suggesting that after statistical controls for economic development are included, the religious impact falls away. See Adam Przeworski et al., *Democracy and Development: Political Institutions and Well-Being in the World, 1950–1990* (New York: Cambridge University Press, 2000). A close reading of actual historical accounts of the democratizing role of Christian churches in Eastern Europe, Latin America, and the Philippines suggests that the way these tests are operationalized fails to capture the reality of the church role. See Weigel, *Witness to Hope,* 1999; and Johnson and Sampson, *Religion: The Missing Dimension of Statecraft.*

85. Samuel Huntington, *The Third Wave*.

86. Freedom House World Survey, *Freedom in the World* (Lanham, MD: Rowman & Littlefield, 2003).

87. Kim Dae Jung, a Catholic, assumed the presidency of the Republic of Korea in 1998, marking a remarkable saga for a man who had been given a death sentence for opposing the military dictatorship seventeen years before; Lee Teng-hui, also a Christian democratizer, led Taiwan through a good portion of the 1990s.

88. The pessimism is epitomized by Robert D. Kaplan, whose articles in the *Atlantic Monthly* etched a dismal view of the international scene. Those essays were collected in *The Coming Anarchy: Shattering the Dreams of the Post Cold War* (New York: Random House, 2000). Lawrence F. Kaplan has criticized Robert Kaplan and other "conservative declinists" who have abandoned the hope of using American power in support of democratization and human rights. See Lawrence F. Kaplan, "Fall Guys," *New Republic,* June 26, 2000.

89. Stephen Rickard, director of the Nuremberg Project, who takes issue with some of the sweeping claims of movement activists that secular groups "ignored" religious persecution, nonetheless lauds the faith-based movement for providing a new constituency for the cause. Interview, September 2003.

90. Putnam, *Bowling Alone*, chapter 4; Robert Booth Fowler, Allen D. Hertzke, and Laura Olson, *Religion and Politics in America* (Boulder, CO: Westview Press, 1999), chapter 2.

91. Putnam, *Bowling Alone*, chapter 4.

92. Verba, Schlozman, and Brady, *Voice and Equality*.

93. Estimates of the total number of houses of worship in the United States range from 350,000 to half a million.

94. The "National Service" for the persecuted church is held in November each year.

95. Finke and Stark, *Churching of America*.

96. Fowler, Hertzke, and Olson, *Religion and Politics in America*.

97. These phrases have been uttered so many times in interviews and printed in so many publications that I would be hard put to provide a single citation. See chapter 5.

98. This description captures what scholars term the ethnographic or "participant observation" method, which is what I employed in this research. What the scholar loses in detached objectivity in such a method is, in my judgment, more than made up in the richness of material gained.

99. McAdam, *Political Process and the Development of Black Insurgency*.

100. Finke and Stark, *Churching of America*.

101. James L. Guth, John C. Green, Lyman A. Kellstedt, and Corwin E. Smidt, "Onward Christian Soldiers: Religious Activist Groups in American Politics," in *Interest Group Politics*, 4th ed., ed. Allan Cigler and Burdette Loomis, as cited in Putnam, *Bowling Alone*, 162.

102. Putnam, *Bowling Alone*.

103. Putnam, *Bowling Alone*, 162.

104. Christian Smith and Michael Emerson, *American Evangelicalism: Embattled and Thriving* (Chicago: University of Chicago Press, 1998).

105. James L. Guth, John C. Green, Corwin E. Smidt, Lyman A. Kellstedt, and Margaret M. Poloma, *Bully Pulpit: The Politics of Protestant Clergy* (Lawrence: University of Kansas Press, 1997). The Pew Trusts Post-9/11 Survey of Evangelical Elites, Post-9/11 Survey of Religion and Politics, University of Akron, 2002, found 55 percent agreeing that "evangelicals are an embattled minority."

106. See Mark Noll, *One Nation under God? Christian Faith and Political Action in America* (San Francisco: Harper, 1988).

107. Phillip Jenkins catalogs how Christians of the global south may contribute to sectarian violence, *The Next Christendom*.

108. John C. Green, Pew Charitable Trusts 2002 Survey of Evangelical Elites. A 2000 survey found 80 percent stating that combating religious persecution should be given priority. Given the post-9/11 priority given to terrorism, it is not surprising that the numbers are down a bit to 73 percent.

109. "Evangelicals in America," a survey conducted for *Religion and Ethics NewsWeekly*, released April 5, 2004.

110. Elisabeth Bumiller, "Evangelicals Sway White House on Human Rights Issues Abroad," *New York Times*, October 26, 2003.

111. The theoretical explanation can be stated in formal scientific language. The dependent variable (the thing to be explained) is the emergence of the faith-based movement for international human rights and humanitarian intervention. The independent variables (which

explain the dependent variable) include: (1) the tectonic shift of the globe's Christian population to the developing and nondemocratic world, which has nested faith communities among the vulnerable and persecuted; (2) the growth of religious social movement networks, both internationally and at home, that facilitate mobilization; (3) the opening of windows of opportunity with the end of the Cold War, accelerating globalization and favorable intellectual trends; and (4) the rise of the United States as the undisputed global leader. The intervening variable (that links the dependent and independent variables) is the leadership of diverse activists—often motivated by religious conviction or a sense of calling—who capitalized on these conditions to funnel pressure on American policymakers to ameliorate human rights and humanitarian abuses in far corners of the globe.

112. The phrase is from John Noonan, as quoted in W. Cole Durham Jr., "A Comparative Framework for Analyzing Religious Liberty" (paper presented at the Inter-American Bar Association Meeting, Santiago, Chile, April 20, 1993).

113. Senator Sam Brownback, interview, summer 2000.

114. As Charles Jacobs, president of the American Anti-Slavery Group, recounted to me in the spring of 2003, groups like Human Rights Watch and allies in the press slighted the massive human rights abuses occurring against Christian populations in such places as Sudan and Indonesia because of what he calls the Human Rights Complex, which is described in chapter 3.

115. One example is the book *The Mobilization of Shame* by Robert F. Drinan (New Haven, CT: Yale University Press, 2001). Drinan provides a valuable exegesis of human rights covenants, but he often uses language ("nullified," "legally binding," "implemented") that implies a real force of law. The reader notices, however, that when he says that a provision has been "implemented," that only means that UN rapporteurs issued reports on particular provisions (chapter 17).

116. Putnam, *Bowling Alone*, chapter 9.

117. See Trafficking in Persons Report, U.S. Department of State, March 2003; and John Miller, director of the Office to Monitor and Combat Trafficking in Persons (speech, Georgetown University, Washington, D.C., February 20, 2003).

118. Kristof, a notable exception to this trend, argued that his cohorts do indeed operate with a caricature of evangelicals and therefore have been blind to the growing international humanitarian work of the community. See "Following God Abroad."

CHAPTER 2

1. This chapter heading, of course, is the title of Paul Marshall's book *Their Blood Cries Out* (Dallas, TX: Word, 1997), which is in turn coined from the Genesis story of Cain and Abel, in which God says to Cain that "the voice of your brother's blood is crying to me from the ground" (Genesis 8:10). Borrowing Marshall's title is appropriate for two reasons: (1) it evokes the sense of innocent blood being shed and (2) it captures how Christian solidarity activists have become motivated to join a movement to respond to persecution.

2. Tomas J. Belke, *Juche: A Christian Study of North Korea's State Religion* (Bartlesville, OK: Living Sacrifice Book Company, 1999).

3. Michael Young, testifying as chair of the Commission on International Religious Freedom, said that when refugees are forced back to North Korea they are asked questions, one of which is "Are you a Christian?" and if they answer yes they are executed. Hearing of Human Rights Caucus, April 17, 2002, chaired by Congressman Mark Kirk.

4. Soon Ok Lee, *Eyes of the Tailless Animals* (Bartlesville, OK: Living Sacrifice Book Company, 1999).

5. Prayer of Soon Ok Lee at the Second Summit of Christian Leaders on Religious Persecution, Mayflower Hotel, Washington, D.C., May 1, 2002.

6. The most comprehensive document, detailing the status of religious freedom in every country on Earth, is the *Annual Report on International Religious Freedom*, November 2002, submitted to the Committee on International Relations, U.S. House of Representatives, and the Committee on Foreign Relations, U.S. Senate, by the Department of State, www.house.gov/international_relations/www.state.gov/g/drl/rls/irf/2001/. Because it is vetted by diplomats, this report sometimes is criticized as soft-pedaling certain situations. More hard-hitting is the report by Freedom House, *Religious Freedom in the World: A Global Report on Freedom and Persecution,* ed. Paul Marshall (Nashville, TN: Broadman & Holman, 2000). Also hard-hitting but with a stronger policy focus are reports and hearings of the U.S. Commission on International Religious Freedom presented each May. See for example: *Annual Report of the United States Commission on International Religious Freedom,* May 2002, www.uscirf.gov. Numerous congressional hearings also highlight a problem.

7. The U.S. State Department annual report provides a good catalog of the distinct sources of religious violations.

8. Certain horrific abuses, such as genocide in Rwanda, are not specifically religious in nature and thus fall outside the treatment in this book. Though religious persons, even Catholic priests, became involved in the Rwanda genocide, the conflict was almost entirely tribal or ethnic rivalry between Hutus and Tutsis.

9. See Freedom House, *Religious Freedom in the World*, 2000; and the most recent report on international religious freedom issued by the U.S. State Department at www.state.gov/drl/rls/irf/2003/.

10. Interview with Norbert Vollertsen, May 1, 2002. Also see Vollertson's article "Memo to Mr. Carter: Evil Exists," *Wall Street Journal*, March 7, 2002; and the most recent U.S. Commission on International Religious Freedom report at www.uscirf.gov/reports/02May03/vietnam.php3.

11. *Persecution of Christians Worldwide*, Hearing before the Subcommittee on International Relations, House of Representatives, 104th Cong., 2nd sess., February 15, 1996, 7.

12. *Persecution of Christians Worldwide*, 10.

13. *Persecution of Christians Worldwide*, 8.

14. U.S. Department of State, *Annual Report on International Religious Freedom* 2001, 122.

15. The website of the Falun Dafa organization is www.falundafa.org/.

16. See Freedom House, *Religious Freedom in the World*, 2000; and the most recent report on international religious freedom issued by the U.S. State Department at www.state.gov/drl/rls/irf/2003/.

17. Akbar S. Ahmed, *Islam Today: A Short Introduction to the Muslim World* (London: I. B. Tauris, 1999).

18. Bernard Lewis, *What Went Wrong: The Clash between Islam and Modernity in the Middle East* (New York, Oxford: Oxford University Press, 2002).

19. Paul Marshall, "The Persecution of Christians in the Contemporary World: Presentation to the Advisory Committee to Secretary of State on Religious Freedom Abroad," as reprinted by the Claremont Institute, 1997, old.claremont.org/publications/Persecution.cfm.

20. Samuel Huntington, "Religious Persecution and Religious Relevance in Today's World," in *The Influence of Faith: Religious Groups and U.S. Foreign Policy*, ed. Elliott Abrams (Lanham, MD: Rowman & Littlefield, 2001).

21. Bassam Tibi, *The Challenge of Fundamentalism*. Berkeley: University of California Press, 1998.

22. Freedom House sponsored a Washington, D.C., conference on July 10, 2002, titled "Prospects for Human Rights under Extreme Shari'a." A number of scholars and thinkers, including Muslim representatives, discussed this growing threat to human rights of militant imposition of Shari'a.

23. Shaykh Muhammad Kabbani, Chairman of the Islamic Supreme Council of America and a Sufi Muslim, has spoken and written extensively about the misapplication of Shari'a by fundamentalists and Wahhabis. See www.islamicsupremecouncil.org.

24. Shaykh Kabbani cites numerous Muslim scholars and historical precedents to back his argument against the extremist interpretation of Shari'a.

25. Stan Guthrie with Obed Minchakpu, "A Blast of Hell," *Christianity Today* (October 7, 2002): 28.

26. Sudanese Anglican Bishop Rt. Rev. Peter El Birish, for example, was thrashed in public after being accused of adultery, Freedom House, *Religious Freedom in the World*, 285.

27. Freedom House, *Religious Freedom in the World*, 171.

28. U.S. Department of State, *Annual Report on International Religious Freedom*, 2002, 430.

29. Freedom House, *Religious Freedom in the World*, 228; U.S. Department of State, *Annual Report on International Religious Freedom*, 2001, 159.

30. U.S. Department of State, *Annual Report on International Religious Freedom*, 2001, 153–54.

31. U.S. Department of State, *Annual Report on International Religious Freedom*, 2001, 479.

32. U.S. Department of State, *Annual Report on International Religious Freedom*, 2001, 529.

33. U.S. Department of State, *Annual Report on International Religious Freedom*, 2001, 440.

34. Freedom House, *Religious Freedom in the World*, 285.

35. *Persecution of Christians Worldwide*, 32.

36. Freedom House, *Religious Freedom in the World*, 123.

37. U.S. Department of State, *Annual Report on International Religious Freedom*, 2002.

38. This individual was Pastor Wally, as he is known and mentioned in chapter 2.

39. Nina Shea, *In the Lion's Den* (Nashville, TN: Broadman & Holman, 1997), 41.

40. Marshall, *Their Blood Cries Out*, 30–31.

41. Bernard Lewis, numerous news articles, letter from Southern Baptist Convention, April 25, 2003.

42. Freedom House, *Religious Freedom in the World*, 282.

43. U.S. Department of State, *Annual Report on International Religious Freedom*, 2001, 148–64.

44. U.S. Department of State, *Annual Report on International Religious Freedom*, 2001, 160.

45. Daniel Pipes and Jonathan Schanzer, "Militant Islam's New Strongholds," *New York Post*, October 22, 2002.

46. Freedom House, *Religious Freedom in the World*, 95.

47. Freedom House, *Religious Freedom in the World*, 94.

48. Commission on International Religious Freedom, Recommendations on Designating Countries of Concern, last modified October 15, 2002, www.uscirf.gov.

49. Freedom House, *Religious Freedom in the World*, 263.

50. Freedom House, *Religious Freedom in the World*; and the State Department report at www.state.gov.

51. Lawrence A. Uzzell and Michael Bordeaux of the Keston Institute in the United Kingdom have documented these problems, www.keston.org. Also see Freedom House, *Religious Freedom in the World*.

52. In Belgium, for example, they have been denied recognition and, therefore, even the right to bring spiritual assistance to their members in hospitals and prisons. Members of non-recognized religions, like the Jehovah's Witnesses, in many nations have even been deprived of legal custody of their children solely due to the public status of their belief system.

53. U.S. Department of State, *Annual Report on International Religious Freedom*, 2001, xxiii.

54. U.S. Department of State, *Annual Report on International Religious Freedom*, 2002.

55. Marshall, *Their Blood Cries Out*, 104.

56. Marshall, *Their Blood Cries Out*, 109.

57. Nina Shea, "Terror against the Church," *Crisis* 15, no. 3 (March 1997): 16–20

58. Kamran Khan, "Gunmen Kill Seven Christians at Karachi Charity," *Washington Post*, September 26, 2002, A23.

59. Paul Marchall, "Motive for Massacre," *Wall Street Journal*, September 27, 2002.

60. Paul Marshall, *Their Blood Cries Out*.

61. These figures are from the *World Christian Encyclopedia*, eds. David B. Barrett, George T. Kurian, and Todd M. Johnson (New York: Oxford University Press, 2001).

62. Huntington, "Religious Persecution."

63. Marshall's combined figures of 600 million living in conditions of persecution and discrimination would equal 30 percent of the 2 billion total Christians. Given that more nominal Christians reside in the free countries, it is probably safe to say that the suffering church constitutes a third of the real whole of Christendom, assuming Marshall's figures are reasonably accurate.

64. Marshall, *Their Blood Cries Out,* 227.

65. Shea, *In the Lion's Den*, x.

66. *Persecution of Christians Worldwide*, 19.

67. *Persecution of Christians Worldwide*, 7.

68. *Persecution of Christians Worldwide*, 41.

69. Marshall, *Their Blood Cries Out,* 25.

70. Marshall, *Their Blood Cries Out*, 79.

71. *Persecution of Christians Worldwide*, 41.

72. Marshall, *Their Blood Cries Out*, 103.

73. Freedom House, *Religious Freedom in the World*, 248.

74. Marshall, *Their Blood Cries Out*, 34.

75. *Persecution of Christians Worldwide*, 2.

76. Marshall, *Their Blood Cries Out*, 69. This is in reference to the 1915 genocide of Armenians.

77. Raymond Bonner, "Indonesian Suspect Agrees to Questioning, Then Collapses," *New York Times*, October 19, 2002, A8.

78. Freedom House, *Religious Freedom in the World*, 2000, 70. The local court interpreted Shari'a as to prohibit women to give witness to an offense and stipulated that to prove rape would require four Muslim men, or eight non-Muslim men, as witnesses.

79. Freedom House, *Religious Freedom in the World*, 247.

80. Freedom House, *Religious Freedom in the World*, 249.

81. Freedom House, *Religious Freedom in the World*, 190.

82. Freedom House, *Religious Freedom in the World*, 189; the U.S. State Department Report, November 2003, echoes the sorry picture of the treatment of Christians in North Korea, but does not present the picture in such vivid terms as the Freedom House report.

83. U.S. Department of State, *Annual Report on International Religious Freedom*, 2001, 169.

84. Freedom House, *Religious Freedom in the World*, 103.

85. When I was in China in 1999 I attended mass at a Patriotic Catholic church. The Vatican has attempted to negotiate the theological thicket of acknowledging the validity of the experience of the believers who attend official churches, even while fighting for recognition of the Catholic Church loyal to the Pope.

86. *Persecution of Christians Worldwide*, 8.

87. Marshall, *Their Blood Cries Out*, 89.

88. See Habib Malik, "Political Islam and the Roots of Violence," in *The Influence of Faith: Religious Groups and U.S. Foreign Policy*, ed. Elliott Abrams (Lanham, MD: Rowman & Littlefield, 2001); William Dalrymple, *From the Holy Mountain: A Journey among the Christians of the Middle East* (New York: Holt, 1997); and Marshall, *Their Blood Cries Out,* 50, for the figure on Syrian Christians.

89. Voice of the Martyrs Annual Conference, Tulsa, Oklahoma, April 1999.

90. In its 2001–2002 report, Freedom House found that 41 percent of the world's population lives in free countries, 23 percent in partly free countries, and 36 percent in not free countries. See Freedom House, "Freedom in the World 2002: The Democracy Gap." Freedom House's Center for Religious Freedom found in 2000 an identical 36 percent of the world's population living in places where religious freedom is fundamentally violated, but a much higher 39 percent reside where conditions are only "partly free." The difference suggests the way that generally free countries are restricting religious practice. See "Religious Freedom 'Deteriorating,' New Freedom House Survey Finds," news release, Washington, D.C., Freedom House, October 26, 2000. This news release summarized findings of the Freedom House publication *Religious Freedom in the World*, ed. Paul Marshall..

91. All of the major international documents on religious freedom are contained in *Religion and Human Rights: Basic Documents*, ed. Tad Stahnke and J. Paul Martin (New York: Center for the Study of Human Rights, Columbia University, 1998).

92. Mary Ann Glendon, *A World Made New: Eleanor Roosevelt and the Universal Declaration of Human Rights* (New York: Random House, 2001). The appendix contains the Universal Declaration.

93. John Hanford III, ambassador-at-large for International Religious Freedom, Introduction to the 2002 State Department Report on International Religious Freedom, www.state.gov.

94. Senator Joseph Lieberman, Prepared Statement, Hearings before the Committee on Foreign Relations, 1998, 84.

95. This version of the oft-quoted epigram of Paul Wolfowitz was made by Senator Lieberman, Prepared Statement, 1998, 85.

96. Robert F. Drinan, *The Mobilization of Shame* (New Haven, CT: Yale University Press), 2001.

97. See T. Jeremy Gunn, "A Preliminary Response to Criticisms of the International Religious Freedom Act of 1998," *Brigham Young University Law Review* (September 2000): 841–66. This article provides a valuably detailed analysis of the criticisms of IRFA. Gunn served as the first research director for the International Religious Freedom Commission, but departed apparently because he had differences with some of the activities of the Commission.

98. The pluralism of denominations and sects in the early Republic, many of which fled to the New World to escape persecution, led the framers of the Constitution to enshrine the legal guarantee of free expression of religion, providing all with a stake in the pluralist system. Though a number of religious minorities suffered discrimination and even persecution in periods of American history, nonetheless the constitutional protection encouraged pluralist vitality.

99. Senator Joseph Lieberman, Prepared Statement, Hearings before the Committee on Foreign Relations, United States Senate, May 12 and June 17, 1998, 84. Not only were the first sixteen words of the First Amendment concerned with religious freedom, but the struggle for religious rights played a crucial role in American democratization by promoting pluralism.

100. Gunn, "A Preliminary Response," 841, 846.

101. Wei Jingsheng, letter, February 4, 1998.

102. Jacob Heilbrunn, "Christian Rights," *New Republic*, July 7, 1997, 23.

103. Speech by Chris Smith at the press conference in front of the Capitol, October 10, 1998, celebrating the passage of the International Religious Freedom Act.

104. *Religious Persecution as a U.S. Policy Issue*, ed. Rosalind I. J. Hackett, Mark Silk, and Dennis Hoover (Hartford, CT: Center for the Study of Religion in Public Life, Trinity College, 2000).

105. One scholar normally fair to religion described the legislative campaign as part of a conservative religious agenda that includes predictions about the coming of the anti-Christ and a fundamentalist paranoia toward the European Union. See William Martin, "The Christian Right and American Foreign Policy," *Foreign Policy* (spring 1999).

106. Speech by Frank Wolf in front of the Capitol, October 1998, at the press conference celebrating the passage of the International Religious Freedom Act.

107. This is the position of Robert D. Kaplan, a correspondent for *Atlantic Monthly*, whose essays paint a picture of anarchy in many places. Kaplan provides a bracing challenge to fuzzy idealistic thinking, but his pessimistic resignation would lead to the abandonment of efforts to ameliorate the tragedies of the current age. See Robert D. Kaplan, *The Coming Anarchy: Shattering the Dreams of the Post Cold War* (New York: Vintage), 2000.

108. In the "Trafficking in Persons Report," issued on July 11, 2003, the State Department cited changes in national laws, crime rings broken up, and the freeing of women and children from forced prostitution.

CHAPTER 3

1. Charles Jacobs, interview, April 2003.

2. Charles Jacobs and Mohamed Athie, "Bought and Sold," *New York Times*, July 13, 1994.

3. The legislative achievements of the faith-based movement include the International Religious Freedom Act of 1998, the Victims of Trafficking and Violence Protection Act of 2000, and the Sudan Peace Act of 2002. The movement failed to block the granting of Permanent Normal Trade Relations to the People's Republic of China in 2000, though it continues to champion the cause of religious freedom in the world's largest Communist country through a variety of initiatives.

4. Nina Shea, *In the Lion's Den* (Nashville, TN: Broadman & Holman, 1997); and interview with congressional staff member involved in drafting the legislation.

5. Jackson-Vanik was an amendment to the Trade Act of 1974 (Section 402, "Freedom of Emigration in East-West Trade").

6. Kenneth Cosgrove, "The Tangled Web: Ethnic Groups, Interest Groups, and Congressional Foreign Policy-Making" (Ph.D. diss., University of Oklahoma, 1993).

7. See Allen D. Hertzke, *Representing God in Washington* (Knoxville: University of Tennessee Press, 1988).

8. Skeptics argue that it was not clear that Jewish emigration from the Soviet Union increased as a result of Jackson-Vanik. Proponents, on the other hand, argue that it kept economic and political pressure on Communist regimes in Eastern Europe and contributed to their ultimate demise.

9. The A. M. Rosenthal columns appeared in the Op-Ed section of the *New York Times* on the following dates in 1997: February 11, February 14, April 4, April 25, April 29, May 13, June 10, June 17, July 25, September 16, October 10, and December 2.

10. "Bill Proposed to Combat Christian Persecution," Report from the Capital, Baptist Joint Committee, vol. 52, no. 11 (July 3, 1997).

11. Roger Finke and Rodney Stark, *The Churching of America, 1776–1990: Winners and Losers in Our Religious Economy* (New Brunswick, NJ: Rutgers University Press, 1992).

12. "Issues before the 209th General Assembly," Presbyterian Church (United States) Conference, June 14–21, 1997, Syracuse, N.Y., www.pcusa.org/pcusa/ga209/97issues.htm.

13. See the work by Andrew Greeley, *The Denominational Society* (Glenview, IL: Scott Foresman, 1972); and Will Herberg, *Protestant, Catholic, Jew* (New York: Doubleday, 1955).

14. See Robert Booth Fowler, *Unconventional Partners: Religion and Liberal Culture in the United States* (Grand Rapids, MI: Eerdmans, 1989).

15. Finding the proper nomenclature for the historically mainline denominations is a challenge. In terms of demographics they are no longer "mainline," having been replaced by the evangelical branch as the predominant branch of Protestantism. Their ministers are trained in theologically liberal seminaries and are generally more liberal than their evangelical counterparts, but the members of these churches are generally moderate to conservative. So it is not accurate to term these churches either mainline or liberal. Old-line is a term some use, but it has a pejorative connotation.

16. "Issues before the 209th General Assembly."

17. "General Conference Issues," 1996 United Methodist General Conference, http://gbgm-umc.org/GC/issues.html.

18. Samuel P. Huntington, *The Clash of Civilizations and the Remaking of World Order* (New York: Touchstone, 1996).

19. H. Richard Niebuhr, *Christ and Culture* (New York: Harper & Row, 1951).

20. Robert Wuthnow, *The Restructuring of American Religion* (Princeton, NJ: Princeton University Press, 1988), 145.

21. Wuthnow, *Restructuring of American Religion*, 132.

22. James Davison Hunter, *Culture Wars: The Struggle to Define America* (New York: Basic Books, 1991).

23. James L. Guth, John C. Green, Corwin E. Smidt, Lyman A. Kellstedt, and Margaret M. Poloma, *Bully Pulpit: The Politics of Protestant Clergy* (Lawrence: University of Kansas Press, 1997). This book analyzes a large set of original surveys by the authors and is the definitive account of the subject.

24. Hertzke, *Representing God in Washington*.

25. Putnam, *Bowling Alone: The Collapse and Revival of American Community* (New York: Simon & Schuster, 2000).

26. Christian Smith, *Christian America? What Evangelicals Really Want* (Berkeley: University of California Press, 2000).

27. Cal Thomas and Ed Dobson, *Blinded by Might* (Grand Rapids, MI: Zondervan, 1999).

28. Horowitz not only spoke and wrote about this, but he also lamented this tendency frequently in personal conversations.

29. According to Gary Bauer in an interview in June 2001, Horowitz got so upset by these evangelical justifications that he broke his pencil in the middle of one discussion.

30. Shea, *In the Lion's Den*, 15. For a similar analysis, see Habib C. Malik, "Political Islam and the Roots of Violence," in *The Influence of Faith: Religious Groups and U.S. Foreign Policy,* ed. Elliott Abrams (Lanham, MD: Rowman & Littlefield, 2001).

31. Gary Bauer, interview, 2001.

32. Charles Colson, *How Now Shall We Live?* (Wheaton, IL: Tyndale House, 1999).

33. Thomas and Dobson, *Blinded by Might*.

34. Duane Oldfield, "Resisting the New World Order: The Emerging Foreign Policy Agenda of the Christian Right," paper delivered at the Annual Meeting of the American Political Science Association, Atlanta, Georgia, September 2–5, 1999.

35. Sam Ericsson, a highly respected former counsel for the Christian Legal Society, is now with Advocates International. As one fellow lobbyist noted, he "caught the devil" when he supported extension of MFN for China. Interview with Oliver Thomas, December 1997.

36. Though Ericsson is widely respected for his advocacy work, some of the activists I interviewed saw his approach as naive.

37. Sam Ericsson, interview, April 2000. Numerous publications and tapes of Advocates International echo these sentiments.

38. Ericsson, interview, 2000. The quote from Tom White is from the March 2000 issue of the *Voice of the Martyrs* publication.

39. Robert Seiple's piece is in the October 2002 issue of *Christianity Today*, www.christianitytoday.com/go/uscirf.

40. In its March 2003 issue, *Christianity Today* featured a debate between Michael Horowitz, who disputed Seiple's argument, and Jeremy Gunn, who backed the quiet diplomatic approach. Gunn, who served for a time as research director for the U.S. Commission on International Religions Freedom but took issue with its approach, characterized Horowitz's approach as "polemical" but never addressed the variety of activities of the Commission that would not seem to fall under such a rubric. See "Breaking Chains: Two Religious-Rights Advocates Differ Sharply on How Best to Help the Persecuted," *Christianity Today* (March 2003): 46–54.

41. Alan Cooperman, "Robertson Defends Liberia's President," *Washington Post*, July 10, 2003.

42. The letter was mailed out in spring 2001 from Coral Ridge Ministries, Fort Lauderdale, Florida.

43. See James Adams, *The Growing Church Lobby in Washington* (Grand Rapids, MI: Eerdmans, 1970); Jeffrey Hadden, *The Gathering Storm in the Churches* (Garden City, NJ: Doubleday, 1969); Harold Quinley, *The Prophetic Clergy* (New York: Wiley, 1974); and Hertzke, *Representing God in Washington*.

44. Oliver Thomas, chief counsel for the National Council of Churches, offered a systematic critique of original antipersecution legislation that raised concerns about unintended consequences—reprisals against vulnerable communities of Christians abroad. Tom Hart, then director of the Washington Office for the Episcopal Church, went even further by endorsing the Senate alternative and helping to line up support for it. He remained exceptional among the mainline leadership.

45. Testimony of Albert M. Pennybacker, Associate General Secretary, National Council of the Churches of Christ in the United States, before the House Subcommittee on Human Rights of the International Relations Committee, Focus on Persecution of Christians, February 15, 1996.

46. Reverend Cannon Patrick Mauney, director of Anglican Global Affairs of the Episcopal Church, in *Episcopal Life*, September 1997.

47. Mark Brown, "Religious Persecution Act Introduced," Legislative Update, Lutheran Office for Governmental Affairs, July 1996; Letter to Members of Congress from Rev. Dr. Thom White and Wolf Fassett, General Secretary, General Board of Church and Society, United Methodist Church, June 23, 1997.

48. Edward Yihua Xu, a scholar of American Studies at Fudan University in Shanghai, China, documented in an unpublished manuscript how the roots of the Three-Self Churches can be traced to the liberal denominations in the United States. He found that a number of the early leaders of the Three-Self Churches received their training at such places as Union Theological Seminary, noting that their liberal theological perspective lent itself to the aims and rhetoric of the Maoist revolution.

49. "Lutherans Back Away from Rebuking China," Special Reports from the Lutheran World Federation Assembly, Hong Kong, July 8–16, 1997, *Ecumenical News International*, www.wcc-coe.org/eni/0316.html.

50. News Release, "Methodist Finds Christians in Hong Kong Have Hopeful but Cautious Attitude," *United Methodist Daily News*, July 17, 1997, www.umc.org/umns/news97/jul/lfran.htm.

51. Mauney, *Episcopal Life*.

52. Kate O'Beirne, "Their Brothers' Keepers: The Conservative Shade of Human-Rights Activists," *National Review*, June 30, 2003.

53. Pennybacker, testimony before the House Subcommittee on International Operations and Human Rights, February 15, 1996.

54. Samuel Huntington, *The Third Wave: Democratization in the Late Twentieth Century* (Norman: University of Oklahoma Press, 1991).

55. Jack Connell, "Getting to Know China—Again," *Maryknoll* (January 1998): 33–35.

56. Written testimony by Reverend Drew Christiansen, U.S. Catholic Conference, September 10, 1997.

57. Some critics have charged that some bishops do not want to upset dialogue with the American Muslim Council, which fears the focus of the campaign against persecution.

58. This theme is developed in Robert Booth Fowler and Allen D. Hertzke, *Religion and Politics in America* (Boulder, CO: Westview Press, 1995), chapter 12.

59. Stephen Carter, *The Culture of Disbelief: How American Law and Politics Trivialize Religious Devotion* (New York: Basic Books, 1993).

60. Paul Marshall, *Their Blood Cries Out* (Dallas, TX: Word, 1997), chapter 8.

61. Secular human rights groups had not totally ignored religious persecution, and State Department human rights reports did include instances of religious rights abuses, including against Christians. But these cases were unfocused and largely lost in the white noise of issues competing for attention.

62. S. Robert Lichter, Stanley Rothman, and Linda S. Lichter, *The Media Elite* (Bethesda, MD: Adler, 1986).

63. Charles Jacobs, director of American Anti-Slavery Group, as quoted in Marshall, *Their Blood Cries Out*, 201.

64. Nina Shea, "Atrocities Not Fit to Print," *First Things* (November 1997): 33, found that over the past year "not a single story on Sudanese religious persecution has appeared from the foreign desks of the *New York Times*, the *Washington Post*, the *Wall Street Journal*, or *USA Today*."

65. A. M. Rosenthal, "Is This a Story?" *New York Times*, December 2, 1997.

66. Laurie Goodstein, "A Move to Fight the 'Persecution' Facing Christians," *New York Times*, November 9, 1998.

67. *New York Times*, September 26, 2003.

68. This is a point I develop more fully in a guest editorial. See Allen D. Hertzke, "On This They Do Agree," *Wall Street Journal*, October 10, 2003.

69. Elisabeth Bumiller, "Evangelicals Sway White House on Human Rights Issues Abroad," *New York Times*, October 26, 2003. This front-page feature story was a remarkable departure from previous *Times* coverage, as it captured the alliances and impact of the faith-based movement in a sympathetic fashion. Also notable is a *New York Times* editorial lauding the potential for peace in Sudan and mentioning pressure by the American Christian community as a factor in getting President George W. Bush to invest his capital in ending the civil war. "Hope from an African Trouble Spot," November 4, 2003, A28.

70. Marshall, *Their Blood Cries Out*, 75.

71. Richard Land, as quoted in Shea, *In the Lion's Den*, 5.

72. Nina Shea, "Atrocities Not Fit to Print," 34–35.

73. Kevin Boyle and Juliet Sheen, eds., *Freedom of Religion and Belief: A World Report* (London: Routledge, 1997), preface, introduction.

74. As of November 2003, the website for Human Rights Watch reflected its increasing attention to religious freedom. Religious freedom is included among its global issues highlighted, and that category includes a number of news bulletins on the denial of religious rights, including of Christians. A month earlier, however, religious freedom was not included on the list of global issues on the site map (though it was elsewhere), suggesting how the topic has been grafted onto a structure that had previously slighted it. Human Rights Watch, www.hrw.org.

75. Charles Jacobs, "Why Israel and Not Sudan is Singled Out," *Boston Globe*, October 5, 2002.

76. Stephen Richard, then director of the Washington Office of Amnesty International, mentioned Sudanese slavery in his testimony before the House Committee on International Relations, September 10, 1997.

77. Jacobs, "Why Israel."

78. Winnifred Fallers Sullivan, as quoted in *Religious Persecution as a U.S. Policy Issue*, ed. Rosalind I. J. Hackett, Mark Silk, and Dennis Hoover (Hartford, CT: Center for the Study of Religion in Public Life, 2000), 52, 54.

79. For a summary of this story, see Allen D. Hertzke, "An Assessment of Mainline Churches Since 1945," in *The Role of Religion in the Making of Public Policy*, ed. James W. Wood Jr. and Derek Davis (Waco, TX: Dawson Institute, 1991). On the movement toward greater church benevolence toward the Soviet Union and its satellites, see Kent Hill, *The Soviet Union on the Brink*, (Portland, OR: Multnomah Press, 1991), part III, 149 onward; K. L. Billingsley, *From Mainline to Sideline*, (Washington, DC: Ethics and Public Policy Center, 1990), 20 onward; Paul Abrecht, "The Predicament of Christian Social Thought," *Ecumenical Review*, 1991; and J. A. Emerson Vermaat, *The World Council of Churches and Politics* (New York: Freedom House, 1989). One of the most stinging critiques of this posture was offered by Roy Howard Beck, a writer for the *United Methodist Reporter*. Beck showed how the double standard of public denunciation of right-wing governments and "quiet diplomacy" with left-wing governments violated Amnesty International guidelines about how to approach human rights abuses. See Roy Howard Beck, *On Thin Ice* (Wilmore, KY: Bristol Books, 1988), 195.

80. Alan Wisdom, ibid.

81. James Rudin, *Commonweal*, February 8, 1991, as quoted in *Religion Watch*, March 1991.

82. Joan Brown Campbell, as quoted by Jeffrey Goldberg, "Washington Discovers Christian Persecution," *New York Times Magazine*, December 21, 1997.

83. News Release, "Activist Speaks Out on Proposed Legislation," September 15, 1997, United Church of Christ, www.igc.org/conferences/wfn.news/entries/10428449910.html.

84. See Charles Lindblom, *Politics and Markets* (New York: Basic Books, 1977).

85. Huntington, *Clash of Civilizations*.

86. Robert D. Kaplan, *The Coming Anarchy* (New York: Vintage, 2000).

87. Congressman Chris Smith, interview, September 2000.

88. Paul Wolfowitz, *The New Republic*, February 5, 2001.

89. Congressman Smith, interview, September 2000.

90. Tarrow, *Power in Movement*, 1994.

91. Preface to the 2002 State Department Report on International Religious Freedom. This language probably comes from Tom Farr, director of the Office of International Religious Freedom, who has been a sympathetic voice for the cause in the State Department but now has an enhanced position to make that case.

92. John C. Green, Pew Charitable Trusts Survey of Evangelical Elites, Post-9/11 Survey of Religion and Politics, University of Akron, 2002.

CHAPTER 4

1. "How Beautiful Are the Feet," *Voice of the Martyrs*, April 2001; Pastor Richard Wurmbrand, *Tortured for Christ* (Bartlesville, OK: Living Sacrifice Book Company, 1967; 1998).

2. Michael Bourdeaux founded and for many years led the Keston Institute, a respected organization that documented human rights abuses of Soviet Communism. His eulogy of the pastor was titled, "On Richard Wurmbrand," *Tablet*, March 3, 2001; see also *First Things* (August/September 2001): 89–90.

3. Tom White, *God's Missiles over Cuba: The Tom White Story* (Bartlesville, OK: Living Sacrifice Book Company, 1981), xiii.

4. The quotes are standard boilerplate from VOM literature. White's story is contained in *God's Missiles over Cuba*.

5. Though raised a Baptist, Eibner now attends an Episcopal congregation in Zurich, Switzerland.

6. From my interview with Eibner, July 2003, and biography at www.csi-int.org.

7. From my interview with Eibner, July 2003, and biography www.csi-int.org.

8. Organizational Profile, Christian Solidarity International Webpage, www.csi.

9. This is how Baroness Cox refers to herself, and how she is introduced at a function. I saw her at two different functions, one in Washington, D.C., and the other in Midland, Texas.

10. This vignette occurred at the annual conference of Voice of the Martyrs, Tulsa, Oklahoma, 1998.

11. See, for example, Steve Cleary and Gary Lane, "The Good Shepherd: Caring for the Persecuted Church in Sudan," *Voice of the Martyrs*, April 2002.

12. Nina Shea, interview, 2003.

13. This was according to an interview with Nina Shea, January 2003.

14. This is what Baroness Caroline Cox argued in speeches to congregations in Midland, Texas, on the weekend of November 4, 2001, as part of the International Day of Prayer for the Persecuted Church. She elaborated on this theme in an interview.

15. Bin Laden's statement was entitled "Jihad against Jews and Crusaders," February 23, 1998, www.fas.org.

16. Though the WEF had begun a modest initiative, Horowitz pressed Charles Colson and other evangelical leaders to create a major, high profile event.

17. See Anthony Lewis, "The Wrong Signal," *New York Times*, September 12, 1997.

18. Eibner, interview, July 2003.

19. Oldfield, "Resisting the New World Order," speech delivered at the 1999 Annual Meeting of the American Political Science Association, Atlanta, September 2–5.

20. George Weigel, *Witness to Hope* (New York: HarperCollins, 1999).

21. Declaration on Religious Liberty, Vatican II, "Dignitatis Humanae," December 7, 1965, as published in *Vatican Council II: The Conciliar and Post Conciliar Documents*, ed. Austin Flannery (Collegeville, MN: Liturgical Press, 1975). For the first time the Catholic Church embraced Protestants as fellow Christians, recognized Jews as brethren, and acknowledged the legitimacy of other faiths.

22. Pope John Paul II, Annual Address to Diplomatic Corps, January 13, 1996, Vatican Information Service.

23. Pope John Paul II, "Tertio Millennio Adveniente: Toward the Third Millennium," Apostolic Letter, November 10, 1994.

24. Testimony of then Archbishop of Newark, Theodore E. McCarrick, before the Subcommittee on International Operations and Human Rights of the Committee on International Relations on the topic of *Persecution of Christians Worldwide*, U.S. House of Representatives, February 15, 1996.

25. Speech of Pope John Paul II, July 23, 2001.

26. This material is taken from several interviews with Shea, along with an extensive public record. See Ronald Radosh, *Commies: A Journey through the Old Left, the New Left, and the Leftover Left*, chapter 11 (San Francisco, CA: Encounter Books, 2002); Carroll Bogert, "Facing the Lions," *Newsweek* (August 25, 1997); Charlotte Hays, "Breaking Ranks: A Fortunate Habit," *National Catholic Register*. I had several conversations with Shea and weave her recollections and observances together.

27. Interview with Nina Shea, 2003.

28. Interviews with Nina Shea, 1999–2003.

29. Stephen Rickard, former director of the Washington office of Amnesty International and current Director of the Nuremberg Legacy Project, lauds the new energy and constituencies provided by the faith-based movement, but disputes that the secular groups were ignoring the issue of religious freedom or the persecution of Christians. He points to the fact that his organization's reports are cited in Nina Shea's book, *In the Lion's Den* (Nashville, TN: Broadman & Holman, 1997). See Ralph Kinney Bennett, "The Global War on Christians," *Reader's Digest* (August 1997) for an example of what Richard sees as "sensationalist" stories drawing upon Shea's work.

30. Interview with Nina Shea, 2003.

31. Bogert, "Facing the Lions."

32. Shea, *In the Lion's Den*, ix.

33. The most systematic source of the demographic distribution of religious adherents around the world (not just Christians), and the one used by Britannica for its yearbooks, is the

World Christian Encyclopedia, produced by David Barrett and associates. The book estimates that some 70 million Christians have been martyred—killed because of their faith—in the past twenty centuries. Of that number slightly less than 65 percent were martyred in the twentieth century. See David B. Barrett, George T. Kurian, and Todd M. Johnson, eds., *World Christian Encyclopedia,* 2nd ed., vol. 1, 2001), 11. (New York: Oxford University Press).

34. Samuel Huntington, "Religious Persecution and Religious Relevance in Today's World," in *The Influence of Faith: Religious Groups & U.S. Foreign Policy,* ed. Elliott Abrams (Lanham, MD: Rowman & Littlefield, 2001), 57.

35. Interview with Nina Shea, 2003.

36. "Religious Persecution as a Violation of Human Rights," Hearings before the Committee on Foreign Affairs and its Subcommittee on Human Rights and International Organizations, U.S. House of Representatives, 97th Cong., 2nd sess., 1982, 747.

37. Shea and Belli wanted to call the organization the John Paul II Institute but could not get the papal nuncio to agree to the use of his name, so Belli proposed Puebla Institute, after the bishops meeting where John Paul II chastised priests who allowed themselves to be co-opted for Marxist revolutionary movements. Shea never liked the name because few people had enough awareness of its origins and got it confused with Pueblo Indians, and so she was happy when the Puebla Institute became absorbed into Freedom House and became the Center for Religious Freedom.

38. This was the standard boilerplate that Puebla staff used in congressional testimony. See testimony of Ann Himmelfarb, Research Associate of the Puebla Institute, before the Subcommittee on Trade of the Ways and Means Committee of the U.S. House of Representatives, June 8, 1993.

39. Interviews with Nina Shea.

40. Characteristic of the kind of work Shea's organization was doing was testimony of Ann Himmelfarb, June 8, 1993. It provided an excellent history of the regime's practices against religious freedom, lists of actual prisoners, and policy recommendations.

41. As an example of its credibility, a *Washington Post* editorial on May 25, 1994, listed Puebla Institute as one of the "reputable organizations" reporting on human rights abuses in China, along with Asia Watch and Amnesty International.

42. Interviews with Nina Shea.

43. Steve Rickard, head of the Nuremberg Legacy Project, coordinator of the Human Rights Executive Directors Working Group, and former Washington director of Amnesty International, noted that Shea used Amnesty reports for some of the examples in her book, *In the Lion's Den.* Phone interview, August 2003.

44. This according to interviews with Paul Marshall, July 2001, and subsequent conversations.

45. Paul Marshall, *Their Blood Cries Out* (Dallas, TX: Word, 1997).

46. Marshall critiqued the secularization paradigm that operated implicitly in elite circles, as well as the anti-Christian animus that prevented a clear-eyed assessment of the problem in his view.

47. Paul Marshall, "The Persecution of Christians in the Contemporary World: Presentation to the Advisory Committee to the Secretary of State on Religious Freedom Abroad," as cited by the Claremont Institute, 1997, www.claremont.org.

48. Samuel Huntington cited Marshall in "Religious Persecution and Religious Relevance in Today's World."

49. Prepared Statement of Senator Lieberman, Hearings before the Committee on Foreign Relations, U.S. Senate, May 12 and June 17, 1998, 85.

50. Interview with Nina Shea.

51. The literature on this is huge, but a good source is Christian Smith and Michael Emerson, *American Evangelicalism: Embattled and Thriving* (Chicago: University of Chicago Press, 1998).

52. Shea interviews.

53. Marshall's first report was published in 2000, and subsequent editions are planned to cover more countries.

54. A. M. Rosenthal, *Thirty-Eight Witnesses: The Kitty Genovese Case,* reissued (Berkeley: University of California Press, 1999). The quotes are from his introduction to the new edition of the original book. In public statements during the campaign for the International Religious Persecution Act, Rosenthal recounted the Genovese case as a searing motivator more than three decades later.

55. A. M. Rosenthal's columns in the *New York Times* include the following: "Persecuting the Christians: The Book of Daniel," February 11, 1997; "Questions Unasked about Persecution of Christians," February 14, 1997, A37; "The Chinese Christians," April 4, 1997, A29; "The Double Crime: Persecution and Acceptance," April 25, 1997, A31; "The Well Poisoners: Copts, and Other Christians," April 29, 1997, A25; "Chance for Americans to Help Persecuted Christians," May 13, 1997, A25; "Questions from West 47th Street: Why So Much about Christians?" June 10, 1997, A35; "The City and the Kingdom: The Royal Embassy Lies," June 17, 1997, A23; "The Position of Worship: A Letter for Congress and the China Lobby," July 25, 1997, A29; "The Right Message: The Importance of the Religious Persecution Bill," September 16, 1997; "Gutless in New York: But Courage in Washington," October 10, 1997; "Shatter the Silence: Two Videos, Two Moralities," October 21, 1997, A21; "Is This a Story?: Eight Million Prayers," December 2, 1997; "A Year of Awakening: America and Human Rights," December 30, 1997; "Feeling Clean Again: Fighting Religious Persecution," February 6, 1998; "The Simple Question: Voting on the American Purpose," May 12, 1998, "Clinton Policies Explained: The Values of Persecution," April 24, 1998; "Clinton's Fudge Factor: Operating for Religious Persecutors," May 1, 1998; "Freedom from Religious Persecution: The Struggle Continues," August 7, 1998, A25; "They Will Find Out," October 2, 1998, A27; "Secrets of the War: Refugees Sold into Slavery," April 23, 1999; "Slaves Stay Out: The U.N.'s New Human Rights Policy," June 25, 1999, A27. After he left the *Times,* Rosenthal continued to write periodically. See A. M. Rosenthal, "Ignoring Religious Persecution Overseas," *Washington Times Weekly Edition,* November 13–19, 2000; "Of Slavery, Oil Money and Human Rights," *Washington Times,* July 20, 2001. Michael Horowitz said this potential connection did not occur to him until well after he was deeply involved in the movement, and he thinks the same is true for Rosenthal.

56. This quote and historical background is provided by Jeff Mankoff, "Russia's Jews since 1973: Jackson-Vanik, Liberation, and Anti-Semitism," Undergraduate Research Day paper, University of Oklahoma, April 8, 2000.

57. Mankoff, "Russia's Jews." There are indications that easing U.S.-Soviet relations may have had as much to do with more emigration as the law itself.

58. These included Nina Shea, Michael Horowitz, Elliott Abrams, who worked for Senator Jackson, and Congressman Chris Smith.

59. The effort came in the wake of the Soviet invasion of Afghanistan and the intensification of the Cold War, the Iranian Revolution, and the election of Ronald Reagan and controversy over his human rights policies in Latin America.

60. "Religious Persecution as a Violation of Human Rights," Hearings and Markup before the Committee on Foreign Affairs and its Subcommittee on Human Rights and International

Organizations, House of Representatives, 97th Cong., 2nd sess., February 10, March 23, May 25, July 27 and 29, August 5 and 10, September 23, December 1 and 14, 1982.

61. Peter Benson and Dorothy Williams, *Religion on Capitol Hill* (New York: Oxford University Press, 1986).

62. The three have belonged for years to the same weekly prayer breakfast group, one of many such groups that have proliferated on the Hill.

63. Statement by Chris Smith introducing hearings on *Persecution of Christians Worldwide*, Subcommittee on International Operations and Human Rights of the House Committee on International Relations, February 15, 1996.

64. This material is from interviews with both Chris Smith, September 2000, and Frank Wolf, September 2000.

65. A fuller discussion of Tony Hall's work is provided by Robert Booth Fowler, Allen D. Hertzke, and Laura Olson, *Religion and Politics in America* (Boulder, CO: Westview Press, 1999), 130–31.

66. Lori Montgomery, "Party Lines Blur for Area Lawmakers," *Washington Post*, May 24, 2000, A15.

67. Interview with Frank Wolf, September 2000. At meetings I have observed these same sentiments expressed by the congressman.

68. Michael Barone with Richard E. Cohen, *The Almanac of American Politics 2002* (Washington, DC: National Journal, 2001).

69. Interview with Sharon Payt, with the office of Senator Brownback, June 2000.

70. House floor debate, Freedom from Persecution Act, May 14, 1998.

71. Wolf does not shy away from tackling issues that might make others cringe, as when he testified about the harvesting of organs from executed Chinese prisoners and the reputed sale of human fetuses for food in China. Though he took this latter material from a reputable Hong Kong newspaper, such accounts are easily dismissed as hysterical by critics of the Christian Right. But Wolf does not tack on the basis of how others will perceive him. Testimony by Frank Wolf before the Subcommittee on Trade of the Committee on Ways and Means, U.S. House of Representatives, on "U.S.-China Trade Relations and Renewal of China's Most-Favored-Nation Status," May 23, 1995.

72. Barone with Cohen, *Almanac of American Politics 2002.*

73. It was striking in my long interview with Chris Smith how much biblical passages and injunctions naturally sprinkled his conversation. Those who work with Smith, and outside observers of his record, agree that he is guided by authentic religious convictions. Barone with Cohen, *Almanac of American Politics 2002.*

74. Interview with Smith, 2000.

75. Interview with Smith, 2000.

76. Interview with Smith, 2000.

77. Interview with Smith, 2000.

78. After the 2000 elections, Smith stepped down from his subcommittee chairmanship to assume the chairmanship of the Committee on Veterans Affairs.

79. Interview with Smith, 2000.

80. *Persecution of Christians Worldwide,* hearing before the Subcommittee on International Operations and Human Rights of the Committee on International Relations, House of Representatives, February 15, 1996.

81. *Persecution of Christians Worldwide.*

82. Interview with Smith, 2000.

83. *Persecution of Christians Worldwide.*

84. Interview with Senator Don Nickles, June 2001. He announced his retirement in October 2003, and at that press conference, he mentioned his interest in continuing to promote religious freedom abroad in new capacities.

85. In one memorable case Nickles secured the release of an Oklahoman imprisoned in Nepal for Christian evangelizing. Interview, 2001.

86. Here again we see movement networks at play. It was former Colorado senator Bill Armstrong's pastor who introduced Horowitz to Tancredo, according to Horowitz.

87. Hanford began his work on the Hill in 1981 and assumed his position as ambassador in 2002.

88. This according to Mike Horowitz, interview, 2001.

CHAPTER 5

1. From a speech delivered by Charles Colson of Prison Fellowship, presenting Horowitz the William Wilberforce Award (for a distinguished contribution to humanity inspired by religious faith) on February 5, 1997, Washington, D.C.

2. Ironically, this is contrary to the thrust of much modern social science, which, in the quest to mimic natural science, explores "factors," marshals "variables," and probes "statistical probabilities." One of the hottest trends, imported from economics, involves making assumptions about the "rational choices" of political actors and then deriving dense mathematical models that purport to predict their behavior. Lost in this research is the potential for individuals to make a difference.

3. Numerous interviews with members of Congress, congressional staff, and national religious leaders, as well as news reports, a large documentary record, and personal observation in a variety of political contexts confirm Horowitz's role as the catalyst of this new movement. Scholarly honesty compels me to note that Horowitz provided tremendous access to me during this research. Aware of how this might be viewed as compromising my objectivity, I consciously strove to balance my account with extended conversations with those critical of Horowitz. The documentary record is unambiguous in demonstrating Horowitz's centrality to the movement. Among the most helpful news profiles and stories are: Samuel G. Freedman, "Horowitz's List," *New York Magazine*, March 31, 1997; Paul Blustein, "A Jew Battles Persecution of Christians," *Washington Post*, October 9, 1997; Michael Cromartie, "The Jew Who Is Saving Christians," *Christianity Today*, March 1, 1999; Charles Colson, "The Jews of the Twenty-first Century?" *Jubilee*, spring 1997; Jeffrey Goldberg, "Washington Discovers Christian Persecution," *New York Times*, December 21, 1997. Unless otherwise cited, all quotations are from personal interviews or public meetings.

4. From interviews and published accounts, this is remarkably how such figures as Charles Colson, Richard Land, and Bill Armstrong speak of Horowitz.

5. The term "moral entrepreneur" was coined by sociologist Howard Becker, *Outsiders: Studies in the Sociology of Deviance* (London: Free Press of Glencoe, 1963). Though Becker's use had some negative connotations, I employ the term in a more neutral way because it seems to capture the entrepreneurial quality of Horowitz's human rights crusades, and the moral fervor with which he pursued them.

6. Though I do not attribute sensitive statements, it is no secret that severe critics of Horowitz include staff members involved in fashioning an alternative to the bill backed by Horowitz. This is discussed in chapter 6. But in the Sudan battle, as well, there were critics

who saw Horowitz as a self-promoter prone to hyperbole and willing to do solo initiatives independent of what the coalition members were attempting.

7. This quote came from a mainline Protestant leader who locked horns with Horowitz on several occasions.

8. Ann Morse, "Screaming People Awake," *World*, February 3, 2001.

9. Freedman, "Horowitz's List."

10. This material is from an interview with Horowitz. I will dispense with citations for the remaining interview quotes. I not only had numerous conversations with Horowitz but attended a number of meetings at which he spoke, and I have attempted to weave these together. Thus, certain phrases might come from an interview, others from a casual conversation, others from a meeting. Repeatedly citing these would be cumbersome.

11. Freedman, "Horowitz's List."

12. Freedman, "Horowitz's List."

13. He was appointed chief counsel for the Office of Management and Budget, the fulcrum of the Reagan revolution of tax and budget cuts.

14. Freedman, "Horowitz's List."

15. Richard Land, interview, March 2001; Gary Bauer, interview, June 2001.

16. Freedman, "Horowitz's List."

17. Letter from Michael Horowitz to 143 mission board directors, July 26, 1995.

18. Plan for the National Day of Prayer, memo from Mike Horowitz, June 5, 1996.

19. Interviews with Charles Colson, the latest on November 13, 2003.

20. Interviews with Charles Colson, the latest on November 13, 2003.

21. Bill Armstrong, interview, February 2001.

22. Charles Colson, interview, November 13, 2003. Colson went on to say that not only did Horowitz not waste his time, but that he "did not embarrass me."

23. The letter to President George W. Bush was drafted by Horowitz and amended and signed by evangelical leaders. It was a hard-hitting and passionate document that illustrated the growing sympathy and even identification that the evangelicals have with Jews.

24. Memo from Sandy Rios to Harry Newman, March 8, 2002, www.geocities.com/vmken/editormail100html.

25. Freedman, "Horowitz's List."

26. Cromartie, "The Jew Who Is Saving Christians."

27. I heard this sentiment in a variety of circles, and there is ample evidence for it. But on the other hand, Horowitz also spends a lot of time on the phone with reporters giving them names of people they need to talk with for a story, and sometimes he offers a story to a reporter that will not contain him at all. Moreover, the story line, "A Jew Battles for Persecuted Christians," was just too good for journalists to ignore and operated independently of self-promotion.

28. From a speech by Horowitz at the National Press Club, October 1998.

29. "Bill Proposed to Combat Christian Persecution," in a report from the Capitol, Baptist Joint Committee, vol. 52, no. 11 (July 3, 1997).

30. Freedman, "Horowitz's List."

31. Freedman, "Horowitz's List," 50.

32. The statement appeared in the *Washington Post*, February 1, 1993, in a story on gays in the military. The quote elicited responses from Ph.D.-bedecked Christians gleefully writing the *Post*, which published a retraction the next day admitting that "there is no factual basis for that statement."

33. Michael Horowitz, "Bridges Crossed—and Yet to Cross," *Crisis*, September 1994.

34. Horowitz, "Bridges Crossed." Since I draw extensively on this article in the next two pages, the reader can assume that all quotations are from this piece.

35. Horowitz, "Bridges Crossed." Horowitz used the phrase coined by Joshua Haberman.

36. Horowitz relayed the vignette of how James Watt, the "lightening-rod Secretary of the Interior under Reagan," shared a draft of a speech he was to give, which contained moving references to the Holocaust. But the speech segued immediately into a discussion of how "the Holocaust still continues" with abortion. Horowitz pleaded with Watt at least to separate the two discussions because "there were deeply caring people, my wife, for example, who grieved over people lost in concentration camps and supported the right to abortion, and that they would never accept the genuineness of his views about the former if he acted as if it were no different from the latter." Because Watt refused to change the speech he "forfeited the chance to persuade people outside his church that he cared about much beside abortion, and wound up, ironically, confirming for many the false view of him as insensitive if not anti-Semitic." "Bridges Crossed."

37. In *Oregon v. Smith*, 1990, the Supreme Court narrowed the grounds of religious exemption from secular laws that burden religious freedom, and for the next decade religious groups worked with Congress and state legislatures to restore the so-called compelling state interest test that would provide more expansive grounds for religious free exercise.

38. Judith Miller, "Jewish Allies of Evangelicals Attack Film on Anti-Semitism," *New York Times*, January 20, 1998.

39. Freedman, "Horowitz's List."

40. Nina Shea, *In the Lion's Den* (Nashville, TN: Broadman & Holman, 1997), 21.

41. Michael Horowitz, "New Intolerance between Crescent and Cross," *Wall Street Journal*, July 5, 1995.

42. Letter from Horowitz to 143 evangelical mission boards, July 26, 1995.

43. Armstrong interview, January 2001.

44. Memorandum from David Stravers, The Bible League, to Michael Horowitz, April 9, 1999.

45. Phone interview with Deborah Fikes, Midland, Texas, April 2004. The award was presented in February 2004.

46. Paul Johnson, *Modern Times*, rev. ed. (New York: HarperPerennial, 1991), 48.

47. Colson, "Jews of the Twenty-first Century?"

48. Cromartie, "The Jew Who Is Saving Christians."

49. Cromartie, "The Jew Who Is Saving Christians."

50. Colson, "Jews of the Twenty-first Century?"

51. Cromartie, "The Jew Who Is Saving Christians."

52. Horowitz utters these phrases so often in speeches and conversations that it is impossible to cite a single source.

53. Paul Marshall, *Their Blood Cries Out* (Dallas, TX: Word, 1997), xxi.

54. Cromartie, "The Jew Who Is Saving Christians."

55. Marshall, *Their Blood Cries Out*, 150.

56. Cromartie, "The Jew Who Is Saving Christians."

57. Mark Noll, *One Nation under God? Christian Faith and Political Action in America* (San Francisco: Harper, 1988).

58. The rest of the quotes from Horowitz, unless specifically cited, are from personal interviews or meetings.

59. Ulysses S. Grant, *Personal Memoirs: Ulysses S. Grant* (New York: Random House Modern Library), 1999.

60. Sidney Tarrow, *Power in Movement* (New York: Cambridge University Press, 1994).

61. Doug McAdam, *Political Process and the Development of Black Insurgency, 1930–1970* (Chicago: University of Chicago Press, 1985).

62. Stravers Memorandum, April 9, 1999.

63. Christian solidarity organizations focused on Sudan from the early 1990s, as did Nina Shea; Charles Jacobs began work in 1993 and formed the American Anti-Slavery Group in response to his discovery of slavery in Sudan.

64. This material is from an interview with Horowitz in April 2001.

65. Horowitz interview, April 2001.

66. That provision was sent to the Ways and Means Committee, historically hostile to trade sanctions, where it struck the provision from the bill.

67. This is a rather widespread complaint one hears among the staffs of organizations, congressional staff members, and individual activists. One does not hear it as often among national leaders—such as members of Congress, top evangelical officials, denominational heads, and so forth, who are either treated with greater deference by Horowitz or whose positions shield them from feeling bullied.

68. This analysis was offered off the record by an activist in the Sudan campaign. In the interview with Charles Colson for the magazine of Prison Fellowship Ministries, *Jubilee*, in the spring of 1997, Horowitz used exclusive examples of Christians suffering slavery and genocide in Sudan.

69. For purposes of ensuring confidentiality I am not attributing to specific people the criticism of Horowitz, but one thing that can be said is that there was no secret about the antipathy between Horowitz and the congressional staffers who drafted the Nickles-Lieberman bill, which I describe in chapter 6.

70. Shea argued that her remarks were made in jest and that the reporter had been following her and Horowitz around for a month trying to find just such an angle for the story, which was blown out of proportion.

71. Goldberg, "Washington Discovers Christian Persecution."

72. This episode, described in more detail in chapter 7, occurred on September 11, 2001.

73. Horowitz, "New Intolerance."

74. Plan for the National Day of Prayer, memo from Mike Horowitz, June 5, 1996.

75. Fax from Mike Horowitz to Steve Haas, August 4, 1997.

76. As late as October 2003, Human Rights Watch seemed to be struggling to elevate religious freedom to the status of other highlighted issues. In one part of its website religious freedom was included under its "Global Issues" category but in another it was not. By November, however, religious freedom was finally incorporated fully into the highlighted "global issues," suggesting that the criticism of the organization and campaign for religious freedom were having an impact. See www.hrw.org.

77. Freedman, "Horowitz's List."

78. Freedman, "Horowitz's List."

79. Letter to Ronald Bernstein, chair of Human Rights Watch, March 28, 1997.

80. Blustein, "A Jew Battles Persecution of Christians."

81. This quote from one religious freedom advocate was not for attribution.

82. See note 76.

83. This quote from the Catholic official was not for attribution.

84. Blustein, "A Jew Battles Persecution of Christians."

85. These vignettes came from off-the-record conversations with a variety of people. The implication was that Horowitz was orchestrating these events.

86. Freedman, "Horowitz's List."

87. Memorandum from Michael Horowitz dated October 28, 1998.

88. Laura Lederer, interview, March 2001.

89. Peter Waldman, "Evangelicals Give U.S. Foreign Policy on Activist Tinge," in *Wall Street Journal*, May 26, 2004, A1; Elisabeth Bumiller, "Evangelicals Sway White House on Human Rights Issues Abroad," *New York Times*, October 26, 2003. I was called by Bumiller at the insistence of Horowitz.

CHAPTER 6

1. Department of State, *Annual Report on International Religious Freedom*, November 2002, 209; on political prisoners see Annual Report of the United States Commission on International Religious Freedom, May 2001, 38.

2. International Religious Freedom Act, Public Law 105-292, 22 USC 6401, signed into law October 27, 1998.

3. For a good overview see T. Jeremy Gunn, "A Preliminary Response to Criticisms of the International Religious Freedom Act of 1998," *Brigham Young University Law Review* (September 2000): 841–66. For an example of the criticism see Peter Danchin, "U.S. Unilateralism and the International Protection of Religious Freedom: The Multilateral Alternative," *Columbia Journal of Transnational Law* 41 (2002).

4. Liminal is variously defined as the "threshold of a physiological or psychological response," or a subtle membrane separating states, or a threshold. *American Heritage College Dictionary* (Boston: Houghton Mifflin, 1997). Because the 1998 legislation marked the threshold of a new era in human rights advocacy, but one barely discerned at the time, it represents a kind of liminal moment. Subsequent initiatives on Sudan and human trafficking especially show this.

5. National Association of Evangelicals, "Statement of Conscience," January 23, 1996, in Nina Shea, *In the Lion's Den* (Nashville, TN: Broadman & Holman, 1997).

6. Interview with Richard Cizik.

7. Laura Bryant prepared an internal document that listed several key items of NAE's Statement of Conscience and noted provisions of IRFA that implement them.

8. Hearing before the Subcommittee on International Operations and Human Rights of the Committee on International Relations, House of Representatives, 104th Sess., February 15, 1996.

9. Some Bush White House officials were upset with Horowitz's claim to have engineered this rhetorical approach, with one saying that Forte was not the only scholar making the kind of argument that Bush ultimately adopted.

10. U.S. Department of State, *United States Policies in Support of Religious Freedom: Focus on Christians*, July 22, 1997.

11. Doug McAdam, *Political Process and the Development of Black Insurgency, 1930–1970*, (Chicago: University of Chicago Press, 1985).

12. One example was Sam Ericsson, head of Advocates International.

13. Interview with Michael Horowitz. The rest of the quotes from Horowitz in this chapter come from numerous conversations I had with him or comments he made at various meetings in Washington, D.C.

14. Rees, interview, May 1998.

15. The key staff included Ann Heiskus of Congressman Wolf's staff; Steve Rademacher, director of the House International Relations Committee (working for Chairman Ben Gilman); and Rees.

16. Rees, interview, May 1998.

17. This was especially Horowitz's argument about why to focus on hard-core persecution as a uniting factor. For examples of the concern about proselytization, see *Religious Persecution as a U.S. Policy Issue*, Proceedings of a consultation held at Trinity College, Hartford, September 26–27, 1999, ed. Rosalind I. J. Hackett, Mark Silk, and Dennis Hoover (Hartford, CT: Center for the Study of Religion, 2000), especially the introduction and the comment by Winnifred Fallers Sullivan.

18. Bryant, *Religious Persecution as a U.S. Policy Issue*, 12. This conference's proceedings contains reflections by the staff cadre that drafted the Nickles-Lieberman bill, including John Hanford, Steve Moffitt, Laura Bryant, and William Inboden.

19. Interview with Horowitz.

20. H.R. 2431, 105th Cong., 2nd sess. Reported from House Committee on International Relations, March 1998, passed the House of Representatives, May 14, 1998.

21. Roger Winter, then head of the U.S. Committee on Refugees, endorsed the Wolf-Specter immigration provisions because he felt that Congress had erected, in its immigration law of 1996, a "burdensome hurdle" for those making asylum claims. Letter to Senator Specter and Congressman Wolf, September 4, 1997.

22. The famous passage from Isaiah 58 starts with verse 6 and contains the divine mandate that the yoke of oppression be lifted.

23. I was in attendance at the event, and this material came from my notes.

24. Some staff members involved in the Nickles-Lieberman bill complained about the lack of grassroots mobilization for the cause, while other congressional sources suggested that a considerable grassroots buzz over persecution attuned members to the salience of the issue. Some of the differences have to do with generalized constituent concern versus letters of support for specific legislation.

25. Senator Sam Brownback told me that he does hear frequently from constituents in Kansas town hall meetings about what the American government is doing about China or Sudan.

26. Prepared Statement, Chairman Jesse Helms, Hearings before the Committee on Foreign Relations, United States Senate, May 12 and June 17, 1998, 81.

27. John Carr, interview, December 1999.

28. Steven A. Holmes, "G.O.P. Leaders Back Bill on Religious Persecution," *New York Times*, September 11, 1997, A3.

29. Saperstein, interview, July 1999.

30. Horowitz liked to depict the campaign as a David versus Goliath, with the "ratty, informal group" meeting in 441 Cannon taking on big business lobby millions.

31. At least this was the claim by Horowitz and others in the coalition. Horowitz drew this conclusion from his work in the White House.

32. Stacie Burdette, interview, December 1999.

33. Mary McGrory, "The Man Who Won't Give Up," *Washington Post*, August 31, 1997.

34. Memo from Mary Beth Markey, International Campaign for Tibet, to Michael Horowitz, January 2, 1998.

35. Letter from the Dalai Lama, February 1998.

36. Holmes, "G.O.P. Leaders Back Bill," A3.

37. House floor debate, May 14, 1998. I was in the gallery and was struck by the tenor of the debate.

38. Ken Silverstein, "So You Want to Trade with a Dictator," *Mother Jones*, May/June 1998.

39. The intensity, though not widely reported in the press, was confirmed by several key congressional staff members involved in pressing the legislation.

40. Silverstein, "So You Want to Trade with a Dictator."

41. These documents were provided to me by activists.

42. Letter to Trent Lott from James Dobson, Charles Colson, Gary Bauer, and Randy Tate, June 16, 1998, as reprinted in Hearings before the Committee on Foreign Relations, U.S. Senate, May 12 and June 17, 1998, on S. 1868: The International Religious Freedom Act of 1998.

43. Jacob Heilbrunn, "The Sanctions Sellout," *New Republic*, May 25, 1998.

44. House staffers noted an intense effort against the bill by the administration, including criticism from John Shattuck, Madeleine Albright, Sandy Berger, and the president himself.

45. Albright cite.

46. According to Horowitz.

47. Testimony of John Shattuck, Assistant Secretary of State for Democracy, Human Rights, and Labor, Hearings before the Committee on Foreign Relations, U.S. Senate, May 12 and June 17, 1998, 11–31.

48. Elaine Sciolino, "On Sanctions, Clinton Details Threat to Truth," *New York Times*, April 28, 1998.

49. Memorandum to James B. Gray, Office of Senator Joseph Lieberman, from Steven Mc-Farland, Center for Law and Religious Freedom, Christian Legal Society, June 10, 1998.

50. Silverstein, "So You Want to Trade with a Dictator."

51. Pennybacker, interview, November 1998.

52. Pennybacker, interview, November 1998.

53. C. E. Carlson, "We Hold These Truths," Scottsdale, Arizona, www.whtt.org.

54. Steve Snyder, interview, May 1998.

55. A letter to Congressman Hyde dated April 22, 1998, from James Robb of Evangelicals for Immigration Reform.

56. Interview with Gary Bauer, June 2001.

57. Jewish and Catholic groups are also attentive to this concern, and sometimes avoid public condemnation of a country for that very reason.

58. Ambassador Edward Perkins, former director general of the State Department, told me that he saw no evidence of reprisals against local religious minorities because of U.S. government exposure and sanction. Discussion, November 2003.

59. Letter to Benjamin Gilman, Chair of the House International Relations Committee, from Robert Rifkind and David Harris of the American Jewish Committee, September 24, 1997.

60. This conclusion comes from conversations with a wide array of insiders to the process.

61. It is fortunate that the views of the three congressional fellows and Steve Moffitt of Senator Nickles's office have been published. See *Religious Persecution as a U.S. Policy Issue*.

62. Internal memo comparing Wolf-Specter with IRFA.

63. Conservatives have been highly critical of the LSC because it supposedly enables welfare claimants to receive more benefits and results in more divorces.

64. This was according to one of the staffers in attendance at the meeting.

65. John Hanford *Religious Persecution as a U.S. Policy Issue*, chapter 1.

66. John Hanford, interview, October 1998.

67. Laura Bryant, *Religious Persecution as a U.S. Policy Issue*, 10.

68. Bryant, *Religious Persecution as a U.S. Policy Issue*, 9.

69. Critics of Wolf-Specter noted that its language about "widespread and systematic" abuse would not capture terrible persecution that might be concentrated in a particular region. Nickles-Lieberman drafters wanted to set a lower threshold to encompass such phenomena.

70. For example, Terrorism Sec. 620A of the Foreign Assistant Act of 1961, Drug Certifications, Foreign Assistant Act, Fishing Zone Violations 16 U.S.C. 1826a (b)(1)(B), Trade Violations Sec. 301–310 Trade Act of 1974, and Arms Export Control Act.

71. Examples of designations involve whether countries are adequately fighting drug trafficking or are violating whaling quotas.

72. Bryant, *Religious Persecution as a U.S. Policy Issue*, 10.

73. That staff including Cecile Shea, a State Department official detailed to his office, and Fred Downey.

74. Bryant, *Religious Persecution as a U.S. Policy Issue*, 2000, 11.

75. "Congress OK's Measure Targeting Religious Persecution Abroad," *Report from the Capital*, vol. 53, Newsletter of the Baptist Joint Committee, October 27, 1998.

76. Letter to Senator Don Nickles from Bill Armstrong, Gary Bauer, Chuck Colson, Jim Dobson, Brant Gustavson, Don Hodel, Pat Nolan, and Pat Robertson, September 2, 1998.

77. Steve Moffitt interview, October 1998, and subsequent conversations.

78. Equal Employment Opportunity Commission, a federal agency that adjudicates charges of discrimination.

79. Bryant, *Religious Freedom as a U.S. Policy Issue*, 10.

80. Testimony of John Shattuck, Assistant Secretary of State for Democracy, Human Rights, and Labor, Hearings before the Committee on Foreign Relations, United States Senate, May 12 and June 17, 1998, 11–31; and subsequent answers to senatorial questions, 69–81.

81. Steve Moffitt, interview, October 1998.

82. Memorandum from Steven McFarland, Center for Law and Religious Freedom, Christian Legal Society, to James B. Gray, Office of Senator Joseph Lieberman, June 10, 1998.

83. Horowitz described his reaction to the bill thus: "You had the ambassador who was basically working for the president, make findings of fact, the president then accepts or rejects them, then the commission makes its fact finding after the president has already dealt with it. It's Rube Goldberg."

84. John Hanford as quoted in *Religious Persecution as a U.S. Policy Issue*, 58.

85. Letter to Nickles from Armstrong et al., September 2, 1998. This letter occurred just a bit more than a month before the Senate finally passed the IRFA, on October 9, 1998.

86. According to a key congressional staffer who helped draft the Nickles-Lieberman bill, on the eve of final consideration of IRFA listeners to James Dobson's radio program called to ask Senators to vote for the "Wolf bill that Horowitz worked on," or even the "Wolf-Horowitz" bill. This also reflects Horowitz's unique access to the evangelical elite, which so exasperated evangelical staffers who didn't like his approach.

87. David E. Rosenbaum, "Senate Puts Aside Bill to Punish Nations That Persecute Religion: Measure Doomed by Split among Republicans," *New York Times*, July 24, 1998, A1.

88. Rosenbaum, "Senate Puts Aside Bill," A1.

89. Rosenbaum, "Senate Puts Aside Bill," A4.

90. I conducted two long sessions with the staff cadre involved in Nickles-Lieberman, once on the day final legislation passed in October 10, 1998, and another time after that. All quotes are taken from these sessions, along with subsequent conversations with them and other staff and religious group leaders involved in the process.

91. Under Senate procedures, unanimous consent is a common way that legislation is brought to the floor, especially toward the end of the session when time gets short. The objection of a single senator can hold up legislation under such arrangements.

92. On the eve of its passage, when many compromises were worked out, three mainline groups endorsed the IRFA—the ELCA, the Disciples, and Methodist Women. These actions were purely symbolic because they had no impact on the legislative process. Most of the other mainline churches, including the National Council of Churches, did not endorse the final bill.

93. Letter to Senator Don Nickles from Tom Hart, Interim Director of Governmental Relations, the Episcopal Church Office of Government Relations, May 5, 1998. The quote from Hart on hearing from partners abroad is from an interview.

94. Tom Hart worked for former California Democratic senator Alan Cranston.

95. Tom Hart, interview, October 1998.

96. Statement of the Right Reverend Munawar Kenneth Rumalshah (Mano), Anglican Bishop of Peshawar, Pakistan, Hearings before the Committee on Foreign Relations, U.S. Senate, May 12 and June 17, 1998, 34–39.

97. Tom Hart, interview, October 1998.

98. That commission was headed up by the venerable president of Notre Dame, Father Hesburgh, who recounts his efforts in his biography. O'Brien, Michael (Washington, DC: Catholic University of America), 1998.

99. Letter to Nickles from Armstrong et al., September 2, 1998.

100. I heard this complaint about secrecy among the Senate bill cadre, even to the point of not sharing drafts, not only from Horowitz but several other members of the steering committee for Wolf-Specter.

101. Letter to Nickles from Armstrong et al., September 2, 1998.

102. To staffers working on Nickles-Lieberman, the commission was "somewhat peripheral to the crux of the bill—the requirement for action." Ironically, it was in part because they did not see the commission as central that the staff cadre agreed to incorporate some of the recommendations of the Wolf-Specter coalition.

103. The members of the first two commissions are listed in the appendix.

104. uscirf.gov.

105. Robert Seiple, the first ambassador for International Religious Freedom, complained that the commission interfered with regular diplomatic efforts, as discussed in chapter 3.

106. Rosenbaum, "Senate Puts Aside Bill," A1.

107. The commission would issue the annual report on religious freedom, designate countries that practice severe persecution, recommend actions to the president, and disclose inadequate responses to Congress. Since Horowitz had come to believe that required presidential actions would result in meaningless steps, his bill only said what the president "should" do, not what he must do.

108. What was bizarre to some observers was that Horowitz apparently contacted those he fought on the House side—the Chamber of Commerce, the National Council of Churches, the State Department—in an attempt to build their support for his last-minute substitute. He

also appealed to those senators still skeptical of Nickles-Lieberman to embrace his bill. This entire effort seemed too Machiavellian by half, even to some of Horowitz's allies. Strengthening the commission was one thing; "gutting" other aspects of Nickles-Lieberman with the help of those who oppose your vision and goals seemed beyond the pale.

109. Tom Hart, for example, orchestrated a key letter from a broad array of religious organizations, notably including all of the major Jewish groups, endorsing Nickles-Lieberman just five days after Horowitz's memo. A number of senators had also gotten engaged in the process, especially when it appeared that legislation might pass, and they negotiated changes that broadened the base of support for the proposed law.

110. Senate Majority Leader Trent Lott, who promised Christian solidarity leaders that he would facilitate passage of legislation, made a conscious decision to "hold back" Wolf-Specter when it was sent from the House. Technically, this meant that Lott could bring it to the Senate floor at any time, and he used this vehicle to bypass the Senate Foreign Affairs Committee that had been hostile to the legislation. When compromises had been worked out between diverse stakeholders, Lott brought forward Wolf-Specter, which was then simply amended to replace its language with the final Nickles-Lieberman draft.

111. Michael Horowitz, and others in his coalition, view the final legislation as better than the original Wolf-Specter bill because it created the new commission.

112. Press conference on the Capitol grounds, October 19, 1998, tape recorded.

CHAPTER 7

1. The title is from a passage Matthew 10:16, where Jesus says that since he is sending his disciples out into the midst of wolves they must be "wise as serpents, innocent as doves" (RSV translation). Other translations read cunning as serpents and gentle as doves. I reversed the order, which seemed appropriate in terms of the order of events.

2. As Francis Bok relayed to me, he asked John Eibner of Christian Solidarity International to try and track down his family, and Eibner, who makes frequent trips to Sudan on slave redemption missions, was able to confirm that his parents were killed in the raid.

3. Abd or abid is the singular Arabic word slave; abeed is the plural. Sometimes Bok uses the singular and sometimes the plural because, as he relayed, his masters sometimes used the plural to convey that he was of slave people.

4. This material is from an interview and a book by Francis Bok with Edward Tivnan, *Escape from Slavery: The True Story of My Ten Years in Captivity—and My Journey to Freedom in America* (New York: St. Martins Press, 2003). This account is as compelling as any slave narrative of nineteenth-century America.

5. Characteristic was Laurie Goodstein, "A Move to Fight 'Persecution' Facing Christians," *New York Times*, November 9, 1998.

6. The feeling of being forsaken echoed in the speeches of Sudan exiles I spoke with or saw speak, and in their writings. See Bok, *Escape from Slavery*, 2003

7. Eric Reeves saw signs of such bad faith in Sudan's depredations of the Darfur Province, located in northwest Sudan. Because it lies outside of the south and involves a conflict that spilled over into Chad, it has not been a part of the peace negotiations between Sudan and the south. Eric Reeves, "Red Flags in Sudan: Threats to the Peace Process; Widening Humanitarian Crisis in Darfur," email, November 11, 2003.

8. *Report of the United States Commission on International Religious Freedom,* 2002, 25.

9. As quoted by Charles Jacobs, "Why Israel and Not Sudan is Singled Out," *Boston Globe,* October 5, 2002.

10. Randolph Martin, "Sudan's Perfect War," *Foreign Affairs* 81 (March/April 2002): 111.

11. "A Working Document: Quantifying Genocide in the Southern Sudan 1983–1993," U.S. Committee on Refugees, October 1993; and "Working Document II: Quantifying Genocide in Southern Sudan and the Nuba Mountains, 1993–1998," U.S. Committee on Refugees, December 1998. The 1998 report estimated 1.9 million dead, and many more have died since then. In his testimony before the Joint Hearing before the Subcommittee on International Operations and Human Rights and Subcommittee on Africa of the Committee on International Relations, U.S. House of Representatives, May 27, 1999, Burr said that he can "hardly speak of these things without choking up."

12. See Jeremy Gunn, "When Our Allies Persecute," *Religion in the News* 4, no. 3 (fall 2001).

13. Karl Vick, "Powell Calls for Reconciliation in Sudan," *Washington Post,* May 27, 2001, A20.

14. Walid A. Phares, "Christian Minorities in the Middle East: Statehood or Assimilation," a paper delivered to the Religion and Politics panel at the 1994 Annual Meeting of the American Political Science Association, 14.

15. The complexities of Sudanese history and the various factions in the country are chronicled by Douglas H. Johnson, *The Root Causes of Sudan's Civil Wars* (Bloomington: Indiana University Press, 2003).

16. The relative proportion of Christians to animists is not known. The CIA report on Sudan suggests that a considerable majority of Africans are tribal religionists, while other sources suggest rapid growth of Christianity has rendered those old figures obsolete. What is clear is that Christian institutions and social networks have provided crucial glue for the African people of Sudan.

17. Sudanese Catholic Bishop Macram Gassis argues that the relations among the Christians, Muslims, and animists of the Nuba Mountains were amicable until the militants took power in Khartoum. Representatives of Bishop Gassis told me stories of how Muslims from the Nuba would go to Khartoum and come back militants, creating discord. Asked why he did not side with the government of Sudan, one Muslim replied that he had seen how the "contagion" of fundamentalism had led to strife in villages where coexistence had been the rule.

18. Martin, "Sudan's Perfect War," 113–14.

19. The Rift Valley Institute, funded by the British government and Save the Children UK, documented over 10,000 abducted in parts of northern Bahr-el-Ghazal, while officials of the SPLM estimate 50,000–60,000 total in that region and upwards of 200,000 in the whole of southern Sudan. See "Groundbreaking Field Research on Abduction and Slavery in Sudan," Rift Valley Institute, news release, May 28, 2003, institute@riftvalley.net; "Enslavement of over 200,000 Estimated," May 28, 2003, FreedomNowNews@aol.com.

20. Nina Shea, *In the Lion's Den* (Nashville, TN: Broadman & Holman, 1997), 34.

21. Shea, *In the Lion's Den,* 33.

22. Charles Jacobs, "Slavery Worldwide," report of the American Anti-Slavery Group, www.aasg@anti-slavery.org/worldwide.

23. Speech on the floor of the House of Representatives, October 7, 2002, debating the Sudan Peace Act.

24. Some of the best summaries are contained in annual reports of the U.S. Commission on International Religious Freedom, May 2000 and May 2001, www.uscirf.gov.

25. The best scholarly treatment of the way Khartoum employed this racist ideology is Jok Madut Jok, *War and Slavery in Sudan* (Philadelphia: University of Pennsylvania Press, 2001). Charles Jacobs, head of the American Anti-Slavery Group, in an interview in the spring of 2003, described this ideology as Islamo-fascist.

26. Clarence Page, "Bin Laden and His Quest for Slaves," *Chicago Tribune*, January 22, 2002. Charles Jacobs of the American Anti-Slavery Group reported that bin Laden himself owned slaves.

27. "The Scars of Death: Children Abducted by the Lord's Resistance Army in Uganda," Human Rights Watch, September 1997; Greg Taylor, "Innocence Stolen," *Christianity Today*, July 10, 2000. The leader of the Lord's Resistance Army, Joseph Kony, uses a cultlike blend of Mosaic, Christian, animist, and Islamic elements to justify his marauding guerrilla war.

28. Some critics of the faith-based movement dismiss the use of the term as rhetorical excess. Jeremy Gunn likens the movement's use of "genocidal" as "like a novice writer enchanted with exclamation points." See Jeremy Gunn, "When Our Allies Persecute," *Religion in the News* 4, no. 3 (fall 2001).

29. "A Working Document: Quantifying Genocide in the Southern Sudan 1983–1993," U.S. Committee on Refugees, October 1993; and "Working Document II: Quantifying Genocide in Southern Sudan and the Nuba Mountains, 1993–1998," U.S. Committee on Refugees, December 1998. See also Millard Burr's testimony before Joint Hearing before the Subcommittee on International Operations and Human Rights and Subcommittee on Africa of the Committee on International Relations, U.S. House of Representatives, May 27, 1999. The Holocaust Museum's genocide alert was issued in October 2000.

30. "Slavery, War and Peace in Sudan," Washington Office on Africa briefing paper, November 22, 1999, www.woaafrica.org/Sudan.htm.

31. This quote is taken from a brochure that corresponds to the Holocaust Museum's exhibit on Sudan, titled "Genocide Warning: Sudan." Committee on Conscience, United States Holocaust Memorial Museum, Washington, D.C., www.ushmm.org/conscience.

32. Macram Max Gassis, "West Ignores Slaughter in Sudan," *Boston Globe*, July 19, 1999.

33. Statement of Charles Jacobs before the Subcommittee on International Operations and Human Rights, of the Committee on International Relations, U.S. House of Representatives, May 27, 1999, 63.

34. Human Rights Watch and Amnesty International issued a number of reports on human rights abuses in Sudan, some quite hard-hitting. But these tended to be scattered among a variety of causes and concerns, so that prolonged high-level exposure depended on the faith-based movement.

35. Jacobs, "Why Israel and Not Sudan."

36. Charles Jacobs, interview, spring 2003.

37. From Jacobs interview, 2003; and Jacobs, "Why Israel and Not Sudan."

38. See "Shepherd under Fire: An Interview with Bishop Bullen Dolli of Sudan," *Touchstone*, April 2002.

39. Tom Hart was a strong backer of the Sudan Peace Act, especially its capital market sanctions provision. But also endorsing the legislation was the Lutheran Office for Government Affairs. While its newsletters during the early campaign against persecution of Christians expressed skepticism, by 2002–2003 the organization joined in promoting tough action against Sudan. See "Sudan Peace Act Signed into Law," Newsletter of the Lutheran Office for Governmental Affairs, January 2003.

40. William Saunders, "The Slaughter of the Innocents," *Catholic World Report*, May 1999.

41. Statement of U.S. Catholic Bishops Delegation to Sudan, Bishop John Ricard of Pensacola-Tallahassee and Chairman of Catholic Relief Services, before a hearing of the House Human Rights Caucus, April 5, 2001; "Pope, Anglicans Agree to Fight Discrimination in Sudan," Associated Press, February 14, 1999; "World Leaders Wake up to Sudan Horrors," Catholic News Service, *Sooner Catholic*, Sunday, December 3, 2000, which quoted a plea by the Pope for the international community "not to ignore this immense human tragedy."

42. Saunders, "The Slaughter of the Innocents"; "Christmas in Sudan," *First Things* (May 1999); "Grace Still More Abounds," *Catholic World Report*, April 2000.

43. The award recognizes those who champion religious freedom and human rights. Wilberforce, of course, refers to the British parliamentarian of the eighteenth and early nineteenth centuries whose Christian convictions motivated him to lead the campaign against the slave trade.

44. *The Hidden Gift: War and Faith in Sudan*, Bishop Gassis Sudan Relief Fund, www.petersvoice.com.

45. Nina Shea, interview, 2003.

46. Nina Shea, "A War on Religion," *Wall Street Journal*, July 31, 1998.

47. Karl Vick, "Ripping Off Slave Redeemers," *Washington Post*, February 26, 2002, A1.

48. Christian Solidarity International, www.csi-int.org.

49. Eibner received his bachelor's degree in history from Barrington College, Rhode Island, and a Ph.D. from the University of London, specializing in national conflicts in foreign policy. His initial involvement focused on Eastern Europe through the Keston Institute. He joined Christian Solidarity International in 1990, and it was an invitation from the New Sudan Council of Churches in 1992 that led him into the redemption issue. From interview, July 2002, and biography, www.csi-int.org.

50. One photograph shows Eibner giving money to redeem a large group of Sudanese and has been widely distributed among religious organizations and publications.

51. Charles Jacobs, interview, April 2003. Jacobs further described Eibner as an intellectual who can deal with tribal chiefs.

52. The UN Children's Fund (UNICEF) criticized slave redemption, but the organization itself came under criticism for being co-opted by Khartoum (because UNICEF does not distribute aid outside of the regime's control) and for its silence on the existence of slavery. Its rationale for opposition seemed to belie its own operations in India to purchase children in bondage. See statement of Charles Jacobs before the Subcommittee on International Operations and Human Rights, of the Committee on International Relations, U.S. House of Representatives, May 27, 1999, 11–15 and 59–73; and "A Double Standard on Slavery," *Boston Globe*, April 27, 1999, an editorial that chastises UNICEF for its double standard.

53. Vick, "Ripping Off Slave Redeemers."

54. Dennis Bennett, head of Servant's Heart, as quoted in Art Moore, "Faith under Fire," WorldNetDaily.com, March 4, 2002.

55. Eric Reeves, "Slave Redemption Won't Save Sudan," *Christian Science Monitor*, May 26, 1999.

56. Eibner uses an elaborate system of photographs and fingerprinting to ensure against abuse, and those who have traveled with him note how it would be impossible for the hundreds of people they interviewed to fake stories, emotional reunions, or scars that were unlikely to have been made by rebels engaged in a ruse. This was especially stressed by Joe Madison to me in an interview on July 7, 2003.

57. Eibner outlines the extensive safeguards he employs at www.csi-int.org.

58. News release of Christian Solidarity International, "Church Leaders Support Christian Solidarity International's Slave Redemption Program," February 28, 2002.

59. John Eibner, interview, July 2003.

60. This report came from the Freedom Action Network, update@iabolish.com. Its website is www.iabolish.com.

61 "President Bush Urged to Help Free Sudanese Slaves Now: Conditions Ripe for Mass Exodus of Slaves," Christian Solidarity International press release, May 28, 2003; John Eibner, interview, July 7, 2003.

62. "Aid Groups Meet to Confront Slavery in Sudan," Christian Solidarity International press release, June 27, 2003.

63. Jacobs, interview, April 2003.

64. Mindy Sink, "Schoolchildren Set Out to Liberate Slaves in Sudan," *New York Times*, December 2, 1998, A28; Richard Woodbury, "The Children's Crusade," *Time*, December 21, 1998, 44; Nat Hentoff, "Anybody Care about Black Slaves?" *Village Voice*, August 12, 1998.

65. In testimony before a combined hearing, "Crimes against Humanity in Sudan," of the Subcommittee on International Operations and Human Rights and the Subcommittee on Africa, of the Committee on International Relations, May 27, 1999, 24–28. Vogel provided this figure.

66. Chuck Colson, "America's 'Little Abolitionists,'" *Jubilee Extra* (May 1999): 8.

67. Nina Shea reported that Sharon Payt, formerly of Brownback's staff, was the one who made the connection with the program producer.

68. The episode aired on September 26, 1999.

69. Joe Madison suggested this, along with the "Christian Right" stigma attached to the movement that made black leaders skittish about alliances.

70. On May 23, 2000, the Sudan coalition held its kickoff rally to inaugurate its campaign for publicity, divestment, and congressional legislation. Chaired by John Eibner, it brought a number of black clergy to Washington, including preachers with huge congregations and broadcast ministries. The press conference and march to the White House included such black pastors as T. D. Jakes of Dallas, Jethro James of Newark, Marvin Williams of Atlanta, Alex Hurt of Boston, Michael Faulkner of New York City, and Chuck Singleton of Los Angeles.

71. American Anti-Slavery Group news release, April 16, 2002.

72. Joe Madison hosts the program, "Joe Madison and Company," on WOL-1450 AM, which is broadcast nationally through satellite and airs at 6:00 a.m. Eastern time.

73. "The Tony Brown Show." This was according to an interview with Joe Madison in July of 2003.

74. He saw Charles Rangel share a platform with Dick Armey, Jesse Helms and saw Henry Hyde join Donald Payne. Joe Madison, interview, July 2003.

75. Walter Fauntroy was a prominent figure in the 1960s civil rights struggle and was elected as the D.C. representative to Congress.

76. Joe Madison, interview, July 2003.

77. Statement by Joe Madison at a Congressional Hearing on Slavery in Sudan in Washington, D.C., on April 26, 2001.

78. I was in the room and can testify to the impact the singing made.

79. This was how Madison described his conversations with some black leaders. The gist of this was corroborated by conversations with others in the coalition.

80. Michael Horowitz, interview, May 2001.

81. These included Jesse Helms, Henry Hyde, and Dick Armey.

82. Madison pointed to a strong statement on Sudanese slavery that appeared on Jesse Jackson's Rainbow Coalition website.

83. The account of the sequence is from Michael Horowitz.

84. Steven Mufson, "3 Arrested in Protest at Sudanese Embassy," *Washington Post*, April 14, 2001, A5; William Raspberry, "The Am-I-Dreaming Team," *Washington Post*, May 5, 2001; "Legal Dream Team," *Good Morning America* broadcast, May 15, 2001.

85. "Cochran, Starr Hint at Protestors' Defense," *Washington Post*, May 16, 2001, B2.

86. Barbara Reynolds, "Making a Stand against Slavery," *Washington Post*, July 15, 2001.

87. The American Anti-Slavery Group operates a "Freedom Action Network," called iAbolish, which takes on slavery in Sudan and Mauritania, debt bondage and sex trafficking, and virtual slavery of children and impoverished workers in certain countries.

88. Charles Jacobs and Mohamed Athie, "Bought and Sold," *New York Times*, July 13, 1994.

89. Charles Jacobs, interview, April 2003.

90. Bok, *Escape from Slavery*.

91. The man's name was Franco Majok. Bok, *Escape from Slavery*.

92. Bok, *Escape from Slavery*.

93. Charles Jacobs, interview, April 2003.

94. Four days after the Kennedy School speech by Bok and the grilling of the National Security Council official, President Clinton, on Human Rights Day, condemned "the scourge of slavery in Sudan." Bok, *Escape from Slavery*, 215–17.

95. Abuk Bak, as told to Michael Weiss, "I Found a New Life," *Ladies Home Journal*, February 2002. This account was picked up by Tony Lewis, "No Greater Tragedy," *New York Times,* March 24, 2002, who had previously described the movement's concern about persecuted Christians as special pleading.

96. Bak, "I Found a New Life."

97. Zoe Ingalls, "Notes from Academe: An English Professor to Call the World's Attention to Sudan's 'Invisible War,'" *Chronicle of Higher Education*, December 10, 1999; Sebastian Mallaby, "Taking Foreign Policy Private," *Washington Post*, May 29, 2000.

98. Ingalls, "Notes from Academe."

99. Every six years or so, most major universities grant a semester's leave with pay for professors to conduct research full time and allow the professor to take a full year leave with the second semester not for pay. Thus Reeves cut his salary in half during his first year of Sudan work.

100. Eric Reeves, interview, spring 2003; and Ingalls, "Notes from Academe."

101. He believes false claims undermine the credibility of legitimate charges that accuse Khartoum of engaging in genocidal crimes.

102. The Sudan Peace Act passed on October 7, 2002. The next day there was no *New York Times* story on the passage of the act; there was only a photograph illustrating the event in a different story.

103. That day was June 13, 2001, when the Bachus Amendment to the Sudan Peace Act was adopted by the House of Representatives, and the Southern Baptist Convention, meeting in New Orleans, adopted a resolution condemning the persecution and genocide sponsored by the militant Islamic regime in Sudan and supporting direct aid for the victims. Bobby Ross, Jr., "Baptists Share United Voice," *Daily Oklahoman*, June 14, 2001.

104. Mindy Belz, "Creating a New 'Market' for International Outrage," *World*, February 19, 2000, 28; "Blue Nile Blackout," *World*, June 10, 2000, 20; "We Have Nothing, But We Have Everything," *World*, June 17, 2000, 46; "Blue Nile Blackout II," *World*, July 29, 2000, 44; "Daniel of the Year," *World*, December 16, 2000, 21; "Memo to Washington," *World*, March

31, 2001, 24; "More than a Warlord," *World*, July 21, 2001, 18; "Nowhere to Run," *World*, August 11, 2001, 32.

105. Joe Madison told me he had invited a number of well-known journalists, such as Geraldo Rivera, but they refused when informed of the hardships and dangers involved.

106. Holly Lebowitz, "A Resurrection of Campus Activism," *Sojourners* (September–October 1999).

107. House International Relations Committee hearing; Shea, interview, 2003.

108. William Lobdell, "Raising Their Voices," *Los Angeles Times*, February 19, 2001; Regina Holtman, "Songwriter Strikes Chord with Sudan," *Washington Times*, February 20, 2001.

109. George Neumayr, "Midland Ministers to the World," *American Spectator*, December 8, 2003.

110. The organization was headed up in 2001 by the Rev. Billy Raies, a charismatic minister who had spent time evangelizing in Mexico, but whose family roots in the Middle East gave him a sense of special mission to the suffering church. He was succeeded by Jerry Hilton, who went on to become a key grassroots lobbyist on the Sudan Peace Act and its implementation.

111. Neumayr, "Midland Ministers to the World."

112. "West Texas Rock," *Sojourners* (November/December 2001): 12.

113. Neumayr, "Midland Ministers to the World."

114. Sharon Denning, "Rock the Desert Gives Voice to Sudan's Lost Boys," *Odessa American*, August 11, 2002.

115. Servant's Heart E-News, August 6, 2002, enews@servheart.org.

116. "Post 9-11 Survey of Evangelical Elites," University of Akron 2002 Survey for the Ethics and Public Policy Center, John Green, Principal Investigator. This survey was funded by the Pew Charitable Trusts in an effort to inventory the engagement in the public square of the major religious communities in the United States. With 349 usable responses, the survey tapped a wide swath of the evangelical elite, and probably indicates that other religious leaders had been made aware of the situation in Sudan, if not in the same numbers.

117. Not suprisingly, Stephen Morrison, director of the African Program for CSIS characterized Horowitz and some of the others in the Sudan campaign as "radicals" who oversimplify. Conversation with Morrison, March 2004.

118. Horowitz's and Fowler's quotes are from interviews.

119. For a quarter of a century Saperstein has been director of the Washington Office of the Union of American Hebrew Congregations, the Reform branch of Judaism.

120. Saperstein provided documentation of this outreach effort; I describe it as stunning because it was the most extensive grassroots effort within the Jewish community.

121. "Remarks by the President to the American Jewish Committee," May 6, 2001, from the website of the White House Office of the Press Secretary, www.whitehouse.gov/news/releases/2001/05/20010504.html. See also "Bush Condemns Suppression of Religious Freedom in Sudan," *New York Times*, May 4, 2001, web version.

122. Eric Alterman, "Blood on His Hands," MSNBC editorial, July 9, 2001.

123. This was the assessment of Ed Corr, former ambassador to El Salvador, and Ed Perkins, former director general of the Foreign Service, ambassador to the United Nations, and ambassador to South Africa during the transition from white rule. Perkins told me that Abrams was very aggressive in promoting human rights, including in governments with friendly relations with the United States.

124. Elliott Abrams, *Faith or Fear* (New York: Free Press, 1997).

125. Elliott Abrams, "Nazi Gold and Chinese Christians," *American Purpose* 11 (fall/winter 1997), Ethics and Public Policy Center.

126. Elliott Abrams, "The U.S. Role in Humanitarian Intervention," *American Purpose* 14 (winter 2000), Ethics and Public Policy Center.

127. Elliott Abrams, interviews, December 1999, April 2001, and subsequent interviews.

128. Elliott Abrams, "What to Do about Sudan," *Weekly Standard*, May 7, 2001.

129. He was appointed Senior Director for Democracy, Human Rights, and International Operations for the National Security Council.

130. Tancredo's quotes are from a speech he gave at a May 23, 2000, rally in Washington, D.C. sponsored by the Sudan Coalition. I also gleaned this information from a conversation with Tancredo, interviews with others, and extensive congressional record.

131. Mary McGory, "Suddenly Sudan," *Washington Post*, March 11, 2001.

132. Laurie Goodstein, "Inaugural Pastor's Youthful Trajectory Was Like Bush's," *New York Times*, January 20, 2001.

133. Elisabeth Bumiller, "Evangelicals Sway White House on Human Rights Issues Abroad," *New York Times*, October 26, 2003, A1.

134. Michelle Cottle, "Bible Brigade," *New Republic*, April 21 and 28, 2003.

135. I drew upon his and other reports in my piece in the *Weekly Standard*. See Allen Hertzke, "Genocide Fueled by Oil," *Weekly Standard*, July 22, 2002.

136. "The NIF Regime Expectedly Has Made Sham of the Machakos Deal," public statement from the Sudanese Civil Society, Nairobi, August 2, 2002.

137. Bennett reported that in one village the region's only Christian pastor and his family were burned to death as soldiers ringed their grass home, while another fifty-nine were killed. The Civilian Protection Monitoring Team investigated and found that the pastor's family was still alive and that evidence suggested that he may have been killed by a renegade rebel group. This was reported by David Hoile, "American Christians Gravely Misled on Sudan," September 11, 2003, world.mediamonitors.net, and he cited the Civilian Protection Monitoring Team, www.cpmtsudan.org.

138. Some of Bennett's reports of violations of cease-fire agreements in 2003 were later refuted or clarified by the Civilian Protection Monitoring Team, www.cpmtsudan.org. These exaggerations provide ammunition to such Sudan apologists as David Hoile, Media Monitors Network, world.mediamonitors.net.

139. Reflecting the movement's religious base and diversity, along with the new participants, those involved at some level of strategizing included: (1) lobbyists for diverse denominations, from the Southern Baptist Convention to the Union of American Hebrew Congregations to the Episcopal Church; (2) representatives of advocacy groups, such as Prison Fellowship, the Institute on Religion and Democracy, the American Anti-Slavery Group, and the William Casey Institute; (3) political leaders, including members of the Congressional Black Caucus; (4) individual activists, such as Michael Horowitz and Smith College professor Eric Reeves; (5) grassroots advocates from New York and Boston to Dallas and Midland; and (6) Sudanese expatriate leaders.

140. Strategy meeting for Sudan coalition.

141. This vignette was relayed independently in pretty much the same way by several people in the room at the time.

142. Albright made this statement at a meeting with religious freedom advocates in Washington, and it was circulated widely from that point onward.

143. In April of 2002, for example, a delegation from Australia's mainstream churches, led by an Anglican archbishop, returned from Sudan with a call for the Australian government to bring pressure on Khartoum to end the war.

144. Eric Reeves, e-mail, March 2003.

145. Eli J. Lake, "Slow on Sudan," *National Review*, July 29, 2002.

146. "Spineless on Sudan," *Washington Post*, September 10, 2000, B6.

147. U.S. Commission on International Religious Freedom, "Report on Sudan," April 2002.

148. Dennis Bennett put this to me during the November 2001 events in Midland, Texas, for the International Day of Prayer.

149. See "Quantifying Genocide," 1993 and 1999 reports, U.S. Committee on Refugees.

150. In an interview in the spring of 2003, Reeves recalls that as the pivotal moment that sparked his role in the divestment campaign.

151. The article was published in the *Globe and Mail*, May 4, 1999. The "bombshell" was how Reeves described its impact in an interview in 2003.

152. Sidney Tarrow, *Power in Movement* (New York: Cambridge University Press, 1994).

153. Eric Reeves, interview, April 2003, along with numerous internal documents.

154. "Exploiting Sudan's Agony," *Washington Post*, editorial, November 15, 1999, A22.

155. "Canadian Oil Company Ordered Ethnic Clean Sudan," March 5, 2002, from the website of the Anti-Slavery Group, www.iabolish.com/news/global/2002/talisman03-05-02.htm.

156. "Judge: Talisman Can Be Held Liable for Genocide," *Dow Jones International News*, March 20, 2003.

157. Material from various interviews and meetings, along with reports by Reeves. See "Genocidal Ambition on Wall Street," *Intellectual Capital*, November 11, 1999; and "Goldman Sachs, China National Petroleum Corp., and the Destruction of Sudan," *Newark Star-Ledger*, April 27, 2000.

158. Interviews with Dennis Bennett, 2001, and Eric Reeves, April 2003. Estimates vary widely about how much of a cut CNPC took in its IPO. Most put the figure as well below half of what it wanted, depending on how much was hoped for in the first place.

159. Letter from Laura Unger, Acting Chair of the Securities and Exchange Commission, to Congressman Frank Wolf, May 8, 2001.

160. "Their Finest Hour: Financial Times Describes Emerging Forces in Global Finance and National Security/Human Rights Nexus," news release from the William Casey Institute, May 11, 2001. The action was also reported by Edward Alden, "SEC Seeks Closer Watch on Overseas Group," *Financial Times*, May 11, 2001.

161. "Report of the United States Commission on International Religious Freedom," U.S. Commission on International Religious Freedom, May 1, 2001. The commission repeated this call in its 2002 report as well.

162. Elliott Abrams, "What to Do about Sudan," *Weekly Standard,* May 7, 2001, 27.

163. Michael Young, testimony before the House International Relations Committee, June 5, 2002.

164. National Association of Evangelicals Summit on Religious Persecution, May 1, 2002, Washington, D.C.

165. The Bachus vote took place on June 13, 2001.

166. Letters from House members to Senate leaders, 2002.

167. This was how Horowitz described Powell's appointment of Crocker.

168. Jane Perlez, "Candidate as Envoy for Sudan Wants a Shield from Politics," *New York Times*, May 31, 2001.

169. This quote by the Goldman Sachs lobbyist was supposedly mentioned in confidence but was ultimately shared by Michael Horowitz during a debate over Sudan on national public radio. My own interviews corroborated the story.

170. Charles Jacobs, interview, spring 2003.

171. Chris Smith, interview, September 2000.

172. A. M. Rosenthal, "Of Slavery, Oil Money, and Human Rights," *Washington Times*, July 30, 2001.

173. This agreement was the Machakos Protocol, which set the stage for later peace pacts between the Khartoum government and rebel groups.

174. Joshua Green, "God's Foreign Policy," *Washington Monthly* (November 2001): 32.

175. Letter to the president sponsored by Freedom House and the Institute of Religion and Democracy, November 19, 2001, 2.

176. E-mail report from Eric Reeves, April 16, 2003.

177. Eric Reeves, interview, April 2003.

178. Hearing of the House International Relations Committee with testimony given by Walter Kansteiner, Assistant Secretary for African Affairs, June 5, 2002. Diane Rehm Show, August 16, 2001.

179. Gassis said this in a talk to Wilberforce Fellows, students studying at the Family Research Council, in a meeting hosted by William Saunders in 2002.

180. The term, of course, comes from Samuel P. Huntington, *The Clash of Civilizations and the Remaking of World Order* (New York: Touchstone, 1996).

181. Mindy Belz, profile of John Garang, "More Than a Warlord," *World,* July 21, 2002.

182. Steve Cleary and Gary Lane, "The Good Shepherd: Caring for the Persecuted in Sudan," *Voice of the Martyrs* (April 2002).

183. MSNBC interview, November 2001.

184. Laurie Goodstein, "Top Evangelicals Critical of Colleagues over Islam," *New York Times,* May 6, 2003.

185. The American Muslim Council sponsored a panel on June 1, 2001, in Washington, D.C., titled, "Slavery in Sudan Is a Sham," as reported by the American Muslim Council, e-mail announcement, June 1, 2001, amc@amconline.org. The panel was organized by a group called the Committee for Truth about Sudan.

186. David Forte, testimony before the Subcommittee on International Operations and Human Rights, House Committee on International Relations, February 15, 1996. In the wake of 9/11 Michael Horowitz faxed Forte's testimony to numerous White House officials. Though reports cited Forte's testimony as influencing the Bush administration, one Bush official told me that there were also others, such as Daniel Pipes, who were making similar arguments.

187. This is taken from an e-mail message from Charles Jacobs, September 29, 2001.

188. Letter to the president sponsored by Freedom House and the Institute of Religion and Democracy, November 19, 2001, 2.

189. Letter to Nina Shea from Condoleezza Rice, January 22, 2002, 1.

190. Led by Western military commanders, the Civilian Protection Monitoring Team included members from Britain, France, Italy, and Norway, and was directed on the ground by Western military officers.

191. Eric Reeves, "Monitoring in Southern Sudan: Confusion Abounds, Khartoum Benefits," e-mail release, May 30, 2002.

192. See Allen Hertzke, "Genocide Fueled by Oil," *Weekly Standard*, July 22, 2002.

193. Letter to First Lady Laura Bush and President George W. Bush, dated July 10, 2002, and sent to the First Lady's scheduling secretary that the group had dealt with before from the Ministerial Alliance of Midland, Rev. Billy Raies, Midland Association of Churches, Fr. Jon Stasney, Hispanic Evangelical Church Association, Pastor Jose Chavez, African-American Pastors Association, Rev. Leroy Lengyon, BASIC Ministries International, Deborah Fikes, FACES OF CHILDREN Advocacy Group, Margaret Purvis, St. Ann's Parish Lay Leaders, Rhett and Janice Gist.

194. Twelve House Members, May 13, 2002.

195. Black caucus letter, May 12, 2002.

196. Michael Horowitz, who entertained the position that making Sudan a pariah state would be sufficient to end its war and possibly even bring the regime down, was the exception in believing that the Bachus Amendment could never pass the Senate but could be valuable trading bait for other substantive legislative language. Indeed, Horowitz was meeting with Senator Brownback on the September 11, 2001, while Shea and others were preparing for their scheduled press conference. This bit of solo diplomacy upset others in the coalition, who had to do "damage repair" with Brownback about their continued commitment to Bachus.

197. H.R. 5532, the revised Sudan Peace Act, passed the House on October 7, 2002, by a vote of 359–8 and then was adopted unanimously by the Senate on October 9.

198. Speech on the floor of the House of Representatives, October 7, 2002, in debate over the Sudan Peace Act.

199. Coalition leaders heard from several members of Congress who conveyed that the vigil helped keep the issue on the agenda and therefore was pivotal to the outcome.

200. A cogent summary of this record was amassed by Dennis Bennett, Executive Director of Servant's Heart. See his September 2002 letter, www.servheart.org.

201. The *New York Times*, October 22, 2002, did not have a story on the signing, but only embedded a photograph of the event in another story.

202. One of those battles occurred almost immediately after the signing of the Sudan Peace Act. A letter issued by the White House and signed by President Bush seemed to suggest that the president might not implement certain provisions of the bill. Activists, especially Michael Horowitz, demanded an explanation. What they learned is that the White House counsel had been attaching stock qualifiers asserting the president's discretion over foreign policy against congressional initiatives. Horowitz secured a promise from Walter Kansteiner, Bush's African specialist at the State Department, that they intended to fully implement the new law, but subsequent actions suggested an anemic effort to do so.

203. Chris Regner, "Bush Signs Sudan Peace Act in the Presence of Activists," news release, Institute on Religion and Democracy, October 29, 2002.

204. Press release, Center for Religious Freedom, Freedom House, October 10, 2002.

205. This was recounted to me by Faith McDonnell, who attended the ceremony.

206. Tom Hart, then director of the Washington office of the Episcopal Church, was the only mainline Protestant church leader present. As noted in chapter 6, his involvement in the new religious freedom campaign was exceptional among the liberal Protestant churches, in part because the Anglicans in Sudan brought their plight to the world Anglican community. Hart helped promote the Sudan Peace Act among Democrats with whom his office had good relations.

207. "Bush Signs Sudan Peace Act, Meets Francis Bok," October 22, 2002, Freedom Action Network of the American Anti-Slavery Group, www.iabolish.org.

208. "Bush Meets Former Slave for Signing of Sudan Peace Act," news release, American Anti-Slavery Group, Boston, Massachusetts, October 21, 2002.

209. Charles Jacobs and John Eibner, "Sudan Enters a New Era," *Washington Times,* November 27, 2003.

210. These are cataloged by the Civilian Protection Monitoring Team: "CPMT Final Report: Military Events in Western Upper Nile, 31 December 2002 to 30 January 2003," Khartoum, February 6, 2003; "CPMT Report to IGAD: Military Events in Leer, 26 January to 30 January 2003," Khartoum, February 2, 2003. These are cited in Eric Reeves, "Monitoring in Southern Sudan: Confusion Abounds, Khartoum Benefits," e-mail release, May 30, 2002.

211. John Eibner, "Another Front: Genocidal Jihad in the Sudan," *National Review Online,* March 25, 2003.

212. Reeves, "Monitoring in Southern Sudan."

213. "From Joseph Farah's G2 Bulletin: U.S. to Forgive Sudan for 2 Million Deaths?" WorldNetDaily.com, June 2, 2003.

214. I am indebted to a University of Oklahoma student, whose senior thesis systematically reviewed the possibilities for peace in Sudan. See Michael English, "Evolving Objectives: An Examination of America's Policy Towards Sudan," senior honors thesis, May 10, 2003, on file at the Honors College, University of Oklahoma.

215. April 22, 2003.

216. Memos from Nina Shea to Sudan Coalition, April 30 and May 22, 2003; e-mail note from Faith McDonnell, May 9, 2003.

217. Dennis Bennett, "Servant's Heart," news release, June 4, 2003.

218. Ministerial Alliance of Midland, open letter to the government of Sudan, March 7, 2003. Reported by Julia Duin, "Bush's Hometown Seeks Sudan Peace," *Washington Times,* March 7, 2003.

219. Neumayr, "Midland Ministers to the World."

220. The Midland approach to quiet diplomacy was criticized by some in the coalition, who feared that the government of Sudan would co-opt the locals. But the Midland folk, while speaking softly, carried an implicit big stick, enabling them to convey hard messages to the Sudanese government.

221. Neumayr, "Midland Ministers to the World."

222. Neumayr, "Midland Ministers to the World."

223. On the meeting see Andrew England, "Sudanese President and Rebel Leader Meet for First Time in More than Eight Months," Associated Press, April 2, 2003, as reported in www.Sudan.net, May 5, 2003. On Bush initiative see Richard W. Stevenson, "Bush Calls for Changes in Africa to End Wars and Promote Trade," *New York Times,* June 27, 2003.

224. Charles Jacobs and John Eibner, "Sudan Enters a New Era," *Washington Times,* November 27, 2003.

225. Both Amnesty International and Human Rights Watch vigorously documented the tragedy in Darfur. Eric Reeves drew heavily from Amnesty reports in his reportage on Darfur. Eric Reeves, "Another Chance to Combat Genocide," *Baltimore Sun,* April 1, 2004. On media coverage of Darfur see Barbara Borst, "750,000 Displaced in Sudan," Associated Press Story, *The Oklahoman,* April 4, 2004; Somini Sengupta, "War in Western Sudan Overshadows Peace in the South," *New York Times,* January 17, 2004; Samantha Power, "Remember Rwanda, but Take Action in Sudan," *New York Times,* April 6, 2004; "Peril in Sudan," editorial, *New York Times,* April 7, 2004; Nicholas Kristof, "Ethnic Cleansing, Again," *New York Times,* March 24, 2004; Nicholas Kristof, "Cruel Choices," *New York Times,* April 14, 2004.

226. *AgenceFrance-Presse,* June 3, 2004, as quoted in Reeves email newsletter, "If the UN Won't Act to Save Hundreds of Thousands in Darfur, Who Will?" June 9, 2004.

227. Nina Shea, "From Sudan to the East River," *The Weekly Standard,* June 21, 2004.

CHAPTER 8

1. International Religious Freedom Act, Public Law 105-292, 22 USC 6401, signed into law October 27, 1998.

2. Elisabeth Bumiller, "Bush, in China, Urges Freedom for Worshipers," *New York Times*, February 22, 2002, A1.

3. See chapter 3.

4. This was not only the view of many I interviewed who worked with the State Department but even of some inside the Diplomatic Corps as well. As one official noted, the view at State was "that religion is bad, that it causes conflict."

5. U.S. Department of State, *Annual Report on International Religious Freedom 2001* (Washington, DC: GPO, December 2001), introduction.

6. Readers might recognize the "Catholic" language here, especially the emphasis on the "dignity of the human person." I suspect this has to do with the influence of Tom Farr.

7. U.S. Department of State, *Annual Report 2001*, introduction, xiii.

8. For a scholarly response to criticisms of IRFA, see T. Jeremy Gunn, "A Preliminary Response to Criticisms of the International Religious Freedom Act of 1998," *Brigham Young University Law Review* (2000): 841–66.

9. From its inception in 1999 through 2002, the Director of the State Department Office of Religious Freedom was Tom Farr. A veteran State Department official and Roman Catholic, he was committed to the issue even before the legislation passed. Drawing upon his contacts in the diplomatic corps, Farr staffed the work of Seiple and Hanford. His vital work illustrates how the new law enhanced the internal clout of individuals who shared its aims. The quote is from an interview with Farr.

10. Report on International Religious Freedom, U.S. Department of State, 2002.

11. Letter from David Saperstein to Allen Hertzke, fall 2003.

12. Conversation with Ed Perkins, former director general of the Foreign Service and former ambassador to South Africa, November 2003. The other sought after document is the Annual Human Rights report.

13. Letter from David Saperstein to Hertzke, September 24, 2003.

14. Particularly notable is the 2003 International Religious Freedom Report, released by the Bureau of Democracy, Human Rights, and Labor, December 18, 2003.

15. This account circulated in the religious presses and was confirmed by inside sources.

16. "2003 Report on International Religious Freedom," Executive Summary, U.S. Department of State, released December 18, 2003.

17. Intriguingly, it was the staff cadre that drafted the original IRFA that commissioners thought were trying to micromanage the commission. Working with Congressman Wolf, the commissioners gained enabling language that secured their independence.

18. Executive Director Joseph Crapa was selected with a charge to aggressively focus staff energies on policy adoption.

19. Three commissioners are selected by the president, two by the leaders of the president's party in Congress, and four by the congressional leaders of the other party.

20. The commission report, purposely less cumbersome than the State Department report, begins with a concise portrayal of each country of concern. The commission then provides full reports on particular countries, enabling the reader to easily navigate through information of special relevance.

21. The commission's third report came out in May 2002.

22. U.S. Commission on International Religious Freedom, news release, August 8, 2003.

23. U.S. Commission on International Religious Freedom, Report on Indonesia, May 2002, 18.

24. This and a wealth of other information is contained on the website of the U.S. Commission on International Religious Freedom: www.uscirf.gov.

25. *Annual Report of the U.S. Commission on International Religious Freedom*, May 2003.

26. *Annual Report of the U.S. Commission on International Religious Freedom*, May 2003, p. 51.

27. U.S. Commission on International Religious Freedom, "Commission Recommends 12 Nations for Designation as 'Countries of Concern,'" news release, September 30, 2002, www.uscirf.gov.

28. U.S. Commission on International Religious Freedom, news release, August 8, 2003.

29. Background interview.

30. For Robert Seiple's criticism of the commission see the October 2002 issue of *Christianity Today*, www.christianitytoday.com/go/uscirf.

31. Addendum to the *Report of the U.S. Commission on International Religious Freedom*, Individual Dissenting View of Commissioner Dr. Laila Al-Marayati Regarding Israel and the Occupied Territories, May 14, 2001, 13.

32. This according to other members of the commission.

33. *Annual Report of the U.S. Commission on International Religious Freedom*, May 2003.

34. Thomas Omestad, "Gulag Nation," *U.S. News and World Report* (June 23, 2003); and Anthony Spaeth, "Kim's Rackets," *Time* (June 9, 2003).

35. On this documentation, see Doug Struck, "Keeping the Faith, Underground: N. Korea's Secret Christians Get Support from South Korea, *Washington Post*, April 10, 2001; Robert Marquand, "Korean Evangelicals Aiming North," *Christian Science Monitor*, as reported in the *Daily Oklahoman*, June 11, 2003; "Christians Brainwashed and Living in Fear, says Defector," *South China Morning Post*, January 26, 2002 (this report was based on testimony of Soon Ok Lee before the U.S. Commission on International Religious Freedom); and James Brooke, "N. Koreans Talk of Baby Killings," *New York Times*, June 10, 2002 (this story also featured eyewitness accounts by Soon Ok Lee). On how Christian Solidarity watchdog groups spotlighted the regime, see "A Martyr's Light: A Glimpse into North Korea," Voice of the Martyrs newsletter, August 2001.

36. Tomas J. Belke, *Juche: A Christian Study of North Korea's State Religion*, Bartlesville, OK: Living Sacrifice Book Company, 1999).

37. Ann Morse, "View from the Axis of Evil," *World*, March 9, 2002; "Gulag Nation," *U.S. News and World Report*, (June 23, 2003); and Spaeth, "Kim's Rackets," *Time* (June 9, 2003). To be fair to the secular press North Korean abuses were documented in prestige outlets, but those accounts did not penetrate as widely as the more popular ones. See Elisabeth Rosenthal, "Beijing Increases Detentions of Illegal North Korean Immigrants, *New York Times*, March 21, 2002; James Brooke, "One German, and His North Korean Conscience," *New York Times*, March 19, 2002; Struck, "Keeping the Faith."

38. North Korea was featured prominently in regular and special commission reports between 2001–2003, and the commission held hearings at which such figures as Soon Ok Lee and Dr. Norbert Vollertsen testified. These received international coverage (www.uscirf.gov). The commission executive director announced commission backing of legislation introduced by Senator Brownback that would expedite asylum for North Korean refugees (June 25, 2003, press conference, Washington, D.C.).

39. Statement of Ambassador John Hanford on the issuance of the 2003 Report of the U.S. Commission on International Religious Freedom, U.S. Department of State, December 18, 2003.

40. Vollertsen went to North Korea with Cap Anamur (German Emergency Doctors), for eighteen months from 1999 to 2001.

41. Anne Morse, "View from the Axis," *World*, March 9, 2002; speech by Norbert Vollertsen at the Second Summit of Christian Leaders on Religious Persecution, May 1, 2002, Mayflower Hotel, Washington, D.C.; Brooke, "One German"; Rosenthal, "Beijing Increases Detentions"; Norbert Vollertsen, "Memo to Mr. Carter: Evil Exists," *Wall Street Journal* (March 7, 2002); Vollertsen, interview, May 1, 2002.

42. Vollertson's videos of these children, dressed in blue-and-white-striped pajamas, hauntingly evoke Holocaust images.

43. Norbert Vollertsen, "Memo to Mr. Carter"; Morse, "View from the Axis."

44. Vollertson's speech before the Second Summit of Christian Leaders on Religious Persecution, Mayflower Hotel, Washington, D.C., May 1, 2002.

45. Brooke, "One German."

46. Vollertson, interview, May 1, 2002.

47. Brooke, "One German."

48. Morse, "View from the Axis."

49. We see this in how Sandy Rios, head of the conservative Concerned Women for America, responded with alacrity to Horowitz's appeals to help lead the grassroots awareness campaign on North Korea. In a memo from Sandy Rios to Harry Newman, March 8, 2003, she wrote enthusiastically about Vollertsen's conversion.

50. On March 14, 2002, Vollertsen and twenty-five North Korean refugees entered the Spanish embassy in Beijing, which received wide coverage of the plight of these people and favorable editorial coverage. See "Asylum in China," *Washington Post*, editorial, May 12, 2002.

51. Senator Sam Brownback, "Mercy in Short Supply: The Plight of North Korean Refugees in China," 2003 Report of the U.S. Committee on Refugees, June 2003.

52. *Annual Report of the U.S. Commission on International Religious Freedom*, May 2003.

53. See "From Helsinki to Pyongyang," *Wall Street Journal,* January 17, 2003. The statement of principles was signed by Leith Anderson, William Bennett, Charles Colson, Nicholas Eberstadt, Robert George, Michael Horowitz, Max Kampelman, Penn Kemble, Dianne Knippers, Richard Land, Richard Neuhaus, Michael Novak, Marvin Olasky, Mark Palmer, Nina Shea, Radek Sikorski, and R. James Woolsey.

54. Ann Morse, "The Abolitionist," *World,* March 1, 2003.

55. Donna Hughes, "Aiding and Abetting the Slave Trade," *Asian Wall Street Journal,* February 27, 2003, A11; Donna Hughes, "Human Sexploitation," *Weekly Standard*, February 24, 2003.

56. John R. Miller, "Sex Slavery in Seattle the Tip of a Global Scourge," *Seattle Times,* October 3, 2002.

57. Kate O'Beirne, "Of Human Bondage," *National Review*, March 11, 2002.

58. Morse, "The Abolitionist"; Hughes, "Aiding and Abetting the Slave Trade"; Hughes, "Human Sexploitation"; Mindy Belz, "No Way Out," *World*, February 23, 2002; O'Beirne, "Of Human Bondage." In her *Asian Wall Street Journal* piece, Hughes documented how a USAID program that attempted to teach women and girls the meaning of "consent" criticized them for being "unwilling to spend time building a community." She also demonstrated how this general approach was taken by such NGOs as the French group *Medecins sans Frontieres* (Doctors without Borders).

59. Hughes, "Human Sexploitation." Hughes provided documentation to members of Congress and the antitrafficking coalition that showed how pro-prostitution groups had received U.S. grants. Hughes obtained copies of actual slides used in a presentation at a conference in New York on April 11, 2002, depicting the work of those groups in the notorious Cambodian village, Svay Pak, providing "assertiveness training" to "sex workers" as young as six. Memo from Michael Horowitz to Congressmen Frank Wolf and Chris Smith, June 12, 2002.

60. Victims of Trafficking and Violence Protection Act of 2000, Public Law 106-386, October 28, 2000. The legislation is divided into two parts, each of which has its own title. So Division A is the Trafficking Victims Protection Act, which is the one cited for our purposes.

61. "Trafficking in Persons Report," U.S. Department of State publication 11057, Office of the Undersecretary for Global Affairs, June 2003. The State Department report conservatively estimates at least 700,000 women and children trafficked per year across international boundaries, while many more are trafficked inside countries, leading John Miller to conclude that the million figure is realistic. Interview with Miller, April 2003.

62. Michael Specter, "Traffickers' New Cargo: Naive Slavic Women," *New York Times*, January 11, 1998; Laura Lederer, "Human Rights Report on Trafficking of Women and Children: A Country-by-Country Report on a Contemporary Form of Slavery," Protection Project of the Nitze School of Advanced International Studies, Johns Hopkins University, 2001.

63. William Branigin, "A Different Kind of Trade War," *Washington Post*, March 20, 1999.

64. Jessica Neuwirth of Equality Now, an international feminist organization, suggested that a strong public/private distinction accounts for the lack of focus by such groups as Human Rights Watch and Amnesty International to trafficking issues. Interview, August 2003.

65. Among the feminist leaders who made this point, in a letter to Madeleine Albright, Secretary of State, January 2000, were Jessica Neuwirth, president of Equality Now; Gloria Feldt, President of Planned Parenthood Federation of America; Patricia Ireland, president of the National Organization of Women; Frances Kissling, president of Catholics for a Free Choice; Dorchen Leidholdt, co-executive director of the Coalition against Trafficking in Women; Robin Morgan, founder of the Sisterhood is Global Institute; Hibaaq Osman, director of the Center for Strategic Initiatives for Women; Julia Scott, president of the National Black Women's Health Project; Eleanor Smeal, president of the Feminist Majority; and Gloria Steinem, founder of *Ms. Magazine*. Laura Lederer documented the deception, manipulation, and force involved in trafficking, in the "Human Rights Report on Trafficking in Women and Children." Gary Haugen of the International Justice Mission observes that brothels present a facade of voluntary prostitution that is belied by the beatings and intimidation inside. Interview, August 2003.

66. Laura Lederer, ed., *Take Back the Night* (New York: William Morrow, 1980).

67. Laura Lederer, interview, March 2001.

68. The head of the Women's Division, Swanee Hunt, has assumed the position after serving as ambassador to Austria, and had expressed interest in trafficking issues.

69. Lederer, "Human Rights Report on Trafficking of Women and Children."

70. Lederer came to these conclusions on the basis of her experience in cataloging global trafficking. Interview, 2001.

71. Gary A. Haugen, *Good News about Injustice* (Downers Grove, IL: InterVarsity Press, 1999).

72. Gary Haugen, interview, August 2003.

73. Haugen works with such groups as Amnesty International and serves on a consortium of all the major human rights groups.

74. As featured in several international news broadcasts, IJM investigators documented how young children were sold to work twelve-hour days rolling by hand Beedi cigarettes, which are a popular export to teenagers in the United States. With documentation in hand, IJM lawyers secured papers to free the children.

75. Human rights groups, especially Amnesty International, took a more aggressive posture as the new faith-based movement mobilized for legislation.

76. From the moment I started conversations with Horowitz in 1998 about the religious freedom campaign, he was talking about sex trafficking, which seemed to me at the time tangential to the movement but which Horowitz saw as central. I observed the way he worked the phones to find allies, connect people, create strange bedfellows coalitions.

77. Specter, "Traffickers' New Cargo."

78. Mariam Bell headed a Christian effort against child pornography called Enough is Enough. She was part of one of the early alliances between Christian conservatives and certain feminists concerned about the effects of pornography on women and girls. Lederer was certainly in that camp, and that relationship provided a linkage to the current struggle.

79. Laura Lederer, interview, 2001. Lederer recalls Bell warning her about how aggressive Horowitz is and not to let him "browbeat her."

80. Laura Lederer, interview, 2001.

81. Both Lederer and Haugen offered cogent testimony and detailed recommendations, versions of which became law. See Hearings before the Subcommittee on International Operations and Human Rights, House Committee on International Relations, September 14, 1999. Joseph Rees, counsel for the subcommittee, worked closely with Haugen and Lederer as refinements were made in the daft legislation.

82. Gary Haugen, interview, August 2003.

83. Testimony of Gary Haugen before the Subcommittee on International Operations and Human Rights, Committee on International Relations, U.S. House of Representatives, September 14, 1999.

84. Victims of Trafficking and Violence Protection Act of 2000, public law 106-386, October 28, 2000.

85. I was in attendance at the meeting.

86. "Army Joins Initiative against Sexual Trafficking," *The Wary Cry*, June 10, 2000.

87. Trafficking strategy session, May 11, 1999, U.S. Capitol.

88. Lederer, interview, 2001.

89. Jessica Neuwirth, interview, 2003.

90. As one person put it, Lederer recruited Neuwirth, who worked with Shifman, who knew Steinem.

91. Letter from Richard Cizik to National Association of Evangelicals members, September 1, 1999.

92. Tony Carnes, "Odd Couple Politics," *Christianity Today* (March 6, 2000).

93. This was the gist of an internal memo that circulated in the State Department.

94. The most prominent of these groups were the International Human Rights Law Group, headed by Ann Jordan, and the Human Rights Watch–Women's Division.

95. Internal documents provided by Laura Lederer and others show this support, which continued into the Bush administration. Particularly aggressive in work with the State Department was Ann Jordan, head of the International Human Rights Law Group, which promotes legalized prostitution.

96. Memo from Pamela Shifman to Laura Lederer, December 9, 1999.

97. See endnote 65.

98. UN Convention of 1949.

99. Swanee Hunt, director of the Women's Division at the Kennedy School, was a Clinton appointee as ambassador to Austria before assuming the Kennedy position, leading some antitrafficking activists to impute the "firing" of Lederer to pressure from the administration.

100. Memo from Michael Horowitz to Sex Trafficking Initiative Steering Committee, May 5, 2000. Some members, such as Chris Smith, needed no such urging. Smith cited Lederer's "painstaking research" as "indispensable to ensuring that we have the facts about this worldwide criminal enterprise and its victims." House floor debate, October 17, 2000.

101. Letter from Senator Sam Brownback (R-KS) to Rand Beers, Assistant Secretary, International Narcotics and Law Enforcement, U.S. Department of State, May 8, 2000.

102. Woolsey is partner for Shea and Gardner and did other work on the trafficking issue, earning plaudits from antitrafficking campaigners. At the October 2000 celebration of the legislation's passage he was referred to as a "knight" in the struggle.

103. Laura Lederer, "Human Rights Report on Trafficking of Women and Children."

104. Laura Lederer, interview, March 2001.

105. Capitol Hill celebration of passage of the trafficking legislation, Indian Room of the Russell Senate Office Building, November 2000.

106. Letter to President George W. Bush, June 28, 2002, from some forty religious and human rights leaders. The letter identified as getting a whitewash Thailand, India, Albania, Honduras, Brazil, and Mauritania, because they were not placed in the Tier III category.

107. "Honesty about Sex Slaves," editorial, *Washington Post Weekly Edition*, June 10–16, 2002.

108. In a March 2002 memo Horowitz described the State Department effort as focused on inputs, such as conferences held, and not focused on outputs—such as shattered trafficking rings. The June 28 letter to President Bush complained that State Department officials were conveying to foreign governments that the cutoff of aid would not be enforced. A June 11, 2002, memo from Donna Hughes cataloged State Department grants to pro-prostitution groups that opposed the legislation. Hughes also provided information on the infamous work of certain NGOs in Svay Pak.

109. The quote on drift is from a memo from Horowitz to Charles Colson, July 17, 2003; the quote on debacle is from an undated summer of 2002 memo from Horowitz to Frank Wolf, Chris Smith, and Sam Brownback. The exasperation of evangelicals and others involved in the trafficking issue with the Bush administration was palpable in conversations I had with them, and it certainly came out in the June 28, 2002, letter, signed by mostly evangelical leaders, along with other trafficking activists.

110. Memo from Michael Horowitz to Chris Santora, May 15, 2002. Horowitz drew upon documentation of Lederer and Hughes on grants.

111. Morse, "The Abolitionist." This article contained rather pointed criticism of Ely-Raphael by movement activists.

112. Ely-Raphael was moved to a different post by Undersecretary for Global Affairs Paula Dobriansky. The decision was communicated to activists in the summer of 2002 but not made official until early in 2003, to coincide with John Miller's appointment.

113. This is according to Horowitz, though Miller wonders if it might have been embellished. Miller did oppose Most Favored Nation Status for China even though Boeing strongly supported the designation. And he even participated in demonstrations at the Chinese embassy. See Morse, "The Abolitionist."

114. John Miller, interview, Washington, D.C., July 2003.

115. John Miller, interview, Washington, D.C., July 2003.

116. John Miller, speech delivered at Georgetown University, February 20, 2003.

117. John Miller, interview, 2003.

118. John Miller, interview, 2003.

119. According to one private e-mail document, Rove told Charles Colson that he opposed Miller and the reason.

120. Letter to Karl Rove, August 16, 2002.

121. "Trafficking in Persons Report," U.S. Department of State publication 11057, Office of the Under secretary for Global Affairs, June 2003.

122. John Miller, interview, 2003.

123. "Trafficking in Persons Report," 2003; John Miller, interview, spring 2003; John R. Miller, "Slavery in 2004," *Washington Post*, guest editorial, January 1, 2004.

124. *World Christian Encyclopedia*, University of Oxford Press, 2001, 2nd ed., David B. Barrett, George T. Kurian, and Todd M. Johnson, Table 1.1 in volume 1, counts 238 countries with Christian populations, followed by 218 for Baha'is and 204 for Muslims.

125. In an infamous vignette, on the eve of the Iranian Revolution in 1979, a proposal to have the CIA investigate the activities of Shiite leaders was vetoed because religion was deemed "unimportant" in modernizing societies. See Edward Luttwak, "The Missing Dimension," in *Religion: The Missing Dimension of Statecraft*, ed. Douglas Johnston and Cynthia Sampson (New York: Oxford University Press, 1994).

126. Barry Rubin, "Religion and International Affairs," in *Religion: The Missing Dimension of Statecraft*, ed. Douglas Johnston and Cynthia Sampson (New York: Oxford University Press, 1994).

127. Douglas Johnston and Cynthia Sampson, eds., *Religion: The Missing Dimension of Statecraft* (New York: Oxford University Press, 1994). Douglas Johnston has become a leading figure in documenting and promoting religious mediation and reconciliation.

128. Samuel P. Huntington, *The Third Wave: Democratization in the Late Twentieth Century* (Norman: University of Oklahoma Press, 1991); Adam Przeworzski et al., in *Democracy and Development* (Cambridge: Cambridge University Press, 2000); take issue with Huntington's view of the role of Christianity, but their analysis stopped in the mid-1990s before the faith-based human rights movement took off.

129. Robert Putnam, *Bowling Alone: The Collapse and Revival of American Community* (New York: Simon & Schuster, 2000).

130. Samuel P. Huntington, *The Clash of Civilizations and the Remaking of World Order* (New York: Touchstone, 1996).

131. The Ethics and Public Policy Center has sponsored a number of symposia featuring Muslim moderates and critics of Islamism and militant Shari'a. See www.eppc.org.

132. Both at the conference on Shari'a, which was held on July 10, 2002, in Washington, D.C., and at an evening dinner hosted by Senator Sam Brownback, I noticed the sense of solidarity among the group of activists that included evangelicals, Catholics, Episcopalians, Jews, Baha'is, Sufi Muslims, and Iranian dissidents. Among those attending the conference were Nina Shea, Paul Marshall, Mike Horowitz, Diane Knippers, and Faith McDonnell. Kabbani, who has written and lectured widely about the misinterpretation of Shari'a by fundamentalists, is increasingly cited by faith-based activists.

133. E-mail letter from Deborah Fikes, December 25, 2003.

134. This Christian realism would have been appreciated by Reinhold Niebuhr, who often criticized Christians as naive about politics.

135. John C. Green, Pew Charitable Trusts 2002 Survey of Evangelical Elites, Post-9/11 Survey of Religion and Politics, University of Akron, 2002.

136. One of the first to notice this trend was Jacob Heilbrunn, "Christian Rights: The Next Big Conservative Issue," *New Republic*, July 7, 1997.

137. Nicholas D. Kristof, "Following God Abroad," *New York Times*, May 21, 2002, A21.

138. Elisabeth Bumiller, "Evangelicals Sway White House on Human Rights Issues Abroad," *New York Times*, October 26, 2003.

139. According to the survey "Evangelicals in America," conducted for *Religion and Ethics NewsWeekly*, released April 5, 2004, evangelicals were more likely than the general public to say that the United States should "promote human rights abroad, like religious freedom" and that it should "promote democracy and freedom abroad, such as for religious minorities."

140. Cal Thomas and Ed Dobson, *Blinded by Might* (Grand Rapids, MI: Zondervan, 1999).

141. Mark Lacey, "In Sudan, Militiamen on Horses Uproot a Million," *New York Times*, May 4, 2004.

142. Mark Noll, ed., *One Nation under God? Christian Faith and Political Action in America* (San Francisco: Harper, 1988).

143. This figure is from the *World Christian Encyclopedia*, 2nd ed., David B. Barrett, George T. Kurian, and Todd M. Johnson (New York: Oxford University Press, 2001), volume 1. Barrett et al., use the term "Great Commission" to connote the broad evangelical rubric, though some of those meeting such a definition might not stress the born-again experience. Still, this is the best figure we have.

144. "Religious Leaders Cheer Debt Relief," *Christian Century*, November 2000. The Jubilee legislative campaign was led by Tom Hart, then director of the national Episcopal office in Washington, who was active on IRFA and the Sudan Peace Act. Hart said that relationships he developed during the lobbying campaign for IRFA were absolutely crucial to his work in assembling the coalition for International Debt Relief. As to informational networks, during an interview with Hart about his work for IRFA, I learned of his upcoming effort on debt relief and shared with him information about Pat Robertson's strong public support for the idea of a Year of Jubilee and forgiveness of debts. Hart wrote the religious broadcaster about the legislation, and though he does not know if Robertson's action was sparked by his correspondence, it certainly was timely and on-message. Intriguingly, White House officials invited Robertson, at Hart's assent, to attend the bill signing ceremony that included Bono and a host of religious leaders, and Robertson offered "on-message" comments to the press afterward.

145. Kevin Bales, *Disposable People: New Slavery in the Global Economy* (Berkeley: University of California Press, 2000).

146. Lanah was about six years old when International Justice Mission investigators captured the transaction on May 8, 2002. Agonizingly, it took a year of continual agitation by IJM and the American government to get Cambodian authorities into the violent village and free Lanah and the other girls. Given corrupt police protection for the gangsters in the area it was not possible to free the girls any other way.

147. "Seek Justice," Quarterly Report, International Justice Mission, spring 2003; *NBC Evening News*, June 13, 2003.

148. *NBC Evening News* and *Dateline* presented an exposé of Cambodian child prostitution and featured the work of Haugen and the International Justice Mission on June 13, 2003.

149. The raid occurred in the spring of 2003.

150. "Seek Justice," Quarterly Report, International Justice Mission, spring 2003.

APPENDIX

Table 1.   Who's Who in the Campaign to Raise Awareness of Persecuted Christians

- Michael Horowitz, neoconservative Jew, former Reagan administration official, and think tank fellow who seized the initiative in sparking and harnessing nascent movement energies toward specific policy goals.
- Nina Shea, a Catholic human rights veteran who created and directs the Center for Religious Freedom at Freedom House and who authored the widely cited *In the Lion's Den*, a narrative with vivid stories of persecution and martyrdom of Christians in Islamic and Communist countries.
- Paul Marshall, a human rights scholar and political theorist who wrote *Their Blood Cries Out*, an account of Christian faith under siege. An evangelically oriented Anglican, he offered trenchant explanations for the inadequate response of Western Christians to the persecution of their counterparts abroad. He now is working for Freedom House to produce reports scaling the status of religious freedom around the globe.
- Charles Colson, the former Nixon counsel who founded Prison Fellowship, a widely praised global ministry for prisoners and prison reform. One of the most esteemed American evangelical leader today, his support became pivotal to the campaign, both for grassroots mobilization and for bringing other leaders to the table. He credits Horowitz with showing him the scope of the problem and sparking his commitment.
- Voice of the Martyrs, a missionary organization begun by a Romanian pastor and his wife, Richard and Sabina Wurmbrand, who endured brutal treatment at the hands of Nazis and Communists in their native land. In exile, the Wurmbrands began a ministry first to countries behind the Iron Curtain, but then expanded assistance to persecuted churches in some eighty countries. The organization, headquartered in Bartlesville, Oklahoma, has grown rapidly to over a hundred thousand members and is currently directed by Tom White, who spent seventeen months in a Cuban jail for smuggling Christian literature.
- Open Doors with Brother Andrew, an international organization begun in 1955 as a support mechanism for the efforts of Holland pastor Andrew Vanderbijl, who

(continued)

smuggled Bibles and other Christian materials behind the Iron Curtain during the

Table 1.   Who's Who in the Campaign to Raise Awareness of Persecuted Christians *(continued)*

Cold War. With offices in seventeen countries, including the United States, its mission now focuses broadly on persecution of Christians in Communist, Islamic, and authoritarian governments. It sponsors Compass Direct News Service, out of Santa Ana, California, which publishes credible monthly reports of incidents around the globe.

- Christian Solidarity Worldwide, headed by Baroness Caroline Cox of the British House of Lords, a grandmother and fervent Christian who describes herself as "a nurse and social scientist by intention, and a Baroness by surprise." She travels to places where some of the worst human rights abuses occur in the world today. For example, she has visited Sudan at least twenty times, flying into unsecured landing strips, sleeping in tents, and hiking miles to reach victims of abuse.
- Christian Solidarity International, an interdenominational organization founded in 1977 and headquartered in Switzerland. Under the leadership of John Eibner, it has been the most heavily involved of all the groups in the practice of slave redemption in Sudan and has helped sponsor the campaign against the Khartoum regime.
- International Christian Concern, founded by the late Steve Snyder in Washington, D.C., an organization with links to underground churches in a number of countries and credibility for early reports of persecution in such places as China, Pakistan, Saudi Arabia, and Algeria.
- Christian Federation International, headquartered in Front Royal, Virginia, which specializes in helping besieged believers in such places as Sudan and Burma. Headed by James Jacobson, a former Reagan administration official, the organization refuses to accept UN or government money, which frees it to deliver supplies outside of bureaucratic channels.
- Antislavery activists, including: Charles Jacobs of the American Anti-Slavery Group based in Massachusetts; Chuck Singleton, Los Angeles pastor of one of the largest black congregations in the country and creator of Congress on Modern Pan-African Slavery; and the late Samuel Cotton, African American scholar from Columbia University who directed the Coalition against Slavery in Mauritania and Sudan. They led a quiet crusade, often ignored by prominent American black leaders, against Arab enslavement of black Africans.
- Prayer for the Persecuted Church, which sponsors the annual "Shatter the Silence" International Day of Prayer, in which congregations receive packets to help them devote a Sunday in November to learn about, and pray for, the persecuted. In 2000 the organization estimated that 300,000 congregations around the world (100,000 of them in the United States) participated in some way in the event.
- Advocates International, a U.S.-based group headed by Sam Ericsson, which takes a nonconfrontational approach to working with foreign leaders to build legal institutions that protect religious rights. Staffed primarily by attorneys, it trains lawyers, judges, and legislators around the world on principles of religious freedom. It identifies and works with professionals who are, or might be, in positions to advance religious liberty.
- Specialized groups, such as the Cardinal Kung Foundation, which monitors treatment of Roman Catholics in China and provides support to its bishops, as well as Iranian Christians International and groups representing Egyptian Copts, which document persecution, assist refugees, and engage in government advocacy on

behalf of these minorities.

- Parachurch Christian broadcasting and direct mail ministries, such as Focus on the Family, the Family Research Council, Coral Ridge Ministries, Christian Broadcasting Network, and the Christian Coalition, which can reach millions of American evangelical citizens on international issues of concern.
- Denominational or church-affiliated organizations, such as the U.S. Catholic Conference, the Anglican Communion, Christian Life Commission of the Southern Baptist Convention (SBC), the National Association of Evangelicals, the World Evangelical Fellowship Religious Liberty Commission, and the Salvation Army, which maintain domestic grassroots constituencies and contacts with communities abroad.
- Catholic bishops around the world, led by Pope John Paul II, who have championed human rights and documented persecution. In Tertio Millennio Adveniente, the Pope especially underscored the "ecumenical inheritance" of modern martyrdom.
- Church mission organizations, numbering by the score, which serve the missionary impulse in evangelicalism. To maintain workable relations with foreign governments—and thus access for evangelical work—mission boards sometimes take issue with other evangelical advocates and counsel against public criticism or sanctions against persecuting countries.
- Relief and development organizations, especially evangelical ones such as World Relief, Mercy Corps, Samaritan's Purse (directed by Franklin Graham), and the largest, World Vision. These organizations have a major presence, not only among the international NGOs but in policy circles as well.
- Christian journalists, such as David Aikman, formerly of *Time* and now with the Ethics and Public Policy Center, and Kim Lawton, with the PBS program *Religion & Ethics NewsWeekly,* whose foreign reportage often illuminates religious dynamics hidden from secular journalists.
- Catholic, Jewish, and evangelical scholars and activists working in such think tanks as the Ethics and Public Policy Center and the Institute for Religion and Democracy, who have sponsored symposia and published reports on international religious freedom issues.
- Jewish human rights activists and organizations.
- A cohort of fervent members of Congress, such as Chris Smith (R-NJ), Frank Wolf (R-VA), Tony Hall (D-OH), Tom Tancredo (R-CO), Joseph Pitts (R-PA), and Spencer Bachus (R-AL) in the House and Joseph Lieberman (D-CT), Don Nickles (R-OK), and Sam Brownback (R-KS) in the Senate, who have conducted fact-finding trips documenting international human rights abuses and championed legislation. They are joined by a cadre of staff, some of whom have become key players in the evolving politics of human rights.

Table 2. Worldwide Adherents of All Religions by Six Continental Areas, Mid-2001 (in millions)

	World	Africa	Asia	Europe and Russia	Latin America	North America	Oceania	%	# of Nations
Christians*	2,019,052	368,244	317,759	559,359	486,591	261,752	25,343	32.9	238
Roman Catholics	1,067,053	123,467	112,086	285,554	466,266	71,391	8,327	17.4	235
Protestants**	737,711	176,465	208,323	103,347	89,365	151,196	9,014	12.0	232
Orthodox	216,314	36,038	14,219	158,375	564	6,400	718	3.5	134
Anglicans	80,644	43,524	735	26,628	1,098	3,231	5,428	1.3	163
Other Christians***	138,312	27,927	8,098	26,377	12,238	59,461	4,211	2.2	>232
Muslims	1,207,148	323,556	845,341	31,724	1,702	4,518	307	19.7	204
Hindus	819,689	2,384	813,396	1,425	775	1,350	359	13.4	114
Nonreligious	771,345	5,170	611,876	105,742	16,214	28,994	3,349	12.6	236
Chinese Folk Religionists	387,167	33	385,758	258	197	857	64	6.3	89
Buddhists	361,985	139	356,533	1,570	660	2,777	307	5.9	126
Ethnic Religionists	230,026	97,762	129,005	1,258	1,288	446	267	3.8	140
Atheists	150,252	432	122,408	22,555	2,787	1,700	369	2.5	161
New-Religionists	102,801	29	101,065	160	633	847	67	1.7	60
Sikhs	23,538	54	22,689	241	0	535	19	0.4	34
Jews	14,484	215	4,476	2,506	1,145	6,045	98	0.2	134
Spiritists	12,466	3	2	134	12,169	152	7	0.2	55
Baha'is	7,254	1,779	3,538	132	893	799	113	0.1	218
Confucians	6,313	250	6,277	11	<1	0	24	0.1	15
Jains	4,281	67	4,207	0	0	7	0	0.1	10
Shintoists	2,732	0	2,669	0	7	57	0	0.0	8
Taoists	2,670	0	2,658	0	0	11	0	0.0	5
Zoroastrians	2,601	<1	2,519	<1	0	79	1	0.0	22
Other Religionists	1,082	67	63	238	100	605	10	0.0	7
Total Population	6,128,512	802,150	3,730,168	728,270	525,878	311,877	30,164	100.0	238

Source: World Christian Encyclopedia, ed. David Barrett, George Kurian, and Todd Johnson (New York: Oxford University Press, 2001).
*The subgroups of Christianity may add up to more than this total due to some individuals claiming more than one affiliation.
**Includes Protestants and Independent members of churches and networks that regard themselves as postdenominationalist and neoapostolic and thus independent of historic, organized, institutionalized, denominationalist Christianity. Thus this category includes evangelicals and mainline denominational Protestants.
***This category includes two groups: (1) marginal Christians, those who are members of denominations on the margins of organized mainstream Christianity (e.g., Church of Jesus Christ of Latter-day Saints, Jehovah's Witnesses, and Christian Science) and (2) unaffiliated (nominal) Christians not affiliated with any church.

Table 3. Regional Distribution of Christian Population (Percent of Total in Each Branch)

	Africa	Asia	Europe and Russia	Latin America	Northern America	Oceania	World (in thousands)
Christians*	18%	16%	28%	24%	13%	1%	2,019,052
Roman Catholics	12%	11%	27%	44%	7%	1%	1,067,053
Protestants	26%	15%	22%	14%	20%	2%	345,855
Orthodox	17%	7%	73%	<1%	3%	<1%	216,314
Anglicans	54%	1%	33%	1%	4%	7%	80,644
Independents**	21%	40%	7%	10%	21%	<1%	391,856
Marginal***	8%	10%	14%	26%	40%	2%	26,623
Unaffiliated****	23%	5%	20%	5%	44%	4%	111,689

Source: World Christian Encyclopedia, edited by David Barrett, George T. Kurian, and Todd Johnson, 2nd ed., vol. 1 (New York: Oxford University Press, 2001).
* This category is subdivided into affiliated Christians (church members) and unaffiliated.
**This term denotes members of churches and networks that regard themselves as postdenominationalist and neoapostolic and thus independent of historic, organized, i
   stitutionalized, denominationalist Christianity.
***Members of denominations on the margins of organized mainstream Christianity (e.g., Church of Jesus Christ of Latter-day Saints, Jehovah's Witnesses, and Christian Science).
****Nominal Christians (professing Christians not affiliated with any church).
Figures for the subgroups of affiliated Christians add up to more than 100% because some Christians claim more than one affiliation.

Table 4. Religious Distribution by Region and Year

Region	1900	2000
Africa		
Christians	9%	46%
Muslims	32%	41%
Ethnoreligionists	58%	12%
Asia		
Christians	2%	9%
Muslims	16%	23%
Hindus	21%	22%
Nonreligious	0%	17%
Chinese Fold-Religionists	40%	10%
Buddhists	13%	10%
Europe		
Christians	95%	77%
Muslims	2%	4%
Jews	3%	<1%
Buddhists	<1%	<1%
Nonreligious	<1%	15%
Latin America		
Christians	95%	93%
Spiritists	<1%	2%
Muslims	<1%	<1%
Ethnoreligionists	4%	<1%
Nonreligious	1%	3%
North America		
Christians	97%	84%
Jews	2%	2%
Muslims	0%	1%
Buddhists	<1%	1%
Nonreligious	1%	9%
Oceania		
Christians	78%	83%
Jews	<1%	<1%
Muslims	<1%	1%
Hindus	<1%	1%
Ethnoreligionists	21%	1%
Nonreligious	1%	11%
Atheist	0%	1%

Table 5. Members of the U.S. Commission on International Religious Freedom, 1999–2004

Member	Term
Elliott Abrams Former President, Ethics and Public Policy Center, and Special Assistant to the President for Near East and African Affairs, 2002–present	5/15/99–5/14/01
Laila Al-Marayati, M.D. Founding member and past President of the Muslim Women's League, a Los Angeles-based nonprofit organization focusing on the dissemination of accurate information about Islam and Muslims, particularly regarding women	5/15/99–5/14/01
Preeta D. Bansal Visiting Fellow, Harvard University's John F. Kennedy School of Government (Institute of Politics); former Solicitor General of the state of New York	5/15/03–5/14/06
John R. Bolton Senior Vice President of the American Enterprise Institute for Public Policy Research and former Secretary of State for International Organization Affairs	5/15/99–5/14/01
Patti Chang President and C.E.O. of the Women's Foundation of California	5/15/03–5/14/04
Most Reverend Charles J. Chaput Archbishop of Denver and First Native American Bishop in U.S. history	5/15/03–5/14/06
Michael Cromartie Vice President, Ethics and Public Policy Center	5/15/04–5/14/06
Khaled Abou El Fadl Visiting Professor at Yale Law School, Professor of Law at UCLA, and a leading authority on Islamic law	5/15/03–5/14/06
Felice D. Gaer Director, Jacob Blaustein Institute for the Advancement of Human Rights; the American Jewish Committee	5/15/03–5/14/06
Firuz Kazemzadeh Senior Advisor, National Spiritual Assembly of the Baha'is of the United States and Professor Emeritus of History at Yale University	5/15/99–5/14/03
Richard D. Land President and C.E.O. of the Ethics and Religious Liberty Commission of the Southern Baptist Convention	5/15/03–5/14/06
Theodore Cardinal McCarrick Roman Catholic Archbishop of Washington, D.C., and member of the College of Cardinals	5/15/99–5/14-01

(continued)

Table 5. Members of the U.S. Commission on International Religious Freedom, 1999–2004 (continued)

Most Reverend William Francis Murphy Bishop of the Diocese of Rockville Centre, New York	5/15/01–5/14/03

Elizabeth H. Prodromou
    Associate Director, Institute on Culture, Religion,
    and World Affairs, Boston University
	5/15/04–5/14/06

Bishop Ricardo Ramirez Bishop of the Diocese of Las Cruces, New Mexico	5/15/03–5/14/06

Leila Nadya Sadat
    Professor of Law, Washington University School of Law, and
    a leading expert in international and comparative law
	5/15/01–5/14/03

Rabbi David Saperstein Director, Religious Action Center of Reform Judaism	5/15/99–5/14/01

Nina Shea
    Director of the Center for Religious Freedom, Freedom
    House
	5/15/99–5/14/06

Justice Charles Z. Smith
    Washington State Supreme Court Temple of Justice, whose
    experience includes serving as Special Assistant to U.S.
    Attorney General Robert Kennedy and two-term service as
    President of the American Baptist Churches, U.S.A.
	5/15/99–5/14/01

Charles R. Stith
    Former Ambassador and Director of the African Presidential
    Archives and Research Center of Boston University
	5/15/01–5/14/03

Shirin Tahir-Kheli
    Former Ambassador and Director of the Near East and South
    Asian Affairs for the National Security Council and Professor
    at the Johns Hopkins University School of Advanced
    International Studies
	5/15/01–5/14/03

Michael K. Young
    Dean, the George Washington University Law School, and
    graduate of Brigham Young and Harvard Universities
	5/15/99–5/14/05

Current Members as of April 2006:
    Michael Cromartie, Chair
    Felice D. Gaer, Vice Chair
    Nina Shea, Vice Chair
    Preeta D. Bansal, Commissioner
    Most Reverend Charles J. Chaput, Commissioner
    Khaled Abou El Fadl, Commissioner
    Richard D. Land
    Elizabeth H. Prodromou, Commissioner
    Bishop Ricardo Ramirez, Commissioner

INDEX

ABOUT THE AUTHOR

An internationally recognized expert on religion and politics, **Allen Hertzke** is professor of Political Science and director of Religious Studies at the University of Oklahoma. He is author of several books, including *Representing God in Washington*, an award-winning analysis of religious lobbies, which has been issued in Chinese language translation; *Echoes of Discontent* (1993), an account of church-rooted populist movements; and coauthor of *Religion and Politics in America*, a comprehensive text on faith and politics now in its third edition. A frequent news commentator, he has been featured in such outlets as the *New York Times, Washington Post, Wall Street Journal, Weekly Standard*, BBC World Service, PBS, National Public Radio, and Swedish Radio. A winner of numerous teaching awards, Dr. Hertzke has lectured at the National Press Club, the U.S. Holocaust Memorial Museum, the Council on Foreign Relations, the Carnegie Council on Ethics and International Relations, and before numerous audiences in China.